Definitive Readings in the History, Philosophy, Theories and Practice of Career and Technical Education

Victor C. X. Wang
California State University at Long Beach, USA

INFORMATION SCIENCE REFERENCE

in cooperation with

ZHEJIANG UNIVERSITY PRESS

Director of Editorial Content:	Kristin Klinger
Director of Book Publications:	Julia Mosemann
Acquisitions Editor:	Lindsay Johnston
Development Editor:	Julia Mosemann
Publishing Assistant:	Travis Gundrum
Typesetter:	Michael Brehm
Production Editor:	Jamie Snavely
Cover Design:	Lisa Tosheff
Printed at:	Lightning Source

Published in the United States of America by
Information Science Reference (an imprint of IGI Global)
701 E. Chocolate Avenue
Hershey PA 17033
Tel: 717-533-8845
Fax: 717-533-8661
E-mail: cust@igi-global.com
Web site: http://www.igi-global.com

Library of Congress Cataloging-in-Publication Data

Definitive readings in the history, philosophy, theories and practice of career and technical education / Victor Wang, Editor.
    p. cm.
"Information Science Reference in cooperation with Zhejiang University Press." Includes bibliographical references and index.
 Summary: "This volume brings together definitive writings on career and technical education by leading figures involved in the history, philosophy, practice and theories of the field"--Provided by publisher. ISBN 978-1-61520-747-3 (hardcover) -- ISBN 978-1-61520-748-0 (ebook) 1. Career education. 2. Vocational education. 3. Education and globalization. I. Wang, Victor.
 LC1037.D44 2010
 370.11'3--dc22
                                     2009053462

British Cataloguing in Publication Data
A Cataloguing in Publication record for this book is available from the British Library.

Table of Contents

Preface

What should be the goals of Career and Technical Education (CTE)? The question lies at the heart of the field of career and technical education, which parallels the efforts of humanity from the Stone Age to modern civilization. A satisfactory answer requires a thorough examination of historical, philosophical, practical and theoretical issues. Almost every community college offers CTE programs in the United States; over two hundred universities offer degree programs in CTE in the nation. Does everyone who practices in this particular field understand the goals of CTE? What about those who make important decisions that will impact those who practice in this field?

CTE has come a long way. Prior to 6000 years ago, there were unorganized CTE programs. Vocational skills were learned from watching one's elders either at the campsite or in a worksite. Learning could be considered an act to gain knowledge or skill by observation. Trial and error could be the best learning method. Then, there were organized programs in Egypt 6000 years ago where scribes were required to copy documentation from documentation so that training and learning would be more effective. It is believed that the ancient Egyptians began to develop a civilization based on scientific knowledge, government, and religion in the valleys of the Nile, the Tigris, and the Euphrates rivers. Prior to the Industrial Revolution, CTE was called manual training. Later at the turn of the 20th century, it was called manual arts. A year later, it was called industrial arts. Scholars and practitioners used the term vocational education for decades. Eventually, in the 1990s, most programs started to call the field Career and Technical Education to distance the field from being closely associated with blue collar workers because the image of a skilled craftsman may not appeal to our high school students. In fact, we also have a large number of CTE learners preparing for careers requiring a baccalaureate or higher level degree. Therefore, the name "vocational education" no longer reflects what we do and practice in the field. Career and technical education is a vivid name that truly reflects the nature of the field in the 21st Century.

From the cotton mills in 1803 to modern factories, principles, philosophies, theories and practice of CTE by leading individuals have helped shape the field. As the ancient nations focused on apprenticeship systems, the Industrial Revolution put a strain on the apprenticeship programs in the then developing nations, including the United States. In this information age, CTE has become a multibillion dollar training enterprise. To make our students more competitive in the labor force and to make our nation economically strong and firms internationally competitive, we have to depend on CTE to train today's workers of various kinds. Without a doubt, CTE has become a vibrant source of workforce development across the globe. It has matured into a sound and meaningful program for high school and post-secondary students across interest areas and abilities. After the first passage of the Morrill Act, CTE programs became available at land grant universities. As our nation's leaders provide more federal funding to this strong field of study, CTE will definitely fulfill its number one objective, that is, to meet the manpower needs of society.

This volume brings together definitive writings on CTE by leading figures and by contemporary thinkers in the History, Philosophy, Practice and Theories of the field. In the past, we had great texts written by prominent figures such as Roy Roberts, Rupert Evans and Edwin Herr. Philosophies and principles advanced by Prosser and Miller reflected the cultural needs of the people in the past. As our society changes, we realize how pervasive technology and information skills are needed to meet the manpower needs of society. At the same time, what we lack is a definitive book on the History, Philosophy, Practice and Theories to prepare people, young and old, for the world of work in the 21st Century. No where can we find a volume like this one. This book has filled a much needed void in the literature and it will equip our scholars and practitioners with knowledge, skills, and attitudes to succeed in the field of CTE.

Victor C. X. Wang, Ed.D.
Associate Professor of CTE and Adult Education
California State University, Long Beach
Long Beach, California, USA

May 29, 2009

Acknowledgment

To ensure quality of books, editors/authors have their books go through the double blind review process so that their books will become refereed books in the field. This book is no exception. All entries are written by knowledgeable, distinguished scholars from many prominent research institutions. The reviewers were invited based on their sustained scholarship in this field. Therefore, I extend a huge thank you to the following reviewers/authors:

- Ernest W. Brewer, University of Tennessee, Knoxville, USA
- Lesley Farmer, California State University, Long Beach, USA
- Janice Frates, California State University, Long Beach, USA
- Kerry Lee, University of Auckland, New Zealand
- James B. Martin, U.S. Army Command and General Staff College, USA
- Gregory Petty, University of Tennessee, Knoxville, USA
- Leane B. Skinner, Auburn University, USA
- James E. Witte, Auburn University, USA
- Maria M. Witte, Auburn University, USA
- Chris Zirkle, Ohio State University, USA

I thank my fellow authors, IGI Global, and Zhejiang University Press, especially Dr. Mary Wu for their contribution to this book. This book is designed for the teacher-practitioner and is written from both a scholar's and a practitioner's perspective. Because of the rich information provided by this book, individual chapters can be selected according to readers' specific needs and interests. Thanks also go to my family, Katie Wang, Anni Wang and Anthony Wang for their continued support and encouragement during the many months it took to give birth to this book. Last but not least, I thank all of our readers who have become consumers of this excellent book. This book will assist you in your educational and scholarly endeavors.

Victor C. X. Wang, Ed.D.
Associate Professor of CTE and Adult Education
California State University, Long Beach
Long Beach, California, USA

May 29, 2009

Chapter 1
The History of Career and Technical Education

Ernest W. Brewer
University of Tennessee, USA

ABSTRACT

This chapter examines the history of career and technical education in the United States beginning with its earliest forms in the 16th and 17th centuries and continuing on through present-day society. Chronologically formatted, the primary focus is on how the nation's domestic and international issues during each time period affected the development of vocational education, leading to major federal government legislation. Following a brief introduction of the subject, the background section will provide the reader with basic definitions of career and technical education as discussed by various authors, noting the changes of such definitions over the years. The main body of the chapter is divided into several sections based upon time periods. Each section will discuss national issues and major legislation reflecting changes in vocational education. Finally, the future of career and technical education will be examined, followed by a brief conclusion.

1.1 INTRODUCTION

Career and technical education programs have been around for hundreds of years in one form or another. Well before this nation was founded, fathers and mothers were passing on important survival skills to their children (Evans, 1971; Keller, 1948). The first forms of formal education of any type were reserved for religious teachings

and groups (Keller, 1948). However, as the needs of the people changed, so did education. In this nation, vocational education began in the form of apprenticeships in an effort to ensure that various aspects of community work were efficiently and effectively completed (Barlow, 1974; Brewer, Campbell, & Petty, 2000; Keller). With the onset of the Industrial Revolution, apprenticeships were no longer capable of providing all of the necessary training to operate the new forms of machinery

DOI: 10.4018/978-1-61520-747-3.ch001

(Barlow). Since that time, technological changes and the nation's workforce needs have dictated the direction of vocational education in the United States.

This chapter will demonstrate the various changes that career and technical education has undergone over the years. It will provide background information on these types of programs, including the changes in definition that vocational education has undergone over time. Furthermore, it will specifically discuss how the issues and controversies related to the history of our nation have affected the status of vocational education, as well as how federal legislation has attempted to solve some of these issues. Finally future trends for the field of career and technical education will be presented, followed by a brief conclusion.

1.2 BACKGROUND

Over the years, vocational education has gone through many changes in meaning and scope. In general, vocational education is characterized by teaching a skill or skills to students that will be useful in the workplace. However, this explanation does not satisfactorily describe the dimensions of vocational education, especially in how it is used in today's society. A review of literature provides a wide variety of perspectives on the subject, as well as descriptions of vocational education as it has changed over time.

F. J. Keller, a notable historian on this subject, looked at vocational education in a unique way. Instead of simply describing a method of educating students, Keller believed that vocational education was actually a way of living one's life (Keller, 1948). He believed that vocational educators were charged not only with teaching specific skills, but also with teaching students how to live and act in the workplace and in society. He attributed the first form of vocational education, to monks, going as far back in history as the 7th century. Even before more structured forms of apprenticeships

evolved, Keller claimed that monks were teaching each other the skills needed to conduct research and teach, along with necessary life lessons needed to live a productive life in the monastery (Keller, 1948).

Eventually, the greater society began to see the benefits of this type of teaching, and apprenticeships became the common standard of passing on vital work skills to others during the colonial period of our nation's history. Several authors have defined apprenticeships as forms of education where a master provides direct instruction of mastering a skill to a student, or apprentice (Barlow, 1974; Evans, 1971; Keller, 1948; Kneller, 1963; Miller, 1993). As discussed in future sections below, some masters expanded their teachings to include other basic educational components, such as reading and writing (Barlow, 1974; Kneller, 1963; Miller, 1993). Many apprenticeships, especially during this time period, also included room and board for the students (Barlow, 1974).

It was during the Industrial Revolution, beginning in the late 18th century, that apprenticeships became obsolete and the more contemporary forms of vocational education were founded (Barlow, 1974). Barlow (1974) attributes much of this change to two movements during the 19th century: the practical arts movement and the trade school movement. While these movements are discussed in more detail in future sections, the core concepts of such movements are important in understanding the early definitions of vocational education. The practical arts movement provided skill-based learning by developing unique curriculum, such as domestic science and agriculture courses (Barlow, 1974). However, this movement also continued to stress the importance of general education. The trade school movement, in contrast, focused specifically on teaching a trade in a more formalized way than apprenticeships had been able to do (Barlow, 1974). Thus began the debate as to how much general education should be included in vocational education.

Throughout the 20th century, the definition and scope of vocational education continued to adjust based upon the workforce needs of the nation. During wartimes, it appeared that vocational education focused less on general education courses and more on skill development. This was due in part to the fact that many men were overseas, and their jobs needed to be quickly filled by new employees (ACTE, 2002; Thompson, 1973). In addition, the government needed a variety of war materials developed in large amounts at a fast pace (Thompson, 1973). Technology has been another driving force that has changed the nature of vocational education. With the advent of modern computers and machinery, new skills have had to be taught in order for employees to remain competitive in the workplace (Calhoun & Finch, 1976). Often, these new skills require more knowledge in the areas of math and science, thus putting the pressure back on the programs to provide adequate general education in addition to skill development (ACTE, 2002; Thompson, 1973). It was during the latter part of this century that Congress defined vocational education as the process of preparing students for employment through instruction by providing skill-based learning. In addition, Congress specified that vocational programs were designed for individuals not interested in careers that required traditional four-year college degrees or higher (Brewer et al., 2000). In 1990, the Carl D. Perkins Act added that such classes should include a variety of academic and work skills, not merely the specific skills required to perform a job function (Brewer et al., 2000).

As our nation entered the 21st century, technological advancements have continued to shape the nature of vocational education programs. So many fields have become dependent on computer technology, ranging from auto mechanics to various medical fields. The types of courses involved in vocational education are constantly changing and adapting to the nation's needs, and the debate continues as to what actually constitutes a vocational education course in some cases. Advanced math and science courses are becoming more vital to our nation's workforce. Technology continues to propel our nation forward, and therefore, the definition, nature, and scope of vocational education will need to adapt in order to prepare students adequately for a technologically-based workforce.

1.3 THE HISTORY OF VOCATIONAL EDUCATION

Although the meaning of vocational education has become more complex, the idea of such education can be found throughout history. Before schools and programs of education were even ideas, generations of families were self-sustained by teaching sons and daughters skills to help the family survive (Evans, 1971; Keller, 1948). Examples of such teachings ranged from mothers showing daughters how to gather and prepare food to fathers teaching their sons how to hunt. In early history, even basic medical needs were often taken care of within the family. As society advanced, family members passed on newer and more efficient ways of completing such tasks. Eventually, however, society's advancements surpassed the family's ability to provide for itself, giving way for the need for families to find assistance outside of the home (Evans, 1971). These and future advancements paved the way for the field of vocational education. This section provides a chronological glimpse at how various stages of our nation's history has shaped the field of career and technical education. The first subsection discusses trends, issues, and problems as related to vocational education, and the remaining subsections add to this a discussion of relevant federal legislation regarding vocational education that attempted to solve such problems and issues.

1.3.1 16th and 17th Centuries

During the 16th and 17th centuries, before America was established as a nation, vocational education was informal at best. Kneller (1963) discusses the impact of the Puritans on education. In the early 1700s, Puritans believed that every person was destined to perform a specific duty, and those that performed that duty to the best of their ability would be rewarded by God. While they did not believe that people should attempt to rise up into other classes of society, this concept of mastering a skill is essential to the field of vocational education even today. The Puritans also impacted education through a "compulsory educational system" (p. 6), and they further required all persons to be involved in "some sort of productive work" (p. 7). Despite such early efforts, our nation did not adapt the idea of compulsory education until the 20th century. Although Puritanism failed in the end, some of the key points can still be found in modern day education.

During these centuries, very few people had the opportunity to take part in a formalized educational program of any type, much less vocational education. As noted in the Puritan system, education was often associated with religion, and more formal education other than the basic reading and writing was reserved for religious leaders. For centuries, monasteries were some of the earliest forms of sophisticated vocational education (Keller, 1948). As noted by Keller, "life was the profession, a most effective kind of professional education" (p. 37). Inside these monasteries, monks learned the basics of reading and writing, and such skills were then passed on to other monks. These skills were essential for the written research and duplication of books that were developed inside the monasteries. According to Keller, it was during the 16th and 17th centuries that monasteries truly became teaching schools that benefited society through their written and scholarly works. The internal teachings that occurred within the monasteries applied both classical and vocational methods of instruction, similar to modern vocational programs.

1.3.2 Apprenticeships in Colonial America

1.3.2.1 National Issues

Apprenticeships were one of the earliest forms of formal training for the general population (Brewer et al., 2000). Typical apprenticeships required the master to teach a trade or skill to the apprentice, while also often providing the student with basic needs, and in return, the student worked and produced for the trainer (Barlow, 1974, 1976; Evans, 1971; Keller, 1948; Miller, 1993). Barlow (1974) suggested that "apprenticeships provided for five basic elements: (a) food, clothing, and shelter; (b) learning to read and write; (c) religious instruction; (d) instruction in the trade; and, (e) secrets of the trade (related science and mathematics)" (p. 16). Barlow also discussed voluntary versus involuntary apprenticeships. Voluntary apprenticeships allowed the apprentices to decide which type of occupation they wished to undertake, while apprentices in involuntary apprenticeships were simply placed with a particular tradesman. Typically, involuntary apprentices were those who did not have caregivers.

Barlow (1974) also demonstrated that early apprenticeships affected modern day vocational education in three ways. First, apprentices learned not only the skill for the specific trade they were involved in, but also many other educational concepts. This intertwining of vocational and general education could be found throughout history and is important in present-day programs. The next important lesson learned from apprenticeships is that "most occupations could be taught in school. It was entirely possible in the school environment to provide the basic instruction necessary for a person to enter an occupation" (p. 16). Apprenticeships could be seen as an example of modern vocational co-op programs that many high school and postsecondary schools offer. The final concept that Barlow focuses on is that vocational education applied to all persons. Barlow's intention behind this concept is that vocational education should not only be for children. Instead, it can extend throughout a person's existence, from early schooling on through adulthood. In addition, this concept can also be interpreted to mean that vocational education is not for one class of people; all people can participate in such programs.

1.3.2.2 Important Legislation

At this point in American History, the American colonies were not united and were still under the control of Great Britain. However, one colony, the Massachusetts Bay Colony, did successfully pass a law regarding apprenticeships (Miller, 1993). In 1642, a "comprehensive apprenticeship law" was passed that forced families and apprenticeship masters to ensure that children were learning not only a specific trade, but also about the colony's laws and religious views (p. 4). This law stressed the importance of combining both technical skill and general education to ensure that all students would be productive members of society, and these two issues continue to be an important part of modern-day vocational education programs.

1.3.3 19th Century America

1.3.3.1 National Issues

At the turn of the 19th century, America began to undergo significant changes that forever changed the way the nation would prepare for work. It was during this time that Americans moved from an agrarian, farm-based society to one of factories and machines, and eventually people moved to the cities to find work (Brewer et al., 2000; Evans, 1971; Miller, 1993). Referred to as the Industrial Revolution, this period in our nation's history marked an increase in technology and efficiency in many occupations. This was the era of mass production, and machines replaced individual

craftsmen efforts (Miller, 1993; Thompson, 1973). New technology and new skills meant that people had to learn to effectively use such devices, and schools and training programs began to replace apprenticeships (Barlow, 1974). Schools began to include "practical arts" in addition to the traditional education curriculum. The practical arts courses resembled basic life skills courses that students could use in their home and community (Barlow).

During the latter part of the 19th century, trade schools also became prevalent. Much more sophisticated than the practical arts courses offered in regular schools, the trade schools more closely resembled vocational education programs. Barlow (1974) described three types of trade schools: "(a) schools that provided trade instruction only; (b) schools that provided trade instruction and general instruction—reading, writing, arithmetic and citizenship; and (c) schools that provided residential facilities for youth" (p. 18). Barlow further explained the impact of such schools on contemporary vocational education by stating again that almost any trade can be taught in school (p. 18), and the nation as a whole benefits from such training.

1.3.3.2 Important Legislation

By the middle of the 19th century, the federal government realized that legislation must be passed in order to provide adequate training and help to develop a competent workforce. At first, the idea of government supported education, referred to as common schools, was met with opposition from some groups (Kneller, 1963). As noted by Kneller, up until this point, religion was a major focus of education, and many educational programs were funded through religious organizations. These groups were wary of the government-funded common schools for two reasons. First, some religious groups thought that one type of religion would become the primary religion for such schools, leading to abandonment of other religions. Second, religious leaders were also skeptical of the common schools because they feared that religion would be exempted from the curriculum all together. Kneller also points out that the lower classes were displeased about the common school movement because they did not believe it should apply to them. Despite these issues, the first piece of legislation passed by the government to promote vocational education was passed during this time period.

Morrill Act

In 1862, the Morrill Act was passed by the federal government, essentially marking the beginning of land grant colleges. The Act provided land to the states, and the states used the income from the sale of such land to develop agricultural and mechanical arts colleges (Barlow, 1976; Brewer & Achilles, 2008; Calhoun & Finch, 1976; Hawkins, Prosser, & Wright, 1966; Miller, 1993). This marked the "first legislation passed by the national government to support vocational education" (Brewer & Achilles; Calhoun & Finch, p. 34). This Act was reinforced by the Second Morrill Act of 1890, which essentially provided additional money to support the colleges (Calhoun & Finch; Hawkins et al.).

Hatch Act

In 1887, the Hatch Act provided funding for states to develop agricultural experiment stations "to provide help to farmers and to upgrade the nation's agricultural methods" (Calhoun & Finch, 1976, p. 34). Another objective of this Act was to disseminate information regarding agriculture to the nation at large (Hawkins et al., 1966). As noted by Hawkins et al. (1966), this Act has been referred to as the Experimental Stations Act. Funding was later increased by means of the Adams Act of 1906 (Hawkins et al., 1966).

1.3.4 Early to Middle 20th Century America

1.3.4.1 National Issues

By the early 20th century, it became obvious to state and national leaders that the nation needed to focus on education. Calhoun and Finch (1976) describe this period as one of "rapid economic and industrial development . . . characterized as a period of conflict in the beliefs of the American people" (p. 32). Americans were torn between wanting freedom from government intervention and wanting the government to take the lead in providing quality education for all citizens (Calhoun & Finch). At this point in history, secondary educational programs were available but not mandatory, and post-secondary educational programs were for the academic elite and were not geared toward vocational education (Barlow, 1976). The majority of students were not motivated to remain in school, and thus they were not learning necessary skills required to be successful in the work industrial work environment (Calhoun & Finch). Even the Agricultural and Mechanical colleges previously established by the Morrill Land Grant Act began to incorporate substantial general educational components, limiting vocational education curriculum (Barlow, 1974). Ironically, many vocational education programs were aimed working with social deviates and known as reform schools (Keller, 1948). The failure of schools to properly educate and train people to perform in the workplace led to a substantially underproductive society (Calhoun & Finch).

In 1906, the National Society for the Promotion of Industrial Education was created to essentially rediscover and revisit the idea of vocational education (Barlow, 1974). In 1914, this group successfully encouraged the federal government to establish the Commission on Vocational Education, whose main purpose was to provide an extensive report on the status of vocational education (Hawkins et al., 1966). This group changed its name over the years and in 1926 became what is now known as the American Vocational Association (AVA) (ACTE, 2002; Barlow, 1976). It was this group of individuals, including the noteworthy "father of vocational education" Dr. Charles A. Prosser, that was responsible for much of the legislation that was passed during the beginning of the 20ᵗʰ century, as discussed in following subsection (Barlow, 1976).

As discussed by Thompson (1973), wars also forced the federal government to take a look at the state of vocational education in the nation. During World War I, the government required trained and skilled craftsmen to supply the military with appropriate equipment, "trained mechanics, technicians, and highly experience supervisory forces would be needed in addition to troops" to fight this "mechanical war" (p. 32). Furthermore, with so many men serving their country in the war effort, factories at home needed skilled replacement workers (Brewer et al., 2000; Thompson, 1973). The solution was to provide short, intensive courses to workers in order to teach them a skill both quickly and efficiently. In addition, the nation turned to women to fill the spots left open by men who had left for the war. This war had a huge impact on vocational education, opening the eyes of both the government and the American people to the importance of skilled workers (Thompson).

The 1930s brought new challenges for the nation as unemployment rates rose to new heights. The Great Depression not only affected the adult population, but the youth population also suffered tremendously as adults took over jobs once held by them (Evans, 1971). Employers would rather have adults with some work experience working for them than youth who were untrained and lacked experience (Evans). It was also during this time period that the federal government recognized the need for youth programs, as noted in the following subsection regarding legislation. It was during the 1930s that vocational education and training truly made a difference in preparing

the nation's youth and adult population for the workforce (ACTE, 2002).

World War II once again brought to light the nation's need for proper vocational education (Brewer et al., 2000, Thompson, 1973). However, by this time, many vocational education programs had been in existence due to the efforts of vocational education commissions and legislation. Instead of needing to create new programs, the federal government was pushed to expand current programs and increase appropriations. Two major training programs were developed to address the rising vocational needs during World War II: Vocational Training for War Production Workers (VTWPW) and Vocational Educational for National Defense (VEND) (Thompson, 1973).

It was also during World War II that women became essential in factories and industries while the men were off fighting in the war (ACTE, 2002). Despite their efforts, there were many people, men especially, who did not necessarily approve of women working in the plants and factories. As noted by ACTE, "some Congressmen saw it as the death knell for the American home if women went to work in factories. Some men feared for their own jobs, and others believed that women simply did not have the mechanical ability required for the tasks" (p. 28). Women proved the pessimists wrong, and "by April 1943, 741,322 women were enrolled in training programs" (p. 29). With women becoming prevalent in the workforce, vocational education programs had to adapt.

While jobs were plentiful during the war, it was in its aftermath that the nation faced a tremendous challenge. All of the men returning from service would need both training and employment in the workforce (ACTE, 2002). This meant that vocational education programs would require more funding and more trained instructors in order to meet the needs of the thousands of veterans returning from war. In order to achieve these ends, the federal government would have to supply additional funding through legislation (ACTE).

1.3.4.2 Federal Legislation

During the first half of the 20th century, the federal government realized the importance of funding vocational programs to increase the productivity of the nation's citizens. It was during this time period that several key pieces of legislation were passed by congress, and in turn, vocational programs became strong entities in the world of education in this country. These particular pieces of legislation laid the foundation for many more government-funded vocational education programs in the future.

Smith-Hughes Act of 1917

After tremendous lobbying by the vocational education supporters in the states, as well as huge efforts from the Commission on National Aid to Vocational Education and the National Society for the Promotion of Industrial Education, the federal government passed the Smith-Hughes Act of 1917 (Calhoun & Finch, 1976; Hawkins et al., 1966). Also known as the Vocational Education Act of 1917, this Act provided funding to the states to support vocational education in secondary schools (Calhoun & Finch; Hawkins et al.). Specifically, this Act allotted funds to develop secondary school programs in agriculture, trade and industry, and home economics, as well as to train instructors to teach such subjects (Calhoun & Finch). The Act further required the state's to submit detailed plans, including plans to evaluate the efficiency of such programs on a regular basis. As noted by Calhoun and Finch, "this example of the federal government's concern of the preparation of the nation's young people for productive adulthood established another precedent for future generations to follow" (p. 36).

Fess-Kenyon Act of 1920

This Act provided funding for the "vocational rehabilitation of industry-disabled persons" (Calhoun & Finch, 1976, p. 41). This Act has also been referred to as the Industrial Rehabilitation Act, and further funding authorizations were made through subsequent acts and amendments (Calhoun & Finch). Because of this act, many disabled persons are able to take part in our nation's workforce.

George-Reed Act of 1929

A decade after passing the Smith-Hughes Act, vocational education leaders lobbied for additional funds to support home economics and agricultural programs. This Act provided funds for such purposes, but only through 1934 (Calhoun & Finch, 1976; Hawkins et al., 1966). Because of this constraint, additional legislation would need to be passed in order for vocational education programs to receive funding.

George-Ellzey Act of 1934

The Act was another extension of the original Smith-Hughes Act, and it provided additional funding following the close of the authorization period set forth by the George-Reed Act of 1929 (Calhoun & Finch, 1976; Hawkins et al., 1966). In addition, the Act included appropriations for trade and industry programs. As with the George-Reed Act of 1929, funding was time-limited and not authorized past 1937 (Calhoun & Finch).

George-Deen Act of 1936

This Act continued the funding for the vocational education programs mentioned in the George-Ellzey Act of 1934. In addition, this Act provided funding for programs in U.S. territories, thus extending vocational education programs into a larger geographic area. In addition, this Act provided additional funding for the training of instructors (Calhoun & Finch, 1976; Hawkins et al., 1966).

Servicemen's Readjustment Act of 1944

What is more commonly referred to now as the G. I. Bill, this Act provided funding to help the soldiers following their service during World War II. Based upon the number of years of service, veterans were given the opportunity to receive education and training in any field of interest. Many veterans over the years have taken, and continue to take, advantage of the services and funding provided by this Act (Calhoun & Finch, 1976).

George-Barden Act of 1946

While this Act provided additional funding following the close of the authorization period of the George-Deen Act, it also expanded the scope of the previous acts. This Act provided the states with the authority to determine how the funds are spent for vocational programs, including training programs for teachers and salaries for program administrators (Calhoun & Finch, 1976; Hawkins et al., 1966). Unlike the Smith-Hughes Act, this Act allows the states to purchase equipment needed to carry out the vocational programs (Hawkins et al.).

1.4 OTHER FEDERAL ACTIVITIES ASSISTING VOCATIONAL EDUCATION

During the first half of the 20th century, the federal government has tremendously expanded its role in preparing its citizens for the world of work. In 1935, the National Youth Administration was created to assist youths who wished to enter the workforce (Calhoun & Finch, 1976). Beginning in 1933, the Civilian Conservation Corps helped "unemployed young men obtain work" (Calhoun & Finch, p. 42). Finally, the creation of the National Science Foundation supported research and education primarily in the mathematical, physical, engineering, biological, and medical sciences (Calhoun & Finch).

1.4.1 Latter 20th Century America

1.4.1.1 National Issues

The beginning of the second half of the 20th century could be characterized by restlessness and chaos as our nation entered the Korean War in the 1950s and the Vietnam War in the 1960s. Once again, the nation was faced with the need to produce war materials and to fill the employment gaps left when the soldiers went off to fight. It became necessary for youth and women to take on more employment roles in the workforce. Due to the nature of the Vietnam War and much of the nation's reaction, many soldiers returned to the country physically and mentally disabled, and they were often unprepared for the workforce (Thompson, 1973). As noted by Thompson (1973), these wars forced the federal government to again focus on vocational programs.

In addition to these actual wars, the cold war began during the 1950s between the U.S. and Russia. Russia was beginning to assert itself by improving "production in order to become a competitor in the world marketplace" (ACTE, 2002, p. 31). The U.S. government and its citizens were scared that Russia would soon surpass the U.S. in production of international goods and services. The American Vocational Association (AVA) took the lead in planning against this possibility, and it was the AVA's efforts that encouraged the federal government to reevaluate vocational education at this time (ACTE).

The second half of the 20th century was also marked by tremendous technological advancements, ranging from assembly lines to computer engineering at the end of the century. Although automation had begun earlier in the century, it was not until the 1950s that its full impact was evident (Thompson, 1973). While automatic machines and assembly lines replaced many hands-on worker, it required that new workers be trained to operate such machines. According to Thompson, "this era produced a number of changes in work and its significance to man. It raised the level of preparation needed by workers, which resulted in more demands for vocational and technical education" (p. 50). The 1960s presented new challenges as our nation, amongst others, began to look towards the sky. In order to be truly marketable in the area of space exploration, the U.S. needed to advance the nations technological skills tremendously (ACTE, 2002). Technology continued to have a huge impact on vocational education, as well as education in general. Several pieces of legislation were passed during this time period to address the changing needs of nation as they related to vocational education. It was no longer possible to simply teach specific skills. General education and career development became key aspects of vocational programming.

Technology continued to become more complex over the years on a massive scale, requiring the need for more education and training in order for employees to remain marketable in such a society (Thompson, 1973). During the 1980s, the first personal computers became available, marking the beginning of a new era in our nation and the world of technology (ACTE, 2002). At the same time, reports such as *A Nation at Risk* showed that schools were failing to adequately teach students the basic academic subjects, essential for living in a technologically-based society (ACTE). Once again, the federal government was forced to revisit education and training programs, and during the 1990s, the federal government passed a series of acts presented by Carl D. Perkins in the 1990s. These Acts were an effort to bring the nation's workforce up to par with the complex world of technology (ACTE; Wonacott, 2003).

1.4.1.2 Federal Legislation

The latter half of the 20th century in the United States was met with huge changes in workforce development and production. The large-scale wars left our nation wanting for workers and materials to support the military, as well as to keep domestic production up to standards. Sweeping technological advancements in both this country and amongst other world powers required major changes in vocational education in order for the United States to remain competitive. Because of these issues, the federal government was com-

pelled to revisit vocational education legislation once again.

Manpower Development and Training Act of 1962
Due to the increase in unemployment in the nation, the federal government sought to train adult workers so that they would have usable skills in the nation's workforce. This Act brought vocational education and training to the job market through state-based vocational agencies (Calhoun & Finch, 1976; Hawkins et al., 1966). Specifically, "training is provided by a project method requiring federal approval for each project" (Hawkins et al., p. 113).

Vocational Education Act of 1963
Hawkins et al. (1966) assert that this particular Act actually supplemented the original Smith-Hughes Act and the George-Barden Act. More flexible than prior legislation, this Act substantially increased funding for vocational education and broadened the scopes of the original acts (Calhoun & Finch, 1976; Hawkins et al.). Under this Act, vocational education included business occupations and nursing, and it focused major efforts on secondary school vocational education. It also specified that funds could be used for those young people who had either graduated or dropped out of high school, as well as for disadvantaged and disabled populations (Calhoun & Finch). As with prior legislation, the Act required states to submit a plan for use of funds, as well as to continuously evaluate the use of such funds.

Economic Opportunity Act of 1964
Essentially, this Act aimed at helping those individuals living in poverty-stricken areas of the country (Hawkins et al., 1966). Under this Act, several programs were created to serve such populations, many of which have been successful over the years. The Job Corps assisted youth by providing housing for youth and young adults while they train in specially designed Job Corps centers. Work-Training Programs also provided

jobs for youth; these jobs were typically under the supervision of community or government-funded programs. Work–Study Programs assisted students in postsecondary education programs by allowing them to work for their postsecondary institution. The Act provided for Adult Basic Education Programs that taught basic reading and writing skills to adults. It also created A Program to Assist Migrant and Seasonally Employed Agricultural Employees by providing funding to state and agencies to work with such populations. Finally, Work-Experience Programs were aimed at training "persons who are unable to support or care for themselves or their families" (Hawkins et al., 1966, p. 114).

Vocational Education Amendments of 1968
Through these amendments, the federal government increased the seats on the National Advisory Council and required that members be appointed directly by the president (Calhoun & Finch, 1976). According to Calhoun and Finch, the council has issued numerous reports dealing with:

(a) *the national attitude toward vocational education as a system designed for someone else's child; (b) the approach of federal funding to reduce the flow of untrained manpower into the pool of unemployment; (c) employment as an integral part of education; (d) the problems involved in local support, state plans, the lack of federal initiative, and the need for effective national planning for vocational education; (e) those forces that appeared to prevent the adoption of some of the recommendations of the first four reports; (f) counseling and guidance and what must be done to provide sound counseling systems; (g) vocational student organizations and their role in vocational and career education; and (h) a national policy on career education.* (p. 47)

These amendments further required states to submit more detailed plans of action for usage of funds. In addition, a major component of the amendments was to help students stay in school and successfully transition to the workplace following graduation. Through these amendments, the federal government provided assistance with defining vocational education courses and for developing adequate curriculum. Provisions were made for vocational education instructors to receive additional schooling, and the amendments encouraged vocational education program personnel to work closely with area businesses and industries in order to provide further training for instructors (Calhoun & Finch, 1976).

Elementary and Secondary Education Act of 1965
While not specifically dealing with vocational education, this Act aimed to improve learning conditions across the nation for those students who were living in poverty. To do so, the Act called for increase in quality of vocational equipment, classrooms, and teaching for all students (Calhoun & Finch, 1976).

Education Amendments of 1972
The federal government realized that vocational counseling needed to start earlier in education, thus amending earlier legislation to include programs to provide such counseling beginning in elementary school. Further, the amendments called for such vocational counseling to continue not only through high school but also through post-secondary school as well. These amendments created the Bureau of Occupational and Adult Education, and they also expanded the definition of vocational education once again. These amendments also brought consumer education to the forefront (Calhoun & Finch, 1976).

Education Amendments of 1974
These amendments further strengthened the previous amendments in the area of career education. It

was no longer enough for students to graduate with a degree and basic skills. With these amendments, educators were charged with the job to ensure that all students who were graduating from high school were prepared to enter into a career that met the students' needs, goals, and abilities. Additionally, it created the Office of Career Education (Calhoun & Finch, 1976).

Education Amendments of 1976

As noted above, the GAO reported on the biases and inadequacies found in vocational education programs. These findings prompted the federal government to pass the 1976 amendments, with primary focus on program evaluation. Unfortunately, the National Assessment of Vocational Education (NAVE) found that the legislation had not been successfully implemented. According to Hayward and Benson (1993), the funding was used inappropriately and ineffectively. Instead of aiding the disadvantaged students, the amendments served to "segregate such persons into training for dead-end occupations" (p. 13). Finally, there were limited efforts towards eliminating sexual discrimination against women (Hayward and Benson, 1993).

Carl D. Perkins Vocational Education and Applied Technology Act of 1984

This Act sought to regain credibility for vocational education in two ways. First, focusing on the need for the nation to improve its workforce productivity, it called for major improvements in the quality of vocational education programs. Secondly, the Act sought to address needs of students who have previously been denied proper vocational education services and to correct such wrongdoings (ACTE, 2002; Hayward & Benson, 1993; Wonacott, 2003).

Carl D. Perkins Vocational Education and Applied Technology Education Act of 1990 (Perkins II)

Perkins II provided additional directives from the federal government to vocational programs regarding implementation. The focus of this Act was to improve not only vocational components but also to increase academic components in vocational education programs in the effort to meet the needs of increasing technology. This Act reinforced the idea that in order to meet such demands, students needed to continue education past high school on into postsecondary programs, and it was the job of the vocational programs to encourage and support this (ACTE, 2002; Wonacott, 2003).

National School-to-Work Opportunities Act (NSTWOA) of 1994

Feeding off of the funds from prior legislation, this Act sought to "address the nation's serious skills shortage through partnerships between educators and employers" (ACTE, 2002). These partnerships developed into learning opportunities for students while still participating in secondary school. Most school-to-work programs were designed to allow vocational education students to attend regular classes for part of the day, and the remainder of the school day was spent interning in a business or industry (ACTE).

Carl D. Perkins Vocational Education and Applied Technology Education Act of 1998 (Perkins III)

Perkins III continued the basic ideas of Perkins I and II, requiring improvements in vocational programs to meet the needs of the nation in the midst of increased technology. As with the prior legislation, vocational education programs were again asked to pair strong academic components with vocational and technical components in an effort to create success in both secondary and postsecondary programs. Again, vocational programs were also asked to work with disadvantaged and other special populations. In addition, this Act required states to provide performance data regarding student aptitude, secondary education completion, postsecondary or military service completion, and other forms of job training program completion (ACTE, 2002; Wonacott, 2003).

1.5 FUTURE TRENDS

As noted from our nation's history, technology is fluid, constantly changing and progressing. With so many technological advancements, vocational education must adapt to such changes in order to be considered essential in our society. Vocational program educators and administrators are responsible for updating themselves and their students on current methods and skills required by a modern workforce. While modern machines and computers may have replaced some vocational workers, new skills can be learned to run those machines and computers. Such skills must be taught in schools and technical education programs (Calhoun & Finch, 1976).

Another important issue to consider is that general education requirements, as well as occupational preparedness, should continue to be included and may need to be increased in order for a vocational student to truly be successful (ACTE, 2002; Calhoun & Finch, 1976). It is already apparent in our nation's society that advanced mathematics and science courses are mandatory educational fields necessary to keep up with the ever-changing world of technology (ACTE, 2002; Wonacott, 2003). It is no longer relevant to simply teach single skills to students and expect that they will be able to survive in society that our nation has created (Wonacott). Vocational programs must continue to provide strong career guidance to students, as well as onsite learning opportunities through internships and partnerships with businesses and industries. It will be through these efforts that vocational education students will truly be successful in their transition from school to the workplace.

A final lesson learned from the history of vocational education is the power of groups. Without the work of groups such as the National Society for Vocational Education, the American Vocational Association, and the current Association for Career and Technical Education, the federal government would not have passed the tremendous amount of legislation that has brought vocational education to where it is today. These groups were also responsible for changing the curriculum and programming aspects of vocational education in order to keep our nation updated with technologically-skilled individuals. Such groups will be assets as vocational education continues in the future (ACTE, 2002).

1.6 CONCLUSION

Vocational education has gone through many changes since its inception, beginning as informal lessons to becoming the formal instruction that it is today. The definition, scope, and audience of vocational education in the past, present, and future fluctuate based upon national and international issues and events. When the nation has required a skillful, competent workforce, vocational education has successfully trained new workers to meet those needs. This will no doubt continue into the future. In addition to training and educating new students, vocational education programs must also focus on retraining and updating existing workers so that they do not become obsolete. Because the nature of our nation's needs is constantly changing, it is imperative for vocational education programs to be abreast of new technologies and skills needed to successfully compete in the international market.

REFERENCES

Association for Career and Technical Education (ACTE). (2002, February). Celebrating 75 years of success. *Techniques, 77*(2), 20–45.

Barlow, M. L. (Ed.). (1974). *The philosophy for quality vocational education programs*. Washington, DC: American Vocational Association.

Barlow, M. L. (1976, February). *Implications from the history of vocational education*. Paper presented to The Center for Vocational Education and the Ohio State University staff, Columbus, OH.

Brewer, E. W., & Achilles, C. (2008). *Finding funding: Grantwriting from start to finish, including project management and internet use* (5th ed.). Newbury Park, CA: Corwin Press.

Brewer, E. W., Campbell, A. C., & Petty, G. C. (2000). *Foundations of workforce education*. Dubuque, IA: Kendall/Hunt Publishing Co.

Calhoun, C. C., & Finch, A. V. (1976). *Vocational and career education: Concepts and operations*. Belmont, CA: Wadsworth Publishing Corp.

Evans, R. E. (1971). *Foundations of vocational education*. Columbus, OH: Charles E. Merrill Publishing Co.

Hawkins, L. S., Prosser, C. A., & Wright, J. C. (1966). *Development of federal legislation for vocational education. Compiled by J. C. Swanson*. Chicago, IL: American Technical Society.

Hayward, B. C., & Benson, C. S. (1993). Vocational-technical education: Major reforms and debates. (Report No. ED/OVAE-93-9). Washington, DC: Office of Vocational and Adult Education. (ERIC Document Reproduction Service No. ED 369959).

Keller, F. J. (1948). *Principles of vocational education*. Boston: D. C. Heath and Co.

Kneller, G. F. (1963). *Foundations of education*. New York: John Wiley & Sons, Inc.

Miller, M. T. (1993). *The historical development of vocational education in the United States: Colonial America through the Morrill legislation*. (ERIC Document Reproduction Service No. ED 360481).

Thompson, J. F. (1973). *Foundations of vocational education*. Englewood Cliffs, NJ: Prentice-Hall, Inc.

Wonacott, M. E. (2003). *History and evolution of vocational and career-technical education: A Compilation*. (Report No. ED-99-CO-0013). Columbus, OH: ERIC Clearinghouse on Adult, Career, and Vocational Education. (ERIC Document Reproduction Service No. ED 482359).

Chapter 2
Principles of Scientific Management and Occupational Analysis

Victor C. X. Wang
California State University, Long Beach, USA

ABSTRACT

As work has become more technical and analytical due to the increased availability of digital information technology, more team-based due to organizational restructuring, increasingly more customer oriented, has made the workforce more diverse, it is necessary and important to show our readers that both principles of scientific management and occupational analysis are driven by the predominant philosophy, behaviorism. Observed behaviors on the part of employees/or trainees in occupational analysis come from searching for the one best method of doing one's job (occupation). Once this one best way is identified, instructors or employers are responsible for training the employees by using the carefully selected science. Although other philosophies do affect occupational analysis, behaviorism coupled with principles of scientific management does remain the predominant guiding principle for occupational analysis.

2.1 INTRODUCTION

As soon as Taylor (1911) published his book on *Principles of Scientific Management*, his principles have been widely studied, borrowed and even applied in the field of Career and Technical Education (CTE). Taylor made the comparison between traditional management and scientific management. Regardless of which type of man-

agement, the principal object of management should be to secure the maximum prosperity for the employer, coupled with the maximum prosperity for each employee (Taylor, 1911, p. 9). While traditional management focuses on the work of the employees, scientific management focuses on the training and development of each individual in the establishment, so that employees can do (at their fastest pace and with the maximum of efficiency) the highest class of work for which their natural abilities fit them (Taylor, 1911, p. 12). Taylor's

DOI: 10.4018/978-1-61520-747-3.ch002

rationale has been although there are many ways of doing the same job, among the various methods and implements used in each element of each trade, there is always one method and one implement which is quicker and better than any of the rest. Further, this one best method and best implement can be discovered or developed through a scientific study and analysis of all of the methods and implements in use, together with accurate, minute, motion and time study (Taylor, 1911). Occupational analysis in CTE shares the same philosophy as principles of scientific management. Occupational analysis addresses standard procedures, narrow span of control, and specific job descriptions instituted to improve efficiency. A standard course is offered in almost every land-grant university, which deals with occupational analysis for students in the field of CTE. In this course, students learn to analyze occupations by breaking down tasks into steps of procedures. In most cases, students are required to use *Dictionary of Occupational Titles* issued by the Department of Labor to assist them in analyzing occupations in order to improve efficiency. The object in analyzing occupations is to emphasize conformity and predictability of employees' contributions to the organization. In doing so, employees are trained to look for structure, rules, and search for the one best way in order to maximize prosperity for both employers and employees. Critics (Berman, Bowman, West, & Van Wart, 2006) argue that principles of scientific management in relation to occupational analysis in CTE may impede achievement of quality performance with their narrow span of controlled job design in today's organizations where customization, innovation, autonomous work teams and empowerment are required (p. 11). Although there is some truth in this criticism, to institute efficiency, occupational analysis has to rely on principles of scientific management. The principles outlined by Taylor (1911) serve to guide occupational analysis in which employers and trainers (human resource

developers, instructional designers, learning specialists) should engage in doing the following:

- First, develop a science for each element of employees' work.
- Second, scientifically select and then train, teach, and develop the employee, whereas in the past employees chose their own work and trained themselves as best they could (prior to Industrial Revolution).
- Third, cooperate with the employees so as to ensure all of the work being done in accordance with the principles of the science which has been developed.
- Fourth, there is an almost equal division of the work and the responsibility between employers and employees. The employers take over all work for which they are better fitted than the employees, while in the past almost all of the work and the greater part of the responsibility were thrown upon the employees. (p. 37)

By following these principles, employers can find the one best way to improve efficiency. Although occupational analysis is changing from emphasis on functional, technical, job-related competencies to a broader range of skills, cross-functional training, and diagnostic, problem-solving capabilities, searching for the one best way (science) in occupational analysis has always had its place in CTE. Without looking for the science of doing one's job, functional, technical, job-related competencies cannot be guaranteed, let alone institute efficiency. Critics may have misunderstood what John Dewey said regarding the goal of CTE. Dewey (Wang & King, 2009) opposed CTE which was limited only to acquisition of job skills. He believed that the underlying principles of the work processes and social significance of work must be included. He further indicated that through vocational studies, culture should be made truly vital for many students (p. 12). From Dewey's analysis, it is obvious that he was advocating that the one best way (science) of doing one's job should be sought after. On the other hand, he was advocating that other job related skills should be taught. Occupational analysis will lead to the one best way. Without efficiency first, other skills will be taught in vain. This chapter will address the dialectical relationship between principles of scientific management and occupational analysis. By reading this chapter, readers will get to the basic idea of how principles of scientific management and occupational analysis have evolved over the years. Above all, this chapter will shed light on some real issues and controversies revolving around occupational analysis. In addition, solutions will be provided and recommendations will be made. With this purpose in mind, the next section will take our readers to some of the historical background of occupational analysis in the field of CTE.

2.2 BACKGROUND

Based on the argument made by Wenrich, Wenrich and Galloway (1988), primitive people did not need much formal education in order to work. Job skills were gained from watching one's elders (Roberts, 1965). Learning is an act to gain knowledge or skill by observation (Wang & King, 2009). During the long Stone Age, it is assumed that people learned their survival skills by observing someone performing on the job (Boyd, 1921). It was after Egyptians developed papyrus and hieroglyphics and started to teach scribes how to write and make the papyrus that documentation of learning and training was possible. By using a written language, people could document the ways that were productive, and the ways that were unproductive could be avoided. Also knowledge and skills that were documented could be passed from generation to generation. Indeed, CTE has paralleled humans' efforts from the Stone Age to modern civilization. However, CTE started out as unorganized programs. It was 6,000 years ago

that apprenticeships started where the students learned on-the-job with an experienced scribe. This kind of apprenticeship lasted until the start of the Industrial Revolution when a large pool of trained workers was needed. The Industrial Revolution prompted rapid development of labor-saving machinery which eventually caused the decline of apprenticeship (Barlow, 1976). Prior to and during the Industrial Revolution, Europeans and North Americans developed the power loom in 1814, the locomotive in 1829, the mechanical reaper and the telegraph in 1835 and the sewing machine in 1846. Trade was expanded by doing business with people inside and outside their countries. Coal and iron mines were developed on a large scale because of machinery. Networks of railroads were developed. The nations' economy was drastically changed. Worthy of note is the fact that in the United States alone between the Industrial Revolution and 1940, the nation's GDP increased by 52% on an annual basis, easily surpassing the United Kingdom. All of these changes contributed much to the decline of apprenticeship. It is obvious that all industrialized nations need well trained workers so that efficiency could be achieved. During the Industrial Revolution, more organized CTE programs were needed in order to train much needed workers. Any organized or planned CTE concerns the identification of areas of training which have relatively broad applicability (Scoville, 1972, p. 11). There is wide recognition that training produces workers with sufficient flexibility to adapt to economic and technological change. As CTE educators and trainers were busy identifying curricula and programs to train workers, it was Taylor in 1911 who reminded educators and trainers and managers that there was a science of doing one's job. Taylor (1911, p. 60) postulated that:

It is now clear that even in the case of the most elementary form of labor that is known, there is a science, and that when the man best suited to this class of work has been carefully selected, when the science of doing the work has been developed, and when the carefully selected man has been trained to work in accordance with this science, the results obtained must necessity be overwhelmingly greater than those which are possible under the plan of the "initiative and incentive."

By the plan of the "initiative and incentive," Taylor referred to the traditional management method. Taylor also indicated that not only principles of scientific management hold the key to maximum prosperity on the part of workers and employers but also the key to harmonious cooperation. He addressed the harmonious cooperation by saying, "the greatest obstacle to harmonious cooperation between the workmen and the management lay in the ignorance of the management as to what really constitutes a proper day's work for a workman" (p. 53).

In response to the Industrial Revolution and in response to searching for the one best way of doing one's job, the *Dictionary of Occupational Titles* (DOT) was developed by the Bureau of Employment Security, U.S. Department of Labor. DOT represents an approach to the area of occupational information. An index of the number of broad bundles of specific jobs (which bundles are termed occupations) exists in significant quantity throughout the U.S. economy. DOT includes a great deal of additional information about job characteristics, broad families of occupations and work fields (Scoville, 1972). According to DOT, job groupings are intended to represent an "occupational-industrial breakdown" of the jobs in U.S. economy, in which work performed is classified by seven basic groups: professional and managerial; clerical and sales; service; agricultural, skilled occupations; semi skilled occupations; and unskilled occupations. While principles of scientific management focus on searching for the one best way, the primary purpose of DOT is to facilitate the placement function of matching job demand and worker attributes. On the other hand, DOT has its weaknesses and readers should

be familiar with these weaknesses. One cannot use DOT well without knowing its strengths and weaknesses. The DOT's major weaknesses were identified as follows:

- Jobs are described at a level of job-specific detail that makes it difficult to conduct cross-occupation comparisons. Thus, it would be difficult to determine to what extent the incumbents of one occupation would have the necessary general skills for easy transition to other work. As a result, the goal of using the system as a resource for workers transitioning from obsolete or down-sized occupations could not be realized.
- Jobs are described solely according to tasks. Information about the skills, abilities, knowledge, and other individual qualities needed to perform jobs is not directly collected. The latter information may be crucial to answer questions inherent in person-job matching, training, skill transfer, and wage and salary administration.
- The DOT provides some information about the physical and ergonomic aspects of jobs, such as noise, temperature, and work schedules. However, other contextual factors, such as interpersonal demands and stressors, organizational influences, and exposure to other hazards, are not covered.
- The time and expense involved in updating descriptive job information ensure that a substantial portion of the information in the DOT is outdated at any given time.
- The discrete, qualitative descriptions in the DOT do not allow for linkages with other occupational or labor-market data-bases. ("Implications for Occupational Analysis," 1999, p. 183)

It can be concluded that DOT does not deviate too much from Taylor's principles of scientific management. Occupational analysis stems from both the Industrial Revolution and principles of scientific management. How does DOT group occupations? It groups occupations according to some combination of required general educational developments, specific vocational preparation, aptitudes, interests, temperaments, and physical demands. Further DOT assesses the degree of involvement of various jobs with data, people and things.

For occupational analysis, additional materials can be found from the following sources:

- The Modules of Employable Skills developed by the International Labor Office.
- The Developing a Curriculum (DACUM) initiated in Canada.
- Competency-based Curricula in Secondary Schools in the United States, Australia and England.
- The Vocational and Technical Education Consortium of States (V-TECS).
- Curriculum Development in CTE developed by professors/scholars.

All these sources including DOT and principles of scientific management share one common goal, that is, competency-based education for students in CTE. As competency-based education has become the norm in CTE, what are the real issues and controversies that need to be addressed in relation to occupational analysis? The next section will take our readers to the main thrust of this chapter regarding these real problems and challenges. Then, solutions will be provided, and recommendations will be made.

2.3 MAJOR ISSUES REVOLVING AROUND OCCUPATIONAL ANALYSIS

Occupational analysis stems from searching for the one best way of doing one's job and begins with task analysis. According to Gagne, Wager, Golas and Keller (2005), there are two major kinds of task analysis. One is referred to as a procedural task analysis or information processing analysis and the other is termed a learning task analysis. Procedural task analysis involves breaking tasks down into steps of procedures that the workers must perform in order to complete the task. Job design characterized by standard procedures, narrow span of control and specific job descriptions instituted to improve efficiency all stem from procedural task analysis and are closely related to principles of scientific management. The so-called observed behaviors cannot occur without procedural task analysis. No doubt procedural task analysis is driven by the behaviorist philosophy that requires job-designers, managers and trainers to focus on observable and measurable behaviors on the part of the employees or trainees. To improve efficiency, procedural task analysis must align with the mission and goal of all the industries in this consumer society, which is characterized by rapid technological changes, innovation, and creativity (Wang & King, 2009). First and foremost, employers would like to hire fully competent workers, and competent workers can achieve efficiency. Efficiency guaranteed by the one best way precedes innovation and creativity. In other words, employers will address innovation and creativity based on tangible profits as a result of increasing efficiency. Procedural task analysis also called information processing analysis because it accounts for the intellectual skills that are components of the total task (Gagne et al., 2005). For detailed procedural task analysis, see DOT. In fact, many universities teach the course titled *Occupational Analysis* by directing students to use DOT for procedural task analysis.

Once procedural task analysis is completed, the second kind of task analysis, a learning task analysis needs to be conducted. Learning task analysis refers to an analysis to identify prerequisites competencies or enabling skills. A prerequisite is a task learned prior to the learning of a target objective and it enables learning. This learning task analysis is useful in CTE because workers are required entry level behaviors before any on-the-job training is needed. If any enabling capabilities have been learned prior to performing any jobs, employers or managers or job designers may just go to procedural task analysis based on the nature of the current jobs. It must be noted that both types of task analysis lead to competency-based education in CTE.

Competency-based education in CTE originated in the 20th Century behaviorism. According to the leader of behaviorism, John B. Watson, the way to understand humans was through observing their behavior, not exploring the inner, unobservable recesses of mind and emotion. Another behaviorist, Skinner addresses the issues of who and what should be taught as well as the administrative concerns of student control and individual differences (Elias & Merriam, 2005). Like John Dewey, Skinner advocates that allowing for novelty and diversity for both cultures and species increase their strength with respect to a far wider range of contingencies when subject to variations and selection (1968, p. 235). Skinner argues that student behavior can and should be controlled through positive rather than negative reinforcement, and that individual differences need to be more efficiently dealt with. Applied to occupational analysis in CTE, behaviorism would translate into:

The roles of employers, managers, trainers and employees are quite defined in the behaviorist framework. The ultimate goal of occupational analysis (training) is to bring about behavior that will ensure survival of the human species, societies, and individuals. The role of the job designer is to design an environment that elicits behavior toward meeting these goals and to extinguish behavior that is not desirable. The trainer (teacher), then, is a contingency manager, an environmental controller, or behavioral engineer who plans in detail the conditions necessary to bring about *desired behavior. (Adapted from Elias & Merriam, 2005, p. 93)*

Behaviorism has been widely used in occupational analysis and CTE since its inception. Since behaviorism focuses on the measurable, overt activity of an employee, training, in behavioral terms, is a change in behavior. Training objectives in occupational analysis or CTE, then, specify the behavior to be exhibited by trainees after completing a series of training sessions. Therefore, any training or instructional objectives in occupational analysis contain three components: (1) the relevant conditions under which a trainee is expected to perform; (2) the behavior a trainee is to perform, including a general reference to the product of the trainee's behavior; and (3) a description of the criteria by which the behavior will be judged acceptable or unacceptable, successful or unsuccessful. The goal of behaviorist is to measure learning outcomes objectively and precisely, thus revealing how much progress has been made on the part of the employee or trainee. Evaluation based on behaviorism eliminates subjective, capricious estimates of employee performance. In occupational analysis, the emphasis is placed on identifying the skills (derived from task analysis) needed to perform in an occupation, teaching those skills, and requiring a certain standard of performance in those skills (Elias & Merriam, 2005). Taylor's principles of scientific management on searching for the one best way do not deviate from this emphasis in occupational analysis. The rapid economic growth between the Industrial Revolution and the 1940s led to the wide adoption of behaviorism in CTE. If efficiency is the goal and mission of CTE, then, competency-based education is the means via which the goal can be reached. First, knowledge, skills and behaviors (competencies) come from analysis of worker roles. Second, criteria used in assessing employee competency are to be provided by employers via the use of DOT and other sources. Third, assessment of employees' competency should focus on performance. All three steps can be conducted via the use of behaviorism. Indeed behaviorism dictates occupational analysis. Behaviorism is well suited to CTE and serves to guide occupational analysis. Some outstanding advantages of employing behaviorism for a detailed task analysis of a specific job are outlined by Elias and Merriam (2005, pp. 100-101):

- It allows for individual differences in terms of the starting point for instruction;
- The time it takes a student to master competencies is flexible and dependent upon individual ability;
- Learning specified competencies may be done in a variety of ways from formal class activities to life or work experiences;
- Criterion-referenced evaluation is non-threatening;
- It is an ideal vehicle for a self-directed individual learning experience.

Based on these advantages of behaviorism, programmed instruction became the norm in the 1960s and technical rational tradition has continued to dominate in the 1990s (Sork, 2000, p. 173). There are always two sides to everything. Elias and Merriam (2005) also listed the disadvantages of behaviorism associated with occupational analysis in CTE:

- It depends on an accurate identification of tasks performed in thousands of occupations and the availability of such task inventories to curriculum developers;
- Some competencies desirable for certain occupations may be difficult to specify from task inventories and, if identified, difficult to perform;
- Identifying what constitutes minimum performance standards for mastery of some tasks may be difficult;
- It predetermines the end product of a learning experience;

- It may be dehumanizing or non-humanistic, lacking in concern for the student, and inhibiting creativity.
- It forces all students into the same mold, and fragments curriculum into bits and pieces while it overlooks the whole.

Despite its advantages and disadvantages, behaviorism has provided theoretical framework for both occupational analysis and principles of scientific management. It leads to accountability in that all employers and trainers involved in an educational activity should be held responsible for its outcomes. Outcomes may be desired behavior, better products, better service or even efficiency in scientific management. To achieve competency-based education in CTE, some instructional methods based on behaviorism have been popular. For example, professionals in the field of CTE have been using programmed instruction, computer-based or computer-assisted instruction and contract learning to elicit desired behavior on the part of students. In this new information age, blended learning, virtual education, instructional technology, vocational training, flexible learning, distance education, and collaborative learning all revolve around behaviorism. The new buzz terms such as IT education, mobile/wireless computing, networking/telecommunication, multimedia technology, social computing are new names for programmed instruction, computer-based or computer-assisted instructor or contract learning, a new version of behaviorism. All these instructional methods may require one format according to behaviorism:

- Step 1: Specify behavioral goals;
- Step 2: Analyze the learning task: sequence material in a logical progression;
- Step 3: Assess entry behavior: identify what your students or you already know;
- Step 4: Plan presentation: provide cues, feedback, reinforcement, and self-pacing;

Table 1. Comparison of different philosophies that may be employed in occupational analysis

Aspect	Behaviorist	Humanist	Progressive	Constructivist
Learning theorists	Pavlov, Watson, Skinner	Maslow, Rogers, Knowles	Darwin, Spencer, Dewey	Piaget, Bruner
View of the learning process	Change in behavior	Learners are responsible for their own learning	Learners' experiences are an equally valid center for education	Construction of meaning from experience
Focus of learning	Provide external stimuli	Cater to learners' developmental needs	Conduct needs assessments for program development and instructional purposes	Individual and social construction of knowledge
Purpose of learning	To achieve student learning outcomes	Become self-directed in learning	To remove learners from passivity and uniformity education	To build knowledge
Instructor's role	Arrange external conditions to elicit desired response	Become a learning facilitator by linking students to learning resources	Helper, guide, encourager, consultant, and resource, not that of a transmitter, disciplinarian, judge and authority	Negotiate meaning making with learners
Manifestation in adult and higher education	Manage teaching by objectives, performance improvement, pedagogical approaches	Andragogy, self-concept, self-actualization, lifelong learning	Vocational adult education, extension education, education of the foreign born and citizenship education, family and parent education, and education for social change	Experiential learning, critical reflection, situated learning, communities of practice

Source: Adapted from Merriam, Caffarella, and Baumgartner, 2007, pp. 295-296.

- Step 5: Evaluate, record, and adjust. (Herman, 1977, pp. 126-128)

Readers of this chapter may be aware that a large number of universities and employers have been using the above instructional methods for skills-based vocational technical instruction. What about other types of philosophies? Have they impacted occupational analysis or principles of scientific management in CTE? It can be said the even the most andragogical type of employers are reluctant to experiment with other philosophies in occupational analysis in CTE simply because our consumer society is driven by efficiency, and maximum prosperity on the part of employers and employees. While other philosophies may lead to innovation and creativity, at least in occupational analysis in CTE, very few professionals would be willing to toy with them. For detailed information regarding prevalent philosophies, refer to Table 1.

A great deal has been said on the issues revolv-ing around behaviorism, occupational analysis and principles of scientific management. This major section particularly addressed how behaviorism has impacted occupational analysis in CTE and the relationship between competency-based education and behaviorism. The next section will take our readers to the future trends.

2.4 FUTURE TRENDS

Writing in 1995, Bagnall (p. 81) argued that "The modern world is characterized by the scientific, industrial, and social programs, institutions, actions, and artifacts generated by the humanistic and Enlightenment search for the universal foundations of truth, morality, and aesthetics." Whereas Newman (1994) postulated that in this postmodern era, things are much more diverse, fluid, illusionary, and contested, including the reality of the world itself. While Bagnall still corroborates with the belief on principles of scientific management and occupational analysis, that is, to survive and thrive in the modern world, one needs to search for the one best method, Newman perhaps indicates that there are multiple ways to truth. In terms of occupational analysis, there may be more than one best method that will lead to efficiency. Perhaps, there are no absolutes or single theoretical framework for examining and analyzing one's occupations. However, are we totally divorced from the modern world and have fully embraced the postmodern era? Will competency-based education characterized by principles of scientific management, job-designs and behaviorism remain the norm in this postmodern era? Are we truly moving from functional, technical, job-related competencies to a broader range of skills, cross-functional training, and diagnostic, problem-solving capabilities while distancing ourselves from searching for the best method of doing one's job? For well over a century, the educational system of the United States has adopted methods from three foreign training systems: the Russian system, the Sloyd system, and the Arts and Crafts Movement (Wang & King, 2009, p. 90). Noteworthy is the fact that these approaches were adopted primarily in response to the sharply increased need for skilled workers during the period of the industrial revolution. All three approaches do not deviate much from competency-based instruction, that is, they all revolve around searching for the one best method. The Russian task analysis approach utilized a systems approach in which a specific curriculum was devised by breaking training into its components and each of those were taught as a separate entity. Documented by Wang and King (2009, p. 92), the Russian task analysis approach involves three stages:

- The study of the materials and tools.
- The acquisition of the skills to use the materials and tools.
- The actual construction of a part of a whole item.

The Sloyd system also involves three key elements:

- Making useful objects.
- Analysis of processes.
- Educational Method.

While the Arts and Crafts Movement stressed the importance of good craftsmanship and aesthetic quality, this movement also involves three principles:

- Unity of art, which defined all forms of art as equal rather than in a hierarchy where one type of art was worth more than other types of arts and which opposed the superiority of professionalism.
- Joy in labor, which was the idea that people could use their imaginations to derive pleasure from the experience of work as opposed to working in stultifying factories.
- Design reform, whereby the designs of objects used by ordinary people were changed to look as if they belonged in the place where they were used (e.g., a kettle looked like it belonged in a kitchen), but objects also were stylized, representing taste as opposed to wealth and refinement and craftsmanship as opposed to ostentation. (Crawford, 1997)

A closer examination of all these states, elements and principles points in one direction, that is, in this postmodern era, occupational analysis is still driven by competency-based education that is inextricably intertwined with observed behaviors, principles of scientific management, standard procedures, narrow span of control, and specific job descriptions. Even if we are moving from functional, technical, job-related competencies to a broader range of skills: cross-functional training, and diagnostic, problem-solving capabilities, acquiring and mastering a broad range of skills, cross functional training and diagnostic, problem-solving capabilities also involve in searching for the best method/or science. Without this one best science, efficiency cannot be achieved. As contemporary scholars argue that there is no truth to be found, perhaps one trend is that occupational analysis in this postmodern era will be primarily driven by behaviorism (principles of scientific management) but at the same time supplemented and complemented by other philosophies such as humanism, progressive philosophy and constructivism. Competency-based education in career and technical education coupled with principles of scientific management and behaviorism has stood the test of time and it should remain a major trend in the future. As the field of career and technical education is advancing quickly with the use of technology, programmed instruction has become all the more important. What is programmed instruction popularized in the 1960s? Like occupational analysis and foreign training systems, it involves in searching for the best method of instruction in order to maximize learning on the part of students. When searching for the best method of doing one's work, we should be mindful of the external contexts of work. The external contexts of work may facilitate or inhibit our search for the best method of doing one's job or occupation:

- We are experiencing increased competition in product and financial markets in this volatile global environment. Employees have increased uncertainty over job stability while, at the same time, employers always call for emphasis on quality, innovation, and flexibility in work processes and outcomes.
- In this technological world with so many digital natives, changing technologies continue to alter skills and eliminate and create jobs at a rapid rate. Technologies raise skills requirements given their sophisticated level. Greater emphasis on cognitive, communications and interactive social

skills is being placed on both employees and employers.
- Demographic changes will increase the diversity of individuals and groups across and particularly within occupations and organizations. Looking for the one best method will involve in managing and addressing diversity in the workplace.
- Inequality of wages and incomes in the workplace may strain the search for the one best way of doing one's jobs or occupations. ("External Contexts," 1999)

2.5 CONCLUSION

This chapter has demonstrated that both principles of scientific management and occupational analysis are driven by behaviorism advanced by behaviorists such as Watson and Skinner. Behaviorism has been considered the American philosophy since the turn of the 20th century in that all people could achieve great accomplishments given the opportunity (stimulus), individual initiative (response), and fair treatment (rewards) (Knowles, Holton, & Swanson, 2005). Translated into teaching or training in career and technical education, those with this philosophy as their guiding philosophy are bound to be frozen into the pedagogical model in the field. In other words, behaviorists are always looking for observable and measurable behaviors on the part of their students or trainees. Observed behaviors could be derived from the one best method of doing one's job in Taylor's terms. In occupational analysis, behaviorists are interested in analyzing duties and tasks. More importantly, they are interested in breaking down tasks into steps of procedures so that students or trainees know exactly how to proceed to learn to perform their jobs. Because of the prevalence of behaviorism, educators and trainers popularized programmed instruction in the 1960s in North America. As technology permeates the field of career and technical education, programmed instruction has proven to be more effective especially in terms of teaching or training with the use of technology. In occupational analysis, course instructors are required to develop specific student performance objectives that can be observable and measurable in behaviorist terms. For example, all instructors in career and technical education are required to write their student performance objectives, using a standardized format: By the end of this lesson, the student/trainee will be able (action verb, preferably a higher level action verb from Bloom's Taxonomy) what (object) under what conditions (can be observable) by what standards (can be measured). In doing so, instructors/trainers are searching for the one best method according to Taylor's principles of scientific management. Although principles of scientific management and occupational analysis are interrelated, this is not to say that other philosophies such as humanist, progressive and constructivist philosophies have no place in career and technical education or occupational analysis. Rather, these philosophies enhance behaviorism in their own way. The majority of the learners in career and technical education are adult learners. If we stress problem-solving skills related to adult learners' developmental tasks or real world problems, we are in a sense using humanistic philosophy to help adult learners learn. When we try to tap into adult learners' prior experience, we are in a sense using constructivist philosophy. If we emphasize the learning environment, we are in a sense using the progressive philosophy. As these philosophies are quietly enhancing behaviorism in occupational analysis, behaviorism has been the predominant philosophy linking principles of scientific management with occupational analysis in the field of career and technical education. All training methods including the three major foreign training systems revolve around searching for the best method of doing one's job (occupation) so that efficiency can be achieved. With the changing nature of work in the 21st century, what are the implications for occupational analysis? Will

behaviorism supported by principles of scientific management remain predominant?

REFERENCES

Bagnall, R. G. (1995). Discriminative justice and responsibility in postmodern adult education. *Adult Education Quarterly, 45*(2), 79–94. doi:10.1177/0741713695045002002

Barlow, M. L. (1976). 200 years of vocational education, 1776-1976: The awakening, 1776-1976. *American Vocational Journal, 51*(5), 23–28.

Berman, B., Bowman, J. S., West, J. P., & Van Wart, M. (2006). *Human resource management in public service: Paradoxes, processes, and problems.* Thousand Oaks, CA: Sage Publications.

Crawford, A. (1997). Ideas and objects: The Arts and Crafts Movement in Britain. [from EBSCO-Host Academic Search Elite database.]. *Design Issues, 13*(1), 1–7. Retrieved April 7, 2009. doi:10.2307/1511584

Elias, J. L., & Merriam, S. B. (2005). *Philosophical foundations of adult education* (3rd ed.). Malabar, FL: Krieger.

Gagne, R. M., Wager, W. W., Golas, K. C., & Keller, J. M. (2005). *Principles of instructional design* (5th ed.). Florence, KY: Thomson Wadsworth.

Herman, T. M. (1977). *Creating learning environments: The behavioral approach to education.* Boston: Allyn and Bacon.

Knowles, M. S., Holton, E., & Swanson, A. (2005). *The adult learner* (6th ed.). Boston, MA: Elsevier Butterworth Heinemann.

Merriam, S. B., Caffarella, R. S., & Baumgartner, L. M. (2007). *Learning in adulthood: A comprehensive guide* (3rd ed.). San Francisco: Jossey-Bass.

Newman, M. (1994). *Defining the enemy: Adult education in social action.* Sydney: Stewart Victor.

Roberts, R. W. (1965). *Vocational and practical arts education* (2nd ed.). New York: Harper and Row Publishers.

Scoville, J. G. (1972). *Manpower and occupational analysis: Concepts and measurements.* Lexington, MA: D.C. Health and Company.

Skinner, B. F. (1968). *The technology of teaching.* New York: Appleton-Century-Crofts.

Sork, T. J. (2000). Planning educational programs. In Wilson, A. L., & Hayes, E. R. (Eds.), *Handbook of adult and continuing education* (pp. 171–190). San Francisco: Jossey-Bass.

Taylor, F. W. (1911). *The principles of scientific management.* New York: Harper & Brothers Publishers.

(1999). *The changing nature of work: Implications for occupational analysis.* Washington, DC: National Academy Press.

Wang, V. C. X., & King, K. P. (2009). *Building workforce competencies in career and technical education.* Charlotte, NC: Information Age Publishing.

Wenrich, R. G., Wenrich, J. W., & Galloway, J. D. (1988). *Administration of vocational education.* Homewood, IL: American Technical.

Chapter 3
Career and Technical Education:
Myths, Metrics, and Metamorphosis

Kit Kacirek
University of Arkansas, USA

Jules K. Beck
University of Arkansas, USA

Kenda S. Grover
University of Arkansas, USA

ABSTRACT

Educational institutions are increasingly challenged to provide relevant and rigorous programs to students who demand variety in learning venues, delivery platforms, degree options, and quality assurance. Like many evolving fields, career and technical education (CTE) is additionally challenged by its history, the scope of its mission, a perceived lack of a unifying definition and purpose, a complex of funding formulas and allocations, and the blurring of boundaries among educational providers. This chapter discusses myths regarding CTE that obscure its mission, provides evidence of CTE effectiveness, and illustrates how CTE is transforming itself to meet the demands of multiple stakeholders having diverse agenda and varying needs.

3.1 INTRODUCTION

Jokinen (2009) laments that career and technical education is too often described as an inferior educational alternative by the public as well as their legislative representatives. Members of the Ohio State Association for Career and Technical Education (ACTE, 2006) often articulate the misconceptions surrounding CTE, explaining that it "is not an alternative. It is a great option and it allows students to figure out what they are passionate about and then go into that passion" (para. 2). Jokinen reports about public and official perception where both parents and state officials see college as the sole option for students, revealing a lack of respect for the educational needs of working men and women.

3.2 MYTHS AND MISCONCEPTIONS ABOUT CTE

Husain (1999) has identified enrollment resurgence in CTE programming since 1990, although

DOI: 10.4018/978-1-61520-747-3.ch003

CTE continues to battle a negative image among students, parents, educators and policy makers. Wonacott (2000) suggests that CTE's negative image is largely due to misconceptions and beliefs about the realities of the labor market, college degrees, and CTE programs in general. Some common misconceptions and assumptions associated with CTE include: it is less challenging than traditional academic preparation, CTE graduates have limited employment opportunities, and CTE preparation constricts salary ranges (Wonacott, 2000). Those misconceptions contribute to a "bimodal thinking" that characterizes CTE and traditional academic programs as mutually exclusive realms when, in fact, they are becoming increasingly intertwined (Harkins, 2002). Clarity and transparency regarding the CTE and academic partnership is essential for understanding the role of each in developing a competitive workforce. That partnership, however, is not without obstacles.

This chapter explores some common misconceptions associated with career and technical education, examines the sources of those myths, and clarifies misconceptions. The evolutionary history of CTE provides a framework for understanding the distortions that obscure CTE's purpose and eclipse its mission. In addition to illuminating the dichotomous nature of CTE, this chapter will also discuss some current and emerging issues likely to shape the metamorphosis of career and technical education over the coming years.

3.3 ORIGINS OF CAREER AND TECHNICAL EDUCATION IN THE U.S.

There is a long history in western society of devaluing disciplines that have roots in application and relegating them to a lesser place in the school curriculum, and in society for that matter. In fact, the roots of such separation between thought-based disciplines and action-based disciplines can be traced to ancient Greek Society. The early Greeks believed that working people didn't think and thinking people didn't work. Of course the Industrial Revolution and later, the rise of the middle class, made any further argument about the value of vocational education purely academic. Yet, even though we live in a nation that largely owes its great wealth and success to those hearty pioneers who were not afraid to roll up their sleeves and carry out real labor, one still feels the sting of this relentless stereotype in schools and in larger society. Michael K. Daugherty, Department Head, Curriculum & Instruction, University of Arkansas (M. K. Daugherty, personal communication, May 19, 2009)

Barlow (1976) outlined the history of the first 200 years of career and technical education in the United States where CTE was designed to prepare people for the workplace. Prior to the Smith-Hughes Act of 1917 that provided federal funding and recognition for vocational education, a great variety of programs had trained individuals in work skills and presented a foundation for the contemporary educational system. Hence, CTE was being developed from uncoordinated efforts that individually responded to discrete workplace needs. Colonial and early nineteenth century public educational institutions had no systematic approach to teach literacy or vocational skills. Barlow (1976a) asserted that individuals were more concerned about basic subsistence needs than personal improvement in those early times, but he came to believe that a blatant consumerism has been the primary educational motivator in contemporary society. In contrast, the citizenry of the fledging Republic recognized the value to the general welfare of an educated workforce. Early movements to create a structured educational system generally relied on a philanthropy that served the indigent, and apprenticeships became the common job-skill transfer mechanism, filling the employment need for both society and indigent youth.

3.3.1 The Industrial Revolution Reshaped Workforce Preparation

As machinery and manufacturing systems increasingly reshaped or replaced jobs, apprenticeships became a less attractive or useful way to provide training. The need to assist the less fortunate and American youth, however, remained. As apprenticeships declined, other institutions developed to care for youngsters. By the mid-1880s vocational education was synonymous with institutional programs for these youth (Gordon, n.d.). Self-reliance in the early U.S. was still the prevalent value, as Barlow (1976a) documented, "the specific educational problems of the farmer, the mechanic, the businessman, and the housewife were solved, as they had been from time immemorial, by themselves" (p. 28), but there were still efforts of individuals and groups that would serve as a foundation for vocational education as it is known today. There were advocates for universal public, tax-supported education; there were schools established for orphaned boys to learn a specific trade; and there were curricula at private schools, for those who could afford it, that included skills and crafts that historically would have been taught through a parent-child relationship or apprenticeship. The end of the colonial period witnessed educational priorities shifting from a private education that advanced the study of the classics to a movement among tradesmen to place the responsibilities of practical education on public schools.

3.3.2 Professional vs. Industrial Class

From the colonial period until today, significant legislation and events have shaped career and technical education in ways that may have perpetuated some of the myths surrounding CTE. During what ACTE (2002b) terms "*The Labor Movement,*" institutions that had a mission to educate mechanics and farmers emerged. While occupations had distinct operational manners, they were similar in their addressing the practical problems of their trades. Private business schools also appeared at that time. Such institutionalizing of labor education increased, and during the middle of the nineteenth century, the vision for industrial education at the post-secondary level was realized, pioneered by Jonathon Baldwin Turner. Turner held that society had two classes, the professional and the industrial. He proposed establishing an industrial university in each state and also suggested "that federal aid be used for the purchase of public lands. The plan attracted widespread attention and the farmers of Illinois supported the idea with enthusiasm" (Barlow, 1976b, p. 38).

3.3.3 Early Government Involvement

The post-Civil War realization of Turner's vision came as the Morrill Act of 1862. That legislation sanctioned the establishment of higher education schools that focused on applied studies such as agriculture and the mechanical arts. "Congress did pass a second Morrill Act (1890), which required states with dual systems of education (all-white and nonwhite) to provide land-grant institutions for both systems" (Gordon, n.d., para. 5).

Following the Civil War a debate raged about how African-Americans should be educated. Should Black youth receive a classical or industrial education? One response to that question became the Hampton Institute, which had as part of its mission a "means whereby the student might learn while in school how to support himself after graduation by the work of his hands as well as by his brains, thus affording an example of industry to his people" (Barlow, 1976b, p. 39). The Hampton Institute offered training in bricklaying, harness making, and plumbing, among other skills, and students were rewarded with a certificate or diploma. Business concepts were also included in the curriculum.

Efforts to establish institutions of this type continued. In the years leading up to the Smith-Hughes Act, creative attempts at manual training and teaching the trades were found in schools that centered only on skills, or on a combination of skills and classical studies. According to Barlow (1976c),

Manual training was not without its critics. Technical education was called a "deceptive farce" by zealous guardians of liberal education who considered it a threat to the intellect and unacceptable in the public schools. In some ways these fundamental arguments are indicative of the problems faced by vocational education even today. (p. 47)

3.3.4 Employer-Sponsored Human Resource Development

Industrial employers found ways to educate their own employees, believing that their efforts would create a better workforce. Often similar to trade school practice, instruction focused on specific, job-related skill-training. Some employers, though, expanded instructional efforts beyond an immediate skill need. For example, a manufacturing firm in New York needed improvements to machinery; the company sponsored some employee intellectual development, offering evening classes in subjects such as English, mechanical drawing, and algebra:

Attendance was not compulsory, but advancement within the firm was measured in part by special preparation for it. The graduates were preferred over other workers because it was felt they were better equipped to do the work entrusted to them. The school proved to be satisfactory and after 30 years of operation the company was convinced that a superior class of workmen was their reward. (Barlow, 1976c, p. 50)

Today, such an employment-sponsored activity is referred to as "human resource development." While not every organization could afford to educate its own work force, many others supported a free public education that emphasized developing both "head and hands."

3.3.5 The Smith-Hughes Act of 1917

The Smith-Hughes Act of 1917 provided for federal funding of vocational education. That legislation was the first of many acts that supported and advanced what is now known as career and technical education. The act reflected a reformist view that youth could prepare for entry-level jobs by learning occupational skills in separate vocational schools. The act "supported the notion of a separate vocational education system" (Gordon, n.d., para. 8).

Subsequent legislation, such as the Vocational Education Act of 1963, and the 1968 and 1976 Amendments to the Vocational Education Act, expanded and improved prior legislation. Gordon (2003) listed activities for the following to be funded by the amendments:

1. high school and post-secondary students
2. students who had completed or left high school,
3. individuals in the labor market in need of retraining,
4. individuals with academic, socioeconomic, or other obstacles,
5. individuals who were considered mentally retarded, deaf, or otherwise disabled,
6. construction of area vocational schools and facilities,
7. vocational guidance, and
8. training and ancillary services such as program evaluations and teacher education. (as cited in Threeton, 2007)

Vocational education themes that address economic and social demands of American life are also found in the Carl D. Perkins Act of 1984, with the intent to provide access to vocational education to all students, including targeted groups, while addressing the needs of the national economy (Threeton, 2007).

The Carl D. Perkins Act defined vocational-technical education as sequential programming that would prepare individuals for paid or unpaid jobs where a baccalaureate or advanced degree was not required. The programs were based on applied learning competencies that would contribute to an individual's academic knowledge, higher-order reasoning, problem-solving ability, and the occupation-specific skills needed to be productive, self-sufficient economically, and a contributing member of society.

3.3.6 The Seminal Perkins Legislation

In 1990, the Carl D. Perkins Vocational and Applied Technology Act (Perkins II) focused on improved integration between academics and vocational education, as well as a clearer transition for students between school and work (Threeton, 2007). Another significant component of the legislation was the concept of "tech prep," an initiative intended to integrate technical education with academics. This legislation may have informed the National School-to-Work Act of 1994 that was "designed to address the nation's serious skills shortage though partnerships between educators and employers. The program components of School-to-Work included school-based learning, work-based learning, and activities connecting the two" (ACTE, p. 42). According to ACTE (2002a), the National School-to-Work Act also returned vocational education to its earlier utilization of apprenticeships.

Perkins was reauthorized in 1998 with a focus on accountability and the need for state systems to adapt to new data collection and reporting requirements (ACTE, 2002a). In 2006, the Carl D. Perkins Act was authorized for six years with an even greater focus on accountability and reporting. The legislation was intended to "strengthen the focus on responsiveness to the economy; while tightening up the accountability statement in regards to the integration of academics and technical standards" (Threeton, 2007, para. 7).

The evolution of career and technical education has mirrored the socio-political eras of the U.S., generating perceptions and misconceptions about the field that are time and context-bound. The following section discusses the contextual roots of those perceptions.

3.4 MYTH ENABLERS

This section examines elements of vocational education that have contributed to the myths that have plagued the evolution and growth of CTE. Organizational name changes, different sponsoring authorities and program administration, and assessment challenges have all contributed to confusion in the popular mind surrounding CTE.

3.4.1 Ill Gotten Names

Association of Vocational and Technical Education (AVTE). From its infant history vocational education was a separate developmental pathway distinct from traditional academics. While the field has evolved to meet the demands of a technologically-intensive marketplace, vocational education and vocational-technical education terminology "may have unfairly developed a certain stigma" that persists today (Lovejoy, 2002, p. 44). For over three decades, the American Vocational Association (AVA) resisted a name change that referenced technology, distancing itself from a stereotypical connotation that had been associated with the vocational label. Lovejoy (2002) described the AVA nomenclature evolution, citing President Richard Nixon, who in 1970 advocated a name change from vocational to career education because "too often vocational education is foolishly stigmatized as being less desirable than academic preparation, and too often the academic curriculum offers very little preparation for viable careers" (p. 44). The proposed name change was resisted by some AVA members who viewed it as divisive and prone to confuse the purpose of the organization and the field (Lovejoy, 2002). Entrenched in its position, AVA prevailed in resisting a 1989 initiative by the U.S. House of Representatives to rename vocational education as an applied technology education.

Association of Career and Technical Education (ACTE). In 1998 AVA members voted to change the name of the organization to the Association for Career and Technical Education (ACTE), acknowledging the fundamental importance of technology to its mission (Lovejoy, 2002). With its new name reflecting the centrality of technology to its purpose and curricula, and with career and technical coursework fully integrated into the public school system, ACTE began a public awareness campaign to dispel misconceptions about CTE and to redefine its image among potential stakeholders. The campaign included an updated website to demonstrate resources that support CTE's work of training challenged and gifted students for careers in contemporary society (Lovejoy, 2002). To underscore the utility of CTE, to correct inaccuracies surrounding the field, and to promote its place in the future of workforce development, ACTE created a web-based resource to promote a better understanding of CTE systems, programs and services (Effectiveness Fact Sheet, 2009). While somewhat dated—2004 is the most recent citation—it was a good faith effort to provide consumers with data supportive to the CTE mission. Additionally, the National Dissemination Center for Career and Technical Education provides resources, reports, and links to information germane to the CTE field.

3.4.2 Prevailing Confusion: What Really Is CTE?

Confusion surrounding CTE is partly a result of questions about the identity of career and technical education providers, the nature of CTE students and consumers, and the administration of CTE programs. ACTE describes the overall purpose of career and technical education as preparing youth and adult learners for careers in diverse fields. Occupational fields covered within CTE include, but are not limited to: agriculture; trade and industry; business and marketing; family and consumer sciences; health; public safety; and technology (ACTE, 2006). CTE programming spans from the middle school years through post-secondary degrees. Post-secondary providers include technical institutes, two-year community colleges and four-year degree-granting institutions.

3.4.3 Administration of CTE

While the Perkins legislation has provided funding for CTE, the responsibility for dissemination of funds, program implementation, and evaluation fall upon individual states. The Division of Academic and Technical Education is responsible for helping students acquire challenging academic and technical skills and prepare for high-skill, high-wage, or high-demand occupations in the global economy. The Office of Vocational and Adult Education (OVAE) initiatives are designed

- to administer state formula and discretionary grant programs under terms of the Perkins legislation;
- to provide assistance to states to improve program quality, implementation, and accountability; and
- to establish national initiatives that help states implement rigorous career and technical education programs.

3.4.4 Inconsistency of Program Assessment and Evaluation

Just as various political and economic factors have influenced CTE's reputation, the lack of explicit and systematic data regarding its performance has stymied the program's ability to demonstrate its effectiveness. This shortcoming is due in part to the lack of consistency in curricula, performance standards, and assessment practices across states. Each state implements CTE within its own implementation systems.

The National Center for Education Statistics (NCES) collects and reports data on career and technical education from various states, a result of the 2006 Carl D. Perkins Career and Technical Education Improvement Act (2006 Perkins Act {P.L. 109-270}, Section 114) that requires the National Center for Education Statistics to collect and report information on a nationally representative sample of CTE students. NCES uses a Career and Technical Education Systems (CTES) program that provides data about CTE from students, faculty, and schools at secondary and post-secondary levels, as well as about adults seeking work-related education and training (Levesque, Laird, Hensley, Choy, Cataldi, and Hudson, 2008).

3.5 THE MYTHOLOGY ATTENDING CAREER AND TECHNICAL EDUCATION

This section discusses some common myths purported to define Career and Technical Education. Each myth is subsequently countered by facts consisting of expert opinion and research data, designated as "metrics."

3.5.1 Myth One: CTE is Less Rigorous than Traditional Academic Programs

Career and Technical Education (CTE) is often on the receiving end of criticism that it is not as challenging or rigorous as other subject areas, or that it should be reserved for underachieving students; however most of those individuals tossing disparaging commentary might be surprised to learn that repeatedly CTE is a major interchange on the road to a successful career. Michael K. Daugherty, Head, Curriculum & Instruction, University of Arkansas (M. K. Daugherty, personal communication, May 20, 2009)

At its inception, vocational education provided alternative training for select groups. However, alternative and rigorous are not mutually exclusive categories. A discussion could focus around outcomes, rather than labels. Just as procedural knowledge is no better or worse than continual knowledge—they are different types of knowledge, each requiring a different blend of pedagogy. As one academic reminds us, "There are many non-rigorous academic programs out there as demonstrated by the reverse transfer of graduates from four-year colleges and universities into CTE programs" (G. Belcher, personal communication, June 3, 2009). Whether a program is rigorous depends on how "rigor" is defined. Rigor is determined by the school that offers the program, whether traditional academic or career and technical education venue.

Today's CTE curriculum meets the same state standards as required for academic programs. Most CTE disciplines also have national standards to guide the integration and application of academic competencies delivered through CTE. CTE has always been designed for all students. It is contextual in its delivery—something I believe all students can benefit from in today's global society. CTE programs are required to meet state and national accountability measures. Many states have established dual credit between general education and CTE. As more states develop models that include competency assessment, you will see a greater recognition for the academic content included in CTE courses. CTE programs [at the forefront] of changing industry, such as automotive, information technology and health occupations, have a much higher knowledge and skill level than most people realize. Often well above the 12th grade reading level. Bryan Albrecht, President, Association for Career and Technical Education; President, Gateway Technical College (B. Albrecht, personal communication, June 5, 2009)

3.5.2 Rigor Revisited: Knowledge Types

To fully understand the discussion about CTE's purpose vis-à-vis rigor, it is helpful to consider the distinction among knowledge types and their related pedagogy. In discussing quality teaching, Biggs (2003) identifies four types of knowledge: *declarative, functioning, procedural,* and *conditional.* Using this typology, the goal of CTE curricula is to enhance procedural or competency-based knowledge instead of the academic goal of developing conditional, broad-based critical thinking skills. Academic courses encompass English, mathematics, science, social studies, fine arts, and foreign languages, while enrichment courses include health, physical, and recreational education; religion and theology; and military science (Levesque et al., 2008).

Vocational education originally concerned itself with non-theoretical, hands-on, skill-based employment training for manual laborers. "Today, many CTE program areas are highly technological and require a combination of procedural and continual knowledge. For example, working on a diesel engine today requires a solid theoretical background in electronics and computers, along with the necessary problems solving skills," according to G. Belcher (G. Belcher, personal communication, May 13, 2009). This comment demonstrates how the "shop" or "trade" connotation that has been synonymous with vocational education has evolved in response to the complex mix of occupations and competencies required to keep workers globally competitive.

3.5.3 Metrics, Myth One: CTE Programs Demonstrate Enhanced Rigor

A 2003 report by the National Research Center for Career and Technical Education (NRCCTE) found that in the 1990's CTE students took more math and science than general education students, and that a CTE concentration is more rigorous academically than a general education program (Wonacott, 2000). A study by Levesque et al. (2008) indicated that 97% of 2005 public high school graduates earned CTE credits and 21% of those students had an occupational concentration.

The Effectiveness Fact Sheet (2009) reported that during the 1990's CTE students increased the number of academic courses taken by 30%, took as much or more high level math and science courses than general education students, and had a greater increase in 12th grade test scores. Further, students with a highly integrated program of study had significantly higher achievement in reading, math, and science than students with less integrated programs.

CTE may still be perceived as "less than" by some, but statistical evidence indicates that CTE programs are as rigorous as their traditional academic counterparts, and according to some, may even be more rigorous. Additionally, this data confirms a degree of integration between the academic and CTE tracks. While a perception may persist that CTE and academic curricula are separate entities, within public schools, they are not.

3.5.4 Myth Two: CTE Programs Provide Fewer Employment Opportunities and Lower Earnings than Four-Year College Degrees

Although many people perceive that CTE graduates have limited options, the reality is that CTE programs prepare students for the full range of career options available through 16 national career clusters. CTE continually adapts to the changing needs of the economy and it develops new courses and programs to meet workforce demands. CTE includes traditional fields like cosmetology, HVAC, and automotive technology, but it also includes careers in sustainable energy, telecommunications, nanotechnology, biometrics, robotics, and computer-aided design, to name a few. Nearly one-third of the fastest growing occupations will require an associate's degree or a postsecondary vocational certificate, according to a 2006 Bureau of Labor Statistics (BLS) report. For example, there will be an estimated 2 million new jobs being created in energy-efficiency and renewable energy. CTE programs around the country have developed sustainability programs and courses to help build a pipeline of workers to fill these positions. Jan Bray, Executive Director, Association for Career and Technical Education (J. Bray, personal communication, May 28, 2009)

CTE, like all of education, is one step in the ladder of life-long learning. In today's world all people must continue to seek ways to expand their knowledge and skill through continued education. The fact that many CTE programs are technical in content positions CTE graduates better in today's society for employment or postsecondary education. Community and technical college have for decades embraced CTE course and credit articulation. Students that earn an associate or apprenticeship degree not only increase their market value but demonstrate to employers their eagerness to continue to learn. Many employers provide tuition incentives for CTE careers to *keep employees at the high end of technology change. Bryan Albrecht, President, Association for Career and Technical Education; President, Gateway Technical College (B. Albrecht, personal communication, May 28, 2009)*

The unflattering myth that CTE programs lead to fewer employment opportunities and lower wages persists despite published evidence to the contrary. Wonacott (2000) suggests that this misunderstanding is due in part to "beliefs about the labor market and about college degrees—and some facts that may or may not support those popular beliefs" (para. 1). West (1996) also found a perception that technical education is inferior to the traditional college experience and that parents encourage a four-year degree as a guarantee of a higher standard of living (Vo, 1997). A study by Gray (1997) found that 50% of high school males and 68% of high school females believed that a four-year degree ensures a professional job by age 30.

3.5.5 Metrics, Myth Two: Increases in Earnings and Improved Employment Outcomes

CTE prepares students for high-skilled, high-wage, high-demand jobs, whereas traditional collegiate programs often prepare students for jobs that don't exist or are very narrow in their opportunity. As the educational sector continues to produce more bachelorette level individuals than what our economy needs, we will continue to see the decline in the average salary of these four-year graduates. Job demand currently outpaces supply in the CTE area. (G. Belcher, personal communication, May, 2009)

The truth of this viewpoint is supported by a number of research reports (Federal Reserve Bank of Chicago (2002), Russell Sage Foundation, (2001); and NAVE, (2004) that found CTE students are more likely to be employed, to earn more, and

Table 1. Fastest growing occupations and corresponding CTE career clusters, 2004-2014

Occupation	CTE Career Cluster
Home health aides	Health Science
Network systems and data communications analysts	Information Technology
Medical assistants	Health Science
Physician assistants	Health Science
Computer software engineers, applications	Information Technology
Physical therapist assistants	Heath Science
Dental hygienists	Health Science
Computer software engineers, systems software	Information Technology
Dental assistants	Health Science
Personal and home care aides	Human Services
Network and computer systems administrators	Information Technology
Database administrators	Information Technology
Physical therapists	Health Science
Forensic science technicians	Law, Public Safety & Security
Veterinary technologists and technicians	Agriculture, Food & Natural Resources/Health Science
Diagnostic medial sonographers	Health Science
Physical therapist aides	Health Science
Occupational therapist assistants	Health Science
Medical scientists, except epidemiologists	Health Science
Occupational therapists	Health Science

to be employed while earning post secondary degrees or certification than their non-technical counterparts.

In looking to the future, ACTE (2006) suggests that CTE programs are instrumental in preparing learners for the 20 fastest growing occupations listed by the 2006–2007 U.S. Department of Labor Occupational Outlook Handbook. Table 1 illustrates the breadth of some of the fastest growing CTE occupations that correspond to CTE career clusters.

3.5.6 The CTE Role in Persistence and Retention

A powerful antecedent and determinant of employment opportunity and future earnings is school completion. High school dropouts earn 30% less than graduates (Education Trust, 2003), adversely impact society's economic infrastructure by contributing significantly less to taxes over a lifetime (Rouse, 2005), and are likely to be less healthy than their peers (Bridgeland, Dilulio, and Morison, 2006), all of which have significant repercussions across the entire socio-economic landscape. Conversely, high school graduates in general earn more than dropouts, contribute more to the tax base, and are more likely to raise healthier children (Haveman, Wolfe, and Spaulding, 2001). Hence, educational programs and services that decrease dropout rates may be critical to both individual and public well-being.

Hart (2006), Kemple (2001) and Plank (2001) explored the relationship between CTE programs and school engagement and persistence (as cited in ACTE, 2006). And, The National Dropout

Prevention Center Network identified CTE as one of 15 strategies capable of helping reverse the staggering dropout rate. CTE is particularly useful in that it accommodates the diverse interest and learning styles of learners while linking academics and vocational learning to relevant real world outcomes, all of which help to maximize engagement (National Assessment of Vocational Education, 2003). These studies illustrate the growing body of evidence that CTE contributes to school persistence, thus reducing the dropout rate.

3.5.7 Myth Three: Separate and Unequal

Berliner and Biddle (1996) suggested that a myopic belief that four-year institutions are the best path to occupational success is a result of fears from highly regarded 1980's reports that decried the state of public education, warning that America's security was directly linked to an erosion of student achievement and competitiveness. An influential 1983 study, The Nation at Risk, compiled by the National Commission on Excellence in Education, spurred education reform by exposing declines in student performance, due in part–according to its analysis–by the educational process, itself. That study recommended specific changes in math and science content, expectations, and teaching while condemning the state of public education in the U.S.

Career and technical education and higher education—one has always complemented the other. A student can learn a trade to pay for college and living expenses or get a degree and learn a skill to operationalize their academic education. The facts show that most CTE concentrators move on to higher education programs. Mark Lynch, Adult Education Director, Franklin Technology (M. Lynch, personal communication, June 10, 2009)

"Economic, educational, and societal issues have repeatedly exerted influence on the defi-

nition of vocational education, as well as how, when, where, and to whom it will be provided (Gordon, n.d., para. 1). Current socio-political norms in the U.S. celebrate expansive individual rights, class equity, and mainstreaming, but it may be difficult to imagine a period in U.S. history when explicit and observable class differences created particular expectations for groups that included laborers, farmers, the poor, the disabled, women, and the ethnically diverse. The historical separation between academic and vocational programs may have been less about 'ability' than 'availability.' "An excellent plumber is infinitely more admirable than an incompetent philosopher," according to John W. Gardner (1961), who suggested that "the society which scorns excellence in plumbing because plumbing is a humble activity and tolerates shoddiness in philosophy because it is an exalted activity will have neither good plumbing nor good philosophy." Gardner claimed that neither society's "pipes nor its theories will hold water" (p. 86).

3.5.8 Metrics, Myth Three: Postsecondary Success Points to CTE Achievements

"More colleges and universities are seeing the benefits of CTE and have put into place articulation agreements with community and technical colleges for the transfer of CTE students to acquire a bachelor degree" (G. Belcher, personal communication, June, 2009).

Today, access to CTE programs is available to all who can benefit from the curricula. The 1963 vocation legislation stated that vocational education was for everyone, but many could argue that it is truly for those who will find utility in those CTE programs. Additionally, CTE is offered at both two and four-year institutions.

ACTE reports that there is ample statistical evidence regarding the positive outcomes from CTE association with post-secondary institutions in studies done by the Center on Education Policy and American Youth Policy Forum (2000), the National Center for Education Statistics (NCES, 2000), and the National Assessment of Vocational Education: Final Report to Congress (NAVE, 2004) (as cited in Effectiveness Fact Sheet, 2009). According to those studies, CTE students enter postsecondary institutions at about the same rate as all high school graduates, while there has been a substantial increase in college enrollment of CTE students. That enrollment increase corresponds with the 2004 NAVE Final Report projection that a 30% employment growth in occupations requiring a vocational associate degree is projected to "be more than double overall employment growth (14%) through 2008 ...[and, that] nearly one-third of the occupations will require an associate's degree or a postsecondary vocational certificate" (p. 1). Further, according to a Bureau of Labor Statistics (BLS) report (2006), the U.S. Office of Vocational and Adult Education (OVAE) reports that a third of college students are taking CTE courses (as cited in Effectiveness Fact Sheet, 2009).

3.6 TRENDS AND ISSUES

The over-riding issue in the U.S. comes from the more than 59 million people—30 percent of adults—who have not participated in postsecondary education. According to the Council for Adult and Experiential Learning (CAEL), "in 35 states, more than 60 percent of the population does not have an associate's degree or higher" (2008, p. 9). How will this significant portion of the population be able to fully participate in a productive capacity? The answer may lie in program affordability, accessibility, state support, employer funding, and technology. Each area can contribute to the greater trend of involvement in post-secondary education.

3.6.1 Affordability

Public community college is generally affordable for the nation's adults, since the average tuition and fees "constitute 7 percent of median income for the poorest 25 to 44-year-olds and 5.4 percent of median income for the poorest 45 to 64-year-olds," according to the CAEL report (2008, p.10). Likewise, public four-year college tuition and fees represent 19.5 percent of median income for the poorest 25 to 44-year-olds and 15 percent of median income for the poorest 45 to 64-year-olds.

3.6.2 State Support

While state support is uneven across the nation—seventeen states do not provide any need-based aid to part-timers, and eighteen others provide less than 10 percent of need-based aid to part-timers—however, "nine states devote between 10 percent and 20 percent of need-based aid to part-time students and six devote more than 20 percent of need-based aid funds to this group" (CAEL, 2008, p. 10).

3.6.3 Employer Tuition Support

According to the 2005 National Household Education Survey, 45 percent of the students attending college degree or certificate programs part-time and 54 percent of those attending vocational or technical programs "had some form of support from their employers" (CAEL, 2008, p. 10).

3.6.4 Accessibility

Nontraditional students—such as people who delayed enrollment in post high school education, those who work full-time while in school, or those who have dependents other than a spouse—were more likely than traditional students both to participate in distance education and to be in programs available entirely through distance education (CAEL, 2008, p. 10).

3.6.5 Technology

The numbers of students enrolled in distance learning courses are increasing, and that trend is expected to continue (Kellogg Commission, 1998). "Those courses can overcome obstacles of family and career schedules, distance to campus, and specific class schedules" (Beck and Biggs, 2009, p. 683). Further, "interactive television, combined with other instructional technology, may be a critical medium for maintaining and improving job skills regardless of the setting" (p. 690), and help rural educational programs serve isolated populations who lack traditional brick and mortar facilities.

State agencies may have to alter data collection policies to address those shortcomings to better plan for future initiatives (CAEL, 2008). Increasing Hispanic and other minority immigrant populations will require policy makers to confront language and education equivalency issues and attendant social norms that will impact educational program initiatives.

The U.S. has important gaps in gathering data about adult participation in degree and certificate programs, since not every state keeps such statistics. Data for noncredit programs, college-going rates, GED recipients, participation in distance learning by age group, or progression in literacy programs are also not universally tracked. National attention to the need for increased technical and support skills should lead to concerted and consistent efforts to remedy the data collection shortcomings over the coming years.

3.7 CONCLUSION

The myths discussed in this chapter were commonly believed by educators, legislators, and the public at large. The first myth maintains that CTE is less rigorous than traditional educational programs. However, as Daugherty noted (M. K. Daugherty, personal communication, May 15, 2009), current CTE curricula meet the same state standards specified for academic programs, and most CTE disciplines also have national standards for integration and application of academic competencies delivered through CTE. In addition, NRCCTE found that CTE students took more math and science than general education students while Wonacott (2000) discovered that a CTE concentration is more rigorous academically than a general education program.

The second myth in the popular mind held that CTE programs yielded fewer job opportunities and lower earnings than the traditional college degree. The employment reality, however, points to CTE not only providing skilled workers in traditional fields like cosmetology, HVAC, and automotive technology, but also generating careers in the hottest contemporary fields, such as sustainable energy, telecommunications, nanotechnology, biometrics, robotics, and computer-aided design. It has been estimated that almost a third of the fastest growing occupations will require an associate degree or a post-secondary vocational certificate, according to a 2006 Bureau of Labor Statistics (BLS) report. Reports from the Federal Reserve Bank of Chicago (2002), the Russell Sage Foundation (2001) and NAVE (2004) found that CTE students are more likely to be employed, to earn more, and to be employed while earning postsecondary degrees or certification than their non-technical counterparts.

The third myth held that college and technical school educations were separate and unequal. In fact, many institutions of higher education have chosen to create articulation pacts with community and technical colleges for the transfer of CTE students, thus providing matriculation mechanisms for technically-skilled students to acquire a bachelor degree, according to the U.S. Office of Vocational and Adult Education (OVAE). OVAE reported that a third of all college students are taking CTE courses. Research has also shown that the U.S. population overwhelmingly supports the need for career and technical education—an indication of its increasing importance as an integral educational choice.

The image of a high-school dropout who became an auto mechanic was popularized in many Hollywood movies of the fifties as well as television shows of that and later eras. The concept of vocational education reserved for those less likely to achieve in college was not a new phenomenon. In the first part of the 20th century, students could be selected to pursue a secretarial or vocational course, while those deemed able to withstand the rigor of higher education were placed in a college-preparation curriculum.

The trends discussed above present a compelling picture of a continued availability of post-secondary education for students seeking challenging careers in vocational occupations. The demand for career and technical education graduates is increasing, and both access to programs as well as the funds to support that access will provide opportunities to meet critical occupational shortages across the U.S. economy. Notwithstanding the myths that have downgraded such occupations, on the one hand, and glorified college degrees, on the other hand, the real and practical work that is accomplished daily argues for the respectability and intellectual challenges that attend those who choose to pursue career and technical education. The employability of CTE graduates, in fact, may be the strongest argument for its societal value, confirming that not only is a CTE path a rigorous one, but one that offers both job security as well as financial rewards.

REFERENCES

ACTE. (2002a). A new age of technology. *Techniques, 77*(2), 38–43.

ACTE. (2002b). An association is reborn. *Techniques, 77*(2), 44–45.

ACTE. (2006). Career and technical education's role in American competitiveness. [from http://www.acteonline.org/uploadedFiles/Publications_and_Online_Media/files/Competitiveness.pdf]. *Issue Brief*, (October): 2006. Retrieved May 20, 2009.

Barlow, M. (1976a). 200 years of vocational education: 1776-1976: The awakening, 1776-1826. *American Vocational Journal, 51*(5), 23–28.

Barlow, M. (1976b). 200 years of vocational education: 1776-1976: Independent Action, 1826-1876. *American Vocational Journal, 51*(5), 31–40.

Barlow, M. (1976c). 200 years of vocational education: 1776-1976: The vocational education age emerges, 1876-1926. *American Vocational Journal, 51*(5), 45–58.

Beck, J. K., & Biggs, B. T. (2009). Serving rural communities using blended technology . In Wang, V. C. X. (Ed.), *Handbook of research on E-learning applications for career and technical education: Technologies for vocational training* (pp. 681–694). Hershey, PA: Information Science Reference.

Berliner, D. C., & Biddle, B. J. (1996). In defense of schools. *Vocational Educational Journal, 71*(3), 36–38.

Biggs, J. (2003). *Teaching for quality learning at university*. New York: Society for Research into Education & Open University Press.

Bridgeland, J., Dilulio, J., Jr., & Morrison, K. B. (2006). *The silent epidemic.* Washington, D.C.: Civic Enterprises, LLC.

Council for Adult and Experiential Learning (CAEL) and National Council of Higher Education Management Systems (NCHEMS). (2008). *Adult learning in focus: National and state-by-state data.*

Education and workforce issues: Public attitudes and awareness. (1997). *Washington State Workforce Training and Education Board.* Olympia, WA: WSWTEB.

Effectiveness Fact Sheet. (2009). ACTE home website. Retrieved May 1, 2009, from http://www.acteonline.org

Gordon, R. D. (n.d.). *History of vocational and technical education-Current trends, preparation of teachers, international context.* Retrieved May 28, 2009, from http://education. stateuniversity.com/pages/2536/Vocational-Technical-Education.html

Gray, K. C. (1997). The gatekeepers. *Techniques, 71*(9), 24–27.

Harkins, A. M. (2002) *The future of career and technical education in a continuous innovation society.* Columbus, OH: National Dissemination Center for Career and Technical Education, the Ohio State University.

Hart, P. D. (2006). *Report findings based on a survey among California ninth and tenth graders.* Research Associates Inc. Retrieved May 5, 2009, from http://www.connected california.org/downloads/irvine

Haveman, R., Wolfe, B., & Spaulding, J. (2001). Childhood events and circumstances influencing high school completion. *Demography, 28*(1), 133–157. doi:10.2307/2061340

Husain, D. D. (1999). Good news on the horizon. *Techniques, 74*(3), 14–17.

Jokinen, B. (2009). *Negative perception still surrounds career tech education.* Retrieved May 18, 2009, from http://www.limaohio.com/news/career-37483-education-technical.html

Kellogg Commission on the Future of State and Land-Grant Universities. (1998). *Student access: Data related to change* (Second working paper). Washington, DC: National Association of State Universities and Land-Grant Colleges, Office of Public Affairs.

Kemple, J. (2001, December). Career academies: Impacts on students' initial transitions to post-secondary education and employment. *Manpower Demonstration Research Corporation.* Retrieved May 22, 2009, from http://www.mdrc.org/publications/105/execsum.html

Levesque, K., Laird, J., Hensley, E., Choy, S. P., Cataldi, E. F., & Hudson, L. (2008). *Career/technical education in the United States: 1990 to 2005. (NCES 2008-035). National Center for Education Statistics, Institute of Education Sciences, U.* Washington, D.C.: S. Department of Education.

National Assessment of Vocational Education Independent Advisory Panel. (n.d.). *Earning, learning, and choice: Career and technical education works for students and employers.* Retrieved May 2, 2009, from http://www.ed.gov/rschstat/eval/sectech/nave/ naveiap.pdf

National Dropout Prevention Center/Network. (n.d.). *Effective strategies for dropout prevention.* Retrieved May 6, 2009, from http://www.dropoutprevention.org/effstrat/default.htm

Plank, S. (2001). *Career and technical education in the balance: An analysis of high school persistence, academic achievement, and postsecondary destinations.* National Research Center for Career and Technical Education. Retrieved April 6, 2009, from http://www.nccte.org/publications/infosynthesis/r&dreport/CTE%20in%20 Blnce_Plank. pdf

Rouse, C. (2005, October). *Labor market consequences of an inadequate education.* Paper presented at the Colombia University Teacher College Symposium on the Social Cost of Inadequate Education, NY.

The Education Trust. (2003). *Telling the whole truth (or not) about high school graduation.* Retrieved May 20, 2009, from http://www2.edtrust. org/NR/rdonlyres/4DE8F2E0-4D08-B3B0-013F6DC3865D/0/tellingthetruthgraduates.pdf

Threeton, M. D. (2007). The Carl D. Perkins Career and Technical Education (CTE) Act of 2006 and the roles and responsibilities of CTE teachers and faculty members. *Journal of Industrial Education, 44*(1). Retrieved May 24, 2009, from http://scholar. lbo.vt.edu/ejournals/JITE/v44n1/threeton.html

U.S. Department of Education, Office of the Under Secretary, Policy and Program Studies Service. (2004). *National assessment of vocational education: Final report to congress.* Retrieved May 20, 2009, from http://www.ed.gov/rschstat/eval/sectech/nave/navefinal.pdf

Verducci, S. (1961). The ability to respond . In Gardner, H. (Ed.), *Responsibility at work: How leading professionals act (or don't act responsibly)* (pp. 43–61). San Francisco: Jossey-Bass.

Vo, C. H. (1997). Not for my child. *Techniques, 71*(9), 20–23.

West, P. (1996). Scholarships for Voc Ed training go untapped. *Education Week, 15*(28), 3–5.

Wonacott, M. (2000). *Vocational Education Myths and Realities. ERIC Clearinghouse on Adult, Career, & Vocational Education Myths and Realities.* Retrieved May 16, 2009, from http://www.fape. org/idea/How_it_works/voced_myths_8.html

Chapter 4
Designing Culturally–Sensitive Career and Technical Career Curriculum

Lesley Farmer
California State University, Long Beach, USA

ABSTRACT

The workplace has become more cross-cultural due to labor costs, outsourcing, and international production. Cultural sensitivity accepts cultural similarities and differences without assigning relative values to them. Culture-sensitive curriculum can optimize organization effectiveness with different populations. In order to design effective culture-sensitive curriculum for CTE, basic information about cultures, curricula, learners, and organizations needs to be understood. The curriculum itself should enhance content meaning through cultural context and provide culture-sensitive learning skills in order to help students learn, and to enable them to address cultural factors when dealing with their potential clientele. Culture-sensitive trainer competencies, resources, instructional strategies, assessment issues, and technological trends are detailed. A focus on healthcare training exemplifies culture-sensitive curriculum that results in more effective service.

4.1 INTRODUCTION

Today's world is truly interdependent. Because of telecommunications, faster travel, global manufacturing and trade, and global politics, cultures are coming into contact with one another more than ever before. At the same time, a growing sense of instability and inequity permeates societies. Traditional mores are butting against institutional ties

and international citizenship (Merriam, Courtenay, & Cervano, 2006). In many cases, the workplace has become more cross-cultural due to labor costs, outsourcing, and international production. Technical expertise is particularly difficult to find, so the field has become global in nature.

The cost of cultural insensitivity is high. Cultural misunderstandings within and between organizations can lead to lower productivity, poor decisions, low morale, and substandard service. Organizations need ways to address cultural diver-

DOI: 10.4018/978-1-61520-747-3.ch004

sity: through recruitment and hiring practices, by removing cultural barriers and inequalities, and by rewarding incentives for diversity (Craig, 1996).

Within these contexts, adult education in general and CTE in specific needs to address these cultural issues, and help pre- and in-service employees and their institutions to become at culturally competent. To that end, culture-sensitive curriculum can foster such a mentality and result in more effective business practices.

4.2 BACKGROUND

In order to design effective culture-sensitive curriculum for CTE, basic information about cultures, curricula, learners, and organizations need to be understood. Adult education is the broader context, and CTE education focuses on the specific applications in the relevant fields.

4.2.1 Culture

Regardless of the scale, when people form together into stable groups with sustained shared value and belief systems and act according to normative expectations, they comprise a culture. UNESCO (2002) defines culture as: "the set of distinctive spiritual, material, intellectual and emotional features of society or a social group, and that it encompasses, in addition to art and literature, lifestyles, ways of living together, value systems, traditions and beliefs" (p. 1). An individual may belong to several cultures: family, worksite, neighborhood, race, profession, social club, political party, country. Likewise, a group may belong to several cultures; technicians may be members of a site staff, a union, a system, a state organization, a national organization, and an international organization. Some of these cultures may overlap or even contradict, in which case, the individual or group must either live with the disequilibrium or resolve the conflict (i.e., reject one or the other, reject both, or incorporate parts

of each). A culture may also be measured in terms of how cohesive it is in terms of inside and outside pressures; if conflict arises from outside its borders, do members stay within the culture or switch allegiance to the other culture?

Groups and individuals perceive and respond to cultures at various levels, both intellectually and emotionally. Ideally, cultural competency consists of a congruent set of knowledge, skills, and dispositions about one's own culture and others' that enable people to work effectively in cross-cultural situations (Isaacs & Benjamin, 1991). Cross et al. (1989) lists the following criteria for cultural competency: (1) cultural self-assessment, (2) cultural knowledge, (3) valuing diversity, (4) management of the dynamics of different, (5) adaptation to cultural contexts. Other terms convey a growing capacity towards such competency:

- Cultural knowledge is intellectual familiarization with selected cultural characteristics, history, values, and behaviors (Adams, 1995).
- Cultural awareness implies a sensitivity and understanding of another ethnic group, and usually involves opening to personal change (Adams, 1995).
- Cultural sensitivity accepts cultural similarities and differences without assigning relative values to them (National Maternal and Child Health Center on Cultural Competency, 1997).

Several self-assessment instruments are listed by the National Center for Cultural Competence lists (http://www11.georgetown.edu/research/gucchd/nccc/foundations/assessment.html) and the New York State Education Department (http://cstl.syr.edu/assessment/index.html).

4.2.2 Curriculum

As its most basic level, curriculum consists of content and the methods to convey that content. Behind the curriculum lies an educational philosophy that reflects a belief system. For career and technical education, that philosophy has largely been pragmatic, reflecting economic need for teaching vocational skills to prepare the workforce. Not surprisingly, the rise in factories paralleled the rise in vocational education as a formal enterprise.

What is driving change in adult education today? Changing demographics probably tops the list. Particularly with NAFTA (North American Free Trade Agreement) and other trade agreements, business has become increasingly international. Materials and labor cross national borders constantly. Downturns in economies and worldwide political upheaval have resulted in growing migration. The message is clear that adult education functions within and as a part of interdependent global realities.

Culture plays a significant role in community attitudes towards education, which informs CTE and practice. Suefert (2002) identified a number of learning system dimensions that can be culturally profiled.

- **Educational epistemology:** to pass on knowledge, to preserve the status quo, to socialize, to prepare workers, to help students self-actualize.
- **Pedagogical epistemology:** instructivism to constructivist.
- **Underlying psychology:** behavioral to cognitive.
- **Goal Orientation:** sharply focused to unfocused, short-term vs. long-term, individualistic vs. society.
- **Experimental Value:** abstract to concrete.
- **Role of Instructor:** Master lecturer to egalitarian facilitator, interpreter to questioner.
- **Value of Errors:** errorless learning to learning from experience.
- **Motivation:** extrinsic to intrinsic.
- **Structure:** high to low.

- **Accommodation of Individual Differences:** none to multi-faceted.
- **Learning Control:** none to unrestricted.
- **User Activity:** rote to generative.
- **Cooperative Learning:** none to integral.

For instance, if a cultural norm about the role of the instructor is to tell students what is right and true, then independent critical evaluation of a design brief might be discouraged. If a culture values independent thinking and competitiveness, then collaborative research might be considered cheating. If the culture believes in a highly-structure educational experience, then students may feel lost in loosely defined or student-defined projects.

Just as the meaning of CTE is culturally contextualized, so too are the conditions for cultural-sensitive curriculum. As adult educators seek support for a culturally-sensitive curriculum, they need to examine the cultural landscape in order to discern—and align with—shared values and expectations. Ignorance or denial of cultural norms will spell disaster for cross-cultural initiatives. If the most influential culture shares the goals and strategies of cultural sensitivity, then the adult educator has a natural "in." If the culture is strong, then the path to success is even better paved. On the other hand, a strong culture that discounts cultural sensitivity and has a closed attitude can pose challenges. A culture that undervalues cultural sensitivity may be won over if they have a more accepting nature and can be persuaded by an overlapping stronger culture to join in the overarching goal.

4.2.3 Globalized Learners

Adults are becoming more mobile in their personal and professional lives. People may renounce their original citizenship, fervently ascribing to their new country's norms, or they may work for a brief time in another culture under duress or mandate until their duty is fulfilled or sufficient money is made to return home. Increasingly, people have dual citizenship, or work across the globe from one project to another. The attitude surrounding migration has changed; the traditional image of the "melting pot" where "foreigners" became acculturated has given way to a tossed salad metaphor in several countries. Cultural heritage has gained status throughout the world. Mexico and other Latin American countries, for instance, are realizing the need to maintain the languages and cultural identities of indigenous peoples before they become extinct. Populations of new Americans in the United States tend to join their first country counterparts who emigrated earlier, so, for instance, significant pockets of Khymer, Samoan and Hmong may be found in Long Beach, Carson, and the Fresno areas of California, respectively. In response, adult educators need to demonstrate competence in teaching second-language acquisition skills and working with diverse populations, just as they need to inculcate cultural awareness and sensitivity in CTE students.

Cultural negotiation can be difficult for students and employees because they want a sense of belonging, but are torn between two or more cultures. Their peers may consider them foreigners and outsiders; their own families may think that they are abandoning cultural values. Not only does each ethnic group have its own identity, but those employees who either immigrate or work for a foreign company have an additional identity to confront and may have to overcome personal obstacles. It should also be noted that immigrants may well be more educated and sophisticated than their parents, which upsets the traditional authority of elders and reverses roles of responsibility.

As students and employees deal with at least two significant cultures, their own and the dominant or employer one, they make decisions as to how to balance their allegiances. Alliman-Brissett and Turner (2005) examined the ways that Native American youth deal with this problem.

- They may stay with their primary culture, withdrawing from the dominant one; they choose to remain social outsiders.
- They may reject their original culture, and whole-heartedly embrace the dominant culture, and thus become over-acculturated. Family stress may well rise as a result.
- They may assume most of the values of the dominant culture, and maintain the trappings of their original culture, thus making them mainstreamed.
- They may reject both cultures, and thus become marginalized.

They may accept both cultures, drawing the strengths from each, and thus become bicultural.

Educational experiences can be problematic for immigrant and transnational students or employees because of first-country differences in practices and values. Not only might learners lack knowledge about these institutions and their benefits, but they may also harbor negative attitudes towards the government of the employer. They also tend to lack guidance in using employment benefits since they might not be members of mainstream social groups. Adult literacy efforts may also suffer, not only because of language differences, but also because U.S. adult education tends to favor English-only instruction. Moreover, in some countries, reading is not considered very important. What with immigrant families focusing on survival and acculturation, education and technology usually take a back seat (Constantino, 1998).

The social aspect of cultural interaction cannot be over-emphasized. In his research on transformative learning and social transformation, Miao (2000) developed a four-step model to analyze individual perspective changes when learning in a different culture. He posited two stages, each of which has two steps: a) deconstruction, during which stage the learner 1) recognizes, and then 2) critically analyzes existing cultural assumptions and limitations; and b) reconstruction, during which stage the learner 3) searches for a new direction, and 4) accepts the new social paradigm. Between the two stages, the learner experiences a personal and social crisis. Adult educators need to recognize the difficulties that learners may feel when trying to resolve conflicting cultural norms, and provide opportunities for learners to resolve their social conflicts. Identifying possible conflicts and consequences is a good first step. Providing a safe environment and critical analysis tools for examining cultural implications is another useful instructional strategy. Facilitating vision-making for personal and social cultural transformation through providing relevant resources and reflective activity rounds out instructional approaches. Adult educators have to balance their roles in giving accurate information with responding empathetically to individual emotional states.

4.2.4 Institutional Issues

Most culture-sensitive curriculum focuses on learners achieving an outcome defined by the institution. Either that institution values culture sensitivity or is mandated to incorporate such values. Furthermore, the degree of that value belief and implementation may vary greatly, from lip service to deep conviction and pro-active internalization. While the institution is comprised of individuals and their personal values, the institution has its own identity that transcends any one person.

Likewise, individual change is simpler than institutional change. Not only do a sufficient number of people (at least five percent) need to be convinced of the importance of cultural sensitivity, but they have to pro-actively support and model its precepts (Craig, 1996). Staff may think that too few people represent a different race, so such a mindset is not necessary, but culture can exist in several "guises" (for example, age, religion, lifestyle). On the flip side, staff may think everyone is diverse so that cultural sensitivity is not needed; nevertheless, learning is contextualized by experience and background so that assumptions make take on unintentional

connotations that can detract from learning, such as analogies to dating or marriage. Particularly in technical professions, employees may want to concentrate on hard science skills, and may not see the impact of cultural-sensitivity training; yet, as technicians do more complex work and need to make decisions or persuade others to make decisions, they are likely to need culturally-sensitive communication skills.

One aspect of organizational culture is its degree of inclusivity. Is the organization a fiefdom or a broad-based collaborative learning community? The type of atmosphere dictates how decisions are made – and thus what approach is needed. For example, if the organization is run by a dictator, then focus group work probably won't work. Instead, adult educators would need to assuage the leader carefully, and plant the idea in his/her head so the "proclamation" will support cultural sensitivity. Jackson and Hardiman (1981) researched multicultural organizations, and categorized different stages of inclusivity. Their list follows, with suggestions for ways to make operations more culture sensitive.

- **Exclusion:** one group has all the power, and rejects all other groups (e.g., white male science-types). The old-boy network is the way to get things done, so adult educators should analyze the power of person-based decision-making in order to find ways to broaden that power base.
- **Club Mentality:** traditional decision-making based on the status-quo: the "right way." Innovation is usually not appreciated, so ideas must align with present expectations. This stage reflects Hofstede's 2001 short-term orientation. Miao (2000) would recommend helping these groups to consider alternative realities.
- **Compliance:** "team players" are keys in this organization; differences are ignored with the emphasis on the "bottom line." To get action here requires knowing and play-

ing the game; adult educators may even get reluctant respect if they make a daring move and are successful. This stage might be labeled the "color blind" stage, so raising awareness about cultural impact might be worth considering at this point.

- **Affirmative Action:** this kind of organization tries to support difference of opinions and avoid discriminatory practices; however, it usually doesn't praise the unusual. This is a safe environment to bring up ideas as long as one stays within the norm's parameters. Testing those parameters and analyzing the consequences might be the next course of action.
- **Restructured:** the entire organization reflects on their practice and develops initiatives to focus action within the system. Adult educators can take calculated training risks in this setting as long as actions are based on sound research and thought. The affective domain would be the next area for consideration.
- **Diversified:** the true learning community, this kind of organization practices strong participatory decision-making, and celebrates unique ideas and persons. Cultural sensitivity and competence are organizational goals, backed by sufficient resources and activities. Adult educators can expect equitable support and encouragement for culture-sensitive resources and services; all employees would be expected to participate in culture-sensitive training and would have opportunities to enhance their application and development (Craig, 1996).

4.3 CURRICULUM AS A CONDITION FOR CULTURAL SENSITIVITY

Cultural sensitivity can be realized through its presence in the curriculum, which is in turn impacted by the educational provider's factors. It needs to be explicitly addressed through direct instruction and meaningful learning activities, and it needs to be integrated throughout the organization rather than isolated in some sort of parallel universe of learning. Its assessment should be an essential aspect of organizational planning and implementation.

4.3.1 Content

To support cultural sensitivity, curriculum throughout the CTE and community at large, needs to be contextualized in order to make meaning. Osborn, Thomas and Hartnack (2005) provide a knowledge management taxonomy to illustrate the kinds of knowledges that are involved when addressing cultural sensitivity in education:

- **General Knowledge:** culture-sensitive learning skills are integrated throughout the curriculum.
- **Subject Knowledge:** domain-specific resources and opportunities for contextualize cultural sensitivity are provided.
- **Technological Literacy:** adult educators provide a full range of resources and services that support a culture-sensitive curriculum.
- **Cultural Knowledge:** curriculum gains meaning through cultural context.
- **Languages:** reading and writing form the basis for accessing, understanding, sharing, and generating information about culture.
- **Intellectual Capital:** administrators hire, train, and promote knowledgeable staff who incorporate cultural sensitivity into the curriculum.
- **Educational Professionalism:** instructional design and implementation reflect culturally sensitive values and practices effectively and ethically; a learning community exists in support of culture-sensitive infused curriculum.

- **Educational Collaboration:** communication and joint efforts among stakeholders support cultural sensitivity incorporation into the curriculum.
- **Leadership and Management Policies:** scheduling facilitates educational collaboration; culture-sensitive resources are allocated.
- **Educational Policies:** boards approve and oversee policies requiring cultural sensitivity student outcomes and curriculum that address those outcomes; boards hold stakeholders accountable for cultural sensitivity efforts.
- **Legal and Religious Policies:** societally-derived regulations and value systems support cultural sensitivity.
- **Knowledge of Communities:** the adult educational system is aware of community-based cultural sensitivity values and practices, and facilities their involvement in the curriculum.
- **Partnerships:** stakeholders seek opportunities for ways to partner in support of curriculum that incorporate cultural sensitivity.

Culture-sensitive subject matter can consist of CTE information as it is practiced in different cultures, such as cuisine techniques or medical interventions. Just as appropriate, culture-sensitive can consist of cultural issues per se that might impact CTE practices, such as group dynamics or personal space. On the part of the CTE student, culture-sensitive subject matter may help them improve their services to their clientele, or it may help them resist cultural oppression at work. CTE learners may want help adjusting to a different culture, or transferring their skills to another setting. Each of those motivations can impact what subject matter is covered, so adult educators should conduct a needs assessment in order to determine how to address cultural sensitivity; the final decision usually rests with the training provider, so

adult educators need to be able to justify their recommendations to authorities with conviction.

In any case, both the dominant and minority cultures should learn about each other's cultural knowledge and values so they can promote mutual respect and understanding. A number of frameworks for multicultural education exist. Typical elements include:

- Cultural pluralism theory, commitment and affirmation.
- Knowledge and identity construction from cultural assumptions and social positions.
- Critical awareness.
- Social and educational issues facing minorities.
- Prejudice reduction, social justice and equity.
- Reconstruction of social structures to facilitate individual and group empowerment.
- Skills and strategies for addressing multiculturalism (Lowenstein, 2009; White, 2002).

Hofstede's 2001 updated model of cultural dimensions can help guide adult educators as they teach culture-sensitive content matter. The concepts themselves should be addressed, and instruction should reflect the impact of these dimensions as well as provide students with the tools to navigate in these differing dimensions.

- **Power distance**. A high power distance distinguishes highly hierarchical societies. In general, U.S. students are used to a low power distance with their instructors. Learners with more hierarchical values prefer more structured and formal classes. Instructors should explain this concept, and provide learners with opportunities to experience a range of power structures.
- **Individualism vs. collectivism**. U.S. students are encouraged to demonstrate their uniqueness and to be competitive with

each other, while other cultures such as Latin ones value group identity and effort. For the latter, helping each other is not considered cheating, for instance. Instructors should provide opportunities for students to discuss issues in small groups, and then report out, in order to acknowledge collective wisdom. Instructors can also discuss group dynamics as a way to address both individual and group contributions.

- **Masculinity**. In some cultures, gender-specific roles are well defined and have narrow norms. In general, these same cultures value teachers, and expect them to be males if teaching adults. Therefore, some non U.S. learners may have difficulty relating to female adult educators. In those cases, women trainers need to display their credentials and may need to be "vetted" by a well-respected male in charge. On the other hand, these same students need to learn that other cultures have a more blended view of roles, and need to learn how to become more comfortable working with colleagues in mixed sex environments.

- **Uncertainty avoidance**. Some cultures value tradition and "the right answer" while others value innovation and flexibility. In today's world, almost all cultures have to deal with uncertainty; some hold on more tightly to unchanging values, perhaps separating their changing professional environment from their stable private lives. Students need to learn how to cope with change while maintaining core beliefs as appropriate; the classroom is a perfect arena for taking calculated risks. Students also need to acknowledge the value of those cultures with differing attitudes, and help their colleagues make appropriate adjustments in order to maintain a sense of security.

- **Long-term vs. short-term orientation**. Perseverance and status mark long-term orientation, while saving face and quick results mark short-term orientation. Providing short and term-long projects of differing values can help students work successfully in both mind views.

4.3.2 Learning Factors

Several cultural factors impact student learning, which the instructor has to address on two levels: 1) to help students learn, and 2) to enable students to address these cultural factors in turn when dealing with their potential clientele. In that respect, the adult educator acts as an expert learner, helping students become instructors or facilitators in their own right. McMahon and Bruce (2002) mention several such factors.

- **Language**. Much of CTE involves a relatively small, targeted vocabulary, so straight-forward and literal communication can comprise most of class time and written expectations. Particularly for students who need to learn the corporation's language, focusing on work-related vocabulary is a practical strategy. Instructors might provide bilingual glossaries, or suggest that students create them for their own reference needs. Instructors can also use visual and multimedia aids to clarify concepts, and students can be encouraged to record lecturers for later review. Online education can also help level the learner playing field as students can look up unfamiliar terms, and translate their writing from their primary language to the target language. However, in workplace interaction, informal and idiomatic conversation is also part of the work culture, so learners need to be aware of commonplace phrases. In discussing technical management issues, Laroche (2003) provides a long list of sports-related statements that would be worth teaching so that learners can survive as a team player, particularly in the U.S. Sample phrases include: ballpark figure, "throw a curve ball," "call a time out," and run interference. Language issues can also arise in non-standard English, where students may feel that their daily speech habits are criticized; instructors need to validate their speech patterns, and explain how work settings may have well-defined norms that preclude such language variations. Instructors also need to mention the importance of working with a variety of clientele, so that non-standard English may well be the most effective way to connect with the target population. In other words, communication should be treated as a situational interaction so that a variety of language behaviors should be considered. In that respect, individuals who use non-standard English regularly may be more facile and equipped than those individuals who speak "broadcast" English only.

- **Educational experience and beliefs**. CTE curriculum differs among cultures, with the English-speaking countries tending to be more student-centered and applied than some more traditional cultures (Laroche, 2003). Educational structures differ as do expectations and assessments. Teacher-student relationships also differ, from authoritative to permissive. The social site of education may differ as well in terms of gender roles, attitudes about age, communication styles, and collaboration norms. Additionally, cultures put varying value on formal and informal education. Instructors should express appreciation for these different learning venues and styles, and help students identify when those learning experience can come in handy in their workplace environment, particularly as they deal with their clientele. Small group work, study "buddies" and mentors can

help ease social discomfort while addressing academic needs (NEA, 2006).

- **Age-related norms**. Millenials might not understand why they have to "pay their dues" in the workplace, particularly if they have newer skills than their supervisors. Helping students understand how different generations have unique work values and practices helps them interact more successfully in increasingly cross-generational work environments. Furthermore, cultures place different values on age and maturity; in some cases, wisdom is associated with age while in other cases, someone over forty is out-of-date. In that respect, online work can minimize ageism. In any case, students need to acknowledge these differing attitudes and figure out ways to accommodate age-related expectations.

4.3.3 Trainers

Culture sensitivity has become increasingly important in CTE, particularly with globalization and technology. However, formal adult education training in this area is less common. Sometimes cultural sensitivity is regarded as a pleasant set of skills and processes to be addressed by specialized trainers. Indeed, some companies outsource culture sensitivity training so that it remains outside its regular business; unfortunately, such specialists may lack knowledge about that field in general or that company specifically, so that the company as a whole might not benefit fully from the training.

To conduct such training, adult educators should have formal or informal education and experience in cross-cultural communication, facilitation and counseling skills, and strong background knowledge about relevant cultures and their norms. Participation in international programs can increase trainers' repertoires of instructional strategies, expand their cultural sensitivity and perceptions, and influence their interpersonal relations in education (Rapaport, 2008). Adult educators also need to confront their own cultural biases and do personal emotional work to improve their own mindset. Adult educators who address cultural issues should have a passion for cultural competence but not a rage. In effect, adult educators must first be learners, coming to understand and appreciate culture-sensitive factors and situations. They must be culturally competent, able to operate cross-functionally and culturally, balancing global and local needs. On a personal level, they should be open to new experiences, patient, empathetic, and psychologically accessible (Craig, 1996).

To actively demonstrate how to value cultural diversity, adult educators who train about culture sensitivity should seriously consider co-training with a person of another culture. Another practice is to enlist the help of a local informant who can translate language and cultural nuances. Either way, different perspectives are more easily experienced. Co-trainers should seek unit in objectives and diversity in instructional style. They should get to know each other personally, and complement each other's identified strengths and weaknesses. A good practice is to switch content and process leadership. Co-training has the potential to show how diversity synergizes groups and improves work outcomes (Craig, 1996).

4.3.4 Instructional Issues

While teaching in an inclusive manner that accommodates all students is good practice, culturally sensitive instruction needs to tease out differences explicitly. Such instruction needs to address ways to help students become more culturally competent as well as address the needs of students from differing cultures. Without knowledge of the learner, the instructor cannot successfully teach culture sensitivity conceptually; likewise, students need to know each other on a more personal level than usual if cultural sensitivity is part of the curriculum. Indeed, individual and collective changes in

attitudes, beliefs and actions are the most effect means for learner empowerment.

In training across cultures, Deal (2005) identified five cultural considerations: ways of communicating, ways of learning, ways of training, trainer-learner interaction, and training context. Deal emphasized the need for trainers to be aware both of culture-specific content matter as well as the underlying values for that information. In developing a course that incorporates culture sensitivity, adult educators should build from the known to the unknown, from the comfortable and value-neutral to more challenging material, from surface interaction to authentic interrelationships. As learners gain knowledge and self-confidence with the group, they build capacity to deal with more complex and culturally sensitive situations.

The SIOP (Sheltered Instruction Observation Protocol) model of instruction for English language learners demonstrates how cultural sensitivity can inform learning. Each lesson or session includes both language and content objectives that are practiced through meaningful learning activities the integrate culture and content. Practice should be highly sensory, involving visual and kinesthetic tasks. The instructor helps learners make connections between new concepts and learners' personal experiences; key vocabulary is used to express those connections. Instructors provide opportunities for group interaction and individual reflection, recognizing different cultural learning styles. Assessment is ongoing, through frequent specific review feedback and authentic demonstration of learning. Students should have multiple ways to demonstrate understanding (Echevarria & Vogt, 2004).

To address cultural sensitivity, adult educators should use a variety of instructional techniques. In this way, students of different cultures can experience learning in comfortable ways as well as learn how to gain knowledge using unfamiliar techniques. Group interaction is one vital strategy so that students can practice interdependence and negotiating skills. Groups need to aim for equal status and mutual respect, and contact should become more personal and authentic over time.

Cultural sensitivity as a content matter also has to be treated in several ways, reflecting the kind of learning to be experienced; that is, the instructional approach should match the kind of knowledge to be gained. In teaching medical students about cultural diversity, Li, Caniano and Comer (1998) used several strategies. Definitions and facts were taught didactically. To address problems of cultural misunderstanding, case studies provided an effective venue for discussing nuanced attitudes and behaviors. Simulated experiences helped students gain first-hand visceral knowledge about cultural issues such as discrimination.

Houser (2008) suggests that students take cultural "plunges": exposure to social and cultural settings where students' norms are in the minority. The learners reflect upon their experiences, and the class analyzes the underlying issues. Such in-depth field experience can lead to courage in the face of fear, social criticism and critical reflections, and empathy with others. Another field-based instructional strategy is service learning whereby students volunteer to help a community agency. To promote cultural sensitivity, the student should work at a site that is unlike his or her usual environment. Part of the experience includes needs assessment and observation so that arbitrary and culture-blind projects are not implemented (and typically doomed to failure). As with cultural plunges, such experiences can be uncomfortable for students, and adult educators need to make sure that students are not at high risk of danger.

CTE education is less likely to prone to engage in highly volatile situations. In fact, technical pre-and in-service professionals may resist role playing games or other activities that smack of "touchy-feely." They tend to focus on data and objective skills. Nevertheless, as technical professionals conduct complex projects in cross-cultural settings, they will need to gain expertise in the "soft" skills of persuasion, negotiation, and team-building. In training this clientele, adult educators

should explain the rationale and clear objective for each learning activity, preferably backing up assertions of benefits through hard evidence (Laroche, 2003).

While some cultures and individual students prefer learning abstract theory, culture sensitivity instruction needs to involve the effective domain and link learners with their personal lives. Moreover, in some cultures, for learning to be authentic, it must have that personal or community resonance. Not only do CTE students have to negotiate their work and personal cultures in any case, but if they learn or work in unfamiliar cultures, that negotiation is a conscious and stressful experience that needs to be acknowledged and supported. This experience can be particularly daunting for women who are being trained for non-traditional jobs; the values expressed in the career can seriously conflict with paternal and spousal expectations. Therefore, adult educators need to help these women find ways to sustain traditional behaviors while practicing possibly cutting-edge technical skills.

The workplace also exists within some kind of community, so that the enterprise as a whole has to negotiate possibly conflicting cultures, such as technical corporations in Bangalore. In examining failed CTE efforts for Native American youth, Fortune and Blecharczyk (1983) found a disconnect between training and the youth's community lives. Only when the researchers recruited local reservation trainers and required that outside (i.e., non-reservation) employers guarantee that the trained youth would have jobs and work support did CTE succeed.

4.3.5 Assessment Issues

Because different cultures and societies teach and learn in different ways, assessments may vary as well. Where collaborative learning is encouraged, normed standardized tests given to each student might be threatening. When individualism is king, getting a group grade may seem unfair. If deadlines are considered more as guides, marking down late work might be culturally insensitive (although frustrating for the assessor). If saving face is paramount, then confidentiality needs to be insured. If students are supposed to spend their out-of-school time helping the family, then take home assessments might not measure performance fairly. If gender impacts class participation, then writing assessments might be more appropriate. If Internet connectivity is scarce, requiring online assessments is embarrassing. For these reasons, adult educators should know their students' backgrounds and community values so they can make assessment adjustments accordingly. In large heterogeneous systems, where one set of standardized assessment instruments and administrative processes are used, contributing elements to be equitable; otherwise, data analysis needs to take into consideration the varying contexts of learners' lives.

For these reasons, people prefer internal assessment ("one of us") to external assessment ("one of them"); they often feel that outsiders cannot accurately capture their contextualized reality and do not have to live with the consequences of the assessment thereafter. In this regard, adult educators may well be considered as outsiders to students if common ground is not established. Inside assessments are usually more aware of subtle organizational behaviors and values, and may be able to elicit deeper data. However, external assessments can provide a more impartial and independent point of view, bring in expertise, and offer new insights unhampered by prior connotations. In any case, group-based cultural and social norms must constitute part of the assessment equation.

This issue becomes critical when comparing competencies across cultures and nations. Evaluation of some CTE programs consists of national standards and assessment instruments. Yet these two factors are culturally sensitive in themselves, and reviewers might not be aware of cultural implications.

Additionally, if instructors or other people in power make negative or condescending remarks about the abilities of specific groups, be they based on gender or ethnicity, those same group members are likely to internalize those negative messages and perform less well. Therefore, adult educators should maintain a respectful learning climate, and they should probably address such stereotyped vulnerabilities head on, and help students gain coping skills to withstand and countermand such harmful statements (Welch, Cleckley & McCLure, 1997).

4.4 ONLINE CURRICULUM ISSUES

CTE curriculum is increasingly delivered online. With international training, such online venues enable all relevant learners to participate and interact in real time as well as at their own convenience. Particularly for in-service training, online curriculum is practically a necessity. Online curriculum can also ameliorate cultural differences because a variety of resources can be posted online for easy access, and students can use translation services on their own time to comprehend materials written in another language and well as to write their own ideas. As bandwidth has increased, instructors can incorporate visual and multimedia materials to illustrate and clarify concepts.

Online curriculum also poses challenges. Some students may be unstable physical access to technology so they cannot compete equitably. Students may be disadvantaged if they have not been trained in using educational technology; older students in particular may feel uncomfortable with newer technology. Cultural expectations about education may impact experience in that face-to-face learning may be considered more valuable than distance learning. If the course reflects an educational philosophy that is unfamiliar to the student, then additional adjustment to this new approach to learning will require more time and effort on the part of the student. Furthermore, most students consider education to be a social phenomenon, and may feel isolated when working online without visual social cues. In that respect, instructors may incorporate group discussions and video conferencing to mitigate that lonely sensation.

In terms of being culturally sensitive, online curriculum needs to focus on instructional design delivery differences. Students should be given opportunities to share information and pictures of themselves or some meaningful image (depending on their need for personal privacy) so that they can connect socially. Instructors should consider holding individual "conferences" in order to make professional connections with students. While courses should have clear expectations and specific deadlines, students should be given choices in the resources they use and the ways that they demonstrate competence. Instructors should also provide opportunities for students to learn independently and in groups. These practices enable students to experience learning that affirms their typical educational backgrounds and introduces new strategies that help them build a repertoire of learning tools. To further "push" on cultural sensitivity, instructors can explicitly address issues of culturally defined educational practices. Students can share their educational background and underlying philosophies as a way to identify culture-specific and universal patterns. At the least, when students understand that different cultures learn differently and value different aspects of education, they can better appreciate the challenges that their peers may be experiencing, and may become more tolerant of unexpected responses during a course (Liaw, 2006).

4.5 CULTURE-SENSITIVE CURRICULUM IMPLEMENTATION: AN ACTION RESEARCH MODEL

By now adult educators should know about culture-sensitive curriculum, and support its use

for lifelong learning and contextualization within the CTE community. On the other hand, some employers may be ignorant of cultural sensitivity *per se,* although they may well be aware of its elements. For that reason, adult educators should focus more on the ultimate goal of student learning, and weave in culture-sensitive concepts as a means to contextualize learners' engagement with CTE content matter. To this end, adult educators should examine relevant educational goals, standards, and indicators, and then match those elements with culturally-sensitive concepts. For instance, for developing design briefs, engineers need to communicate clearly with their foreign counterparts and may need to consider different ways that cultural groups approach problem solving. For cultural sensitivity to impact the rest of the enterprise some kind of need on that entity's part must emerge; the *status quo* cannot remain comfortable. At this point, a needs assessment, even if it consists of staff discussion, should be conducted.

At this point, adult educators can present culturally sensitive best practices that model ways to meet those identified needs: through readings, presentations, workshops, and interactive sessions. For instance:

- Cultural sensitivity can be used as a means to relate work functions.
- Cultural sensitivity facilitates learning that crosses clientele-staff lines.
- Cultural sensitivity helps learners deal with their personal needs.
- Cultural sensitivity is most effective when taught collaboratively.
- Employers can reinforce and use cultural sensitivity daily.

Adult educators can also note valid research-based assessments to use with these models in order to make a case that culture-sensitive training can improve the organization as a whole.

To facilitate organizational change, administrators may start by targeting one of several groups:

- "Early adopters" who like to take intellectual risks.
- Functions that are easy to adjust.
- Groups who have the greatest need.
- Groups most in contact with other cultures.

Adult educators can serve as consultants, develop training interventions, and test the most likely ones out.

Because institutions are organic and dynamic systems, one intervention might impact the rest of the enterprise in unpredictable ways; requiring bilingual signage can impact facilities and graphic design departments, and require that all employees be able to read those signs aloud. Therefore, any education effort should include communication: among the group, with the entities being impacted by the training, with administrators, and any other stakeholders. This communication aspect helps each group define its role within the larger enterprise, provides evidence for accountability, minimizes duplicative or conflicting efforts, and facilitates possible coordination with other bodies. For example, the same training might be used by two groups, or two groups might design a common assessment instrument that can measure the impact of two different trainings.

Even if the training is ineffective or, worse, negatively impacts learner performance, adult educators and administrators can study the reasons for failure and learn from the experiences. They can posit whether a larger test group would have made a difference, in which case they can work on persuading others to join in the project. Perhaps the training required more resources, which would make a strong case for allocating additional funds to the effort. Perhaps the enterprise was not ready for the change, be it because of lack of training or insufficient attention to group norms; prerequisite training might be called for in this situation. And

if the idea was a total flop, at least the whole enterprise doesn't have to suffer.

On the other hand, if rigorous assessment and analysis reflect that the intervention *does* improve learner performance, then the adult educator has a strong case for wider organizational participation and adoption. Using a model of the learning community, the first trainees can act as the veteran experts who can help mentor and support the new participants. Again, the factors for success, including ways to overcome obstacles, need to be determined in order to optimize outcomes on a broader base. At this point in organization change, a formal proposal can be developed by key personnel, to be put into place via approved policies and procedures. Effort needs to be made to prepare potential participants so they will be ready and prepared to implement the plan of action: through staff development in-services, tutorials, guidelines, and coaching. Adequate resources—including materials, facilities, and human—need to be allocated and insured in order to start, implement, and sustain the effort. Influential leaders need to catalyze the enterprise into action. Again, adult educators can take leadership in this process by training their colleagues, suggesting relevant learning resources, and culling best practice.

Only through systematic preparation and support can change be implemented successfully. Especially as the number of successful participants grows, individual assistance can be given to those having trouble with change so they will have the inner and outer resources to persevere past the obstacles. As part of that effort, adult educators can help manage the growing knowledge base so all can access important learning.

As the organization experiences the benefits of the training, they start to value and internalize culture sensitivity. Summative assessment can provide empirically-based evidence of improvement, and longitudinal participants can demonstrate positive change over time. The "new" procedures become the *de facto* norm, the new *status quo*. When new individuals join the enterprise, they are oriented to these actions as part of the organization's routine. Sustained change needs to transcend any vanguard personalities or situational variations; otherwise, the effort will regress to the former status. If, for instance, a change in staffing results in the cultural sensitivity "ball" being dropped, then that is a sign that the enterprise really hasn't developed a sense of ownership for it. One of the most telling pieces of evidence of such ownership is prioritization of resource allocations; when the now accepted process or policy is challenged, as the enterprise affirms its value, then it has a good chance for institutional survival. The learning community can continue to grow.

4.6 CULTURAL FOCUS ON HEALTH CARE

Healthcare exemplifies a culturally sensitive profession. Cultures often hold strong beliefs about health and medical care, from shamanistic practices to standardized technical procedures. In some cultures, health status has moral implications. The care of the ill may be relegated to the lowly or delegated to the specialist. Healthcare staff typically meet people under emotional stress, when communication and behaviors are likely to be muddled even without cultural connotations. Both the staff and the clientele, at least in the United States, have also diversified. In total, cultural sensitivity can determine a person's life.

Health literacy is an emerging term that refers to the ability to think critically, problem solve, advocate, and learn independently about health-related issues. Poverty, low educational status and poor health tend to correlate with low health literacy, so trying to fill the health literacy gap is an equity issue. Adult educators can help healthcare staff train low-literate adult clientele in culturally sensitive ways, and help that clientele develop effective health communication skills. Kerka (2000) found that participatory learning

activities that incorporated the development of culturally-sensitive materials and programs, and fostered collaboration among stakeholders, led to most successful interactions with patients.

McKinney and Kurtz-Rossi (2000) noted the need for health education curriculum and resources for adults who speak limited English, the intent of which was to improve communication between health care staff and their patients. Their resultant guide includes the following content matter:

- Background information about sensitive communication with people of other cultures.
- Specific health information in simple English and world languages.
- Bibliographies and resource guides.
- Curricula to teach health information to people with limited English or literacy skills.
- Multimedia (video, audio, websites) with information and resource lists for healthcare staff working with people having little English skill.

In addressing the needs of African Americans and Latinos with diabetes, three Detroit healthcare systems developed an intervention curriculum that was culturally and linguistically sensitive to the targeted community. They chose a convenient location and trained community residents to deliver the diabetes lifestyle informational meetings. Content matter included dietary recommendations, physical activity, and diabetes self-care. Participants were highly engaged, and were very pleased with the sessions, finding them to be useful and culturally relevant (Feathers, 2007).

To address the needs of rural African American women who risk higher heart disease and stroke rates, The Pine Apple Heart and Stroke Project revised its curriculum content and delivery to make it more culturally relevant. They trained community health workers using a social cognitive theory framework to optimize personal change among the target population. The theory addressed environmental (i.e., community and family), personal (i.e., cognitive and attitudinal), and behavioral (i.e., goal-setting and self-regulation) factors that can impact women's preventative health measures. The training included facts and myths about specific diseases and their risk factors, skills mastery through rehearsal and application, and problem-solving and stress management skills. A manual was also developed to provide reference help. The trainees mentioned the need for tips on taking mediations and spiritual guidance as part of the community training delivery, and those subjects were added to the curriculum. As a result of the co-developed curriculum, community health workers felt more self-confident about their knowledge and skills, improved their own health practices, and were able to provide relevant counseling for their community's women. The researchers concluded that this model can be an effective outreach strategy for rural communities (Kuhajda et al., 2006).

On an international level, a disaster mental health volunteer developed and taught a trauma training curriculum for Sri Lankan mental health professionals and teacher-counselors. The curriculum specifically addressed the health and mental needs of tsunami survivors. Refuge camp adults and children provided valuable input, which helped the trainer refine the curriculum so as to incorporate the local cultural and religious value and behaviors. Due to the cultural sensitivity of the curriculum, participants were highly satisfied and were able to help the disaster refugees (Jordan, 2006).

In an ongoing family medicine consultation in Vietnam by American doctors, cross-cultural challenges emerged and were solved. Little money or resources are available to train family physicians or mental health workers in Vietnam. When U.S. doctors tried to train local health workers, they had to deal with language barriers and differences in health practices and psycho-social beliefs and behaviors. For example, rural Vietnamese depend on their family members to treat them medically, based on herbal substances, acupuncture, and other traditional belief-based practices. Mental health has family and religious connections, with Buddhists believing that mental illness denotes transgressions in a past life. Families may be blamed and shamed by mental problems, so such illnesses are often hidden until they are very severe. In addition, to maintain harmony and respect, patients will agree with the doctor on the surface, but might not implement the treatment out of ignorance. A needs assessment was conducted to ascertain the roles of health providers, availability of resources and services, and the feasibility of trainers. Based on the findings, the consultants worked with Vietnamese health organizations to have native health physicians learn and apply behavioral medial principles that respect local customs. Residency programs built upon local resources, and provided opportunities to work in rural health clinics. The final measure of success is shown in national and local support of such training and improved health practices of the Vietnamese themselves (Schirmer et al., 2004).

4.7 FUTURE TRENDS

As globalization and technology continue to connect people across cultures, cultural sensitivity will continue to grow as a necessary skill. People may accept specific practices of other cultures as they learn about them, and feel comfortable enough about their own identify that they can add a different facet to their lives. As a result, cultures may become more fluid and less well defined, or they may overlap to a larger degree than previously. On the other hand, if cultures feel threatened by competing or conflicting cultures, they may act even more forcefully in defending their own values and beliefs. As more information, particularly in non-English languages, appears on the Internet, individuals can be exposed to a greater variety of ideas. That same deluge of information can also result in individuals finding more information that confirm their existing point of view so that they are less likely to search for other opinions.

The current iteration of the Internet, interactive Web 2.0, amplifies the impact of culture sensitivity. In the United States, Web 2.0 social networking applications have surpassed email in terms of popularity (Nielsen, 2009). In his national survey of distance learners using course management systems, Heo (2009) found that respondents liked sharing personalized, relation-based information, preferring to disclose social awareness specifics with authorities such as teachers. He also noted that younger students used social networking than older students. Heo recommended:

Instructors of online courses and designers of course management systems need to consider these characteristics of today's online learners in their design. This would help online learners to acknowledge themselves as feeling, intentional, thinking, and social human beings. This will cause improved learner interaction and engagement and eventually a successful online learning experience. (p. 293)

While Heo did not address cultural issues, his finding about disclosing to authorities echoes Hofstede's 2001 dimensions of culture. In hierarchical societies, authorities have more stature and more social distances from students. Paradoxically, social awareness information shortens that distance while still recognizing status; in online courses, self-disclosure can also imply compliance with authority and an understanding that the instructor can provide more customized instruction if more details about the student are known.

Other cultural dimensions also apply to Web 2.0 social networking. For instance, in cultures where individualism is not highly valued, students may feel uncomfortable sharing personal information. Students who value privacy may also not want to share such information. In some cases, students may need to have their opinions reviewed by a superior, which may impact the tone and content of their message. In other cases, agencies may routinely scrutinize public communication, which could potentially endanger a naïve writer. Even though Web 2.0 reflects a peer-to-peer relationship, participants remain connected to other existing entities that may conflict with the spirit of social networking; thus, students have to continue to negotiate between cultures.

4.8 CONCLUSION

CTE trainers can contribute significantly to the well-being of industries and agencies through designing and implementing culture-sensitive curriculum. CTE domain subject matter benefits from incorporating cultural aspects because it facilitates the transfer of skills and knowledge across international settings. Cultural sensitivity as content matter helps CTE learners understand the values and belief systems that drive expectations and behaviors of people of different cultures. This knowledge aids in communicating effectively and working together as a team to improve the organization as a whole and to provide effective service to diverse clientele. At the same time, cultural sensitivity can affirm each person's identity and empower them to feel more comfortable about tackling new experiences.

Both culture-specific and general cultural issues should be addressed. While universal cultural values of mutual respect, personal effectiveness, and social equity typically comprise most CTE, culture-specific information offers in-depth techniques that can be applied to targeted populations, be they new employees or directed clientele. In the same spirit, CTE learners gain cultural sensitivity not only to improve their own effectiveness but also to provide more relevant service to their clientele.

As technology further connects CTE, cultural sensitivity needs to be considered. Online training and social networking require technical expertise, and they also impact social interaction. At the same time that people can communicate across distances, the quality of that communication may suffer because it lacks sensory and cultural cues. Adult educators will need to research effective ways to address this paradox at the learner level as well as the organizational level.

The future of cultural interaction is unknown, with scenarios of blended cultural aspects to narrowly-defined cultural norms that can crash against conflicting ideologies. Culturally sensitive CTE holds promise as a way for people to work effectively together towards a common goal by leveraging differences. Education is the key.

REFERENCES

Adams, D. (Ed.). (1995). *Health issues for women of color: A cultural diversity perspective*. Thousand Oaks, CA: Sage.

Alliman-Brissett, A., & Turner, S. (2005). Supporting the career aspirations of American Indian Youth. *CURA Reporter* (Spring).

Constantino, R. (Ed.). (1998). *Literacy, access, and libraries among the language minority population*. Lanham, MD: Scarecrow Press.

Craig, R. (Ed.). (1996). *ASTD training and development handbook*. New York: McGraw- Hill.

Cross, T., Bazron, B., Dennis, K., & Isaacs, M. (1989). *Towards a culturally competent system of care: A monograph on effective services for minority children who are severely emotionally disturbed (Vol. 1)*. Washington, DC: Georgetown University Child Development Center.

Deal, C. (2005). Training across cultures: Designing training for participants from China, India, and Mexico. *Dissertation Abstracts International*, *65*(08), 2836.

Echevarria, J., & Vogt, M. (2004). *Making content comprehensive to English language learners: the SIOP model* (2nd ed.). Boston: Allyn & Bacon.

Feathers, J. (2007). The development, implementation, and process evaluation of the REACH Detroit Partnership's diabetes lifestyle intervention. *The Diabetes Educator*, *33*(3), 509–520. doi:10.1177/0145721707301371

Fortune, J., & Blecharczyk, S. (1983). The effect of setting-culture interaction on the vocational education of American Indians. *Rural Educator*, *2*(1), 1–2.

Heo, M. (2009). Design considerations for today's online learners. *International Journal on E-Learning*, *8*(3), 293–311.

Hofstede, G. (2001). *Culture's consequences, comparing values, behaviors, institutions, and organizations across nations*. Thousand Oaks, CA: Sage Publications.

Houser, N. (2008). Cultural plunge. *Race, Ethnicity and Education*, *11*(4), 465–482. doi:10.1080/13613320802479034

Isaacs, M., & Benjamin, M. (1991). *Towards a culturally competent system of care: programs which utilize culturally competent principles* (Vol. 2). Washington, DC: Georgetown University Child Development Center, CASSP Technical Assistance Center.

Jackson, B., & Hardiman, R. (1981). *Organizational stages of multi-cultural awareness*. Amherst, MA: New Perspectives.

Jordan, K. (2006). A case study: How a disaster mental health volunteer provided spiritually, culturally, and historically sensitive trauma training to teacher-counselors and other mental health professionals in Sri Lanka, 4 weeks after the tsunami. *Brief Treatment and Crisis Intervention*, *6*(4), 316–325. doi:10.1093/brief-treatment/mhl012

Kerka, S. (2000). *Health and adult education*. Columbus, OH: ERIC Clearinghouse on Adult, Career, and Vocational Education.

Kuhajda, M. (2006). Training community health workers to reduce health disparities in Alabama's black belt. *Family & Community Health, 29*(2), 89–102.

Laroche, L. (2003). *Managing cultural diversity in technical professions.* Boston: Butterworth Heinemann.

Li, B., Caniano, D., & Comer, R. (1998). A cultural diversity curriculum: Combining didactic, problem-solving, and simulated experiences. *Journal of the American Medical Women's Association, 53*(3), 127–129.

Liaw, S. (2006). E-learning and the development of intercultural competence. *Language Learning & Technology, 10*(3), 49–64.

Lowenstein, K. (2009). The work of multicultural teacher education: Reconceptualizing white teacher candidates as learners. *Review of Educational Research, 79*(10), 163–196. doi:10.3102/0034654308326161

McKinney, J., & Kurtz-Ross, S. (2000). *Culture, health and literacy: A guide to health education materials for adults with limited English literacy skills.* Boston: World Education.

McMahon, C., & Bruce, C. (2002). Information literacy needs of local staff in cross-cul-tural development projects. *Journal of International Development, 14*(1), 113–137. doi:10.1002/jid.864

Merriam, S. B., Courtenay, B. C., & Cervero, R. M. (Eds.). (2006). *Global issues and adult education.* San Francisco: Jossey-Bass.

Miao, C. (2000). Transformative learning and social transformation: A cross-cultural perspective. *Masters Abstracts International, 36*(06), 1415. (AAT MZ50488).

Nielsen. (2009). *Global faces and networked places.* New York: Nielsen. Retrieved June 25, 2009, from http://blog.nielsen.com/nielsenwire/wp-content/uploads/2009/03/nielsen_globalfaces_mar09.pdf

Osborn, M., Thomas, E., & Hartnack, D. (2005). An evolving model of knowledge management in education and the South African reality . In Lee, S. (Eds.), *Information leadership in a culture of change: IASL reports* (pp. 1–15). Erie, PA: International Association of School Librarianship.

Rapoport, A. (2008). The impact of international programs on pedagogical practices of their participants. *Teachers and Teaching: Theory and Practice, 14*(3), 225–238.

Schirmer, J. (2004). A collaborative needs assessment and work plan in behavioral medicine curriculum development in Vietnam. *Families, Systems & Health, 22*(4), 410–418. doi:10.1037/1091-7527.22.4.410

Suefert, S. (2002). Cultural perspectives . In Adelsberg, H., Collis, B., & Pawlowski, J. (Eds.), *Handbook on information technology for education and training* (pp. 411–424). Munich, Germany: Springer-Verlag.

Texas Department of Health, National Maternal and Child Health Resource Center on Cultural Competency. (1997). *Journey towards cultural competency: Lessons learned.* Vienna, VA: Maternal and Children's Health Bureau Clearinghouse.

The changing world of international students. (2006). *NEA Higher Education ADVOCATE* (December), 6-8.

UNESCO. (2002). *Universal declaration on cultural diversity.* The Hague: UNESCO.

Welch, L., Cleckley, B., & McClure, M. (1997). *Strategies for promoting pluralism in education and the workplace.* Westport, CT: Praeger.

White, L. (2002). *Engaging black learners in adult and community education.* Leicester, England: National Institute of Adult Continuing Education.

Chapter 5
Teaching Philosophies of Career and Technical Education

Gregory C. Petty
University of Tennessee, USA

ABSTRACT

Teaching philosophies as applied to career and technical education are more complex than teaching philosophies studied for a liberal arts teacher. Adult learners present challenges not often encountered by elementary or secondary teachers. Contact with the world of work presents teachers with the paradox of preparing young people directly for work but maintaining a nurturing classroom environment. This challenge often requires unique and innovative solutions to the educational problem presented by adult learners. This chapter presents philosophical approaches the career and technical education teacher can use in the classroom or laboratory.

5.1 INTRODUCTION

To understand teaching philosophies one should begin with the Greek *philosophos*, "lover of wisdom". In the intellectual traditions of ancient Greece, philosophy has related meanings such as: the study of the truths or principles underlying all knowledge, being, and reality; a particular system of philosophical doctrine; the critical evaluation of fundamental doctrines; the study of the principles of a particular branch of knowledge; a system of principles for guidance in practical affairs; and a

philosophical spirit or attitude (Brewer, Campbell, & Petty, 2000; Kneller, 1971).

Philosophers of education maintain that the task of the philosophy of education is solely to try to study and explain approaches to education and educational issues. Educational philosophy does, however, include broader areas of study such as historical writings on education by important philosophers. The philosophy of education and the history of education cannot be clearly separated (Thompson, 1973).

The improvement of educational decisions, policies, values, and methods must be an objective of educational philosophy if it is not to be merely

DOI: 10.4018/978-1-61520-747-3.ch005

an intellectual exercise. The relationship between educational theory and practice—how theory is applied and tested in practice and how practice improves theory should be a focus of educational philosophy (Kneller, 1971).

From its most basic beginnings with the pre-Socratics, the study of philosophy sought to find fundamental, natural principles that could explain what individuals know and experience about the world around them with a comprehensive set of principles that would account for their knowledge of both the natural and the human world (Hyslop-Margison, 2002).

Philosophers believe that asking questions and not providing answers sharpens our inquiring mind. We are, by nature, inquisitive beings. Philosophers have questioned the ways people lived and sought the most acceptable conclusion. Ancient philosophers, beginning with Socrates (469-399 B.C), studied the "good life" and realized their thinking could be a mechanism for criticizing or refuting common myths or thoughts of their predecessors. It was with this beginning that Socrates became the first genius of philosophy (Taylor, Hare, & Barnes, 1998).

This chapter will begin with a review of perspectives of philosophy: Speculative; Prescriptive; and Analytic. This is followed by a brief discussion of systemic and holistic perspectives and a detailed examination of four basic systemic philosophies: idealism; realism; pragmatism; and existentialism.

It is important that philosophy be studied with values and ethics, therefore a short presentation of these components is presented along with logic and philosophy. The chapter then moves to common educational philosophies: perennialism; progressivism; conventionalism; and recontructionism.

The last section of this chapter is an examination of the philosophers themselves and their influence on philosophical methods, the branches of philosophy, and the philosophy of education. The meaning of philosophy is presented along with discussions of the philosophies of ideal-ism, realism, pragmatism, progressivism and existentialism.

5.2 BACKGROUND

From the earliest of times humans have sought to find fundamental, natural principles that explain what they know and experienced in the world around them. We as a people are constantly striving to find the scope of the universe or we try to conceptualize the world and our place in it. In short–to see how the world looks and how we fit (Brewer, Campbell, & Petty, 2000; Kneller, 1971).

Philosophy is a product of the human mind, such as a theory in geometry. What the human mind produces depends on its general competence, the information and other raw material with which it works, and the general setting in which it works. Philosophy is found in its consideration in the nature of humans, our world, our values and the good life (self actualizations). What do we live for? What is the purpose of life? What sort of life should it be (Brewer, Campbell, & Petty, 2000; Kneller, 1971)?

As educators we must try to comprehend philosophy in its entirety. Our task is to interpret these finding which affect education. There are three modes or styles of philosophy:

- Speculative.
- Prescriptive.
- Analytic.

Speculative Philosophy. Speculative philosophy is the oldest mode of philosophy. This philosophical mode is the study of what should be. Applying this mode helps us to build a systematic way to think about the universe in general and the humans in it. It is the attempt to think in the most general and systematic way about everything in the universe–about the whole of reality, because the human mind wishes to conceptualize all things. We seek a pattern to help us conceive all things.

We structure our lives. Speculative philosophy is the attempt to find coherence in the whole realm of thought, knowledge and experience (Kneller, 1971).

In education speculative philosophy works by seeking generalized theories (order) in our total experience in education (Kneller, 1971). To practice speculative philosophy we must understand what it is to:

- Exist.
- Know.
- Value.
- Inquire.

Since CTE is involved with the nature of humans, our education, work, and society we must consider the factors that affect teaching: These are:

- To exist → nature of humans.
- To know → nature of education.
- To value → nature of work.
- To inquire → nature of society.

Prescriptive Philosophy. Prescriptive philosophy states what something ought to be (or must be) and says which qualities are worthwhile and why. This philosophical mode states the ends that CTE ought to follow and the general means it must use to obtain them (Kneller, 1971). Prescriptive philosophy seeks to determine a basis for establishing standards for:

- Accessing value.
- Judging conduct.
- Appraising art.

Analytic Philosophy. Analytic philosophy seeks to qualify what we know already and points to inconsistencies between beliefs and actions. This philosophy suggests that we not take anything for granted. Wherever there is a margin for error there is room for question or inquiry in all our relationships and all our beliefs. This mode deals with the affective domain (Venn, 1964). Analytic philosophy focuses on words and meanings by examining concepts such as:

a. Cause.
b. Mind.
c. Equality of opportunity.
d. Academic freedom.

5.2.1 Systemic and Holistic Perspectives

Epistemology is the type of philosophy that concerns the person who comes from industry (such as a CTE teacher) and has little knowledge about formal education (Morton, 2002). In CTE most often the use of knowledge is associated with replicated uses of knowledge. This concept is usually recognized as OJT, or on the job training and may be loosely interpreted as the science of human action, also known as praxeology (Cherwitz, & Hikins, 1979; Venn, 1964).

Praxeology is the science of human action and is not often used with CTE discussions of teaching philosophies. However we must consider that praxeology plus knowledge is equal to CTE. Mises (2006) concluded that decisions are made on an ordinal basis. In other words, the conscious mind is only capable of one decision at a time. And even though decisions can be made in rapid order, it is impossible to carry out more than one action at once.

Axiology is concerned with values, both objective and subjective values. Subjective values are relative to personal desires (i.e. to be valuable is to be valued by somebody). And whatever is valuable is so because we happen to *assign* a certain value. Some values are absolute and eternal, constants that never change. An example is charity, a value that is good for all people for all times (Brewer, Campbell, & Petty, 2000; Kneller, 1971).

- Matter of choice and not to choose is a choice.

- Human beings are the only organism that can perceive nothingness.
- Highly personal.
- We can achieve an ideal society if we can make ideal persons of all of us.

5.2.3 The Perspective of Values to Philosophy

Values are relative to human desire. According to Brewer et al. (2000) the hierarchy of values to human desire is fixed with spirituality on top and materialistic on the bottom. However, others say there is no fixed hierarchy of values (Brewer, Campbell, & Petty, 2000; Kneller, 1971).

Idealistic. An idealist will state that values and ethics are absolute, not manmade. Values are part of the university and are fundamental and do not change.

Realistic. A realist states there is a universal moral law that is basically permanent and available to reason. A religious realist believes this moral law is established by God whereas a scientific realist believes this moral law is established by nature. Both believe moral law is timeless, unchangeable and universal.

Pragmatic. A pragmatist believes that values are relative to the situation and time, and that we must be flexible and willing to change our values based on consequences. If the consequences are not desirable then we must drop or change our values. Ethics too, must change when consequences are not what we want.

Existentialistic. An existentialist will state that not to choose is a choice, and do not look for the way but look for your way. For an existentialist, values are a personal matter and if you choose to do something you should expect and accept the consequences.

- Deductive.
- Inductive.

5.2.6 Philosophical Teaching Theories

Helpful for the professional or instructor of CTE is an examination of classic educational theories. These theories, as shown below, have their basis in the three oldest philosophies; idealism, realism, and pragmatism (Kincheloe, 2008). These theories are:

- Perennialism
  a. Knowledge should be the same everywhere.
  b. Basic subjects should be taught and used to cultivate students' reason.
    •Progressivism
  c. A critical issue is the lack of fixed goals.
  d. Postulates the questionable belief that reason must be learned.
  e. Based on the belief that humans are social animals.
  f. Force cooperation nurtures conformists–makes us all alike.
  g. Does not favor self discipline.
  h. Humans learn best in real life activities with other people.
    •Conventionalism
  i. Educators believe that fundamental principles are grounded on societal agreements rather than on external reality.
    •Reconstructionism
  j. Believe the primary goal of education is to help create a new social order.
  k. Leads to collective society with very limited individual involvement.
  l. Educators focus on a curriculum that highlights social reform as the aim of education.

5.2.7 The Philosopher

To be a philosopher is to be impervious to the challenges of ordinary life and to be capable of calm reflection. A philosopher's goal is to center upon providing an organizing principle and perspective for a given issue. Philosophically a pessimist might establish safeguards and alternatives to help students, simply because he or she expects the worst. An idealist on the other hand, might look for the best in students and seek ways to reward performance.

The study of philosophy is the effort to fulfill a questioning mind. We should accept that nothing should be taken for granted and that everything should be carefully studied. The philosopher asks questions–and does not provide answers. This process sharpens the inquiring mind (Kazanas, Harris, & Lomons, 1973).

As a discipline of study, philosophy provides a:

- Characteristic way of thinking.
- Conceptual framework for attacking problems.
- Process for describing, defining, and classifying information.
- Means for predicting outcomes and of testing predictions.

It is the objective of this chapter to explore and illuminate teaching philosophies used in CTE. Career and technical education (CTE), formerly vocational education, is not a discipline per se. The origins of CTE come from multiple disciplines such as philosophy, economics, anthropology, history, political science, sociology, and psychology. These disciplines are synthesized into a common philosophy of CTE.

Ancient philosophers such as Socrates questioned the ways people lived and sought the most acceptable one. Their philosophical attitudes and theories served as guides to practical living for their time. Philosophers today devote their studies to identify the good life for humans as individuals and as social beings. Early philosophers realized their thinking could be a mechanism for criticizing or refuting common myths or thoughts of their predecessors.

Socrates proposed that if people do not examine and critically evaluate the principles by which they live, they cannot be sure that worthwhile principles exist. Greek thinkers saw that for each science or study such as history and art there could be a corresponding philosophy of this science or study which involved examining the fundamental principles of a discipline to see if they are logical, consistent, or true (Taylor, 2001).

To understand philosophy as teachers practice it today, one must first study Socrates (469-399 B.C.). The Socratic method of teaching is commonly used by teachers and has heavily influenced CTE teaching styles. This method is a type of pedagogy in which a series of questions are asked to draw individual answers and to encourage fundamental insight into the issue at hand. What is most interesting, particularly today as we utilize this strategy in our classrooms is that Socrates published very little. It was his student Plato who documented for all history the accounts of Socrates (Kofman, 1998).

A couple of interesting things about Socrates should be mentioned: 1) he was a military veteran; and 2) he had a vocational trade of stonemason. Although teachers around the world have followed his thinking, few may be aware he was a tradesman and a veteran. He is noted not only as a founder of Western philosophy but also someone who made lasting contributions to epistemology or the theory of knowledge, and logic i.e. the study of the principles of valid demonstration and inference (Cohen, 2008).

Socrates believed that *ideas* were the only true reality. His methods of question and answer were focused on examining the full extent of meaning for all ideas so teachers could form a dialog of full discussion of the concept. He proposed that if people did not examine and critically evaluate the principles by which they lived, they could not be sure that worthwhile principles existed. He postulated that for each science or art there could be a corresponding philosophy of that science or study examining the fundamental principles of a discipline's logic, consistency and truth (Bruell, 1999).

Socrates was true to his beliefs to the end. Placed on trial for crimes against the country he was convicted of treason and sentenced to death. He had publically questioned authorities and embarrassed them turning the leadership against him. He questioned the Athenian collective notion that "might make right". He irritated the government to stimulate their sense of justice but was punished for his efforts (May, 2000).

Originally, Platonic metaphysics claimed that the body and the mind were two separate and distinct entities. **Plato**, in fact, claimed the body was the prison house of the soul or mind. In the 17th century, **Rene Descartes** contended that mind and body were two separate and distinct substances that had nothing in common although they interact. Several Indian schools of philosophy hold a similar view. In the West this problem was gradually taken over by psychologists and neurophysiologists. The present tendency is to reduce mental phenomena to brain phenomena and thereby reduce the problem from a mind-body problem to a body problem (Bergen, 1981).

Philosophers have traditionally raised questions about **values**:

- What is good?
- How can good be distinguished from bad or evil?
- What is justice?
- What would a just society be like?
- What is beauty?
- How can the beautiful be distinguished from the ugly?

These questions all deal with **matters of evaluation** rather than fact. Scientific investigation is of only slight help in determining if abortion is bad or if Whistler's Mother is a beautiful picture. The values that are at issue are not perceived in the same way as facts. If they were, much more agreement would exist about the specific answers to value questions. The philosopher seeks to find some means of answering these sorts of questions, which are often the most important ones that a person can ask and which will exhibit the basis of a theory of values (Hansen, 2005).

A constant philosophical question, from Greek times up to the present, has been to try to **establish the difference between appearance and reality**. Once people learned about sense illusions, the question arose of how to tell what seems to be from what really is. Skeptical thinkers have pressed the claim that no satisfactory standard can be found that will actually work for distinguishing the real from the apparent in all cases. On the other hand, various philosophers have proposed many such criteria, none of which has been universally accepted (Kneller, 1971).

Another type of question raised by philosophers is: What is truth? Various statements about aspects of the world seem to be true, at least at certain times. Yet experience teaches that statements that have seemed to be true have later had to be qualified or denied. Skeptics have suggested that no evidence would be able to tell, that a given statement is in reality true. In the face of such a challenge, philosophers have sought to find a criterion of truth, especially a criterion of truth that would not be open to skeptical challenge (Brewer, Campbell, & Petty, 2000).

5.3 MAJOR PHILOSOPHERS OF THE ANCIENT WORLD

Three philosophers of the ancient world should be noted for influencing the CTE teacher. These are: Socrates (469-399 B.C.); Plato (427-347 B.C.); and Aristotle (384-322 B.C.). Much of their philosophical basis came from an understanding and appreciation of the trades and the early foundations of education.

Socrates was an Athenian who was primarily interested in value questions that affected what a person should do. Though he did not write anything, he was vividly portrayed by his pupil Plato. He was finally arrested and accused of heresy and corrupting the young of Athens. At his trial for life or death he dramatically stated that he was the wisest of the men because he alone knew nothing and knew that he knew nothing, whereas everybody else thought they knew something. Although, as reported by Plato he was very eloquent and wise, he was convicted and sentenced to death.

Plato was a disciple of Socrates who developed the first comprehensive philosophical system and founded the Academy, the first formal philosophical school. Plato contended that knowledge must be of universals (that is, of general types or kinds) and not of particulars. According to Plato, these universals were the basic elements from which the world was formed. His example was that to know a particular cat, Miranda, the individual must first know what it is to be feline in general, otherwise one will not be able to recognize the particular feline characteristics in Miranda. This line of thinking is called the Forms, or Platonic Ideas.

Plato believed that mathematics provides the most obvious cases of Forms. They are known not by sense perception but by reasoning. Forms are known by the mind, not by the bodily organs and the world of Platonic Ideas is the unchanging Forms of things. He thought he philosopher should turn away from this world of appearance and concentrate on the world of Forms. Plato, in The Republic, said that the world would be perfect when philosophers are kings and kings are philosophers. He believed that the philosopher-kings would know what justice really is, and, based on their knowledge of the Forms, they could then achieve justice in all societies.

Aristotle was Plato's leading student. He developed the most comprehensive philosophical system of ancient times. He later broke with Plato, stressing the importance of explaining the changing world that humankind lives in as opposed to the Platonic Ideas. He spent years studying the natural sciences and collecting specimens, and about 90 percent of his writings are on scientific subjects, mostly on biological ones

Aristotle was noted for believing that he could account for the changes and alterations in this world without either having to deny their reality or having to appeal to another world. For Aristotle all natural objects were composed of form and matter, and the changes that take place in matter are the substitution of one form for another. Substitution takes place because every natural object has a goal, or telos, which it is its nature to achieve. An example of his teaching was that stones, because they are essentially material, seek the lowest point, which is why they fall down. Each species is ultimately trying to achieve a state of perfection which for Aristotle was a state of perfect rest. The cosmos is an ordered striving for this perfection.

5.4 PHILOSOPHICAL METHODS

In view of the kinds of questions that philosophers deal with, what methods does the philosopher use to seek the answers? The philosopher's tools are basically logical and speculative reasoning. In the Western tradition the development of logic is usually traced to Aristotle (384-322 B.C.), who aimed at constructing valid arguments and also true arguments if true premises could be uncovered. Logic has played an important role in ancient and modern philosophy—that of providing a clarification of the reasoning process and standards by which valid reasoning can be recognized. It has also provided a means of analyzing basic concepts to determine if they are consistent or not (Taylor, Hare, & Barnes, 1998).

Logic alone, however, is not enough to answer philosophers' questions. It can show when philosophers are being consistent and when their concepts are clear and unambiguous, but it cannot ascertain if the first principles or the premises are correct. Here philosophers sometimes rely on what they call intuition and sometimes on a speculative reasoning process. From their initial premises, philosophers then try to work out a consistent development of their answers to basic philosophical questions, following the rules of logic.

5.4.1 Branches of Philosophy

Different branches of philosophy correspond to the different problems. One of the most basic is epistemology, the theory of knowledge (episteme is Greek for knowledge). It deals with what can be known, how it can be known, and how certain the individual can be about it. It has special branches like the philosophy of science. The kinds of answers that emerge from a particular epistemology usually structure its metaphysics.

Metaphysics is the study of nature of reality, the study of what features of experience are real and which are apparent. Aristotle called metaphysics the study of being as such; the term ontology is often used to describe this branch of philosophy today. How a person gets to know about pure being (an epistemological problem) colors what it is that is known. The reverse is also the case. What the individual thinks the world is really like colors what he or she thinks can be known about it. How the individual reasons about the world and how he or she can certify knowledge belongs to the branch of philosophy called logic. **Logic** provides the rational framework for all philosophical discussion, but is also itself open to metaphysical interpretations about what sort of world it is explaining.

Other branches of philosophy such as ethics, aesthetics, and political philosophy deal with evaluative aspects of the world such as what is good conduct, what is beautiful, and what is socially and politically correct. The proposed answers to these questions are much involved with the philosopher's epistemological and metaphysical theories, and the values the philosopher espouses color his or her epistemology and metaphysics. Sometimes the pursuit of particular aspects of experience (such as sensations) or the use of particular tools (such as the analysis of language) will reorient philosophical inquiry or give birth to new branches of philosophy. Thus philosophy is never reasoned in a vacuum. It is concerned not only with abstract questions; it is also conditioned by history.

5.4.2 Philosophy of Education

The philosophy of education is a field of applied inquiry in which the method is philosophical and the subjects of inquiry are educational. Inherent in the philosophical method is an attempt to think, speak, and write precisely and thoroughly. The philosophy of education seeks to make people more conscious of important issues in education and to help them evaluate arguments.

The term education has had a variety of definitions. The traditional view of education is expressed in the formal instructional activities conducted in schools and universities. A better definition is that education is a lifelong process that includes both formal instruction and the broad range of other experiences. These experiences include television viewing, video game playing, peer relationships, and family living that usually occupy more time and often exert more powerful influences than formal schooling (Brewer, Campbell, & Petty, 2000; Kneller, 1971).

Education can be viewed as a product, a process, or both. Philosophers of education who focus on education as a product—the result of teaching and learning activities—look particularly at such factors as goals, aims, competence, effective teaching, and standards. Those who view education as a process are concerned primarily with the quality of the learner's experience, the nature of methodologies, and the relationships between teachers and students and among students. To some extent, conservative philosophers of education see education mainly as a product; progressive philosophers of education tend to see it mainly as a process. Others argue that product and process are inseparable (Brewer, Campbell, & Petty, 2000; Kneller, 1971).

Philosophers of education have offered diverse theories of human nature that carry implications for educational purpose, policy, and practice (Brubacher, 1939; Dupuis, 1996; Kneller, 1971; Nash, 1966; Woods & Barrow, 2006). Career and technical education philosophy has been largely dominated by the economic point of view; therefore, this theory of vocational development has been largely ignored. What the *human mind* produces depends on its general competence, other raw material with which it works, and the general setting in which it works (Brewer, Campbell, & Petty, 2000).

5.4.3 Vocational (Career and Technical) Philosophy

The best application for any of us could be to use our philosophy to provide one simple answer to a very basic question: What should be taught? That is to determine what knowledge is of most value to most students in a workforce/vocational education program. Should students be involved in training to get and hold a job? Many vocational education professionals suggest that individuals need more than job skills to be a productive society member (Petty, 1993; Petty, 1997).

Another question that should be asked is: If we provide an education for those who go to college, why not provide it for those who go to work? The image, prestige, purpose, and the place of career and technical education, all stem from this very basic argument (Petty, 1983; Petty, 1995c).

We seek to comprehend philosophy in its entirety in order to understand our position in it. We then can interpret our findings and determine which affect education (in our view). Our summary of philosophical descriptions of human beings gives us an overall description of mankind and hopefully a better understanding of where we, as individuals fit, along with career and techni-

cal education, our profession, and our students (Petty, 1995b).

5.5 MEANING OF PHILOSOPHY

Perhaps the meaning of philosophy is best examined in its consideration of the nature of mankind, world, value and the good life (self-actualization). Maslow in his hierarchy of needs indicated that self-actualization is what humans strive for. Philosophers suggest that only through understanding our own philosophy and what people live for, the purpose of life, and seeking what sort of life we should have, can we achieve this plateau (Kneller, 1971).

5.5.1 Idealism

Idealism is considered the first organized philosophy (Kincheloe, 2008). It is defined as the philosophical view that the mind or spirit constitutes the fundamental reality. In recent years idealism has taken several distinct but related forms. Objective idealism accepts common sense realism (the view that material objects exist) but rejects naturalism (according to which the mind and spiritual values have emerged from material things), whereas subjective idealism denies that material objects exist independently of human perception and thus stands opposed to both realism and naturalism. Idealists believe that ultimate happiness is reality and can only be achieved through education.

Plato is often considered the first idealist philosopher, primarily because of his work with metaphysics. Plato considered the universal Idea or Form—for example, redness or goodness—more real than a particular instance of the form—a red object, a good action. According to Plato, the world of changing experience is unreal, and the Idea or Form—which does not change and which can be known only by reason—constitutes true reality.

Plato considered reality to lie in ideal Forms that constitute the essential nature of the transient, physical objects that most people identify as reality. The purpose of education, he asserted, should be to attempt to perceive and understand these ideal Forms, even though only a few people might be able to achieve such understanding. According to Plato, people can be divided into categories according to their ability to pursue education successfully. In the Republic and the Laws Plato outlined his hierarchical model, a system in which those who were the most able would receive the most education and become the rulers or guardians of society. Those with less talent for intellectual training would become warriors. Those with the least capacity would receive the least schooling and would become the workers (Brewer, Campbell, & Petty, 2000).

Since Plato's time most educational systems in the West have emulated his model. Schooling has been predominantly abstract and intellectual. Many students find difficulty in relating such subject matter to their notion of the real world. Those least adept at this process leave the educational system. The dropouts often go on to occupy the lowest positions in the economic hierarchy. Hierarchical, selective, and segregated educational systems reflect and serve to perpetuate the societies of which they are an essential part.

The 18th-century epistemologist George Berkeley was one of the major exponents of idealism. He held that the object of knowledge is an idea and that ideas can exist only in the mind; therefore, objects can exist only as objects of consciousness. Berkeley's dictum esse est percipi ("to be is to be perceived") has clear metaphysical implications. Indeed he called his theory immaterialism and intended it as a refutation of traditional materialism (Ewing, 1957).

Immanuel Kant held that it is impossible to gain knowledge of the world by either reason or sense experience alone. Whereas in ordinary idealism the individual subject's awareness is the basic element of reality, in Kant's transcendental idealism the subject in general—not a particular subject, but the universal structure of all subjects—is the basic element of reality. This universal subject, the transcendental self, is the precondition of any knowledge of an objective world (Allison, 2004).

5.5.2 Realism

Realism is perhaps the second philosophy recognized as such. It beginnings are over 1000 years old. Realism philosophy is subject centered and attempts to develop essentials. Realism denotes two distinct sets of philosophical theories, one regarding the nature of universal concepts and the other dealing with knowledge of objects in the world. In the classroom the teacher is absolute authority and the student assimilates prescribed subject matter. Students are expected to exhibit certain amounts of mental discipline.

In late-classical and medieval philosophy, realism was (as was idealism) a development of the Platonic theory of Forms and held, generally, that universals such as "red" or "man" have an independent, objective existence, either in a realm of their own or in the mind of God. Medieval realism is usually contrasted with nominalism, and the classic critiques of realism from this point of view were provided by Peter Abelard and William of Occam (Marenbon, 1999).

In modern philosophy realism is a broad term with more emphasis on social heritage and is adjustment oriented. Modern realism encompasses several movements whose unity lies in a common rejection of philosophical idealism. In its most general form realism asserts that objects in the external world exist independently of what is thought about them. The most straightforward of such theories is usually known as naive realism. It contends that in perception humans are made directly aware of objects and their attributes and thus have immediate access to the external world.

This view of realism fails to explain perceptual mistakes and illusions, and most realists argue that causal processes in the mind mediate, or interpret, directly perceived appearances. Thus the objects remain in essence independent, although the causal mechanism may distort, or even wholly falsify, the individual's knowledge of them. Realism has had considerable influence on career and technical education as it is practiced today. It has also given rise to pragmatism and is basically adjustment oriented.

5.5.3 Pragmatism

Twentieth-century philosophy has been characterized in the United States by Pragmatism. Pragmatists wanted an earthy theory—that the truth is that which works—as an expeditious way of solving problems. From William James to John Dewey pragmatism dominated American thought in the first half of this century (Baldacchino, 2008; Thayer-Bacon, 2003).

Developed in the United States, pragmatism is a closer match for most career and technical educators. Most Americans think pragmatism agrees with our way of life–the way we look at the world. It was thought in the 70's that no other philosophy could approach pragmatism in the U.S., especially in career and technical education (Norvack, 1975).

Charles Sanders Peirce is considered the founder of pragmatism. He developed it as a theory of meaning in the 1870s, holding that an intrinsic connection exists between meaning and action—that the meaning of an idea is to be found in its "conceivable sensible effects" and that humans generate belief through their "habits of action." William **James** gave a further direction to pragmatism, developing it as a theory of truth. True ideas, according to James, are useful "leadings"; they lead through experience in ways that provide consistency, orderliness, and predictability. The classical American pragmatists are, in addition to Peirce and James, John Dewey, George Herbert Mead, and Clarence Irving Lewis (Rosiek, & Atkinson, 2005; Stanage, 1994; Wirth, 1974).

Pragmatism has tended to criticize traditional philosophical outlooks in the light of scientific and social developments. The development in science most influential on pragmatism is the theory of evolution. Its impact can be seen in the pragmatic emphasis on action rather than entity, emergent effect rather than cause, process and development rather than finality and permanence. Focusing on the fullness of experience and the richness of nature, pragmatism sees humankind not as a spectator separated from nature but as a constant creative interactor with it. Pragmatism thus tends toward a naturalism in which process plays an important role Norvack, 1975).

The influence of Darwinism on pragmatic thought is further seen in its evolutionary approach, which holds that what is true for one time or place may not be true for another—that reality, as well as human knowledge of it, is constantly evolving, as is morality. What is good or evil, as well as what is true or false, is dependent on its practical outcome—in the case of ethics, its effects on human behavior. Pragmatists do not regard this relativism, whether in epistemology, ethics, or metaphysics, as subjective. Real, true, or good ideas, they maintain, have developed in the course of humanity's interactions with the environment, emerging because they work to lead humans successfully through their experiences. One major pragmatic criterion for truth is agreement on the part of the community of investigators in the long run. Truth tends to be that which gets accepted in the free competition of ideas. Politically, pragmatists usually advocate democracy as the system best suited to change with the needs of the majority (Norvack, 1975).

5.5.4 Progressivism

The term progressive education refers to a diverse group of theories and practices that took shape in Europe and the United States during the late 19th century. Progressive educational theory is not derived from any single source but comprises beliefs that are alike only in their common opposition to traditional schooling, which emphasizes mastery of an academic curriculum within a disciplinary system, and in their concern for the emotional and physical well-being of the child. In the United States the term is applied to a movement whose intellectual leader was the philosopher John Dewey, and that constituted one expression of a widespread reform movement known as Progressivism (Law, 1975; Lynch, 1997).

The intellectual origins of progressive education may be traced to Jean Jacques Rousseau, the principal critic of 18th-century rationalism. In his treatise Emile (1762), Rousseau argued that the spontaneous impulses of children were healthy and should not be repressed by adult demands for emotional restraint, intellectual precision, and social conformity. Rousseau's romantic naturalism provided a justification for the work of such educators Johann Heinrich Pestalozzi and Maria **Montessori**, who created special classroom environments in which children were encouraged to develop their faculties through experience (Jervis, & Montag, 1995).

The principal forerunner of progressive education in the United States was Francis Wayland Parker, who in Massachusetts and Chicago replaced the formal curriculum with a flexible program that included self-expression and claimed to teach pupils rather than subjects, respecting individual differences in the needs and abilities of children. Many of the liberal educational policies of the latter 20th century, such as head start, compensatory education, and early-childhood schooling, draw extensively on progressive assumptions and methods, which remain a major influence on educational thought (Brewer, Campbell, & Petty, 2000).

5.5.5 Existentialism

Existentialism is the popular name of a philosophical attitude primarily associated with the 20th-century thinker Jean Paul **Sartre**, but with a history that goes back to the 19th-century Danish philosopher Soren Kierkegaard. The name itself was coined by Sartre, although the expression "existence philosophy" had been used earlier by Karl Jaspars, who belonged to the same tradition. Existentialists have differed widely from one another on many basic philosophical issues, but they have shared a concern for human freedom and personal responsibility and have stressed the importance of the individual's need to make choices (Brewer, Campbell, & Petty, 2000; Kneller, 1971).

Twentieth-century existentialism is largely defined—in its form if not its expression—by the movement known as phenomenology, originated by Edmund Husserl and pursued into the existential realm by his student Martin Heidegger. His method, simply stated, was to find and examine the essential structures of experience, with the aim of establishing the universal truths necessary to basic consciousness. Heidegger borrowed the phenomenological method and applied it to more personal problems—questions about how human beings should live, what they are, and the meaning of life and death (Burstow, 1983).

Sartre combined existentialism with Marxism. Following both Husserl and Heidegger, he used the phenomenological method to defend his central thesis that human beings are essentially free, free to choose (though not free not to choose) and free to negate the given features of the world. One may be cowardly or shy, but one can always resolve to change. One may be born Jewish or black, French or crippled; it is an open question what one will make of oneself, whether these will be handicaps or advantages, challenges to be overcome or excuses to do nothing (Brewer, Campbell, & Petty, 2000; Burstow, 1983).

Camus borrowed from Heidegger the sense of being abandoned in the world, and he shared with Sartre the sense that the world does not give meaning to individuals. But whereas Sartre joined Heidegger in insisting that one must make meaning for oneself, Camus concluded that the world is "absurd," a term that has (wrongly) come to represent the whole of existentialist thinking. For Sartre, however, the heart of existentialism is not gloom or hopelessness, but a renewed confidence in the significance of being human (Burstow, 1984). Some major points of existentialism are: it is quite different from pragmatism; it was developed in France and Germany; one of the most extreme reactions came from the Danish thinker Soren Kierkegaard (1813-1855).

Kierkegaard believed that all metaphysical systems are unsuccessful, but that to avoid despair an individual had to opt for some sort of belief, by taking a "leap of faith". Kierkegaard's emphasis on subjectivity, confrontation, and despair has greatly influenced the school of thought of existentialism. It is interesting to note that although Kierkegaard was a religious Christian, many of those who have used his basic approach are irreligious.

The most notable reaction to existentialism is phenomenology, developed by Edmund Husserl. Bracketing questions about the self and other transcendental ideas, Husserl attempted to elaborate a method for the analysis of experience as it presents itself. His most important student, Martin Heidegger, developed a philosophy of "being-in-the world," which has also influenced Jean Paul Sartre (1905-1980) and other existentialists. The death of Sartre in 1980 has caused some to question the viability of existentialism as a distinct philosophy for the future.

5.6 FAMOUS PHILOSOPHERS SUMMARY

- **Saint Thomas Aquinas** (1224-1274), known as the Angelic Doctor, synthesized religious and philosophical thought during the Middle Ages.
- **Aristotle** (384-322 B.C.), one of the greatest Greek thinkers, wrote philosophical treatises that through the ages have exerted a major influence on Western thought. He advocated moderation in behavior and the use of logic as the proper tool of investigation.
- **Henri Bergson** (1859-1941), French philosopher, won the 1927 Nobel Prize for literature. He emphasized the value of intuition in scientific thinking and argued that reality is beyond rational understanding.
- **Martin Buber** (1878-1965), was a 20th-century Jewish existentialist who was influenced by Hasidic mysticism. After being expelled from Nazi Germany in 1938, he taught at Hebrew University in Jerusalem.
- **Rene Descartes** (1596-1650) proposed a method for guaranteeing knowledge. He argued that in order to provide a secure foundation for knowledge it was necessary to discover "clear and distinct ideas" that could not be doubted and could serve as a basis for deriving further truths. He found such an idea in the proposition "I think, therefore I am." Descartes is often considered the founder of modern philosophy.
- **Thomas Hobbes** (1588-1679), a 17th-century English political philosopher, justified absolute government as the sole means of protecting a society from the selfish nature of its individual members. In his most famous work, Leviathan published in 1651, Hobbes argues that in their natural state humans lead lives that are "solitary, poor, nasty, brutish, and short"; fear of death, however, leads them to enter into a social contract to create a government whose powers must of necessity be absolute.
- **David Hume** (1711-1776), an 18th-century Scottish philosopher, combined ideas from British empiricism and French skepticism to advance his theory that moral distinctions cannot rest on rational grounds. Although the full impact of Hume's inquiries was not evident during his lifetime, his influence on Kant and philosophers of the 20th century has been profound.

- **John Stuart Mill** (1806-1873), a 19th-century English philosopher and economist, advocated utilitarian reforms in his many writings and as the member of Parliament. A child prodigy, Mill had mastered Greek by the age of 7 and studied economics at the age of 13. His works express his social thought with great clarity and thoroughness.

- **Baron de Montesquieu** (1689-1755) exerted considerable influence on the U.S. Constitution through his analysis of human behavior and institutions, The Spirit of the Laws published in 1748. A member of lively intellectual circles in Enlightenment Paris, he spent two years in England before commencing the work that is now regarded as a precursor of many branches of modern social science.

- **Friedrich Nietzsche** (1844-1900) was among the most influential figures of German philosophical thought. Nietzsche formulated the concept of the ubermensch, or "superman," whose creative impulses were propelled by the "will to power" and were grounded in the material world.

- **Plato** (c.428-347 B.C.), the Greek philosopher, remains one of the most influential thinkers in Western civilization. Plato's dialogues, in their exploration of the basic questions raised by philosophical inquiries, were seminal works in the history of thought. Plato was a pupil of Socrates, and his interest in education led to his founding (387 B.C.) of the Academy in Athens.

- **Jean Jacques Rousseau** (1712-1778), one of the great French philosophers of the 18th century, emphasized the primacy of individual liberty in such writings as his major political treatise, The Social Contract and his work on education, Emile, both published in 1762. This emphasis and his introspective autobiographical works anticipated the focus of later romantic writings.

- **Bertrand Russell** (1872-1970), a seminal figure in the development of 20th-century philosophical thought, made major contributions in the areas of mathematics, logic, education, and social reform. Russell, who received the 1950 Nobel Prize for literature, endorsed the application of rationality to all aspects of thought and language. His early pacifism, which led to his imprisonment in 1918, evolved into a dedicated activism against nuclear armament, for which he was again briefly incarcerated in 1961.

- **Arthur Schopenhauer** (1788-1860), a German philosopher, held that the world is governed by the strivings and conflicts of a universal will, whose irrational impulses cannot be understood by science. His thought, which influenced a generation of intellectuals and artists, was derived in part from the work of Immanuel Kant and from Indian philosophy.

- **Socrates** (c.469-399 B.C.), the great philosopher of classical Athens, reportedly spent his life in conversation with Athenian citizens, seeking true knowledge and exposing the errors of those who claimed to have wisdom. His persistent questioning so antagonized the city fathers that he was accused of heresy and of corrupting the youth; Socrates was sentenced to death by poisoning in 399 B.C..

- **Baruch Spinoza** (1632-1677) was an early advocate of intellectual freedom. The 17th-century Dutch metaphysician was formally expelled for heresy by the traditionalist Jewish community of Amsterdam in 1656. Thereafter, he supported his lifelong rationalist inquiries by working as a lens grinder, refusing any compromising scholarly patronage.

Table 1. Identifying components of teaching with major philosophies of Career and Technical Education Philosophy

Components of Teaching	Realist	Idealist	Pragmatist	Existentialist
Educational approach	Prepare for the world of work	Technical command over fixed body of knowledge	Meet current market needs but exert a force for change	Expose to world of work; Technology Education, Marketing education, FACS
Teacher Type/Qualities	Generalist, is teacher centered Emphasizes detail	Generalist, to be emulated by students, technically competent	Generalist, is student centered, Innovator, Synthesizer	Student centered, sensitive, relate closely, participates with class
Student Selection	Limited, all have limits, only so much demand	Open admission since all must contribute to economy	Open. All must learn to relate and contribute	Limited. Student "selects" himself out of other activities and into CTE class
Course Selection	Core courses in technology, FACS, Marketing/ Retailing	Core courses based on the current industry needs, Formalist	Progressive. Elective by student from controlled core subjects	Offer courses on sign-up basis on student interest. Progressive core
Course Construction	Highly structured. Much repetition. Process practice instead of projects.	Structured. Text oriented. Much reading. Teacher paced.	Cluster concept. Co-op programs. Real world work at same time as academics	Topical with the student selecting areas and rate of progress. Open lab with variety of self-selection
Teaching methods and techniques	Teacher centered, Lecture, demo, audio-visual image	Printed instructions, lecture. Reading followed by practice	Programmed texts, group projects, problem solving activities.	Conferences, individual instruction, self-study. Demo followed by student experimentation
Learning level emphasized	Principle learning	Concept/Principle learning	Problem solving	Problem solving/ synthesis
Discipline	Teacher imposed rules on class/lab acts	Teacher sets rules, uses self-run way	Controlled by student from self-interest	Maximum freedom while accepting responsibility for own actions
Evaluation	Objective testing	Subjective by teacher/essay.	Subjective by performance on tasks/projects	If it worked it is correct regardless of method
Attitudes/ Morals	Taught student/ imposed rules	By example/ self-inspect	Self-developed greatest good to all	Self-developed with guidance

5.7 CONCLUSION

The philosophies presented above provide but a short examination of teaching philosophies of CTE. Table 1 may help further illuminate the differences in philosophies as contrasted by components of teaching. Also included (Table 2.) is a set of definitions taken from various sources

Table 2. Definition of terms used in teaching philosophies of CTE (these have been taken from various sources from Table 1.)

Term	Definition
A priori	Prior to experience. Known without reference to experience.
A posteriori	Reasoning or knowledge which is derived from experience. Generally opposed to a priori.
Agnostic	Of or relating to the belief that the existence of any ultimate reality is unknown and probably unknowable.
Agnosticism	The doctrine that knowledge about God is not possible. Sometimes confused with atheism.
Archetype	The model or form of which other things are viewed as copies. Platonic ideas are frequently cited as examples.
Atheism	The doctrine which denies the existence of God.
Authoritarianism	The doctrine that authority of some type is the most valid source of knowledge. For example, the Bible or the Koran.
Axiology	The theory or study of value of all kinds.
Behaviorism	The psychological theory which insists that all knowledge of human beings must be based on an objective observation of their behavior.
Being	Used to refer to the category of reality or whatever is. Sometimes used in contrast to "becoming" or change.
Cartesian	Refers to the philosophy of Rene' Descartes (1596-1650).
Category	A basic mode or type of being or existence, or (in Kant) a fundamental form or understanding (Smeyers, 2008).
Cognition	The act of perceiving or knowing. Generally contrasted with other modes of consciousness such as conation and affection.
Coherence theory of truth	The view that "truth" constitutes a coherent, integrated system and that the truth of any given statement is determined by its coherence with other accepted truths.
Concept	The general idea of a class of objects. Generally distinguished from percept or sensation.
Confirmation	The process of establishing the probable truth of a proposition by reference to evidence.
Contingent	That which can be equally well conceived as not existing. Generally contrasted with necessary.
Contradiction	A false proposition which can be shown to be false by an examination.
Correspondence theory of truth	The theory that the truth of a proposition is determined by its correspondents to facts sometimes called the semantic theory of truth.
Cosmological argument	An effort to prove the existence of God by using the principle of causality the argument that the existence of the universe requires a cause and that this cause is God.
Cosmology	The part of philosophy which requires both the origin and the Constitution of the universe generally contrasted with ontology and effort to discover the nature of being.
Critical or analytical philosophy	Examines such concepts as mine self and cause in education motivation adjustment and interest.
Deduction	The process of reasoning in which conclusions are drawn from accepted premises sometimes defined as reasoning from the general to the particular contrasted with induction.
Deductive logic	A form of reasoning that moves from a general statement to a particular instance.
Determinism	The thesis that every event and the world are totally conditioned by its cause or sequence of causes is called the "whole principle"; this doctrine applies to all phenomena.
Deism	The doctrine that God created the universe but left it unattended. For the deist, God is not a being to whom one can properly pray; nor is He a moral being or the source of goodness.
Dialectic	A dialogue in which the meaning and truth of concepts and beliefs are subjected to critical examination. Frequently associated with Socrates method of buttonholing persons and drawing out the implications and presuppositions of their statements.
Dualism	Duality is any theory that reduces a field to two irreducible ultimates, such as reality seen as "mind" and "matter."
Eclecticism	The bringing together of different philosophical doctrines into one theory.
Education	Broad sense: any act or experience that has a formative effect on the mind character or physical ability of individual. Technical sense: the process by which society through schools colleges universities and other institutions deliberately transmit its culture heritage its accumulated knowledge values and skills from one generation to another.

continued on following page

Table 2. continued

Term	Definition
Egoism	In the area of ethics a theory which states that the good is one's own pleasure of well-being.
Empiricism	A doctrine which maintains that the source of all knowledge is experience also that human knowledge is limited to the possible scope of human experience.
Epicurianism	A way of life or ethic taught by Epicurus (342-270 B.C.) which advocated a moderate and enlighten kind of a Hedonism.
Epiphenomenalism	The doctrine that the mind is simply a byproduct or effect of the brain and that all mental activity is simply physical change.
Epistemology	Concerned with the nature sources and limitations of knowledge sometimes called the theory of knowledge. Types of: • Revealed knowledge: that which God has disclosed to man by His word. • Authoritative knowledge: accepted as being true because it came from experts. • Intuitive knowledge: subconsciously we believe we know, intuition tells us, must be complemented by analytical thinking. • Rational knowledge: a knowledge derived by deduction and reason. •Empirical knowledge: Knowledge derived from the senses and experience.
Essence	The essential are necessary nature of the thing, in contrast to its accidental or nonessential qualities.
Aesthetics	A study of theoretical beauty and art.
Ethics	A philosophical study of moral values and conduct, concerned with providing the right values as the basis for right actions. There are two types: • Intuitionism: an inborn moral stance telling us whether our values or right or wrong. • Naturalism: everything can be explained in natural terms without the need for any appeal to the supernatural; moral values must meet the real needs of bin and women living now.
Existentialism	The philosophical theory which states that existence is prior to essence. Human beings are viewed as having no fixed nature but as being free and creative.
Fatalism	The doctrine that all events are determined by nonhuman causes.
Great books theory	A set of books that the perennalists say are going to be read because they are as contemporary to us as they were when they were written and that because the problems they deal with than the ideas they present are not subject to the law of perpetual and interminable progress.
Hedonism	In ethics, the view that pleasure is the only intrinsic good. In psychology, the view that all of man's actions are motivated by desire for pleasure and to avoid pain.
Hedonistic calculus	A theory or device formulated by Jeremy Bentham to calculate pleasure as opposed to pain a method for evaluating the rightness of an action.
Humanism	In philosophy, this frequently indicates a naturalistic or non-theistic philosophy. Emphasis upon man is growth and development, as opposed to God and the supernatural.
Idealism	A philosophical theory which reduces all existence to mind. Also used more generally to refer to any theory formulated on the basis of an ideal.
Ideology	Generally refers to a set of social or political ideals.
Indeterminism	The thesis that man has free choice and is not determined.
Induction	Inference from observation of particular instances to general conclusions inductive inference is generally seen as yielding probable knowledge.
Inductive logic	Reasoning that moose from particular instances to a general conclusion.
Instrumentialism	Another name for pragmatism.
Interactionism	A view of the mind-body relation in which mind and body are viewed as distinct substances which interrelate generally associated with the philosopher Descartes.
Knowledge	•Revealed: knowledge that God has disclosed a man. • Intuitive: knowledge that a person finds within himself in a moment of inside. • Rational: knowledge that we obtained by the exercise of reason alone unaccompanied by observation of actual states of affairs. • Empirical: knowledge that is confirmed by the evidence of the five sensors. • Authoritative: knowledge that is accepted as being true because it is vouched for by authorities in their field.

continued on following page

Table 2. continued

Term	Definition
Logic	The study of correct thinking.
Materialism	The philosophical doctrine which maintains that the entire universe including life and mind can be explained by terms of matter in motion.
Metaphysics	The study of being as such the study of ultimate reality generally contrasted with the study of a particular part of nature as in a given science.
Methodology	The study of the basic principles of inquiry frequently involving issues concerning logic classification and basic assumptions sometimes used loosely to mean the means whereby the activity in any given field is carried on.
Mind	Consciousness as an element in reality contrasted with matter.
Mysticism	The view that fundamental truth about reality cannot be had by sense experience or reason but only through a kind of intuitive experience.
Naturalism	The thesis that human beings and the universe can be explained in purely natural terms without the need for any appeal to the supernatural.
Nihilism	A philosophical theory which denies the value of human life and activity.
Normative	That which relates to any norm or standard of evaluation.
Objective values	These values exist regardless of our feelings.
Ontology	The study of the reality.
Pantheism	The doctrine that the universe and God are identical.
Perennialism	Maintains that the basic principles of education are changeless or perennial.
Phenomenalism	The view that reality and our knowledge are of a reality and limited to phenomena or appearances.
Phenomenology	A view generally identified with the philosophy of E. Husserl described as the science of the subject is and it's intended objects.
Philosophy critical or analytic	Examine such concepts as mining the self and cause an education motivation adjustment and interest.
Philosophy prescriptive	Examines good and bad, right and wrong, beautiful and ugly; are actually what they are or are they what our minds sees them?
Philosophy speculative	And a tip to think in the most general and systematic way a bout everything in the universe about the whole of a reality.
Pluralism	Generally used to mean a view that read is comprised of several independent or ultimate substances.
Positivism	A theory which limits all knowledge to the scientifically verifiable. In the past eight treated all metaphysical claims as meaningless. In recent years proponents of this view no longer insist upon conclusive verification.
Pragmatism	A philosophical view normally associated with Peirce, James, Dewey, Schiller, and Mead which emphasizes that meaning and truth depend upon consequences or result.
Prescriptive philosophy	Examines good and bad, right and wrong, beautiful and ugly; are they actually what they all are or are they what our minds seized them?
Rationalism	The epistemological doctrine that truth and knowledge are to be tested not by sensory methods, but by a deduction and "reason". Generally opposed to empiricism.
Realism	A belief in the physical reality of matter.
Relativism	The thesis that absolute final truth is impossible and that truth is relative to time, place, and group.
Skepticism	The doctrine that certain or absolute knowledge cannot be attained by human beings. Sometimes limited to only parts of human experience. Generally distinguish from cynicism.
Solipsism	An extreme form of subjectivism which holes at the mind can know only its own experiences. In metaphysics, the doctrine that oneself or mind and his perceptions are all that exist.
Soul	An entity which is regarded as being the immortal or spiritual part of the person and, though having no physical on material reality is credited with the functions of thinking and willing, and hits determining all behavior.

continued on following page

Table 2. continued

Term	Definition
Substance	That which constitutes the essential nature of a thing and makes it what it is. That which underlies the properties or modifications of the thing, but which itself is not a property or modification.
Summum Bonum	The highest good. The ultimate goal of human conduct.
Teleological Argument	One of the proofs for the existence of God which holds that the existence of order and design in nature constitutes evidence that there is a creative God.
Teleology	The doctrine of final causes. It holds that certain ends and purposes govern the universe.
Theism	The doctrine that a God exists. Generally conceives of God is infinite, personal, eminent and transcendent.
Theodicy	A theory our effort to justify the goodness of God and the face of the existence of evil in the world.
Transcendent	Generally used to refer to that which lies beyond human experience and knowledge. In theology, it designates the doctrine that God is outside of nature. Used by Kant (Transcendental) to refer to the "a priori" eye categories of mind.
Utilitarianism	The ethical doctrine which holds that the fundamental norm of human conduct should be "the greatest good for the greatest number". Generally identified with Jeremy Bentham (Taylor, 1979) and John Stuart Mill (Carbone, P. F. 1983).
Validity	In logic, a valid proposition is one which necessarily follows from accepted premises. An argument is called valid under the circumstances.
Verifiability	The possibility of a statement been in principle establishes true or false. Sometimes identified with confirm-ability. Generally identified with a philosophical movement known as "logical empiricism" in which verifiability is the criterion of empirical meaningfulness.
Verify station	The process of determining the truth or falsity of a statement.
Veltanschauung	Generally used to designate any systematic worldview.

from Table 1 that should help you in your studies (Brewer, Campbell, & Petty, 2000; Kneller, 1971).

REFERENCES

Allison, H. E. (2004). *Kant's transcendental idealism*. New Haven, CT: Yale University Press.

Baldacchino, J. (2008). The power to develop dispositions: Revisiting John Dewey's democratic claims for education. *Journal of Philosophy of Education, 42*(1), 149-163. Retrieved June 5, 2009, from http://dx.doi.org/10.1111/j.1467-9752.2008.00602.x

Bergen, D. (1981). *The dialogue of metaphysics and empirics: Librarianship as platonic and Aristotelian*. Retrieved May 24, 2009, from http://www.csa.com

Brewer, E. W., Campbell, A. C., & Petty, G. C. (2000). *Foundations of workforce education: Historical, philosophical, and theoretical applications*. Dubuque, IA: Kendall/Hunt Publishing Co.

Brubacher, J. S. (1939). *Modern philosophies of education*. New York: McGraw-Hill.

Bruell, C. (1999). *On the socratic education: An introduction to the shorter platonic dialogues*. Lanham, MD: Rowman & Littlefield Publishers Inc.

Buford, T. O. (1969). *Toward a philosophy of education*. New York: Holt, Rinehart & Winston, Inc.

Burstow, B. (1983). Sartre: A possible foundation for educational theory. [from http://www.csa.com]. *Journal of Philosophy of Education, 17*(2), 171–185. Retrieved April 24, 2009. doi:10.1111/j.1467-9752.1983.tb00028.x

Burstow, B. (1984). Adult education: A Sartrean-based perspective. [from http://www.csa.com]. *International Journal of Lifelong Education, 3*(3), 193–202. Retrieved May 26, 2009. doi:10.1080/0260137840030303

Butler, J. D. (1969). *Four philosophies and their practice in education and religion* (3rd ed.). New York: Harper and Row.

Cherwitz, R. A., & Hikins, J. W. (1979). John Stuart mill's "on liberty": Implications for the epistemology of the new rhetoric. *The Quarterly Journal of Speech, 65*(1), 12–24. doi:10.1080/00335637909383455

Cohen, M. (2008). *Philosophical tales.* Oxford: Wiley Blackwell. doi:10.1002/9781444301045

Dupuis, A. M. (1996). *Philosophy of education in historical perspective* (2nd ed.). Lanham, MD: Rowman & Littlefield Publishers Inc.

Eaton, T. H. (1926). *Education and vocations: Principles and problems of vocational education.* New York: John Wiley & Sons.

Evan, R. N. (1971). *Foundations of vocational education.* Columbus, OH: Charles E. Merrill.

Ewing, A. C. (Ed.). (1957). *The idealist tradition: From Berkeley to Blanshard.* London: Free Press.

Green, J. (2004). Critique, contextualism and consensus. *Journal of Philosophy of Education, 38*(3), 511-525. Retrieved June 24, 2009, from http://dx.doi.org/10.1111/j.0309- 8249.2004.00401.x.

Hansen, F. T. (2005). The existential dimension in training and vocational guidance—when guidance counselling becomes a philosophical practice. *European Journal of Vocational Training, 34*(I), 49–62.

Hyslop-Margison, E. J. (2002). Liberalizing career education: An aristotelian approach. *The Alberta Journal of Educational Research, 48*(4), 350–363.

Jervis, K., & Montag, C. (Eds.). (1995). *Progressive education for the 1990's: Transforming practice.* New York: Teachers College Press.

Kankkunen, M. (2001). Concept mapping and Peirce's semiotic paradigm meet in the classroom environment. *Learning Environments Research, 4*(3), 287–324. doi:10.1023/A:1014438905784

Kazanas, H. C., Harris, J. N., & Lomons, D. (1973). *The philosophy and foundations of vocational education.* New York: MSS Information Corporation.

Kincheloe, J. L. (2008). *Critical pedagogy* (2nd ed.). New York: Peter Lang. doi:10.1007/978-1-4020-8224-5

Kneller, G. F. (1971). *Introduction to the philosophy of education.* New York: John Wiley & Sons.

Kofman, S. (1998). *Socrates: Fictions of a philosopher.* New York: Cornell University Press.

Kymes, N. (2004). The no child left behind act: A look at provisions, philosophies, and compromises. *Journal of Industrial Teacher Education, 41*(2), 58–68.

Law, C. J., Jr. (1975). *A search for a philosophy of vocational education.* (Report: ED126368).

Lucas, C. J. (1969). *What is the philosophy of education?* New York: Macmillan Co.

Lynch, R. L. (1997). *Designing vocational and technical teacher education for the 21st century: Implications from the reform literature. Information Series No. 368 Publications.* Columbus, OH: Center on Education and Training for Employment.

Marenbon, J. (1999). *The philosophy of Peter Abelard.* West Nyack, NY: Cambridge University Press.

May, H. (2000). *On Socrates.* Belmont, CA: Wadsworth.

Miller, M. D. (1984). *Principles and philosophy for vocational education. Special publication series No. 48.* Columbus: Ohio: Center for Research in Vocational Education. (ERIC Document Reproduction Service No. ED 250 497).

Mises, L. (2006). *Human action: A treatise on economics* (4th ed.). Indianapolis, IN: Liberty Fund, Inc.

Morton, A. (2002). *A guide through the theory of knowledge* (3rd ed.). Oxford, UK: Blackwell Publishing.

Nash, P. (1966). *Authority and freedom in education: An introduction to the philosophy of education.* New York: Wiley.

Norvack, G. E. (1975). *Pragmatism versus Marxism: An appraisal of John Dewey's philosophy.* New York: Pathfinder Press.

Ozmon, H. A., & Craver, S. M. (2007). *Philosophical foundations of education* (8th ed.). Columbus, OH: Prentice Hall.

Peters, R. S. (1966). *Ethics and education.* Australia: Allen and Unwin Pty., Limited.

Petty, G. C. (1983). Affective work competencies of workers and supervisors from metalworking, building and construction, and maintenance/repair industries. *Journal of Industrial Teacher Education, 21*(1), 28–36.

Petty, G. C. (1993). Technical education delivery systems . In Campbell, C. P., & Armstrong, R. (Eds.), *Workforce development in the Federal Republic of Germany* (pp. 122–138). Pittsburg, KS: Press International.

Petty, G. C. (1995). Adults in the work force and the occupational work ethic. *Journal of Studies in Technical Careers, 15*(3), 133–140.

Petty, G. C. (1995b). Education and the occupational work ethic. *SAEOPP Journal, 14*(2), 47–58.

Petty, G. C. (1995c). Vocational-technical education and the occupational work ethic. *Journal of Industrial Teacher Education, 32*(3), 45–58.

Petty, G. C. (1997). Employability skills . In Campbell, C. P. (Ed.), *Best practices in workforce development* (pp. 144–164). Lancaster, PA: Technomic Publishing, Co.

Rosiek, J., & Atkinson, B. (2005). Bridging the divides: The need for a pragmatic semiotics of teacher knowledge research. *Educational Theory, 55*(4), 421–442. doi:10.1111/j.1741-5446.2005.00004.x

Smeyers, P. (2008). Child-rearing: On government intervention and the discourse of experts. *Educational Philosophy and Theory, 40*(6), 719–738. doi:10.1111/j.1469-5812.2008.00465.x

Stanage, S. M. (1994). Charles Sanders Peirce's pragmaticism and praxis of adult learning theory: Signs, interpretation, and learning how to learn in the post-modern age. *Thresholds in Education, 20*(2-3), 10–17.

Taylor, C. C. W. (2001). *Socrates: A very short introduction.* Oxford, UK: Oxford University Press.

Taylor, C. C. W., Hare, R. M., & Barnes, J. (1998). *Greek philosophers — Socrates, Plato, and Aristotle.* New York: Oxford University Press.

Thayer-Bacon, B. (2003). Pragmatism and feminism as qualified relativism. [from http://www.csa. com]. *Studies in Philosophy and Education, 22*(6), 417–438. Retrieved June 22, 2009. doi:10.1023/A:1025735417682

Thompson, L. H. (1973). *Foundations of vocational education: Social and philosophical concepts.* Englewood Cliffs, NJ: Prentice Hall.

Venn, G. (1964). *Man, education, and work: Post secondary vocational and technical education.* Washington, DC: American Council on Education.

Vlastos, G. (1991). *Socrates, ironist and moral philosopher*. Ithaca, NY: Cornell University Press. doi:10.1017/CBO9780511518508

Wilson, G. (1997). *The metanarrative of consequences in the pragmatism of Charles Sanders Peirce.* (ERIC ED413607). Retrieved May 12, 2009, from http://www.csa.com

Wirth, A. G. (1974). Philosophical issues in the vocational-liberal studies controversy (1900-1917): John Dewey vs. the social efficiency philosophers. [from http://www.csa.com]. *Studies in Philosophy and Education, 8*(3), 169–182. Retrieved June 22, 2009. doi:10.1007/BF00368858

Woods, R. G., & Barrow, R. S. (2006). *Introduction to philosophy of education* (4th ed.). London: Routledge.

Chapter 6
Career and Technical Education's Role in Alternative Teacher Licensure

Edward C. Fletcher Jr.
Illinois State University, USA

Chris Zirkle
The Ohio State University, USA

ABSTRACT

The preparation of teacher candidates is highly differentiated among teacher preparation programs across the country. With the increasing development of alternative teacher licensure (ATL) programs, these practices have been the source of considerable debate and contention. The purpose of this chapter is to: (a) provide a historical overview of teacher licensure; (b) review the literature regarding alternative teacher licensure and the needed knowledge base for teachers; and (c) discuss the role Career and Technical Education (CTE) plays in regards to ATL, as well as point out a misconception regarding the original inception of ATL. Further, future trends and implications for future research regarding ATL and the preparation of teachers are outlined.

6.1 INTRODUCTION

A seemingly ongoing issue in regards to teacher education is the challenge to supply current schools with competent teachers to meet the demands of public schools (Chin & Young, 2007; Tissington & Grow, 2007). As a result, teacher preparation programs in institutes of higher education (IHE) across the country are charged with the tasks of recruiting, training, and retaining prospective teachers that have the knowledge, skills, and

dispositions needed to maximize student learning in P-12 settings (Tissington & Grow, 2007). In order to fulfill this mission, teacher preparation programs are increasingly turning to alternative teacher licensure (ATL) as a solution (Dai, Sindelar, Denslow, Dewey, & Rosenberg, 2007; Humphrey & Wechsler, 2007; Steadman & Simmons, 2007). According to Legler (2002),

The often-cited need for 22 million teachers over the next ten years has spurred educators to seek alternative routes to fill teaching vacancies, which has led supporters to suggest that we need

DOI: 10.4018/978-1-61520-747-3.ch006

to supplement the pool of potential new teachers with an approach that brings in people from other fields. (p. 3)

In fact, currently, every state in the country has enacted an ATL program with approximately 59,000 individuals entering teaching by way of an ATL program in 2004 (National Center for Alternative Certification [NCAC], 2007).

The purpose of this chapter is to: (a) provide a historical overview of teacher licensure; (b) review the literature regarding ATL; and (c) discuss the role Career and Technical Education (CTE) plays with regard to ATL. The primary emphasis of this chapter is to point out a misconception regarding the original inception of ATL. More specifically, the overwhelming majority of discussions in the ATL literature have reported that ATL has its origins in 1987 with the New Jersey ATL project. However, a deeper investigation of ATL's historical roots has revealed that vocational education has been at the forefront of ATL since 1917 with the passage of the Smith-Hughes Act.

6.2 BACKGROUND

6.2.1 Essential Definitions

It is important to define and distinguish between the terms certification and licensure—as these terms are often used interchangeably. According to Bartlett (2002),

Certification: In education, certification means possessing qualifications beyond those required for a license...certification is the process by which a nongovernmental agency or association grants special professional recognition to an individual who has met certain predetermined qualifications.

Licensure: The official recognition by a state governmental agency that an individual meets state-mandated requirements and is, therefore,

approved to practice as a professional in that state. (p. 107)

6.2.2 A Historical Overview of Teacher Licensure

During the late 18th century, the church was the source for education in the United States (Dial & Stevens, 1993). The ministers that facilitated the education had no formal pedagogical training.

However, free public schools were established in the first quarter of the 19th century, thus creating a demand for teachers (Dial & Stevens, 1993). At that time, the only requirements for recruiting teachers were that they possessed certain values and had an accepted moral character. The preparation of teachers dates back to the 1830s with the development of normal schools for teacher education (Dial & Stevens; McCaslin & Parks, 2001; Pushkin, 2001). However, the quality of preparation for teaching was quite questionable. By the end of the 1890s, undergraduate teacher preparation programs emerged as a function of growing developments of land-grant institutions.

The requirements for teacher training became increasingly more substantive and the duration of the programs became lengthier. In fact, teacher training sessions began with short (ten to twelve week) periods and evolved into longer durations ([e.g., two years] Dials & Stevens, 1993). These later programs were intended to prepare teachers instead of merely training them. In addition, the normal schools initially were designed to prepare teachers for elementary teaching.

It was not until the 1920s in which teacher education was considered to be a professional field of study (Pushkin, 2001). In 1940, according to Pushkin (2001), "recommendations were made for teachers to become content specialists in order to have sufficient expertise to teach assessment-related subject matter. However, it would be another two decades before teachers commonly pursued bachelor's degrees in specific subject area" (p. 35).

In the latter half of the 19th century, the granting of teaching licenses transformed from a citizen's committee to state licensure boards (Dial & Stevens, 1993). This change was due to the concern for an appropriate and competent set of individuals qualified to grant teacher licensure. According to Dial and Stevens (1993), "By the first quarter of the 20th century, certification had more requirements: high school diplomas, normal school diplomas (or at least some training in pedagogy), and examinations" (p. 6).

During the mid-1980s to presently, major teacher education reform proliferated. One major examination of teacher education came from the Holmes Group in 1986. The Holmes Group consisted of university administrators from research universities representing each of the 50 states (Mayes, 1998). This group crafted three major reports: *Tomorrow's Teachers* (1986), *Tomorrow's Schools* (1990), and *Tomorrow's Schools of Education* (1995). In these reports, the main issues that surfaced included discussions of the idea of Professional Development Schools (PDSs) and the implementation of graduate teacher education or fifth-year programs. The main objectives of the reports were three-fold: (a) to promote collaborative research efforts between schools and universities; (b) to encourage teacher candidates to engage in professional development; and (c) to enhance teacher preparation.

Currently, the No Child Left Behind (NCLB) Act of 2002 is considered the most comprehensive educational reform initiative in history (Fletcher, 2006; Fletcher & Zirkle, 2009). The primary objective of the legislation is to improve student academic achievement through increased accountability (Fletcher, 2006; Fletcher & Zirkle, 2009). To achieve this goal, NCLB mandates that students be assessed on an annual basis in grades three through eight (Schoen & Fusarelli, 2008) and once in grades 10 through 12 (U.S. Department of Education, 2004). In addition to achievement

tests, NCLB requires that teachers teaching core academic content become Highly Qualified. To be Highly Qualified, teachers must have licensure in the content in which they teach, have earned a bachelor's degree, and have demonstrated competence in their subject areas based on a standardized assessment (Hammerness, Darling-Hammond, Bransford, Berliner, Cochran-Smith, McDonald et al., 2005; Scott & Sarkees-Wircenski, 2008). This provision only affects core academic teachers, teachers that teach at least one core academic course, or those who teach courses for academic credit (Scott & Sarkees-Wircenski, 2008). Core academic content areas are: English, reading or language arts, mathematics, science, history, civics, government, geography, economics, the arts, and foreign language (U.S. Department of Education, 2004).

6.3 ISSUES, CONTROVERSIES, AND PROBLEMS

6.3.1 Defining Alternative Teacher Licensure Programs

Due to the ever-increasing divergence among types of ATL programs (based on their structure and content) and requirements for obtaining licensure, attempts at defining ATL become highly problematic (Darling-Hammond, 1990; Feistritzer, 2005; Fenstermacher, 1990; Hawley, 1990; Humphrey & Wechsler, 2007; Miller, McKenna, & McKenna, 1998; NCAT, 2007; Selke & Fero, 2005; Zeichner & Schulte, 2001). In fact, ATL programs vary on a continuum with some programs offering a crash summer course acclimating students into the teaching profession while other programs may offer programs that lead to a master's degree (Abell et al., 2006). The underlying philosophy of ATL programs that require little training prior to embarking on a teaching career (also referred to as fast-track programs) is that teachers need a command of the subject matter in which they teach and pedagogical knowledge will be acquired on the job (Darling-Hammond, 1990).

Darling-Hammond (1990) discussed two types of ATL programs and distinguished the two by alternative route and ATL programs. Alternative route (AR) programs are those that have the same licensure requirements, but change the pathway (route) in which these individuals proceed in gaining licensure. On the other hand, ATL programs have completely different licensure requirements for their participants.

Humphrey and Wechsler (2007) defined ATL as "programs or licensing routes that allow persons to enter the teaching profession by earning a standard license or teaching certificate without completing a traditional 4- or 5-year university-based program" (p. 485). Cornett (1990) defined ATL programs as,

state programs that alter licensure requirements through:

(a) completing a different set of standards (i.e., limiting the number of education courses required); and (b) meeting licensure requirements by demonstrating competency (i.e., passing tests for certification, on the job evaluations, and/or completing a supervised internship). (pp. 57-60)

In addition, Hawley (1990) asserted, "the distinguishing characteristic of ATL programs is their intent to provide access to a teaching credential that essentially circumvents participation in conventional or traditional college- or university-based preparation programs." (p. 5)

Other researchers have defined ATL programs more broadly. Ruhland and Bremer (2002) defined ATL programs as a non-traditional route for individuals without a baccalaureate degree in education. Dai et al. (2007) defined AR programs as "a heterogeneous set of programs that differ in some way from traditional campus-based, pre-service teacher preparation" (p. 424).

6.3.2 Characteristics of Alternatively Licensed Teachers

ATL programs differ from traditional licensure programs in their purposes as well as the target population they seek (Hawley, 1990; Suell & Piotrowski, 2006). Driven by the immense teacher shortage and the reluctance of graduates in teacher preparation programs to teach in urban settings, a main objective of ATL programs is to recruit and retain more teachers of color (Abell et al., 2006; Dai et al., 2007; Feistritzer, 2005; Humphrey & Wechsler, 2007; Ilmer, Elliott, Snyder, Nahan, & Colombo, 2005; Jorissen, 2003; Natriello & Zumwalt, 1993; Shen, 1997; Stoddart, 1993; Suell & Piotrowski, 2006; Wayman, Foster, Mantle-Bromley, & Wilson, 2003; Zeichner & Schulte, 2001; Zumwalt, 1996). According to Stoddart (1993), "A key difference between alternative routes to teacher licensure and traditional teacher education programs is in the relative emphasis placed on personal background characteristics as qualification for teaching" (p. 29). In fact, many scholars argue that ATL programs have been successful in this mission by recruiting more African American and Hispanic teachers compared to traditional teacher licensure programs in urban settings (Wilson, Floden, & Ferrini-Mundy, 2001; Zeichner & Schulte, 2001). Shen (1997) found, in a nationally representative sample, that 87.2% of traditionally certified teachers were White, while only 12.8% were non-White. Among ATL teachers, 79.3% were White and 20.7% were non-White. In addition, Shen's research indicated that teachers from ATL programs tend to have more positive dispositions in regards to teaching in urban settings.

One of the virtues supporters of ATL programs tout is the ability to attract older and possibly more mature individuals (Hawley, 1990; Ilmer et al., 2005). Research findings regarding the average age of ATL teachers in comparison to traditionally certified teachers appear to be mixed (Shen, 1997; Stoddart, 1993). Findings from Stoddart's

(1993) research suggest that teachers from ATL programs tend to be older than their traditionally certified counterparts, with over 50% being older than 26 years of age. In addition, these individuals are more likely to be male. In contrast, Shen (1997) found that a higher percentage of young individuals were certified through ATL programs in comparison to traditional licensure programs, suggesting that ATL programs may not attract older individuals into teaching.

In examining the reasons why individuals in ATL programs decide to teach, Humphrey and Wechsler (2007) found that the majority of ATL teachers cited that "teaching had always been their calling" (p. 503), with the exception of Teach for America (TFA) participants. However, only 20 to 30% actually had plans on teaching as a career, with TFA participants as the exception. In regards to teacher retention in ATL programs, research indicates that it is highly dependent on the subject matter in which the teacher teaches. Shen (1997) found that ATL teachers were unsure whether or not they intended on staying in the field of teaching until retirement. In fact, 26% of ATL teachers reported that they were "undecided at this time", while only 22.3% of traditionally certified teachers responded this way.

In regard to credentials earned, Shen (1997) found that 99% of ATL teachers had a bachelor's degree compared to 96.7% of traditionally certified teachers. When examining prior work experience and professional preparation, Shen (1997) reported,

A higher percentage of TC [traditionally certified] teachers (68.7%) than AC [alternatively certified] teachers (51.0%) were studying at college. However, a higher percentage of AC teachers were holding teaching or education-related positions (23.8%) and outside-of-education jobs (22.2%) than were TC teachers (16.5% and 11.2% respectively)…[Surprisingly,] among AC teachers, 51% came right out of college, another 23.8% already

held teaching or education-related positions, and only 22.2% came from occupations other than education. (p. 279)

6.3.3 Quality Concerns

Quality concerns from a vast array of educational constituents have made the issue of ATL a widely scrutinized and highly debated conundrum (Abell, Boone, Arbaugh, Lannin, Beilfuss, Volkman, & White, 2006; Bremer, 2006; Dai et al., 2007; Dial & Stevens, 1993; Ferraro, 1998; Hawley, 1990; Henke et al., 2000; Houston, Marshall, & McDavid, 1993; Humphrey & Wechsler, 2007; Jelmberg, 1996; Jorissen, 2003; Ruhland & Bremer, 2002; Ruhland & Bremer, 2003; Shen, 1997; Sokal, Smith, & Mowat, 2003; Stoddart & Floden, 1995; Tissington & Grow, 2007; Wayman et al., 2003; Zeichner & Schulte, 2001; Zumwalt, 1996). The increased focus on the quality of teacher preparation programs may be warranted, particularly due to the growing body of research that suggests effective traditional teacher preparation programs reduce attrition rates among novice teachers (Dai et al., 2007; Henke et al., 2000). Henke et al. (2000) set the context by explicating a number of quality concerns regarding the current environment of teacher preparation and licensure. They stated,

Although teacher preparation and certification have received considerable scrutiny in recent years, teaching remains a profession that is relatively easy to enter. Teaching in private schools is not regulated by state or local governments; in these schools teachers are hired at the discretion of the principal or governing board. In public schools, states set standards for teacher certification. However, public school districts, particularly in large urban areas often hire college graduates with little or no teacher training who have emergency or temporary teaching certificates in order to staff their classrooms. (p. 27)

The increasing focus on improving teacher quality is apparent through the establishment of reform initiatives for teacher education programs; these reform initiatives are structured around standards designed to uncover what it is that teacher candidates need to know and be able to do (Adams, Liston, & Hall, 2005). It is well known that highly qualified teachers are essential to educate students in any field of study. Hence, professional development is needed to strengthen teachers' content knowledge (American Educational Research Association [AERA], 2005). In fact, the AERA (2005) stated,

In a study of a federal program supporting professional development, teachers reported that a focus on content knowledge was one of two elements that had the greatest effect on their knowledge and skills and led to changes in instructional practices. (p. 3)

Darling-Hammond (2000) noted that studies which compare teachers with and without formal teacher preparation programs typically found higher student learning gains for those with more formal teacher preparation. However, defining teacher quality is quite problematic. The No Child Left Behind (NCLB) legislation utilizes the term *Highly Qualified*. Teachers are highly qualified, according to NCLB, if they have a bachelor's degree, are state certified, and have exhibited a specific level of competency for each content area they teach in (Fletcher, 2006; Reese, 2004; U.S. Department of Education, 2004). In a teacher quality publication by Educational Testing Services ([ETS], 2004), they defined teacher quality in terms of verbal ability, student achievement, knowledge of content, content-based pedagogy, and teachers with considerable experience. The National Council for Accreditation of Teacher Education (2007), in identifying effective teachers, stated, "Research indicates that teacher preparation/knowledge of teaching and learning, subject matter knowledge, experience, and the combined

set of qualifications measured by teacher licensure are all leading factors in teacher effectiveness" (p. 3).

6.3.4 What Do Beginning Teachers Need to Know and Be Able to Do?

The discussion of what it is that teacher candidates need to know and be able to do is well documented in the growing teacher education literature (Daniels & Shumow, 2003; Hammerness et al., 2005; Freeman, 2002; Hiebert, Gallimore, & Stigler, 2002). However, there still is little consensus of what this knowledge base entails. Freeman (2002) argued,

...the preparation of teachers is largely animated by popular perception and belief. Moves to improve such professional preparation often seem to be based more on fad or opinion than on any solid research-based understanding how the work of teaching is actually done. (p. 1)

Central to the profession of teaching, teacher preparation candidates must have substantial knowledge in all four of the essential knowledge bases: (a) pedagogical knowledge, (b) pedagogical content knowledge, (c) content knowledge, and (d) professional knowledge (National Council for Accreditation of Teacher Education [NCATE], 2006). The *integration* of these 4 knowledge anchors that candidates must exhibit is highly contested in the educational literature (Ball, 2000; Zeidler, 2002). In fact, the topic of merging theory into practice is the source of an age-old debate of early philosophers such as John Dewey (Ball). In response to this debate, Ball (2000) argued, "Clearly, the answer must be that it depends on both [content and pedagogical content knowledge]. Yet, across the country this tension has continued to simmer, with strong views on both sides of what is unfortunately often seen as a dichotomy" (p. 241). Smylie, Bay, and Tozer (1999) further complicated the matter by stating,

The management of dilemmas is complicated, too, by the fact that the knowledge base of teaching is not systematically codified nor universally recognized...In teaching, the body of relevant knowledge is more than in flux; there is substantial debate about what belongs in it. (p. 37)

Critics of ATL programs argue that teacher candidates must gain skills, knowledge, and dispositions in all facets of teaching provided by teacher preparation programs to become an effective teacher. These individuals cite a host of essential components necessary for developing effective teachers, including the following: pedagogical knowledge; real-world experience in the field through observations as well as internships; supportive teacher preparation cohorts; induction prior to gaining full control of a classroom; licensure; and continuous professional development (Koballa, Glynn, Upson, & Coleman, 2005; Wilson, Floden, & Ferrini-Mundy, 2001). Torf and Sessions (2005) when assessing principals' perceptions of teaching ineffectiveness, indicated that pedagogical knowledge (implementation of lessons, rapport with students, and classroom management) were the most frequently cited deficiencies; whereas, deficiencies in content knowledge were the least cited cause.

On the contrary, proponents of ATL tend to believe that the increase in state licensure requirements are unnecessary and serve as barriers for very talented individuals interested in teaching (Humphrey & Wechsler, 2007). Further, many proponents applaud the many talented individuals entering ATL programs who have forfeited high salaries for the rewards of teaching and believe their real-world experiences enhances their teaching effectiveness.

6.3.5 Pedagogical Knowledge

Cruickshank and associates (1996) defined pedagogical knowledge as, "the application of concepts, theories, and research about effective

teaching. It also has been called "teaching and learning theory" (p. 22). In addition, a wealth of personal experience in teaching has substantial value in the teaching profession; Cruickshank et al. (1996) called this "craft knowledge". Based on the concept of teachers' holding craft knowledge, Mullock (2006) suggested that pedagogical knowledge is related to an accumulation (hence, occurring over time) of knowledge regarding the act of teaching including the objectives, procedures, and strategies of classroom practices. Furthermore, she noted dispositions inherent in pedagogical knowledge in shaping this process. Daniels and Shumow (2003) argued that teacher education must prepare teacher candidates in the area of child development as well as focusing on developing more sophisticated teacher candidate beliefs and attitudes.

6.3.6 Professional Knowledge

Recently the topic of professional knowledge has been at the forefront of the literature on teacher education (Hiebert et al., 2002). According to Shulman (2005), "professional education involves teaching ideas, facts, and principles so that they can contribute to skilled professional practice" (p. 18). NCATE (2006) posited professional knowledge as including the, "historical, economic, philosophical and psychological understandings of schooling and education". Smylie et al. (1999) argued that teachers should have four universal dispositions: (a) teachers should have a student-centered perspective; (b) teachers should accept uncertainty and ambiguity inherent in the varied circumstances that arise in teaching; (c) teachers should be collaborative with their colleagues, administrators, parents, and students; and (d) teachers should be committed and show care regarding their profession. Hiebert et al. (2002) advocated for beginning with practitioners' knowledge in building the professional knowledge base. This knowledge base may be built by teachers utilizing research to inform their practices as well as teachers utilizing their pedagogies and craft knowledge to create the wisdom of practice. Freeman (2002) contends that researchers must be concerned with teacher learning and teacher knowledge. He further recommended that teacher education emphasize reflection and the ability to articulate (which functions as a reciprocal process), establish collaboration among novice and veteran teachers, and consider the school context to bridge theory and practice. As apparent throughout this discussion, the unified body of professional knowledge effective teachers must possess has been a playground for much debate (Cruickshank et al., 1996).

Research findings regarding the level of professional knowledge of ATL teachers, perceived challenges of teaching, ratings of teachers, and student achievement are mixed (Zeichner & Schulte, 2001). Contrary to popular belief, some researchers have even questioned ATL teachers based on their actual preparedness to teach the content (Miller et al., 1998). ATL programs modify or entirely omit certain coursework or internship requirements. However, most ATL post-baccalaureate programs include a fairly substantial overview of educational foundation courses, provide courses in the methods of teaching, as well as structure internships for their students. These programs are based on the ideology that teacher candidates must have a broader knowledge base regarding pedagogy, pedagogical content knowledge, professional knowledge, and content knowledge. Wilson et al. (2001) noted that studies investigating the correlation between a teacher's level of pedagogical knowledge and effective teaching practices (including high student achievement) have been positive. According to Darling-Hammond (1990),

These differing assumptions suggest that, ultimately, the design of teacher licensure programs should rest on answers to two related questions: What kinds of knowledge and training play important roles in the development of teachers' skills

and abilities? And how are these best acquired? (p. 130)

6.3.7 Pedagogical Content Knowledge

Pedagogical content knowledge, according to Hogan, Rabinowitz, & Craven (2003) "is defined as the ability to convey one's understandings of the content knowledge through multiple models of teaching for student understanding, comprehension, and achievement" (p. 236). Grossman, Schoenfeld, and Lee (2005) added that pedagogical content knowledge is the capacity of a teacher to be predisposed to common uninformed understandings that students may have regarding the content combined with the skill of representing concepts in multiple, challenging ways for diverse learners. Pedagogical content knowledge differs from general pedagogical knowledge in that it is situated in the content. Segall (2004) argued that teacher education programs should transcend beyond the focus of teaching teacher candidates pedagogical content knowledge through content free pedagogy; instead, teacher education programs should enable teacher candidates to see the inherent nature of pedagogy in all content, including the pedagogy in textbooks.

6.3.8 Perspectives on the Knowledge Bases

Nakiboglu & Karakoc (2005) reported that there are dichotomous endpoints on the continuum of philosophies regarding content knowledge and pedagogical knowledge. They described two models; one model is the integrative model that involves the integration of subject matter, pedagogy, and context without regard to the term pedagogical content knowledge. In this model, teaching is considered at the intersection of interaction among the three. On the other hand, the transformative model emphasizes that pedagogical content knowledge is at the center of all knowledge teachers must have to be an effective teacher.

Ball (2000) argued that the challenge for teachers regarding content knowledge and pedagogical content knowledge is that novice teachers are expected to independently combine two knowledge areas together into pedagogical content knowledge essential for teaching in a real classroom setting. Having an extensive knowledge of the particular content and knowledge of good teaching practices does not necessarily translate into effective strategies to use in a particular discipline to promote rich understanding of the content or to clarify misconceptions that students may possess. Ball addressed this issue by stating, "Not being able to do this undermines and makes hollow the efforts to prepare high-quality teachers who can reach all students, teach in multicultural settings, and work in environments that make teaching and learning difficult" (p. 243). McAllister and Irvine (2002) in their study found that empathetic *dispositions* are needed to reach students in diverse settings and is typically manifested in teachers promoting caring relationships with their students. Nevertheless, Hogan, Rabinowitz, & Craven (2003) cited Shulman (1986) in emphasizing that the domains of content knowledge, pedagogical content knowledge, and pedagogical knowledge are indispensable for competent teachers to possess.

6.4 SOLUTIONS AND RECOMMENDATIONS

6.4.1 Critical Components of Alternative Teacher Licensure Programs

Selke and Fero (2005) outlined five main indicators of an effective ATL program. These components include the following: (a) rigorous requirements for admission; (b) extensive preparation prior to induction into a teaching career; (c) an internship component with continuous support; (d) compre-

hensive support in teacher induction; and (e) program evaluation through follow-up of graduates.

Hawley (1990) noted that ATL programs may be improved by implementing three main components. These components include: (a) increasing the amount and quality of mentoring; (b) exposing ATL participants to more exemplary teaching practices as well as giving them the opportunity to reflect on them; and (c) providing more opportunities for teacher candidates to learn about pedagogy.

6.4.2 The Role Career and Technical Education Plays with Regard to ATL

The Origins of Alternative Licensure

It is generally agreed on in the educational literature that ATL began in 1984 with the establishment of the New Jersey ATL project (Abell et al., 2006; Darling-Hammond, 2001; Dial & Stevens, 1993; Dill, 1996; Feistritzer, 2005; Humphrey & Wechsler, 2007; Selke & Fero, 2005). However, upon further examination, it is less known in the literature that ATL has its roots in vocational education (currently called Career and Technical Education [CTE]) with the passage of the Smith-Hughes Act of 1917 (Lynch, 1996; Lynch, 1997; Lynch, 1998; Ruhland & Bremer, 2002; Stoddart & Floden, 1995; Zirkle, 2005). According to Ruhland and Bremer (2002), "Teachers in trade and industrial education and health fields [areas within CTE] were typically certified on the basis of their occupational experience, and were required to complete a minimal number of course hours in pedagogy" (p. 21). This 1917 provision was in alignment with Charles Prosser's (the first administrative director of the federal board of vocational education) essentialistic ideology that industry experience in the teacher's respective field would correlate with positive student outcomes (Lynch, 1996). Lynch (1996) noted, "Today, some vocational-technical educators subscribe to that philosophy, while others lean more toward John Dewey, who promoted a more general education to prepare teachers to help students ready themselves for a lifetime of learning and change" (p. 7).

Lynch (1996) further explained that many vocational teachers are not subject to the same teacher licensure and teacher preparation requirements as traditional academic teachers throughout the history of its federal funding. Many CTE teachers instead are hired primarily for their years of experience and specialization in their profession. Lynch (1996) stated, "In effect, then, vocational and technical education always has had a nontraditional or alternative approach to preparing and certifying its teaching force" (p. 5). Lynch (1998) noted, "Demonstration and verification of occupational competence and experience is considered to be proof of the teacher's mastery of the subject matter to be taught" (p. 51).

Some states enable CTE teachers to gain licensure in public schools with a high school diploma, or its equivalency, and extensive work experience (ranging from two to nine years) in their respective fields (Lynch, 1996). In addition, most states require CTE teachers to participate in professional teacher training. This may range from short workshops to for-credit coursework and eventually to college degrees.

In addition to CTE teachers' work experience requirements, many states have also adopted the National Occupational Competency Testing Institute (NOCTI) examination as a requirement (Lynch, 1998a). This examination includes a written portion that assesses technical knowledge as well as a performance portion for candidates to demonstrate their proficiency in their respective trades. NOCTI administers 56 various occupational specific examinations in fields such as auto mechanics, carpentry, and cosmetology. IHEs preparing CTE teachers typically grant credit based on successful completion of these examinations. In addition, some colleges and universities require an acceptable passing score for initial licensure.

CTE also has traditional routes to teacher licensure that require general education, content knowledge coursework, as well as field and clinical experiences (Zirkle, Martin, & McCaslin, 2007). These areas include agriculture education, business education, family and consumer sciences education, and marketing education. These individuals may or may not be required to have formal work experience. However, the requirement of relevant work experience is unique to CTE teacher preparation programs compared to their traditional academic counterparts.

Characteristics of Career and Technical Education Teachers

Historically, CTE teachers were charged with the responsibility of teaching and preparing students to meet the demands of the workforce (McCaslin & Parks, 2002). On the contrary, contemporary CTE teachers have unique expectations of (a) supporting the career development of their students in order to prepare students for any career they may choose upon graduation; (b) developing students who are academically strong in mathematics, science, and technology along with fostering higher-order thinking skills; (c) accommodating an increasingly diversified student body; and (d) revamping the curriculum to reflect current technological advances (McCaslin & Parks, 2002). CTE teachers teach an array of CTE courses that are typically categorized into eight major programs of study: (a) agriculture education, (b) business education, (c) marketing education, (d) family and consumer science, (e) trade and industrial education, (f) health occupations education, (g) technology education, and (h) technical education (Association of Career and Technical Education, 2006; Fletcher, 2006; Gordon, 2003).

According to Walter and Gray (2002), approximately 25% of teachers in the United States are classified as CTE teachers, with 75% of those teachers placed in comprehensive high schools while the remainder is in various types of CTE high schools. Overall, there are a total of 100,000 CTE teachers nationwide in middle and high schools (Gray & Walter, 2001). Walter and Gray (2002) explicated, "The point being that CTE is not a homogenous profession, rather it is a diverse set of programs with differing missions, making the development of a consensus regarding teacher preparation and licensure extremely difficult" (p. 128).

Zirkle, Martin, and McCaslin (2007) found that traditionally licensed CTE teachers followed a similar pathway as their traditional academic counterparts, including earning a bachelor's degree. The primary differences included work experience requirements, assessment requirements, and professional certification. CTE ATL programs on the contrary had very different licensing requirements state to state. In addition, these programs were very dissimilar to traditional academic licensure programs. According to Zirkle, Martin, and Mc-Caslin (2007), "…53 of 105 alternative pathways did require them [bachelor degrees], whereas 22 pathways required only a high school diploma or GED" (p. 14).

As stated previously, one of the distinguishing features of CTE teachers is that these individuals typically have substantial amounts of work experience (Walter & Gray, 2002). This is often in exchange for academic credits and degrees. Nevertheless, CTE teachers may possess strong content knowledge as a result; however, the assumption that increasing work experience will positively increase technical competence may be quite questionable.

The Importance of Content Knowledge

According to Grossman et al. (2005), "to argue that teachers need to know the subject matter they teach seems almost tautological, for how can we teach what we do not understand ourselves?" (p. 205). Teachers specialized knowledge, including working analogies, illustrations, metaphors, and addressing misconceptions is necessary

for fostering understanding. It is essential for teachers to possess a strong epistemic view of their subject matter (Perrone & Traver, 1996). Despite the inherent need of teachers to obtain sufficient content knowledge, there is a savage shortage of research regarding the essentiality of a content knowledge base for teachers. Based on the limited nature of research regarding content knowledge of teachers, the majority of research shows a positive relationship between the level of content knowledge a teacher possesses and student achievement (Wilson, Floden, & Ferrini-Mundy, 2001). However, other research studies show no relationship between teacher content knowledge and student learning (Darling-Hammond, 2000; Mullens, Murname, & Willett, 1996).

The Preparation of Teachers Regarding Content Knowledge

The overwhelming majority of studies regarding the preparation of teachers in the area of content knowledge indicate that there is a lack of deeper understanding of the subject matter that teachers are certified to teach (Wilson et al., 2001). However, Adams et al. (2005) found in a qualitative study of the Georgia Systemic Teacher Preparation program that most CTE teachers had perceived this program to adequately prepare them to be effective student teachers in regards to curriculum and content knowledge.

Ruhland and Bremer (2002) indicated that alternatively certified CTE teachers reported higher levels of content knowledge preparedness than their traditional certified counterparts. In fact, in examining CTE teacher perceptions' of understanding teacher knowledge bases, Ruhland and Bremer (2002) found that only 18% of ATL teachers felt they were adequately prepared in the area of pedagogy. However, 74% of ATL respondents felt as though they were adequately prepared with subject matter knowledge. In contrast, 56% of teachers from baccalaureate programs and 61% of post-baccalaureate or fifth-year programs felt they were adequately prepared with subject matter knowledge.

In addition, CTE teachers rated their likelihood of remaining in teaching. Fivety-three percent of CTE teachers indicated that they planned to continue teaching for eight years or more, six percent of CTE teachers indicated they intended to seek a non-teaching position, while three percent anticipated leaving teaching within two years (Ruhland & Bremer, 2002).

National Data on CTE Teachers

According to the National Center for Education Statistics (NCES, 1994), 66% of vocational teachers had paid work experience in the field in which they taught in comparison with 19% of their core academic counterparts. Eighty-eight percent of vocational teachers held a bachelor's degree; whereas, virtually all academic teachers held a bachelor's degree and 60% held a post baccalaureate degree. Sixty-six percent of vocational teachers majored in education. However, the authors found no national data that examined traditionally versus alternatively licensed CTE teachers.

6.5 FUTURE TRENDS

One of the biggest prevailing challenges in the realm of teacher education is determining what constitutes traditional teacher licensure as well as ATL programs. The education community could benefit from a more comprehensive and agreed upon definition of both traditional teacher preparation and ATL programs. Particularly, consensus is needed regarding the categorization of post-baccalaureate programs; while some may conceive these as traditional teacher licensure programs, others tend to classify these as ATL programs. Further, these definitions should also include characteristics of CTE ATL and traditional licensure programs, as well as other non-traditional education programs, in its re-conceptualization.

With a better understanding of what ATL and traditional teacher licensure programs entail, as well as their distinguishing features, findings from research on ATL may be more generalizable across teacher preparation programs. Thus, a major implication for research regarding CTE is to identify and describe the types of ATL programs that exist in CTE.

Due to the diversity of ATL programs, conducting research on this topic becomes problematic in that researchers define ATL programs differently. Many researchers conceptualize ATL programs as programs that prepare teachers whom have a baccalaureate degree in a field other than education. It is evident in this chapter that many educational scholars are not aware, or choose not to include CTE ATL teachers in their discussions. Thus, some researchers are failing to acknowledge that ATL programs do not necessarily require students to have earned a baccalaureate degree. In contrast, many CTE ATL teachers are able to earn a teaching certificate with no formal education subsequent to a high school diploma or its equivalency. In addition, some researchers may not conceive ATL programs to include post-baccalaureate programs, and further complicating the matter is the distinction between ATL routes and programs. Consequently, a strong need exists for a common definition that incorporates the diversified nature of ATL.

As is apparent in the discussion of CTE ATL teacher characteristics, there is a lack of research in regards to distinct characteristics of CTE ATL teacher candidates. It would be beneficial to identify their average age, their perceptions regarding their intentions to stay in the field, and their self-efficacy.

As indicated previously in this chapter, the discussion of CTE's influence on ATL has been largely overlooked by the broader educational literature (particularly traditional academic areas). A systems approach is needed to better understand the implications of ATL programs compared to traditional teacher preparation. Due to the fact that many CTE teachers, particularly those without academic degrees, are being hired based on their work experience, future research may be beneficial in determining these teachers' impact on student learning. Further, in an era focused on meeting the *Highly Qualified* teacher provision of the No Child Left Behind (NCLB) legislation, it may be helpful to examine the future ramifications this policy may have on CTE teachers as well as ATL programs.

Of great importance is the charge of identifying the essential knowledge bases for prospective teachers, which is critical for informing teacher preparation programs as well as ATL programs for the challenge of preparing teachers with the competencies needed to become effective teachers. With this insight, it would also enable teachers, administrators, researchers, and policymakers to make more informed decisions regarding the appropriate licensure standards for teacher candidates. Thus, this might enable guidelines to be followed for the purpose of establishing programmatic initiatives aimed at providing teacher candidates with the right balance of coursework, content knowledge, pedagogical knowledge, professional knowledge, field experiences, and professional development needed for their teaching careers. In addition, teacher preparation programs that exclude these critical components would no longer be in existence or be revamped. Further, adding work experience to the essential knowledge base of teacher preparation programs across IHEs in teacher preparation programs may also enhance the development of teacher candidates, particularly in CTE teacher preparation programs.

6.6 CONCLUSION

As presented throughout the discussion of ATL and traditional teacher licensure programs and teacher characteristics, ATL and traditionally licensed teachers differ greatly. The most recognizable distinctions between the two groups include the differences in their backgrounds. ATL programs have potentially facilitated the diversification of the teaching pool by employing more teachers of color. ATL teachers also tend to have more work experiences that might promote higher levels of content knowledge within their teaching pool. However, these individuals typically perceive that they lack the needed pedagogical knowledge to become effective teachers. On the contrary, traditionally licensed teachers often cite that they lack the necessary content knowledge to be more effective teachers. In regards to degree attainment, the overwhelming majority of ATL teachers do indeed have bachelor's degrees.

The essence of this chapter was to revisit the nature of ATL and remind educational scholars that CTE has been in the forefront of ATL for nearly a century. As indicated previously, this realization does not appear to be evident throughout the teacher licensure/education literature base. A critical component that has been left out of the discussion regarding the underlining ideology of ATL is the inclusion of work experience as a factor impacting teacher effectiveness. Instead, currently the recognition of increased content knowledge is the only component typically mentioned as a positive outcome of ATL programs.

The limited exposure of CTE, in regards to the issue of ATL, to the broader educational community may stem from the negative stigmatization of CTE programs that has plagued CTE for decades. Oftentimes, CTE is considered to have irrelevant curricula and may also be perceived as counterproductive to the growing need for students to attain postsecondary education experience. Further, CTE is often perceived as appropriate for special needs' students or those students that experience little success in the traditional academic areas. According to Fletcher (2006),

Once considered as a program to assist students who were non-college bound into occupations, career and technical educators are now struggling to convince policymakers, elected officials, admin-

istrators, teachers, and students of a dual mission to prepare students for their future aspirations, regardless of ones postsecondary path. (p. 168)

CTE might also be overlooked because it is not a core academic area and the provisions of the majority of educational legislation, such as the NCLB Act, do not directly impact CTE teachers or programs (Fletcher, 2006; Fletcher & Zirkle, 2009).

Based on the minuscule literature regarding CTE teacher perceptions of ATL programs, most CTE teachers perceived they were indeed prepared in the realm of content knowledge. However, these individuals believed they were lacking in pedagogy. Thus, CTE ATL programs may need to consider the inclusion of more pedagogy in their curricula to adequately prepare their prospective teachers.

REFERENCES

Abell, S., Boone, W., Arbaugh, F., Lannin, J., Beilfuss, M., Volkmann, M., & White, S. (2006). Recruiting future science and mathematics teachers into alternative certification programs: Strategies tried and lessons learned. *Journal of Science Teacher Education, 17,* 165–183. doi:10.1007/s10972-005-9001-4

Adams, E., Liston, J., & Hall, H. (2005). Preparing accomplished career and technical education teachers. *Proceedings of the Association for Career and Technical Education Research Conference, 141-155.*

American Educational Research Association. (2005). *Teaching teachers: Professional development to improve student achievement.* Retrieved November 13, 2007, from http://www.aera.net/uploadedFiles/Journals_and_Publications/Research_Points/RPSummer05.pdf

Association of Career and Technical Education. (2006). *What is career and technical education fact sheet.* Retrieved November 23, 2007, from http://www.acteonline.org/career_tech/upload/CTUFactSheet.doc

Ball, D. L. (2000). Bridging practices: Intertwining content and pedagogy in teaching and learning to teach. *Journal of Teacher Education, 51*(3), 241–247. doi:10.1177/0022487100051003013

Bartlett, J. (2002). Preparing, licensing, and certifying postsecondary career and technical educators. *Journal of Vocational Education Research, 27*(1), 105–125.

Bremer, T. (2006). Teacher preparation solutions: Rumbling for quality just won't do. *Studies in Art Education, 47*(3), 269–285. doi:10.2307/25475785

Chin, E., & Young, J. (2007). A person-oriented approach to characterizing beginning teachers on alternative certification programs. *Educational Researcher, 36*(2), 74–83. doi:10.3102/0013189X07299192

Cornett, L. (1990). Alternative certification: State policies in the SREB states. *Peabody Journal of Education, 67*(3), 55–83. doi:10.1080/01619569009538692

Cruickshank, D. R., & Associates. (1996). *General studies, content studies, and professional education* (pp. 4-28). Preparing America's Teachers. Bloomington, IN: Phi Delta Kappa Educational Foundation.

Dai, C., Sindelar, P., Denslow, D., Dewey, J., & Rosenberg, M. (2007). Economic analysis and the design of alternative-route teacher education programs. *Journal of Teacher Education, 58*(5), 422–439. doi:10.1177/0022487107306395

Daniels, D., & Shumow, L. (2003). Child development and classroom teaching: A review of the literature and implications for educating teachers. *Applied Developmental Psychology, 23*, 495–526. doi:10.1016/S0193-3973(02)00139-9

Darling-Hammond, L. (1990). Teaching and knowledge: Policy issues posed by alternative certification for teachers. *Peabody Journal of Education, 67*(3), 123–154. doi:10.1080/01619569009538694

Darling-Hammond, L. (2000). Teacher quality and student achievement: A review of state policy evidence. *Education Policy Analysis Archives, 8*(1). Retrieved October 7, 2007, from http://epaa.asu.edu/epaa/v8n1/

Darling-Hammond, L. (2001). Standard setting in teaching: Changes in licensing, certification, and assessment. In Richardson, V. (Ed.), *Handbook of research on teaching* (pp. 751–776). Washington, DC: American Educational Research Association.

Dial, M., & Stevens, C. (1993). Introduction: The context of alternative certification. *Education and Urban Society, 26*(1), 4–17. doi:10.1177/0013124593026001002

Dill, V. (1996). Alternative teacher certification. In Sikula, J. (Ed.), *Handbook of research on teacher education* (pp. 932–960). New York: Macmillan.

Educational Testing Services. (2004). *Where we stand on teacher quality: An issue paper from ETS.* Retrieved December 3, 2007, from http://www.ets.org/Media/News_and_Media/position_paper.pdf

Feistritzer, C. (1993). National overview of alternative certification. *Education and Urban Society, 26*(1), 18–28. doi:10.1177/0013124593026001003

Feistritzer, C. (2005). *Alternative routes to teacher certification: An overview.* Washington, DC: National Center for Education Information.

Fenstermacher, G. (1990). The place of alternative certification in the education of teachers. *Peabody Journal of Education, 67*(3), 155–185. doi:10.1080/01619569009538695

Ferraro, J. (1998). I already have a bachelor's degree, how can I obtain a teaching license? *ERIC Clearinghouse on Teaching and Teacher Education: Washington, DC.* Retrieved December 21, 2007, from http://www.ericdigests.org/1999-3/degree.htm

Fletcher, E. (2006). No curriculum left behind: The effects of the No Child Left Behind legislation on career and technical education. *Career and Technical Education Research, 31*(3), 157–174.

Fletcher, E., & Zirkle, C. (2009). Career and technical education in light of the No Child Left Behind legislation. In Wang, V. (Ed.), *Handbook of esearch on E-learning applications for career and technical education: Technologies for vocational training* (pp. 495–507). Hershey, PA: Information Science Reference.

Freeman, D. (2002). The hidden side of the work: Teacher knowledge and learning to teach. *Language Teaching, 35*, 1–13. doi:10.1017/S0261444801001720

Gordon, H. (2003). *The history and growth of vocational education in America* (2nd ed.). Long Grove, IL: Waveland Press.

Gray, K., & Walter, K. (2001). *Reforming career and technical education teacher licensure and preparation: A public policy synthesis.* Columbus, OH: National Dissemination Center for Career and Technical Education.

Grossman, P., Schoenfeld, A., & Lee, C. (2005). Teaching subject matter. In Darling-Hammond, L., & Bransford, J. (Eds.), *Preparing teachers for a changing world: What teachers should learn and be able to do* (pp. 201–231). San Francisco, CA: Jossey-Bass.

Hammerness, K., Darling-Hammond, L., Bransford, J., Berliner, D., Cochran-Smith, M., McDonald, M., & Zeichner, K. (2005). How teachers learn and develop . In Darling-Hammond, L., & Bransford, J. (Eds.), *Preparing teachers for a changing world: What teachers should learn and be able to do* (pp. 232–274). San Francisco: Jossey-Bass.

Hawley, W. (1990). The theory and practice of alternative certification: Implications for the improvement of teaching. *Peabody Journal of Education, 67*(3), 3–34. doi:10.1080/01619569009538690

Henke, R., Chen, X., Geis, S., & Knepper, P. (2000). *Progress through the teacher pipeline: 1992-93 college graduates and elementary/secondary school teaching as of 1997 (NCES 2000-152).* Washington, DC: National Center for Education Statistics.

Henke, R., Choy, S., Chen, X., Geis, S., Alt, M., & Broughman, S. (1997). *America's Teachers: Profile of a Profession, 1993-94 (NCES 97-460).* Washington, DC: U.S. Department of Education, National Center for Education Statistics.

Hiebert, J., Gallimore, R., & Stigler, J. (2002). A knowledge base for the teaching profession: What would it look like and how can we get one? *Educational Researcher, 31*(5), 3–15. doi:10.3102/0013189X031005003

Hogan, T., Rabinowitz, M., & Craven, J. A. (2003). Representation in teaching: Inferences from research to expert and novice teachers. *Educational Psychologist, 38*(4), 235–247. doi:10.1207/S15326985EP3804_3

Houston, W., Marshall, F., & McDavid, T. (1993). Problems of traditionally and prepared and alternatively certified first-year teachers. *Education and Urban Society, 26*(1), 78–89. doi:10.1177/0013124593026001007

Humphrey, D., & Wechsler, M. (2007). Insights into alternative certification: Initial findings from a national study. *Teachers College Record, 109*(3), 483–530.

Ilmer, S., Elliott, S., Snyder, J., Nahan, N., & Colombo, M. (2005). Analysis of urban teachers' 1st year experiences in an alternative certification program. *Action in Teacher Education, 27*(1), 3–14.

Jelmberg, J. (1996). College-based teacher education versus state-sponsored alternative programs. *Journal of Teacher Education, 47*(1), 60–67. doi:10.1177/0022487196047001010

Jorissen, K. (2003). Successful career transitions: Lessons from urban alternate route teachers who stayed. *High School Journal, 86*(3), 41–51. doi:10.1353/hsj.2003.0003

Koballa, T., Glynn, S., Upson, L., & Coleman, D. (2005). Conceptions of Science Teacher Education. *Journal of Science Teacher Education, 16,* 287–308. doi:10.1007/s10972-005-0192-5

Legler, R. (2002, November). The impact of alternative certification in the Midwest. *NCREL Policy Issues, 12,* 1–16.

Lynch, R. (1996). Vocational teacher education: At a crossroads. *Vocational . Education Journal, 71*(1), 22–24.

Lynch, R. (1997). *Designing vocational and technical teacher education for the 21st century: Implications from the reform literature. (ERIC Clearinghouse on Adult, Career, and Vocational Education).* Columbus, OH: U.S. Department of Education.

Lynch, R. (1998). Vocational teacher education in U.S. colleges and universities, and its responsiveness to Carl D. Perkins Vocational and Applied Technology Education Act of 1990 . In Gamoran, A., & Himmelfarb, H. (Eds.), *The quality of vocational education: Background papers from 1994 National Assessment of Vocational Education* (pp. 15–43). Washington, DC: U.S. Department of Education.

Mayes, C. (1998). The Holmes reports: Perils and possibilities. *Teaching and Teacher Education, 14*(8), 775–792. doi:10.1016/S0742-051X(98)00029-8

McAllister, G., & Irvine, J. (2002). The role of empathy in teaching culturally diverse students: A qualitative study of teachers' beliefs. *Journal of Teacher Education, 53*(5), 433–443. doi:10.1177/002248702237397

McCaslin, N., & Parks, D. (2001). *Teacher education in career and technical education: Background and policy implications for the new millennium. (National Dissemination Center for Career and Technical Education).* Columbus, OH: U.S. Department of Education.

Miller, J., McKenna, M., & McKenna, B. (1998). A comparison of alternatively and traditionally prepared teachers. *Journal of Teacher Education, 49,* 165–176. doi:10.1177/0022487198049003002

Mullens, J., Murname, R., & Willett, J. (1996). The contribution of training and subject matter knowledge to teaching effectiveness: A multilevel analysis of longitudinal evidence from Belize. *Comparative Education Review, 40,* 139–157. doi:10.1086/447369

Mullock, B. (2006). The pedagogical knowledge base of four TESOL teachers. *Modern Language Journal, 90*(1), 48–66. doi:10.1111/j.1540-4781.2006.00384.x

Nakiboglu, C., & Karakoc, O. (2005). The fourth knowledge domain teachers should have: The pedagogical content knowledge. *Educational Sciences: Theory and Practice, 5*(1), 201–206.

National Center for Alternative Certification. (2007). *Alternative teacher certification: A state by state analysis.* Retrieved December 19, 2007, from http://www.teach-now.org/ overview.cfm

National Center for Education Statistics. (1994). *Public secondary school teacher survey on vocational education.* Retrieved August 11, 2008, from http://nces.ed.gov/pubs94/ 94409.pdf

National Council for Accreditation of Teacher Education. (2006). *Professional Standards for the Accreditation of Schools, Colleges, and Departments of Education.* Retrieved November 6, 2006, from http://www.ncate.org/documents/standards/ unit_stnds_ 2006. pdf

National Council for Accreditation of Teacher Education. (2007). *What makes a teacher effective?* Retrieved December 3, 2007, from http:// www.ncate.org/documents/resources/ teacherEffective.pdf

Natriello, G., & Zumwalt, K. (1993). New teachers for urban schools? The contribution of the provisional teacher program in New Jersey. *Education and Urban Society, 26*(1), 49–62. doi:10.1177/0013124593026001005

Perrone, V., & Traver, R. (1996). Secondary Education . In Sikula, J. (Ed.), *Handbook of Research on Teacher Education* (pp. 392–409). New York: Macmillan Library Reference.

Pushkin, D. (2001). *Professional development / professional disillusionment. Contemporary education issues: Teacher training a reference handbook.* Santa Barbara, CA: ABC CLIO.

Reese, S. (2004). The highly qualified teacher under NCLB. *Techniques, 79*(8), 33–35.

Ruhland, S., & Bremer, C. (2002). *Alternative teacher certification procedures and professional development opportunities for career and technical education teachers*. Columbus, OH: National Dissemination Center for Career and Technical Education.

Ruhland, S., & Bremer, C. (2003). Perception of traditionally and alternatively certified career and technical education teachers. *Journal of Vocational Education Research*, 28(3), 285–302.

Schoen, L., & Fusarelli, L. (2008). Innovation, NCLB, and the fear factor: The challenge of leading 21st-century schools in an era of accountability. *Educational Policy*, 22(1), 181–203. doi:10.1177/0895904807311291

Scott, J., & Sarkees-Wircenski, M. (2008). *Overview of career and technical education* (4th ed.). American Technical Publishers.

Segall, A. (2004). Revisiting pedagogical content knowledge: The pedagogy of content/the content of pedagogy. *Teaching and Teacher Education*, 20, 489–504. doi:10.1016/j.tate.2004.04.006

Selke, M., & Fero, G. (2005). A collaborative alternative-path program for career-changing mathematics and science professionals: Context, design, and replication. *Action in Teacher Education*, 27(1), 26–35.

Shen, J. (1997). Has the alternative certification policy materialized its promise? A comparison between traditionally and alternatively certified teachers in public schools. *Educational Evaluation and Policy Analysis*, 19(3), 276–283.

Shulman, L. S. (2005). Pedagogies. *Liberal Education*, 91(2), 18–25.

Smylie, M., Bay, M., & Tozer, S. (1999). Preparing teaches as agents of change . In Griffin, G. (Ed.), *The Education of Teachers* (pp. 29–62). Chicago: National Society for the Study of Education.

Sokal, L., Smith, D., & Mowat, H. (2003). Alternative certification teachers' attitudes toward classroom management. *High School Journal*, 86(3), 8–16. doi:10.1353/hsj.2003.0004

Steadman, S., & Simmons, J. (2007). The cost of mentoring non-university-certified teachers: Who pays the price? *Phi Delta Kappan*, 88(5), 364–367.

Stoddart, T. (1993). Who is prepared to teach in urban schools? *Education and Urban Society*, 26(1), 29–48. doi:10.1177/0013124593026001004

Stoddart, T., & Floden, R. (1995). *Traditional and alternate routes to teacher certification: Issues, assumptions, and misconceptions*. East Lansing, MI: National Center for Research on Teacher Learning.

Suell, J., & Piotrowski, C. (2006). Efficacy of alternative teacher certification programs: A study of the Florida Model. *Education*, 127(2), 310–315.

Tissington, L., & Grow, A. (2007). Alternative certification teachers and children at risk. *Preventing School Failure*, 51(2), 23–27. doi:10.3200/PSFL.51.2.23-27

Torf, B., & Sessions, D. (2005). Principals' perceptions of the causes of teacher ineffectiveness. *Journal of Educational Psychology*, 97(4), 530–537. doi:10.1037/0022-0663.97.4.530

U.S. Department of Education. (2004, May). *No Child Left Behind: A toolkit for teachers*. Retrieved August 10, 2008, from http://www.ed.gov/teachers/nclbguide/nclb-teachers- toolkit.pdf

Walter, R., & Gray, K. (2002). Teacher preparation/licensure in career and technical education: A public policy analysis. *Journal of Vocational Education Research*, 27(1), 127–149.

Wayman, J., Foster, A., Mantle-Bromley, C., & Wilson, C. (2003). A comparison of the professional concerns of traditionally prepared and alternatively licensed new teachers. *High School Journal*, 86(3), 35–40. doi:10.1353/hsj.2003.0005

Wilson, S., Floden, R., & Ferrini-Mundy, J. (2001). *Teacher preparation research: Current knowledge, gaps, and recommendations: A research report prepared for the U.S. Department of Education.* Seattle, WA: Center for the Study of Teaching and Policy.

Zeichner, K., & Schulte, A. (2001). What we know and don't know from peer-review research about alternative teacher certification programs. *Journal of Teacher Education, 52*(4), 266–282. doi:10.1177/0022487101052004002

Zeidler, D. L. (2002). Dancing with maggots and saints: Visions for subject matter knowledge, pedagogical knowledge, and pedagogical content knowledge in science teacher education reform. *Journal of Science Teacher Education, 13*(1), 27–42. doi:10.1023/A:1015129825891

Zirkle, C. (2005). Web-enhanced alternative teacher licensure. *Teacher Educator, 40*(3), 208–219. doi:10.1080/08878730509555361

Zirkle, C., Martin, L., & McCaslin, N. (2007). *Study of state certification/licensure requirements for secondary career and technical education teachers.* St. Paul, MN: National Research Center for Career and Technical Education.

Zumwalt, K. (1996). Simple answers: Alternative Teacher Certification. *Educational Researcher, 25*(8), 40–42.

Chapter 7
Workforce Competencies and Career and Technical Education

Maria Martinez Witte
Auburn University, USA

James E. Witte
Auburn University, USA

Leane B. Skinner
Auburn University, USA

ABSTRACT

The need for workforce ready students can be met through the use of Career and Technical Education (CTE) programs. Identification of workplace skills that are rewarded and required by employers will foster relationships between CTE programs and workforce employers. These relationships will also impact economic growth, school-to-work efforts, and the global workforce. This chapter addresses the workforce competencies of business and industry and CTE programs as well as addressing shortfalls in these areas. Future trends are also identified in regards to workforce competencies in CTE programs.

7.1 INTRODUCTION

Current workforce needs anticipate more than a high school diploma or GED to be competitive in the workplace. Workforce skills and career options are and can be reinforced through CTE programs. High school CTE students are more likely to remain in school than those enrolled solely in academic programs (Earning, Learning, and Choice, 2004). Traditional curriculum high school students interested in engaging, experiential activities can often find successful experiences through CTE programs. Developing marketable and competitive skills through CTE programs is an excellent way to meet workforce development needs.

The purpose of this chapter is to identify the role CTE programs have in preparing the workforce; the importance of retaining high school students through graduation; workforce competencies needed in business and industry and career and technical education; and, the issues that will challenge and shape CTE programming. The chapter is organized using the following sections: background, workforce competencies, proposed solutions, trends, and a conclusion.

DOI: 10.4018/978-1-61520-747-3.ch007

7.2 BACKGROUND

A skilled workforce is the key to a viable and healthy economic local, regional, national and global position. Competing internationally is dependent on the skills of our workforce (Adult Learning, 2008). Heinrich, Jordan, and Smalley (2005) emphasized the need for quality mathematics education since U.S. high school students, when compared to students from other countries, were not competitive in mathematics knowledge. It is unrealistic to expect students, who only complete basic high school requirements to be sufficiently ready to meet progressive workforce needs. The role of education has remained constant as Venn (1970) stated "We must accept the belief that it is a responsibility of education to help young people find a meaningful role in society in which they can make increasing contributions and accept increasing responsibilities" (p. 16).

Career and Technical Education (CTE) programs can serve as a retention option to keep some students from dropping out of high school. CTE programs can be a conduit to specific fields and allow flexible curriculum content (Benson, Johnson, Taylor, Treat, Shinkareva, & Duncan, 2004; Peters, 2008). These programs are geared to prepare students for both employment and college experiences and can provide a workforce with skills necessary to gain and sustain employment. CTE is part of the larger secondary school reform effort (Peters, 2008) and exposes and attracts students to academic areas and can also aid in keeping students in school (Salopek, 2007).

It is important that Career and Technical Education administrators recognize that students can achieve academically through a wide range of learning experiences. CTE courses supplement required coursework and promote increased student involvement and interest. Emphasis is on "CTE leadership that maintains the secondary delivery system and improves or initiates the relationship with the adult CTE student, economic development initiatives, and postsecondary occupational education" (Career and Technical Education Administration, 2006, A-1).

Advisors or counselors also influence students to participate in CTE areas as possible career paths. High school teachers can draw parallels between academic coursework and the world of work (Peters, 2008). The competency-based education (CBE) model is often associated with secondary and postsecondary workforce education and begins with an assumption of providing instruction to students and an analysis of the task to be taught. Gray and Herr (1998) listed CBE characteristics as:

- The goal is to teach essential outcomes.
- Outcomes are described in behavioral, observable, or criterion-referenced learning objectives.
- Outcomes are taught in a prescribed sequence.
- Instruction is focused on learning objectives.
- Assessment is defined by the behavioral objectives and usually in the form of demonstration or application.
- A minimal level of competence is established which all students must obtain before continuing to the next behavioral objectives.
- Students or clients are provided with frequent/timely feedback regarding their performance.

Contextual learning is an educational philosophy and strategy that centers on assisting students to find meaning in their education. The major task of the teacher is to broaden the student's perceptions so that the meaning of the task becomes evident and understandable. Learning needs to be connected to the larger meaning in life such as how it relates to real-life issues and actual life roles (Parnell, 1995). Career and workplace information typically comes from a variety of sources such as employer partnerships, community members, and parents. Coordination between educational agencies, employers, and CTE programs is essential to deliver services and trained personnel in business, industry, and labor forces.

The National Center for Educational Statistics considers adult learners, individuals aged 25 or older, as non-traditional students and their characteristics include one or more of the following: financially independent of parents; delayed post-secondary education enrollment; work full-time; have dependents other than a spouse; may be a single parent; and does not have a high school diploma (Adult Learning, 2008). Ensuring that students do not leave high school prior to graduation or obtaining a GED is enhanced through the use of CTE courses as these experiences prepare students for continued success as adult learners and employees following high school. The Council for Adult and Experiential Learning's (CAEL) (Adult Learning, 2008) comprehensive examination reports that there are more than 26 million individuals in the United States who do not have a high school diploma and an additional 32 million who have not attended college. These statistics have a tremendous influence on the workforce readiness and job placement rates.

Career and Technical Education (CTE) programs are offered in several hundred vocational-technical high schools, 11,000 high schools, and approximately 1,400 area vocational-technical centers. Post-secondary institutions such as community colleges and technical institutes also offer technical programs (Salopek, 2007). Salopek revealed that although the nation-wide high school graduation rate is approximately 70%; due to projected retirements, expected number of new jobs, and post-secondary education enrollment, there could be a shortage of 12 million workers by the year 2020.

Enrollment for adult learners in post-secondary education, including part and full-time in community colleges, is approximately 43% (Adult Learning, 2008). Between the years of 1982 and 1992, college attendance among CTE students

has increased by 32% (Earning, Learning, and Choice, 2004). Compton, Cox, and Laanan (2006) identified possible reasons for the increase in post-secondary education as a decrease in the number of high school graduates and a decline in the blue-collar sector due to outsourcing and layoffs requiring individuals gain new skills.

Career and Technical Education can be considered similar to corporate training since CTE provides knowledge and skills needed to be successful in the workplace; however, it is typically not workplace specific (Salopek, 2007). CTE allows students to explore career options and to clarify career goals. It also promotes learning in the workplace with experiences such as internships, cooperative education, and apprenticeships (Earning, Learning, and Choice, 2004). Salopek identified the following fastest growing occupations as: home health aides, medical assistants, computer software engineers, dental hygienists, physical therapists, database administrators, and forensic science technicians. In Texas, trades such as welding, plumbing, heating ventilation and air conditioning (HVAC) and auto mechanics are in high demand and the pay scale is substantial. Entry-level workers, as well as career employees, can find positions in aircraft maintenance, architecture, construction, transportation, distribution, and logistics (*Barriers to Implementing College and Workforce Readiness Initiatives in Texas*, 2009).

According to the U.S. Bureau of Labor Statistics (2008), the shift will continue from goods-producing to service-providing positions. During the 2000-2016 time period, the goods-producing industry will see an overall job loss; however, the service-providing industries can expect 15.7 million new wage and salary jobs. The report of the National Commission on Adult Literacy (2008) revealed that jobs requiring a high school diploma or less will be around 10 percent even though they will account for about 40 percent of the job openings. Approximately half of all employment is in the middle-skill occupations. "If America does not produce the workers, the global market will furnish them, off our shores or over the internet. And if America fails to educate new workers from the adult ranks, nearly half of the U.S. workforce will continue to struggle with only a high school education or less and with low English proficiency" (p. 10).

7.3 WORKFORCE COMPETENCIES

The Workforce Readiness Initiative (2007) stakeholders strategy meeting reported workforce competencies would no longer guarantee success in the workforce, they were just the price of admission. Workforce competencies are the measurable knowledge, skills, and abilities needed to decrease the work skills gap and increase efficiency and productivity within the business and industry sector. "The competency-based movement is a way of returning to a personalized, individualized approach to transmitting skills from a master to a novice" (Blank, 1982, p. 8). The applied skills, such as the ability to communicate, to think creatively, and to work with diverse teams, are considered essential and necessary to succeed on the job. "We must redefine school success beyond the acquiring of basic skills and include assessments for teamwork, civic involvement, professionalism, communication, and analytical thinking" (p. 5).

The job marketplace can be unkind for those without knowledge and skills and individuals may not find employment or spend time "churning" or going from one low-paying position to another. Churning is a dilemma that affects individuals who lack skills or knowledge and "It affects high school dropouts, high school graduates, and college grads. Churning is an even more devastating condition in an inner city urban environment where there may be more competition for low-paying dead-end jobs" (Wichowski, Kormanik, & Evans, 2008, p. 39). In 2000, 50 percent of high school seniors had expected to continue their educational efforts, either in graduate or professional schools. Based

on labor market data, only 10 percent would have been able to participate in this level of educational efforts (Wichowski et al., 2008). Without clear career awareness or direction, individuals will develop inappropriate career expectations and end up in churning positions.

"The changing nature of jobs, education that lags behind skill needs, a slow rate of growth in the workforce and ineffective training investments by employers all cause skills gaps" (Association for Career and Technical Education, 2008, p. 2). These gaps impact at the local, state, and national levels and as businesses experience reduced innovation and growth, productivity and profits will also be reduced.

The report, *Are They Really Ready to Work?* (Workforce Readiness Initiative, 2007), provides survey results of the skill sets that were considered the most important for new workforce entrants, such as recently hired graduates from high schools, two-year colleges or technical schools, or four-year colleges. Approximately 400 U.S. employers were surveyed and the following were listed as the important skills for new employees to be successful: professionalism/work ethic, communications, teamwork/collaboration, and critical thinking/problem solving. The applied skills are oral and written communication, teamwork/ collaboration, diversity, information technology application, leadership, critical thinking/problem solving, creativity/innovation, lifelong learning/ self direction, professionalism/work ethic, and ethics/social responsibility. The basic knowledge/ skills are: English language (spoken), reading comprehension (in English), writing in English (e.g., grammar, spelling), government/economics, humanities/arts, foreign languages, history/ geography, science, and mathematics (Workforce Readiness Initiative, 2007).

7.3.1 Business and Industry

There is a workforce shortage in specific areas throughout the country. Wichowski et al. (2008)

indicated that almost 50 percent of the available health care positions are vacant and within the next 10 years one out of every eight jobs will be in a health-related area. Recruitment efforts seek employees from worldwide sources due to the unavailability of qualified individuals in the United States. As the workforce ages, the shortage will continue. "As of 2007, 52 percent of all engineers and scientists are over the age of 50, 44 percent of all government workers are 45 or older, and the average age of all construction workers is 47" (p. 39). It is predicted that within the next decade, close to 50 percent of all nurses and manufacturing process managers will retire and 40 percent of the entire United States workforce will likely retire. "In addition to these retirement projections, there are already critical shortages in the areas of precision machining, heating ventilation and air conditioning, welding, and automotive service technicians" (p. 39).

The American Society for Training and Development (ASTD) is considered the world's largest association dedicated to workplace learning and performance professionals. Members are from 100 countries, with 130 U.S. chapters and 30 international partnerships (American Society for Training and Development, 2008). Workplace learning and performance (WLP) is conducted by a variety of individuals such as HRD practitioners, line managers, hourly workers, training and development professionals, employment counselors, supervisors, operating managers, school-to-work coordinators, educators, and counselors. The American Society for Training and Development sponsored a research-based competency study entitled *Models for Excellence* in 1983 and promoted the awareness of roles, work outputs, and competencies. Revisions and updates since then have included *ASTD Models for Human Performance Improvement: Roles, Competencies, Outputs*; *ASTD Models for Learning Technologies: Roles, Competencies, and Outputs*, and *ASTD Models for Workplace Learning and*

Performance: Roles, Competencies, and Outputs (Rothwell & Sredl, 2000).

Rothwell and Sredl (2000) reported the seven roles of WLP professionals which were: manager, analyst, intervention selector, intervention designer and developer, intervention implementer, change leader, and evaluator. Each role is associated with specific competencies and the corresponding WLP competencies are grouped in the following categories:

- **Analytical Competencies:** analytical thinking; analyzing performance data; career-development theory and application; competency identification; intervention selection; knowledge management; model building; organization-development theory and application; performance gap analysis; performance theory; process consultation; reward-system theory and application; social awareness; staff-selection theory and application; standards identification; systems thinking; training theory and application; work environment analysis; and, workplace performance, learning strategies, and intervention evaluation.
- **Business competencies:** ability to see the big picture, business knowledge, cost/benefit analysis, evaluation of results against organizational goals, identification of critical business issues, industry awareness, knowledge capital, negotiating/contracting, outsourcing management, project management, and quality implications.
- **Interpersonal competencies:** communication, communication networks, consulting, coping skills, and interpersonal relationship building.
- **Leadership competencies:** buy-in/advocacy, diversity awareness, ethics modeling, goal implementation, group dynamics, leadership, and visioning.
- **Technical competencies:** adult learning, facilitation, feedback, intervention moni-

toring, questioning, and survey design and development.

- **Technological competencies:** computer-mediated communication, distance education, electronic performance support systems, and technological literacy.

Workplace learning and performance expert professionals' perceptions of current important competencies reflected (in order of importance): analytical thinking, leadership, interpersonal relationship-building, facilitation, communication, performance gap analysis, buy-in/advocacy, visioning, identification of critical business issues, and systems thinking. The WLP's perceptions of future important competencies reflect the following (in order of importance): leadership, technological literacy, systems thinking, visioning, identification of critical business issues, knowledge management, interpersonal relationship building, analytical thinking, buy-in/advocacy, and the ability to see the big picture. As the field has evolved from Training and Development (T&D) to Human Resource Management (HRD) to now Workplace Learning and Performance (WLP), the focus has changed to performance improvement and problem identification, and implementing intervention strategies to correct human performance problems (Rothwell & Sredl, 2000).

The Marine Advanced Technology Education Center (MATE) located in Monterey, California has identified and defined marine technical occupations and the knowledge, skills, and abilities that individuals need in order to perform in these specific occupations (Sullivan, Ford, & Murphree, n.d.). The MATE is a national partnership of educational institutions, businesses, and government agencies that work to improve marine technical education and to meet workplace needs of marine-related workforce in the United States. The occupations include marine technicians, hydrographic survey technicians, aquarists, and aquaculture technicians. The sets of competencies that have been developed include safety and seamanship,

computer systems, data processing, oceanography, meteorology, marine biology, technical writing, navigation, hydraulic equipment, electronics, surveying, submersibles, and geographic information systems. These competencies serve as a critical link between the workplace and the classroom and serve as the basis for development of instructional materials, assessments, and instructional modules. The competencies were identified and validated by practicing marine technicians and involved a thorough process of development. Competency levels include basic which are fundamental abilities gained from initial coursework or on the job training, intermediate which are abilities acquired through advanced coursework or substantial on the job training and specialized which are advanced abilities gained through major work experience, advanced coursework, or advanced degrees (Sullivan, Ford, & Murphree, n.d.).

7.3.2 CTE Programs

Aligning classroom instruction with real world applications will assist in maintaining higher student motivation levels as well as establishing instructional content validity. Mohr (2008) indicated that for students who do not plan to attend college after high school, CTE can provide employment opportunities with competitive salaries, benefits and job security. It is the role of CTE instructors, using a core curriculum, to work closely and connect workplace skills and classroom instruction. Workforce competencies include those identified by the national States' Career Clusters Initiative (2009). In addition, the need for construction, auto mechanics, technology competencies are also highlighted.

The national career and technical education model contains 16 career clusters with corresponding competencies (States' Career Clusters Initiative, 2009). The clusters provide a framework for what students need to know and be able to do in order to be successful in the 21st workplace. These clusters were initially developed through coordinated efforts of the Office of Vocational and Adult Education (OVAE) and the National Association of State Directors for Career Technical Education Consortium (NASDCTEc) (Ruffing, n.d.). The OVAE released the sixteen clusters in 1999 and efforts have continued to refine career pathways, plans of study, and alignment with other appropriate standards. This initiative reflects the new role of education and seeks to ensure that "CTE maintains a high level of excellence supported by the identification of academic and workplace standards, measurement of performance/accountability, and high expectations for participant success" (p. 1). The career clusters (States' Career Clusters Initiative, 2009) are:

- **Agriculture, Food and Natural Resources:** competencies refer to the production, processing, marketing distribution, financing, and development of agricultural commodities and resources.
- **Architecture and Construction:** competencies refer to designing, planning, managing, building and maintaining the built environment.
- **Arts, Audio-Video Technology, and Communications:** competencies refer to designing, producing, exhibiting, performing, writing, and publishing multimedia content including visual and performing arts and design, journalism, and entertainment services.
- **Business, Management, and Administration:** competencies refer to planning, organizing, directing and evaluating business functions essential to efficient and productive business operations.
- **Education and Training:** competencies refer to planning, managing, and providing education and training services, and related learning support services.
- **Finance:** competencies refer to planning, services for financial and investment plan-

ning, banking, insurance, and business financial management.
- **Government and Public Administration:** competencies refer to executing governmental functions including governance, national security, foreign service, planning, revenue and taxation, regulation, management and administration at the local, state, and federal levels.
- **Health Science:** competencies refer to planning, managing, and providing therapeutic services, diagnostic services, health information, support services, and biotechnology research and development.
- **Hospitality and Tourism:** competencies refer to management, marketing and operations of food services, lodging, attractions, recreation events and travel related services.
- **Human Services:** competencies refer to preparing individuals for employment related to families and human needs.
- **Information Technology:** competencies refer to designing, developing, supporting, managing hardware, software, multi-media, and systems integration services.
- **Law, Public Safety, Corrections, and Security:** competencies refer to planning, managing, and providing legal, public safety, protective services and homeland security, including professional and technical support services.
- **Manufacturing:** competencies refer to planning, managing and performing materials and related professional and technical support activities such as production planning and control, maintenance and manufacturing process engineering.
- **Marketing, Sales, and Service:** competencies refer to planning, managing, and performing marketing activities to reach organizational objectives.
- **Science, Technology, Engineering, and Mathematics:** competencies refer to plan-

ning, managing, and providing scientific research and professional and technical services including laboratory and testing services, and research and development services.

- **Transportation, Distribution, and Logistics:** competencies refer to planning, management, and movement of people, materials, and good by road, pipeline, air, rail and water and related professional and technical support services such as transportation infrastructure planning and management, logistics services, mobile equipment and facility maintenance.

Career options after high school may be unclear for students and parents as well as the relationship between education and careers or education and being workforce ready. The career clusters include courses that identify academic and technical knowledge and skills to identify and explore career possibilities. The Virginia Department of Education created a resource to assist students in their career education (*ready or not*, 2009). It provides information on the nature of career development and encourages students to participate in activities that will assist them in making the best career decision at the time. "The major concept is that the next stage of their life will happen anyway…whether they are ready or not. They can get ready through an action plan that is the result of guided career study and exploration, or they can let their life and career just happen" (p. iii). This tool is a flexible plan for using the national and state career classification system and should be coordinated with business and industry organizations to present specific career fields.

The state of Alabama's Career and Technical Education program also uses the career clusters in courses that identify academic and technical knowledge and skills to assist students in pursuing a variety of career options. The Alabama Course of Study for Career and Technical Education (2007), which was a revision of the 2002 Alabama courses

of study, contains a narrative and chart for each of the clusters. The narratives provide an overall description of the cluster and the chart provides information regarding optional and foundational courses, pathways, and a list of courses included in each of the pathways and elective courses.

All CTE courses are identified in the career cluster narratives and charts. In the Architecture and Construction cluster, students can choose one of three pathways, Construction, Design and Pre-construction, or Maintenance and Operations. The coursework, as identified in the Alabama Course of Study (2007), leads to careers in welding, electrical technology, drafting design, heating, ventilation, air-conditioning, and refrigeration (HVACR), carpentry, cabinetmaking, masonry, plumbing, and pipefitting. "Students work together to build a community of learners…Students in this cluster affiliate with SkillsUSA as the cocurricular Career and Technical Student Organization (CTSO). SkillsUSA provides additional opportunities that enhance classroom instruction, develop leadership skills, and further career development" (p. 11). Another example is the Education and Training cluster. Students choose one of three pathways, Teaching and Training, Professional Support Services, or Administration and Administrative Support and additional credentialing is available through post-secondary educational institutions. Students will gain knowledge of current technology and information, observe and master proficiencies required for success, apply academic and critical/creative thinking skills to solve real-world problems, and use reading skills required in the content area (Alabama Course of Study).

Employment of new residential and commercial building construction workers is expected to grow 9.5 percent, adding 785,000 new jobs. Construction trades and related workers will account for nearly 4 out of 5 of these new jobs, or 622,000, by the year 2016 (U.S. Bureau of Labor Statistics, 2008). Within the building construction industry, carpentry is a trade that would be in high demand and would require individuals to perform tasks such as preparation, foundation, framing, interior and exterior work (Mohr, 2008). Students preparing for this field would need math as an area of study. Math skills and operations that would be used most frequently in the carpentry trade include basic math, mental math and estimations, fractions, angles, trigonometric and geometric ratios, functions such as the Pythagorean Theorem (the 3, 4, 5, Rule), calculation and volume of an area, and the use of a protractor to measure and construct angles (Mohr).

Career technical education programs use industry-driven models, such as those used in the automotive industry. In partnership with the National Automotive Technicians Education Foundation and the nonprofit organization Automotive Youth Educational Systems (AYES), a set of curriculum standards were established to align with workforce needs. The AYES certification programs are available in brakes, steering and suspension, electrical systems and power train (Stone, 2009).

Guidelines for Essential Learnings in Technology (Nebraska Student Competencies in Technology, n.d.) from the Nebraska Department of Education and Education Technology Center are based on the International Society for Technology in Education (ISTE) and the National Education Technology Standards for Students (NETS). Competencies are provided by grade level (pre K-2, Grades 3-5, Grades 6-8, and Grades 9-12) with respective general indicators and examples of performance. The six technology competencies are as follows: basic operations and concepts; ethical, cultural, and societal issues; productivity tools; technology communication tools; technology research tools; technology problem-solving and decision-making tools.

Student technology competencies can also be used when individuals transition from high school to post-secondary education settings. The University of Alaska Fairbanks uses student technology competencies based on International Society for Technology in Education (ISTE) descriptors and

goals in the areas of Management, Instruction, Integration, and Professional Practice (University of Alaska Fairbanks, 2009). Information Technology (IT) certification has also been created in networking and program language such as used in Cisco, Novell, and A-Plus. The National Health Care Curriculum Consortium partnered with the National Occupational Competency Testing Institute (NOCTI) to create a health care occupation certification examination that is used in 35 states (Stone, 2009).

Bybee and Starkweather (2006) addressed the need for technology education skills to be provided in the classroom for the 21st century workforce. "Technology education must be seen as fundamental to achieving workforce competencies, especially when the competencies include critical thinking, solving semi-structured problems and reasoning" (p. 27). An expert panel reviewed twelve major reports that included, Achieve, Inc, and National Governors Association—*America's High Schools, An Action Agenda for Improving America's High Schools, and Rising to the Challenge: Are High School Graduates Prepared for College and Work?;* Business-Higher Education Forum; Business Roundtable; Committee for Economic Development; The Secretary's Commission on Achieving Necessary Skills (SCANS); and the Task Force on the Future of American Innovation. Based on the analysis of these reports, the need for technology education is clear and it is what is needed to keep the U.S. from losing its competitive edge in the global economy. "The global economy is largely driven by technological innovation. One reasonable extension of this proposition is that the United States needs engineers. Another implication is that all citizens need higher levels of technological literacy...and K-12 education must play a significant role" (p. 27).

Hoerner and Wehrley (1995) indicated the SCANS report established workplace know-how and listed competencies, skills, and personal qualities that were needed for job performance. These competencies and qualities would be part of the curriculum and the classroom would a much different place than before. "With many work-based learning strategies, the classroom will be without walls; many of the activities will be done outside the classroom. This educational system will demand new and innovative curriculum materials. Such materials will need to be applied and contextual in nature and relate to workplace know-how skills" (p. 72). The current educational system has been refocusing and bringing classrooms without walls in order to adequately provide skilled workforce members to business and industry.

7.4 PROPOSED SOLUTIONS

7.4.1 Business and Industry

The global economy is currently unsteady and organizations are striving to accelerate team performance to increase revenues. U.S. businesses spend $15 billion per year to train their sales forces; however, some of the training may not be as effective as needed or is approached in a reactive manner (Salopek, 2009). In response to this need, the American Society for Training and Development (ASTD) has developed a World-Class Sales Competency Model to provide business leaders a new approach to sales training and development. The training considers the entire business system and centers the learning function on developing the skills needed for sales successes and to eventually help organizations succeed (Salopek).

The sales occupation is defined as effectively developing, managing, enabling, and executing mutually beneficial exchanges of goods or services and assumes that a systems approach is needed to be effective; the focus will be on the individuals involved in the interactions; and that there is an exchange of value between a buyer and seller (Salopek, 2009). The ASTD Sales Competency Model involves everyone who directly or indirectly generates organizational or company

revenue. By developing the sales capacity and competence of employees, they will be better equipped to sell products and services. The model defines the knowledge, skills, and abilities needed for sales competence beginning with foundational competencies and focusing on areas of expertise. The competencies are listed by skills, abilities, and behaviors in four groups to include: Partnering (aligning to customers; building relationships; communicating effectively; negotiating positions, setting expectations); Insight (analyzing capacity, building a business case, evaluating customer experiences, gathering intelligence; identifying options, prioritizing stakeholder needs); Solution (articulating value, facilitating change, formalizing commitment, leveraging success, managing projects, resolving issues); and Effectiveness (accelerating learning, aligning to sales processes, building business skill, embracing diversity, executing plans, solving problems, making ethical decisions) (Salopek).

Higher education institutions are beginning to use competencies and career clusters to organize academic programs. According to Paulson (2001), there has been an accelerating trend where postsecondary education institutions reduce offerings of a liberal education but more towards credentialing efforts for students. The University of Alaska Anchorage (UAA) is connecting education and career success pathways in order to prepare their students for workforce demands. Since students and parents are overwhelmed at times in selecting the most appropriate major and possible career options, UAA provides drop down menus with career cluster titles and career pathways to assist students in making an informed decision about their future educational and occupational endeavors (University of Alaska Anchorage, 2009).

The National Postsecondary Education Cooperative Working Group in Competency-Based Initiatives in Postsecondary Education's report entitled *Defining and Assessing Learning: Exploring Competency-Based Initiatives* (Jones, Voorhees, & Paulson, 2002) provides a basic guide to post-secondary competencies and establishing competency-based initiatives at educational institutions. Competencies were defined as the combination of skills, abilities and knowledge that are needed to perform a task. Competency-based initiatives were defined as the "purposeful actions undertaken by post-secondary institutions directed at defining, teaching, and assessing competencies across their system" (p. vii). Compelling reasons to use competency-based initiatives at colleges and universities would be to articulate specific competencies to inform and guide assessment and programs; to assist faculty, students, employers, & policymakers with a common understanding about the specific skills and knowledge that students should master as a result of the learning experiences; and to provide directions for designing learning experiences to ensure students apply the competencies in appropriate settings. This project initiated a review of competency-based learning initiatives in selected U.S. higher educational institutions and offers a set of principles that support successful implementation for future consideration.

7.4.2 CTE Programs

Educators can no longer just offer classes and grant diplomas as evidence of their students meeting workforce needs. "Employers increasingly view diplomas and degrees with skepticism and want different measures to use when recruiting and retraining employees. Competencies can offer a suitable alternative" (Paulson, 2001, p. 42). The National Occupational Competency Testing Institute (NOCTI) conducted a study to identify whether students gain knowledge and skills in CTE program and if those skills were adequately preparing them for the workplace (Foster, Kiker, Ruffing, & Kelley, 2006). The three-year study was conducted throughout five states at eleven different sites. The results indicated that the schools in the study were successful in providing students with the knowledge they needed to begin their careers.

In addition, it was evident that the CTE programs in this study were successful in assisting students prepare for skilled positions and gaining skills.

Businesses can benefit by becoming informed and involved with CTE programs in their immediate area. Salopek (2007) cited a Californian-based Toyota company that has developed and supported automotive technician CTE programs for the past 20 years. In addition, Toyota has technician training and an education network at 58 locations nationwide. There is a two-year Toyota-certification program and a 16-week internship at a local Toyota or Lexus dealership. "Although there is no explicit guarantee of employment upon graduation, 626 of last year's 791 graduates were hired" (p. 23).

The Association for Career and Technical Education's (ACTE) business-education partnership combines education and business leaders to build a collaborative network between businesses and schools. The purpose of this network is to build a workforce that has the requisite skills that America needs to compete in the global marketplace. The partnership's strategic plan stresses the fact that only 20-25 percent of high school graduates will complete four-year baccalaureate degrees; therefore, the goal must be to provide all students the opportunity to attain core academic and technical skills they need to connect their education and careers. Doing so will provide additional career options and continuous learning opportunities (Salopek, 2007).

The purpose of the Carl D. Perkins Career and Technical Education Improvement Act (2006) was to develop the academic, career, and technical skills of secondary and postsecondary education students in CTE programs. One method of doing so is for states and localities to develop challenging academic and technical standards to help student meet the standards so that they are prepared for high skill, high wage or high demand occupations in current or emerging professions. The purpose also includes supporting partnerships and providing individuals with opportunities throughout their lives to develop the knowledge and skills to keep the United States competitive in the world (Carl D. Perkins, 2006). Businesses are encouraged to be proactive and when they partner with CTE programs, it ensures that potential workers will have the foundational and technical skills that would be required.

In 2006, the Academic Standards for Career Education and Work (CEW) were created as a component of the Pennsylvania School Code and were developed by an expert panel of academic, CTE, guidance counselors, business community members, and governmental agencies. According to Wichowski et al. (2008), these standards were designed to include age appropriate (Grades 3, 5, 8, and 11) learning experiences to promote career areas. Educators, not just the guidance counselors, support each K-12 student to their maximum potential and develop the knowledge and skills as addressed in the standards. The standards address the areas of career awareness and preparation, career acquisition, career retention and advancement, and entrepreneurship. For example, in the area of Career Awareness and Preparation, Grade 3 students would need to recognize that individuals have unique interests and identify current personal interests. In Grade 5, students would need to describe the impact of individual interests and abilities on career choices; and relate the impact of change to traditional and nontraditional careers. For Grade 8, students would need to be able to explain the relationship of career training programs and employment opportunities and analyze the economic factors that impact employment opportunities. For Grade 11, the students should be able to evaluate school-based opportunities for career awareness/preparation and analyze the relationship between career choices and career preparation opportunities.

There are tools available for Pennsylvania educators to implement the CEW standards. One is an electronic online resource that is managed by the Pennsylvania College of Technology which includes a curriculum resource lending library, teacher planning guides, open-ended career-related calendar events, career development Internet resources by grade level as well. Another tool is the CareerLinking Academy and was developed by the Lehigh Valley Workforce Investment Board (LVWIB), a state sponsored workforce development system comprised of a 46-member board including employers, business leaders, educators, and community stakeholders. The academy is an innovative career exploration program that is targeted to students in the Grades 10-12 and is aligned with the CEW standards. The academy can be customized to meet the school district's curriculum requirements and can be implemented in either a week-long model or delivered in segments throughout the school year. Also linked to this academy is a Career Cruising website, a web-based career exploration site that is being implemented throughout Lehigh Valley's 17 school districts (Wichowski et al., 2008).

Wichowski et al. (2008) indicated that the model used in the innovative CareerLinking Academy also meets high school senior graduation project requirements in Pennsylvania. Students are encouraged to take leadership roles in their future career whether by joining the workforce, or attending college, university, technical or trade school. Quality career decisions can be made through the use of interactive activities such as career assessments, interviewing skills, preparing resumes, and job shadowing. The Society for Human Resource Management in Lehigh Valley collaborates with the academy students to help them explore different career paths and the face to face interaction develops an understanding of the nature of work and how to make career choices.

Providing options for educators, business and industry leaders, parents and community stakeholders to address and identify career possibilities for students is mutually beneficial. Students who are prepared for the workplace and workforce will serve to replace industry employment needs and students will have a clearer career direction and expectations in the workplace.

7.5 TRENDS

One trend is for CTE programs to prepare students for "green" positions. The Association for Career and Technical Education (ACTE) mentioned CTE's contributions to preparing students for green technology-related jobs. These positions would focus on reducing societies' imprint on the environment, economy, and to decrease dependence on foreign oil. In 2007, the third largest area of venture capital investment was in the area of clean energy with approximately $71 billion invested in new renewable energy capacity worldwide. The leading areas include: solar power, wind power, building retrofitting, mass transit, and energy-efficient vehicles. These positions require strong skills, offer high wages and are in high demand. ACTE is calling for support of green-related workforce training, beginning at the high school level. Career and Technical Education programs are currently preparing students for green careers such as in Western Slope, Colorado where 500 students meet business and industry representatives on the annual Energy Career Day for hands-on, interactive presentations. South Tahoe High School in California provides an introduction to careers in green construction, technology, and auto mechanics (Peckman, 2006).

Christie (2009) identified challenges that would drive upcoming legislative sessions throughout the nation. These challenges included ensuring job opportunities and a workforce with the right skills; reducing dropouts; seeking world-class status for high school graduates; and, ensuring dollars go beyond what is expected in schools. In the current economic times, job opportunities are not as available and the primary method of being competitive in the job market is to possess current and applicable skills. The Ohio Skills Bank Data Tool provides occupational needs information for the state's economic development regions. This tool provides data on employment, wages, licensing, plant closings, training, layoffs, and education.

In Ohio, there are 92 Career-Technical Planning districts that serve as career centers and joint vocational and technical training sites. These types of schools provide career counseling, planning, and new skills training. In addition to equipping the workforce with the right skills, states will be asked to consider implementing early warning indicators to monitor the number of dropouts and to have students earn graduation credits by demonstrating proficiency throughout high school. Some high schools provide a Career Readiness Certificate which serves as a framework for aligning curriculum, graduation requirements, and job readiness. This certificate notifies employers that the applicant possesses basic 21st-century workplace skills (Christie, 2009).

"CTE programs have also been on the frontlines of offering new workforce readiness credentials, and should be considered leaders in the growth of this endeavor" (Association for Career and Technical Education, 2008, p. 3). Each workforce readiness credential, such as the ACT National Career Readiness Certificate, National Work Readiness Credential, CASAS Workforce Skills Certificate, and SkillsUSA Workplace Readiness Certificate, measures a different set of skills; however, almost all of them measure some form of work-related literacy and numeracy skills. CTE educators consider literacy and numeracy skills as technical literacy. Technical literacy is defined as the ability to apply academic knowledge and skills to technical studies; being able to read, understand and communicate in the appropriate technical field; being able to understand technical concepts and principles; and be able to use technology for projects in that specific technical field (Association for Career and Technical Education, 2008).

Technical literacy skills are introduced and reinforced in CTE classrooms and prepare students for workforce readiness assessments such as WorkKeys readiness for information and applied math or the ACT National Readiness certificate's read with understanding and using math to solve problems. Other states mandating some form of workforce credentialing before CTE students graduate from high school are West Virginia, Florida, Arkansas and Georgia. Without the support of business and industry, workforce readiness credentialing has little or no value. "While the skills learned are still vitally important to future career success, the payoff in the actual certificate or credential can only be realized with employer support leading to preferential status in hiring decisions" (Association for Career and Technical Education, 2008, p. 6). Massachusetts also uses an employability certification program that was developed in conjunction with employers. The state identified nine competencies that form the foundation for its work-based learning plan (Stone, 2009).

Establishing connections between local business leaders and educational providers is one method of employee screening and increased employee retention. The Association for Career and Technical Education (2008) article highlighted the VF Jeanswear's production and distribution center in central Oklahoma. It was undergoing high employee turnover and it was affecting company profits. Working with the Gordon Cooper Technology Center and the local workforce One-Stop Center, workforce readiness assessments were designed for the pre-screening hiring process at VF Jeanswear. This has allowed VF Jeanswear to identify employees who are able to meet specific job standards and reduce training costs.

Dividends are doubled when businesses and educational institutions form partnerships such as work-study programs. Having high school students gain experience in real work-world situations is advantageous; however, Rogov (2009) cautions against the lack of knowledge sharing between the older generations and those just entering the workforce. This lack of sharing is a critical factor in the skill gap crisis and "…a Randsland survey identifies that important knowledge is not being transferred between today's multigenerational work force (traditionalists, baby boomers, and generations X and Y) many times because they

either do not interact with each other or they just simply do not recognize each other's skills and work ethic" (Rogov, 2009, p. 3). An institution's greatest asset is the individual expertise and talents within the organization and should be included in collaborative enterprises. "Corporations need to realize they bring a unique set of capabilities and expertise to the partnership table—something that no other sector has. It is important for corporations to share not just cash, but also other resources at least as valuable—time, talent, and experience" (Workforce Readiness Initiative, 2007, p. 6).

One way to improve lines of communication between varying levels of workers is through peer mentoring programs. Electronics & Integrated Solutions (E&IS), a defense electronics company with 17,000 employees in 16 states and overseas locations, began using a peer mentoring program for its younger employees to work with more experienced employees. This future senior leaders plan used a set of competencies to model specific behavior and qualities. "Employers should be providing specialized training to older workers to help them better understand the work ethic and expectations of younger workers, and the public school system should be providing more education to the young entrants to the workforce to better prepare them for working with the older generations" (Rogov, 2009, p. 4).

Measuring a student's workplace readiness skills should be considered just as important as academic standards. State standards are typically used to measure students' adequate progress in schools; however, there is an interest in comparing those standards against students in high-performing countries. Parents and other interested constituents would like assurances that high school graduates are comparable to graduates worldwide. The remaining challenge is to make financial outlays stretch and to have accountable commitments. New initiatives should provide results as promised. There should also be cost savings from energy efficient "green" efforts as well as funds will actually be directed to schools in need (Christie, 2009).

The Association of Career and Technical Education (ACTE) reported that nations with higher enrollments in work-based learning vocational programs will have an increased school and college attendance and upper-secondary completion rates (Slaopek, 2007). Career and technical education programs provide beneficial experiences for our students. The National Assessment of Vocational Education (NAVE) independent advisory panel (Earning, Learning, and Choice, 2004) had suggested that approved, high-quality CTE programs of study should become a focus of federal CTE legislation. The CTE programs should be incorporating a multi-year sequence of courses integrating academic with technical and occupational knowledge. Doing so will promote elevated levels of skill development, specifically around a central career theme.

Continued partnerships with employers and the community will provide relevant and timely information about the workplace and career tracks. "The growing movement to redesign America's high schools includes recognition of CTE as an integral component in providing meaningful educational opportunities for all students" (Stone, 2007, p. 44). This redesigning of high schools would target personal relationships, academic rigor, and course relevance. The elevated high school dropout rate stresses the need for change and CTE programs can motivate and encourage students to be better prepared for the workplace (Stone, 2007).

7.6 CONCLUSION

America has evolved from an industrial economy to a knowledge-based economy and the impact on the U.S. businesses and industries continues to be realized. Being able to compete in the global economy through technology, communications, and business partnerships has further flattened the world and improved the ability to do so. Friedman (2006) indicated that this flattening or globalization of the world will continue to drive individuals to become more responsible for managing their own career, risks, and economic security. The projected shortage of skilled workers is a major concern for the U.S. and one solution is for individuals to develop competitive and workplace skills through CTE programs. Students engaged in CTE programs are less likely to drop out of school and demonstrate increased levels of involvement and interest. "Every year, one in three young adults, more than 1.2 million people, drops out of U.S. high schools. The problem shows no signs of abating" (National Commission, 2008, p. 5). Even if students graduate from high school they may lack basic skills and readiness for work, training or college. These individuals will need to reengage in education or it will affect the economic status of our nation and states.

Career and technical education programs are similar to training used in business and industry settings. Encouraging students to explore career possibilities enhances occupational awareness and clarifies career goals. In order for students to develop workplace skills, the specific skills and competencies have to be identified. There have been initiatives at the local, regional, and national levels to identify, measure, and assess workforce readiness competencies. Workforce competencies refer to distinct knowledge, skills, and abilities that are required for specific jobs in economic markets. Association directors have collaborated with employers, secondary, and post-secondary educators to develop standards that could be used as a benchmark. Community colleges are proactively responding to CTE programs and students due to the changing economy. Friedel (2006) identified the state of Iowa has identified three primary industry clusters which were life sciences (e.g., food, pharmaceuticals, medical technologies, and biotechnologies); information solutions (e.g., financial services, insurance services, software development, and telecommunications); and advanced manufacturing (e.g., developing and applying technology and training a highly skilled workforce). Results of this type of collaboration have reduced the skills gap and enhanced meeting academic, technical and employers' needs.

Employers project that the new entrants to the 21st century U.S. workforce will have to demonstrate beyond basic knowledge and skill sets. The most important skills, as identified by the Workforce Readiness Initiative (2007), were:

- Professionalism/work ethic, teamwork/collaboration and oral communications.
- Knowledge of foreign languages.
- Making appropriate choices concerning health and wellness.
- Creativity/innovation.

Workplace learning and performance professionals, as identified by ASTD, have recognized competencies that would be appropriate in specific roles such as manager, change leader, evaluator, or intervention selector. These competencies include analytical, business, interpersonal, leadership, technical and technological abilities.

The development and implementation of competency-based programs will bridge academic or technical instructional activities and required workplace skills.

CTE instructors align classroom instruction with specific business and industry work requirements. The national States' Career Clusters initiative (2009) identified 16 career clusters and competencies for each cluster. Depending on the individual's interest and awareness, there are career pathways and plans of study to guide the student in coursework and experiences. Industry-driven models are used in CTE programs which further align with workforce needs. Workforce readiness credentials will continue to be used by states to measure work-related literacy and numeracy abilities. The identification of academic and workplace standards continue to establish performance and accountability within educational institutions and workplace settings.

Some states have created tools for CTE educators and stakeholders to use in preparing students for higher skilled and compensated occupations. Whether it is a guidance counselor, parent, business community member, educator, or leader, it is in the best interest of all to become involved and build partnerships to ensure a strong workforce for the future. Christie (2009) stipulated that the upcoming legislative sessions will focus on the importance of matching jobs with an appropriately skilled workforce, reducing the dropout rate, and ensuring the U.S. remains competitive within the global economy. The role of education, government, and business will be to support and assist the workforce of tomorrow today with core knowledge and skills that can be used in a variety of work environments. "Our economy cannot afford to have a workforce that consists primarily of unskilled labor. We must prepare our workforce for the realities of today's, and tomorrow's, economy" (Foster, Kiker, Ruffing, & Kelley, 2006, p. 3).

REFERENCES

Adult Learning in Focus. *National and State-by-State Data*. (2008). Council for adult and experiential learning (CAEL) in Partnership with NCHEMS. Retrieved August 25, 2008, from http://www.cael.org/pdf/State_Indicators_Monograph.pdf

Alabama Course of Study. *Career and technical education*. (2007). Retrieved on May 15, 2009, from ftp://ftp.alsde.edu/documents/54/3-CTE%20 Clusters%20Pathways%20and% 20Courses.doc

American Society for Training and Development. (2008). *About us*. Retrieved May 17, 2009, from http://www.astd.org/ASTD/aboutus/

Association for Career and Technical Education (ACTE). (2008). *Issue brief: Career and technical education's role in workforce readiness credentials.* Retrieved May 15, 2009, from http://www. acteonline.org/uploadedFiles/Publications_and_ Online_Media/files/WorkReadinessCredentials. pdf

Barriers to Implementing College and Workforce Readiness Initiatives in Texas. (2009). Texas association of school boards. Retrieved March 24, 2009, from http://www.tasb. org/issues/resource_center/college_readiness/index.aspx

Benson, A., Johnson, S., Taylor, G., Treat, T., Shinkareva, O., & Duncan, J. (2004). *Distance learning in postsecondary career and technical education: A comparison of achievement in online vs. on-campus CTE courses.* St. Paul, MN: National Research Center for Career and Technical Education.

Blank, W. (1982). *Handbook for developing competency-based training programs. Englewood Cliffs.* NJ: Prentice-Hall.

Bybee, R., & Starkweather, K. (2006). The twenty-first century workforce: A contemporary challenge for technology education. *Technology Teacher, 65*(8), 27–32.

Career and Technical Education Administration. (2006). *Section A.* Retrieved May 1, 2009, from http://www.michigan.gov/ documents/Section_A_CTE_Administrators_-_ Admin_ Guide_169117_7.doc

Carl, D. *Perkins Career and Technical Education Improvement Act.* (2006). Retrieved May 13, 2008, from http://frwebgate.access.gpo. gov/cgi-bin/getdoc.cgi?dbname=109_cong_ bills&docid=f:s250enr.txt.pdf

Christie, K. (2009). Stateline: Anticipating 2009's top 10. *Phi Delta Kappan, 90*(5), 317–319.

Compton, J., Cox, E., & Laanan, F. (2006). Adult learners in transition. *New Directions for Student Services, 114,* 73–80. doi:10.1002/ss.208

Earning, Learning, and Choice: Career and Technical Education works for students and employers. (2004). Report of the national assessment of vocational education (NAVE), Independent Advisory Panel. Retrieved September 21, 2008, from http://www.ed.gov/ rschstat/eval/sectech/ nave/index.html

Foster, J., Kiker, J., Ruffing, K., & Kelley, P. (2006). *Preparing tomorrow's skilled workforce: NOCTI outcomes demonstrate consistent improvements in secondary career and technical education.* Retrieved May 3, 2009, from http:// whitenergroups.net/PDFs/Preparing%20Tomorrows%20Skilled%20Workforce.pdf

Friedel, J. (2006). The role of career and technical education in Iowa community colleges. *Community College Journal of Research and Practice, 30,* 293–310. doi:10.1080/10668920500479184

Friedman, T. (2006). *The world is flat: A brief history of the twenty-first century.* New York: Farrar, Straus and Giroux.

Gray, K., & Herr, E. (1998). *Workforce education: The basics.* Boston: Allyn and Bacon.

Heinrich, G., Jordan, K., & Smalley, A. (2005). Prepare students for technical careers. *Quality Progress, 38*(10), 33–38.

Hoerner, J., & Wehrley, J. (1995). *Work-based learning: The key to school-to-work transition. New York.* Glencoe: McGraw-Hill.

Jones, E., Voorhees, R., & Paulson, K. (2002). *Defining and assessing learning: Exploring competency-based initiatives.* National Postsecondary Education Cooperative Working Group in Competency-Based Initiatives, National Center for Education Statistics (NCES). Retrieved May 2, 2009, from http://nces. ed.gov/pubs2002/2002159.pdf

Mohr, C. (2008). Aligning classroom instruction with workplace skills: Equipping CTE students with the math skills necessary for entry-level carpentry. *Techniques: Connecting Education and Careers, 83*(8), 34–38.

National Commission on Adult Literacy. (2008). *Reach Higher, America: Overcoming crisis in the U.S. workforce.* Retrieved April 30, 2009, from http://www.nationalcomm issiononadultliteracy.org/report.html

Nebraska Student Competencies in Technology. (n.d.). *Guidelines for essential learnings in technology, Nebraska Department of Education.* Retrieved May 10, 2009, from http://www.nde.state.ne.us/techcen/documents/student_essential.pdf

Parnell, D. (1995). *Why do I have to learn this? Teaching the way people learn best.* Waco, TX: Cord Communications.

Paulson, K. (2001). Using competencies to connect to workplace and postsecondary education. *New Directions for Institutional Research, 110,* 41–54. doi:10.1002/ir.10

Peckman, S. (2006). Technically speaking. *Tech Directions, 66*(5), 5–6.

Peters, S. J. (2008, Summer). The promise of career/tech. *ASCD educational leadership.* Retrieved September 15, 2008, from http://www.ascd.org/portal

Ready or not. (2009). *A teachers resource for r u ready? and Career Education.* Richmond, VA: Virginia Department of Education.

Rogov, K. (2009). *HR.com: Workforce readiness skills gap issues.* Retrieved June 23, 2009, from http://www.hr.com/sfs?t=/contentManager/onStory&e=UTF-8&i=1116423256281 &l=0& ParentID=1119278152254&StoryID=12361026 62055&highlight=1&keys=workforce+%2Brea diness+%2Bskills+%2Bgap+%2Bissue&lang= 0&active=no

Rothwell, W., & Sredl, H. (2000). *The ASTD reference guide to workplace learning and performance: Present and future roles and competencies* (3rd ed.). Amherst, MA: HRD Press.

Ruffing, K. (n.d.). *The history of career clusters.* Retrieved May 17, 2009, from http://www.careerclusters.org/resources/publications/TheHistoryofCareerClusters2006.pdf

Salopek, J. (2007). Education for work and life. *Training & Development, 61*(2), 22–24.

Salopek, J. (2009). The power of the pyramid: ASTD unveils world-class sales competency model. *Training & Development, 63*(5), 70–75.

States' Career Clusters Initiative. (2009). Retrieved on April 13, 2009, from http://www.careerclusters.org

Stone, J. (2009). A Perkins challenge: Assessing technical skills in CTE. *Techniques, 84*(2), 21–23.

Stone, M. (2007). E-Learning applications for career and technical education. *Techniques, 82*(5), 44–48.

Sullivan, D., Ford, B., & Murphree, T. (n.d.). *Educational competencies for marine science and technology occupations.* Marine Advanced Technology Education Center (MATE). Retrieved May 15, 2009, from http://www.marinetech.org/marineworkforce/pdf/educational_comps.pdf

University of Alaska Anchorage. (2009). *Academics.* Retrieved May 16, 2009, from http://www.uaa.alaska.edu/pathways/career_connections.cfm

University of Alaska Fairbanks. (2009). *Student technology competencies.* Retrieved May 3, 2009, from http://www.uaf.edu/educ/technology/tech-competencies.html

U.S. Bureau of Labor Statistics. (2008). *Occupational Outlook Handbook.* Retrieved May 13, 2009, from http://www.bls.gov/oco/oco2003.htm

Venn, G. (1970). *Man, education, and manpower*. Washington, DC: American Association of School Administrators.

Wichowski, C., Kormanik, G., & Evans, C. (2008). Pennsylvania's career support tools: An asset to students, parents, the workplace and the economy. *Techniques: Connecting Education and Careers*, *83*(8), 39–42.

Workforce Readiness Initiative. (2007). *Meeting summary report: Stakeholders strategy meeting*. The Conference Board, Research Report E-0014-07-RR, Washington, D.C.

Chapter 8
Certification and Licensure Requirements for Career and Technical Educators

Chris Zirkle
Ohio State University, USA

Edward C. Fletcher Jr.
Illinois State University, USA

Kristina L. Sander
Ohio State University, USA

Jane Briggs
Ohio State University, USA

ABSTRACT

Teacher certification/licensure requirements are in a constant state of change. This is true of both the traditional academic disciplines and vocational/career and technical education. The goal of this chapter is to provide the reader with a historical and current overview of vocational/career-technical teacher certification/licensure through both the traditional and alternative routes. Discussion of expectations of post-secondary institutions and variances in those expectations are shared. A detailed explanation of requirements for alternative certification is provided, specifically with reference to educator preparation requirements, including customized coursework, work experience, entrance requirements and induction programs. Testing for licensure is discussed, as well as details regarding licensure renewal. Issues facing career and technical education referenced in this chapter focus on the highly qualified teacher designation, the need for modifications of testing requirements, employment opportunities, teacher attrition, standards in teacher preparation programs, reform in career and technical teacher preparation, and the need to focus on preparing future CTE teacher educators.

DOI: 10.4018/978-1-61520-747-3.ch008

8.1 INTRODUCTION

Obtaining career and technical teacher certification/licensure (hereafter referred to as licensure) in the United States can be achieved through two different pathways. The first is the traditional education route, in which an individual obtains a baccalaureate or master's degree and meets all requirements mandated by the state to earn a teaching credential, very much like that of other teaching disciplines. The second route to becoming a career and technical teacher is what some would term "alternative licensure"[1] (although that term now has many interpretations), in which a license is granted primarily based on occupational work experience in the subject area to be taught. These types of alternative licensure programs give individuals opportunities to earn their teaching certificates in abbreviated periods of time, often teaching while completing program requirements (Education Week, Alternative Teacher Certification, 2007). In career and technical education this type of teacher training dates back to the Smith-Hughes Act of 1917. Alternative licensure programs typically involve some period of intensive, condensed academic coursework or training, a period of supervised, on-the-job training, and candidates are typically expected to pass certification tests to become fully certified (Legler, 2002).

Legislative initiatives also impact teacher training in CTE. One focus of recent Carl D. Perkins legislation was on improving the transition from business and industry into teaching for CTE educators. This transition is most easily accomplished through the various "alternative" licensure pathways offered by the approaches employed by career and technical education. Alternative licensure programs "allow new teachers to learn in the 'real world'" (Legler, 2002). Citing Haberman (1991), Legler argued that alternative licensure programs are needed for those who want to change careers. Haberman stated that the availability of these highly skilled individuals wanting to move to the classroom should be accommodated through alternative licensure. As we consider these traditional and alternative methods for teacher certification, a look at history, background and current issues facing career and technical teachers is relevant.

The main objective of this chapter is to discuss the licensure requirements of CTE teachers. However, it is important to note that the preparation of CTE teachers in many programs is markedly different than core academic and teachers in other content areas. In fact, McCaslin and Parks (2002) stated,

There has been a great deal of separatism in the way vocational education teachers and general education teachers have been prepared. For years, vocational education teacher requirements have mandated a number of years of experience in their craft or trade outside the classroom prior to their employment as a teacher. (p. 74)

8.2 BACKGROUND

8.2.1 Historical Overview of Career and Technical Teacher Education and Licensure

A teaching license is the conceptual equivalent of a license to practice. The purpose of licensure is to allow individuals to perform specific functions for which they have demonstrated specific skills, knowledge, and abilities. When speaking of educators (both teachers and administrators), requirements for teacher licensure are established and monitored by states (McNergney & Herbert, 1995).

The concept of educator licensure has been in existence for over 175 years. Licensure of teachers first began in 1825, as local counties set up agencies to examine and license candidates for teaching positions. As normal schools began to grow in the mid-1850s, states began to develop guidelines for the licensing of teachers. By 1927, 33 states had specialized requirements, such as four years of college and professional education coursework, for secondary school teaching (Kinney, 1964). By 1950, college graduation was a requirement to begin secondary teaching in all states (Armstrong & Stinnett, 1957). Since that time, licensure of teachers has become largely a state function, with candidates completing a state-approved teacher education program at a college or university. Teacher education programs typically consist of a general studies component, content courses in an area of specific study, a set of professional studies courses taken in schools, colleges or departments of education, and a period of clinical practice or field experience. Many states also require some type of exit exam for full licensure.

Vocational/career and technical education (CTE) teachers have not always followed the same pathways to teacher licensure as educators in other subject areas (Lynch, 1997). While the first general teacher preparation school can be traced back to 1839, CTE's original teaching roots exist in the family, from the beginning of mankind. Fathers and mothers teaching sons and daughters trades are the earliest known forms of vocational (career-technical) education. McCaslin and Parks (2002) shared, "Fathers and mothers have always transmitted the knowledge and skills of their culture to their children in order to teach them to survive, and each new generation added something to the total of the knowledge and skills base" (McCaslin & Parks, 2002, p. 11). While these individuals were not trained as teachers, they inherently knew what needed to be done to educate their families on survival and sustainability. As the industrial revolution began to impact the economy, factories needed employees. Many family businesses were abandoned as family members went to work in factories. The family tradition of passing on work skills to the next generation became less and less of a factor in vocational education.

The move toward formalized teacher training in CTE occurred with the Smith-Hughes Act of 1917. A mindset was established early on that teachers in vocational education (CTE), specifically trade and industry and health occupations, would best benefit students with their knowledge of the trade, and not necessarily the academic knowledge provided in teacher preparation programs. Teacher preparation in these areas focused on trade and employment skills and not related academics. The experience of the teacher in their trade was viewed as more valuable than their educational preparation. This work experience in the occupation to be taught has long been a major consideration in the licensure of CTE teachers, primarily due to the Smith-Hughes Act which stated that only personnel with practical work experience were permitted to teach in programs that were federally funded (Miller, 1982). The Smith-Hughes Act was the first to supply federal funding for CTE teacher training and was administered by the Federal Board for Vocational Education. The Board's first leader, Charles Prosser, emphasized the importance of developing the skills necessary in a craft or trade. The Federal Board itself "indicated that teachers should be knowledgeable of the skills needed by crafts or trades if they were to be successful as teachers and that college and university courses contributed little or nothing to the training of secondary vocational education teachers" (McCaslin & Parks, 2002, p. 13). Alternatively, CTE areas such as agricultural education, business education, family and consumer science education, and marketing education have been prepared under the philosophy of Dewey, that "education should prepare students for a lifetime of learning" and "teachers must be prepared in general education and in professional education courses dealing with the context and understandings related to students' activities" (McCaslin & Parks, 2002, p. 13). These areas represent a more traditional approach to licensure, requiring baccalaureate degrees in a related subject area with professional education coursework (Ruhland & Bremer, 2002) and more closely resemble the traditional requirements of academic teacher licensure in areas such as mathematics, language arts, and science.

8.2.2 Description of Career and Technical Teacher Licensure Pathways: Traditional and Alternative

Zirkle, Martin and McCaslin (2007) conducted a research study involving all 50 states and the District of Columbia to compare the requirements of teacher preparation pathways in CTE among the states, as well as the requirements of CTE teacher preparation pathways in comparison with traditional teacher preparation pathways. The research found, as discussed in the introduction, two distinct pathways to licensure exist. First, CTE teachers may be prepared through a pathway in which one obtains a license through a four-year baccalaureate program or an M.Ed program at the graduate level. This approach is common in agricultural education, business education, family and consumer science and marketing education. Some of these degree-based programs also required work experience in the teaching field, but not all.

The second pathway actually offered a myriad of approaches to allow an individual to obtain a career-technical teaching credential. Generally, an individual with a high school diploma and a minimum number of years of work experience (defined by individual states) was able to obtain an initial license to teach and was (generally) required to simultaneously enroll in a teacher licensure program. This approach capitalizes on the experience of the educator, by requiring work experience to apply toward their teaching credentials and allowing individuals to teach while participating in coursework or professional development for teacher licensure. The work experience requirement, regardless of pathway, emphasizes the importance of experience in a quality CTE educator.

Colleges and universities may offer either traditional or alternative CTE teacher licensure pathways or a combination of both. Most traditional teacher licensure programs offered by post-secondary institutions have the same basic requirements. Students complete a specified number of hours in post-secondary general education courses, such as English composition, college algebra, history, and psychology. In addition, students develop a content specialty such as mathematics, physical education, or business education through content-area coursework. Finally, as part of teacher preparation, students take courses in teaching pedagogy and complete field experiences and supervised student teaching. Some licensure programs are found only at the graduate level, usually as a master's of education program. Students in these programs have usually earned a baccalaureate degree in a subject area and complete the courses in teaching pedagogy as the primary focus of the master's degree.

A comparison of the traditional preparation pathway for CTE teachers and other disciplines found that requirements for all traditional preparation pathways are similar, with minor variations. Some of these differences between CTE educator preparation and teachers of other disciplines included a work experience requirement for CTE teachers (in some states), modifications in testing requirements, and the actual process of obtaining professional licensure. However, every state that offered a traditional preparation pathway for CTE teachers required those teachers to hold a bachelor's degree in addition to completing a teacher preparation program (Zirkle et al., 2007).

In that same study, while investigating alternative preparation programs, Zirkle, Martin and McCaslin (2007) found a total of 105 alternative licensure pathways nationwide. Within these significant numbers of pathways, there were also significantly different standards/requirements for licensure. In some cases, a set of education course were required to give alternatively prepared CTE teachers foundational knowledge in pedagogy, teaching philosophy, practice, and CTE in general. The specific courses required were often based upon the individual's past experience and background and varied from person to person. This type of customized additional coursework was utilized in 55 of the 105 alternative preparation pathways. The required years of work experience varied by state and even within a given state, depending on the educational background of the applicant. Ohio, for example, required an individual with a high school diploma to possess five years of work experience related to the subject area to be taught, while an individual with an associate degree in a related field is required to possess three years of experience. A baccalaureate degree, on the other hand, reduces the work experience requirement to two years (State of Ohio Office of Career-Technical Education, 2006). In many states, prospective teachers with relevant work experience may be hired and granted a provisional or temporary license while concurrently completing a series of courses focused on teaching skills and knowledge. Upon satisfactory completion of these requirements, they may be issued a professional or permanent license. Twenty of the pathways investigated varied the level of work experience required depending on the level of the degree the teacher candidate held. As with the Ohio example, teacher candidates with more advanced degrees were not required to have as much work experience as others. In total, 74 of the 105 alternative preparation pathways required teachers to have at least some occupational work experience (Zirkle, Martin & McCaslin, 2007).

Degree requirements for alternatively licensed CTE teachers have often more flexible than those for traditionally prepared teachers. Often, there has not been a degree requirement for teachers in CTE areas such as trade and industry, where actual associate and bachelor's degrees are rare or nonexistent (such as cosmetology and certain building trades). This differential has often been justified through the use of competency-based credentials in the given occupation (ASE certifica-tion in automotive technology, AWS certification in welding, for example) or through occupational testing via assessments such as NOCTI, or the documentation of extensive work experience (Zirkle, Martin, & McCaslin, 2007).

As novice teachers begin their careers, as part of the process, new teacher induction or mentoring programs are also often required. These can be required for both traditionally-prepared CTE teachers, along with those from alternative certification/licensure pathways. Mandates vary nationally, but states are seeking to ensure new teachers are prepared for the classroom. Many of these induction and mentoring programs include a formal program of support, including mentoring, to foster professional growth of the individual and to prepare them for performance-based assessments of their actual teaching (Briggs, 2008).

Teacher induction may constitute formal programs or informal acclimation. Nevertheless, teacher induction serves as a bridge between pre-service teaching and practice and from student of teaching to teacher of students (Feiman-Nemser, 2001; Ingersoll & Smith, 2004). The first two to three years are extremely critical for new teachers; hence, this is the time that new teacher induction programs must facilitate teacher development.

The implementation of induction programs is growing rapidly (Feiman-Nemser, Schwille, Carver, & Yusko, 1999; Ingersoll & Smith, 2004; Joerger & Bremer, 2001; Roehrig & Luft, 2006); hence, a majority of new teachers have participated in some type of teacher induction program (Ingersoll & Smith, 2004). However, the quality and duration of these programs vary widely (AFT, 2001; Ingersoll & Smith, 2004; NASBE, 2000).

In addition to an induction program that acclimates a new teacher into their new teaching career, ongoing mentoring is critical in reducing the attrition rate. A myriad of studies show that providing mentoring for novice teachers may be a significant factor in the promotion of teacher retention and in ensuring the development of quality teachers by improving their dispositions, efficacy, and instructional skills (Carver & Katz, 2004; Darling-Hammond, 2003; Darling-Hammond & Berry, 1999). In fact, Odell and Ferraro (1992) administered questionnaires to investigate what novice teachers found to be the most helpful (regarding mentoring) during their first year. The categories given were "emotional, instructional, resources, discipline, parental, management, and system" (p. 202). The majority of novice teachers selected emotional support as the most helpful function of their mentors. Out of the 100 teachers surveyed, 96 percent continued teaching. Andrews, Gilbert, and Martin (2006) found in a survey research study regarding the perceptions of novice teachers and principals of what types of support they value, that both agreed that providing new teachers with opportunities to co-plan with other teachers were most highly valued. In addition, Fieman-Nemser (2001) created the construct "educative mentoring"; she defined it as, "an explicit vision of good teaching and an understanding of teacher learning" (p. 2). She further noted that educative mentoring cultivates a long-term, continuous disposition of inquiry among novice teachers. Despite the need for mentoring, Darling-Hammond and Berry (1999) indicated that inner-city schools which have the most inexperienced teachers typically do not offer mentoring support for their novice teachers.

Despite the overwhelming positive attributions of mentoring relationships, Hawkey (1997) pointed out the need for qualitative research regarding the aspects of support and challenge in a mentoring relationship. This type of research may clarify the aspects of a mentoring relationship teacher candidates would greatly benefit from to create a more effective relationship between the mentor and mentee. Correspondingly, Bullough and Draper (2004) investigated the politics of what they call a "triad" relationship, a relationship among the cooperating teacher, student teacher, and the university supervisor. In their findings, they cited communication problems as inherent in mentoring relationships. They further stated that despite differences, "Each [the mentor and supervisor] is essential for the other's growth as much as for the intern's development; together they can come to understand teaching more richly and in more interesting ways than they can alone" (p. 13).

8.2.3 Testing Requirements for Career and Technical Teacher Certification Licensure

The testing of candidates for teaching credentials dates back to 1834, when Pennsylvania became the first state to require future teachers to pass a test of basic academic skills. By the end of the nineteenth century, most states required teachers to pass a locally administered test—usually consisting of basic skills and American history, geography, spelling, and grammar—to get a state teaching certificate (Ravitch, 2002). CTE teacher preparation, with its primary focus on vocational knowledge, appears to have avoided some of the early calls for teacher testing. However, in 1945, the first call for some type of vocational competency testing came from the University of California (Klehm, 1974). An emphasis on the vocational knowledge of teachers in the field and its relationship to teacher testing became very evident in 1966, when conferences were held at Rutgers University to determine methods to assess and certify the non-degreed teacher in the vocational education field (National Occupational Competency Testing Institute, 2005, cited by Zirkle, Martin & McCaslin, 2007). These conferences eventually led to the development and implementation of occupational competency examinations nationwide.

Most teachers in all areas must pass various entry or exit assessments to obtain initial licensure regardless of status in an alternative or traditional licensure track. The teacher tests most commonly used to assess an individual for the teaching profession are the Praxis assessments, developed by the Educational Testing Service (ETS). Accord-

127

ing to the latest data, the Praxis Series tests are currently required for teacher licensure in more than 40 states and U.S. jurisdictions (ETS, 2009).

Different states require different combinations of the tests. Twenty-five states require traditionally prepared CTE teachers to pass the Praxis I Pre-Professional Skills Test (PPST). In addition, many colleges and universities require a qualifying score on this test for entrance into a teacher licensure program regardless of state requirements. Twenty-eight states require traditionally prepared teachers to pass the Praxis II Subject Assessment (PSA), and 27 require them to pass the Praxis II Principles of Learning and Teaching (PLT), a test of teaching pedagogy knowledge, for licensure. With respect to CTE, ETS has developed subject assessments for agricultural education, business education, family and consumer science education, technology education, and marketing education. ETS has also developed an assessment of Vocational General Knowledge, designed for those completing four-year vocational education programs to assess their knowledge and understanding of various disciplines and their interrelationships, including knowledge of fundamental facts. In lieu of any Praxis-developed CTE assessments, 15 states have their own state-developed tests that they require traditionally prepared CTE teachers to pass.

Common assessments in the alternative CTE preparation pathways were the Praxis Series, including Praxis I, Praxis II Subject Assessment and Praxis II PLT. In addition to the Praxis exams, CTE alternative pathways also utilized occupational exams such as those given by the National Occupational Competency Testing Institute (NOCTI), state-designed exams, and assessments of classroom performance, including the Praxis III (Zirkle, Martin & McCaslin, 2007).

In reviewing CTE teacher licensure requirements from previous studies, it appears that the use of tests and assessments has increased in recent years. CTE leaders nationwide may want to determine which of these are most suitable and,

if appropriate, advocate for their inclusion in all CTE teacher licensure requirements. Doing so may make reciprocity between states more uniform and may help to make teacher preparation curriculum more consistent across states (Zirkle, Martin & McCaslin, 2007).

8.2.4 Licensure Renewal and Upgrades in Career and Technical Education

Licensure renewal and upgrade requirements for CTE teachers vary from state to state, and even from pathway to pathway within each state. In addition, the renewal requirements are often different for traditionally and alternatively prepared CTE teachers. Many states also have separate requirements for temporary or substitute licensure. The most common requirements for renewing a license obtained under a traditional route to certification/licensure are completion of college coursework and/or completion of various professional development activities. Also, completion of a set number of hours of college credit is a renewal requirement in 26 states, and completion of professional development activities is a renewal requirement in 36 states. College coursework is also often an option for professional development. Some less common renewal requirements are National Board Certification (four states), completion of an organized professional development program (three states), the completion of a higher degree (two states), and teaching experience (one state).

Renewal of licensure for traditionally prepared CTE teachers often requires a combination of the requirements described above. Many states required teachers to choose between several of the requirements in order to renew their licensure. Often, different levels of licensure within the same state have different renewal requirements. Renewal requirements for alternatively prepared teachers are similar to those for traditionally prepared teachers

Requirements for upgrading from one level of licensure to another vary quite a bit for both the traditional and alternative pathways. Often different combinations or choices of requirements are available under the same pathway. The requirements are usually different when upgrading to different levels of licensure within the same pathway

The most common requirement for licensure upgrades under the traditional pathway was teaching experience; many states required teachers to have a set number of years of classroom experience before advancing to the next level of certification/licensure. Another common requirement is that teachers earn a higher degree to advance their licensure to a higher level. Certification by the National Board for Professional Teaching Standards is also a requirement or an option for upgrading a certificate/license in some states. Some states require additional testing or completion of an induction or mentorship program for certification/licensure upgrades. Upgrade requirements are similar in alternative CTE preparation pathways (Zirkle, Martin & McCaslin, 2007).

8.3 ISSUES, CONTROVERSIES AND PROBLEMS

8.3.1 Career and Technical Teacher Licensure and Highly Qualified Designation

The No Child Left Behind Act stipulates that teachers must be highly qualified in their teaching discipline: if they teach a core academic area (math, science, social students, language arts). To be highly qualified, educators must meet a variety of credentials, including being fully certified and demonstrating competency in their subject area through methods defined by the Act. Zirkle, Martin and McCaslin (2007) addressed the issue of whether CTE educators were required to maintain the designation of being a highly qualified teacher. States were asked in a questionnaire

if a definition of a highly qualified CTE teacher had been created in their state. Forty-three states had no such definition, with most stating that CTE teachers were not required to have "highly qualified" status because they were not teaching in a core academic area. The seven states with requirements for highly qualified CTE teachers were Alabama, Arizona, Louisiana, Missouri, Montana, Oklahoma, and South Dakota. As we consider issues in CTE, the need not to have the high qualified designation sends a negative message. For the betterment of the field and in order to overcome negative stereotypes, CTE teachers should be required to meet some type of highly qualified teacher (HQT) designation based on their specific area of certification. This could be accomplished in a similar format for student credentialing in some fields.

8.3.2 Licensure Testing Challenges

Research by Gray and Walter (2001) brought to light issues related to CTE teacher preparation testing. In CTE, teachers entering teaching through the alternative route frequently do not fare well on competency tests for teaching. This could be a result of the demographics of the alternative CTE teachers, who are more likely to be older, further removed from college (if they have college preparation at all), and less likely to have a baccalaureate degree and at least 60 hours of general education (both norming variables for teacher exit tests) (Gray & Walter, 2001). The Carl D. Perkins Act of 1998, Perkins III, had initiatives in place to improve academics in vocational education and acknowledge the need for vocational teachers to be better prepared academically. Cramer (2004) emphasized that consistency in teacher preparation is needed to insure a well-prepared CTE workforce. CTE educators perform at lower levels in testing on reading levels, writing and mathematics than their academic counterparts (Cramer). Of additional concern is that the CTE educators also scored lower on the testing compared to their elementary education counterparts.

8.3.3 Financial Constraints for CTE Teachers Needing to Meet Licensure Requirements

A current offer of teaching employment is a common requirement for CTE alternative preparation pathways. A CTE teacher is generally required to have a current offer of employment in order to begin completing requirements of the pathway. Many CTE teachers in this pathway are also required to attend classes or summer workshops/programs prior to beginning teaching in a school's early fall (August-September). This can create financial constraints on new teachers, who must resign from jobs in order to begin teacher preparation. In addition to a potential loss of income, the cost of classes and materials creates a hardship for many CTE teachers in their new career.

In addition, many CTE teachers involved in alternative pathways are engaged in a long-term process of obtaining full teacher licensure (in some states, the process can take three to four years). During this time, classwork and/or professional development is usually required. CTE teachers may face financial issues due to these requirements. While some schools may offer part or full tuition reimbursement, many do not, and the cost is incumbent upon the teacher.

Many CTE teachers entering the profession left the work world where their prior salary was higher than their teaching salary. The attraction of returning to the private sector for monetary purposes is one reason cited by CTE teachers for leaving the teaching profession. School districts need to be cognizant of these financial issues when working with CTE teachers on licensure issues.

8.3.4 The Challenge to Prepare CTE Teacher Educators

Another issue that has been neglected in the literature of CTE teacher preparation and licensure is the need to develop CTE individuals to fulfill the roles of teacher educators. This is an important topic because CTE teacher educators are essential in preparing future CTE teachers. Bartlett (2002) discussed the challenge of recruiting CTE teacher educators for teaching in postsecondary classrooms, particularly in community college settings. These individuals would need to have competence in technical areas, as well as teaching and learning related to adolescents and adults. Bartlett stated the need to develop national certification for postsecondary career and technical educators. He further acknowledged the need for further research, consistency of requirements for states throughout the nation, and identification of competencies needed for effective career and technical educators.

Bruening, Scanlon, Hodes, Dhital, Shao, and Liu (2001a) examined characteristics of CTE teacher educators in their national study. They found that CTE teacher educators shared similar characteristics to the general population of teacher educators. The overwhelming majority of CTE teacher educators (97%) were white, 4% were African American, and three percent were Hispanic. Their research showed an increase in women; however, not increase was found in the racial makeup of minority CTE teacher educators. In terms of age, the average was 50 years and more than half of CTE teacher educators were tenured, with a ten percent increase in adjunct faculty. The majority of professional time CTE teachers devoted were spent on teaching.

8.3.5 Teacher Attrition in CTE: Providing Effective Teacher Training Programs

While a need for alternative licensure has been well documented, educational institutions must maintain stringent teacher preparation programs and high standards in preparing an individual for work in the field (Legler, 2002). To promote high standards in CTE teacher preparation, the framework for the alternative licensure program must consider pedagogy, content knowledge and pedagogical content knowledge. "Content knowledge in combination with content pedagogical knowledge appears to make contributions to student learning that exceed the contributions of either component individually" (Darling-Hammond, 2002). The lack of either pedagogy or pedagogical content in an alternative CTE licensure program would seemingly deem it ineffective.

8.3.6 Retention of Teachers in CTE: Impact of Teacher Preparation Programs

In a symposium of The National Commission on Teaching and America's Future (NCTAF, 2002), it was stated that, "the fact is, an alarming number and unsustainable number of teachers are leaving teaching during their first few years of teaching" (p. 3). Ingersoll (2003) reported, "The data suggest that after five years, between 40 and 50 percent of all beginning teachers leave teaching altogether" (p. 148). Further, Tye and O'Brien (2002) stated,

The substantial literature on teacher attrition has consistently shown a bimodal curve: most of those who leave teaching in any given year are either disillusioned beginners with just two or three years in the classroom or 30-year veterans ready to retire. (pp. 702-3)

In fact, the rate of teacher turnover is higher than any other occupational field and teachers leave the profession at much earlier stages than other fields (Dove, 2004; Ingersoll, 2002). High teacher turnover is damaging because it typically signals underlying issues in how well schools function as well as its negative impact on school cohesion and student performance (Ingersoll, 2003; Jalongo & Heider, 2006).

Extensive research has been underway to find the sources of teacher shortages. Among the many directives of investigation into this problem, several areas of research include looking at teacher preparation programs (Darling-Hammond, 2003), examining the structure and placement of field and clinical experiences, ensuring teacher candidates' preparedness for teaching in an urban setting, teacher characteristics (Strunk & Robinson, 2006) and studying school organizational factors (Darling-Hammond, 2003; Ingersoll, 2002, 2003). According to Darling-Hammond (2003),

Four major factors strongly influence whether and when teachers leave specific schools or the education profession entirely: salaries, working conditions, preparation, and mentoring support in the early years. (p. 9)

Darling-Hammond (1996) concluded that the quality of teachers and teaching depends heavily on workplace factors such as teacher networks, enriched professional roles, and more efficiency in gaining essential teacher knowledge bases. Roehrig and Luft (2005) discussed the importance of teacher induction to serve as a baseline for the increasing number of teachers being certified through various types of teacher preparation programs. Despite the laundry list of solutions for teacher preparation programs, an agreed upon list of coherent teacher candidate proficiencies or a professional knowledge base has yet to emerge (Ruhland & Bremer, 2003).

Cochran-Smith (2004) noted that teacher attrition rates are highest in hard-to-staff schools. Ingersoll (2003) argued that the large teacher attrition rate is not due primarily to increasing student enrollment and teacher retirement. Instead, he contended that it is a function of systemic organizational issues. Utilizing the Schools and Staffing Survey (SASS) and the Teacher Follow-up Survey (TFS), Ingersoll found that high poverty schools have much higher teacher turnover rates than affluent schools and urban schools have higher rates than rural or suburban schools. In addition, he found that school staffing cutbacks contribute to turnover at a much greater rate than teacher retirement. These cutbacks include organizational dynamics such as layoffs, terminations, school closings, and reorganizations. Furthermore, motivational issues such as job dissatisfaction due to low salaries, lack of support from administrators, classroom management issues, a lack of decision-making autonomy as well as a desire to pursue a different career accounted for half of the reasons for leaving the profession. Despite the research that has examined the reasons why teachers leave the profession, much more research is needed to determine what factors contribute to this phenomenon.

The retention of CTE teachers is also mentioned in the Perkins legislation. It is well-known that almost half of all teachers leave the profession within their first five years of teaching. Darling-Hammond (2002) cites high attrition rates by those involved in Teach for America, an alternative licensure program. The result of this analysis is the suggestion that teacher preparation is best served by having some type of student teaching experience. Darling-Hammond suggests that those prepared through an alternative route are likely not to have a student teaching experience, which Darling-Hammond also argues makes a strong difference in teacher retention. She goes on to say that those who enter teaching through alternative licensure programs, "leave teaching at rates nearly twice as high" as those who have had clinical student teaching experience (Darling-Hammond, 2002).

Education Week's article *Alternative Teacher Certification* (2007) referenced the idea that alternative routes to teacher certification do nothing more than thrust participants "into the classroom before they are adequately prepared", thus negatively affecting student learning. To counter this, educational institutions must insure that the structure of the teacher preparation program through a traditional or alternative route implements strategies to counter reasons for teacher attrition, as well as creates evaluation tools for determining the effectiveness of preparing the educator certified through an alternative route. Identifying connections between the preparations of the educator, their degree of satisfaction in their teaching experience and the rate of retention in the field are all critical components for advancing the field of CTE.

8.3.7 Need for High Standards for Career and Technical Education Licensure

Many states require only a high school credential, such as a diploma, with appropriate work experience for initial licensure in their alternative pathways. This requirement has long been one reason the CTE teaching profession has been seen as of lesser quality by its academic counterparts. States may wish to examine ways to encourage these alternatively licensed CTE teachers to continue on to a degree, as Ohio has recently done by instituting the requirement of an associate degree in the CTE teaching field/area or in education for the professional certificate/license.

8.3.8 CTE Teacher Preparation Programs in Colleges and Universities

Colleges and universities may offer traditional or alternative CTE teacher certification/licensure pathways or a combination of both. The pathways can be located at state-supported or private educational institutions. Some two-year technical and community colleges are also becoming involved in teacher preparation (St. Arnauld, 2004), and, given these two-year institutions' connection to technical education, this involvement may increase.

CTE teacher preparation programs in colleges and universities have also been the subject of research, including, most recently, research on the declining number of such programs. Over the past 20 years, research has documented the status of vocational teacher certification/licensure pathways and the various requirements in educational institutions (Anderson, 1986; Bruening, Scanlon, Hodes, Dhital, Shao, & Liu, 2001b; Gray & Walter, 2001; Hartley, Mantle-Bromley, & Cobb, 1996; Lynch, 1991, 1996, 1997; Miller, 1982; Pratzner, 1987; Pratzner & Ryan, 1990; Ruhland & Bremer, 2002). In most of these studies, the news was not positive: most programs had seen reductions in the numbers of faculty, course and program offerings, and licensure programs available to CTE teacher candidates.

8.4 SOLUTIONS AND RECOMMENDATIONS

To counter some of the issues a detail discussion is provided. In addition to specific recommendations below, states must define a highly qualified teacher designation for CTE: without it, programs and teacher stand to lose credibility.

8.4.1 Considerations for Career and Technical Teacher Certification Licensure Reform

The responsibilities of CTE teachers have prompted discussions of appropriate preparation, both for alternatively and traditionally prepared teachers. CTE teachers are expected to have a wide variety of skills in educating and engaging students. CTE teachers are expected to develop students' technical skills, meet the career development needs of students, help students improve their academic achievement, develop higher order thinking skills,

meet the needs for greater accountability in student performance, serve a more diverse student clientele, and revise curricula to include additional and new technology (McCaslin & Parks, 2002). With the extensive nature of the CTE teacher's responsibility, determination of the best method of preparing CTE teachers for the classroom must be considered.

Gray and Walter (2001) offered several recommendations for the reform of CTE teacher preparation. They suggested organizing licensure around two missions: a traditional pathway that relies upon a college/university preparation program that generally consists of general education, content/technical specialty coursework, and teaching pedagogy; and a pathway focused on "education through occupations" (p. ix) that has much in common with the alternative pathways now being utilized in academic areas such as mathematics and science. This latter pathway recognizes occupational work experience as equivalent to the content/technical specialty coursework taken within a traditional pathway. The authors list the required preparation for CTE teachers enrolled in either pathway, including training/education in the teaching of academic subjects and of special needs students, supervision of work-based learning, and workforce education and career development (Gray & Walter, 2001).

Cramer (2004) questioned the academic preparation of the next generation of vocational teachers. The study yielded three key findings:

- Candidates for licensure in vocational fields are not as academically or pedagogically prepared as candidates for certification/licensure in secondary fields.
- Candidates for licensure in vocational fields are not as academically prepared in reading and writing as candidates for certification/licensure in elementary education.
- A potential disconnect may exist between the academic and pedagogical skills of vo-

cational education teacher candidates and the direction of federal policy, which has increasingly emphasized the importance of academic skills for vocational students.

With the present federal and state emphasis on developing mathematics and science knowledge and skills to a high degree in all students, it appears that it is necessary for career-technical teachers to have a firm grounding in these and other academic areas. In addition, in this era of accountability and increased emphasis on academic skill development, the findings from Cramer (2004) present challenges for the field. CTE teachers need to be partners in students' academic preparation, and CTE offers many opportunities for this to occur through curricular integration. However, if CTE teachers lack appropriate preparation in this area, their students' performance may suffer.

In examining the research on CTE teachers' use of integrative strategies in teaching, Silverberg, Warner, Fong, and Goodwin (2004) found that CTE teachers believed that basic fundamental courses such as math, science, and reading were strongly needed for students' achievement in CTE courses and for the workforce. However, the majority of CTE teachers also believed they should not be held responsible for providing instruction on core academic content and held accountable for student achievement in core academic areas. Hence, CTE teachers typically do not report that the attainment of academic concepts is reflected in students' grades in CTE courses.

8.4.2 Assessing Teacher Preparation Programs in Career and Technical Education

Understanding why teachers leave the field of education is important to the development of teacher education programs with conceptual frameworks that counter reasons for teacher attrition. The fact that the rate of attrition in teachers new to the profession is so high that an August 2005 Issue

Brief from the Alliance for Excellent Education states "nearly half of all teachers who enter the field leave it within a mere five years, and the best and brightest teachers are often the first to leave" (Alliance for Education, 2005). Parks and McCaslin (2002) argued that reasons for teacher attrition could be due, in part to general working conditions and unrealistic expectations regarding what the teaching profession entails.

All teacher preparation programs should be designed with an element to aid in improving teacher retention rate, regardless of whether they are classified as traditional or alternative. In the 2002 symposium paper on teacher retention, Linda Darling-Hammond is cited for her reference to the need for strong teacher preparation programs. Specifically, "those who complete well designed five-year and four-year teacher education programs stay in teaching at much higher rates" (National Commission on Teaching and America's Future, 2002). Continuing, the paper states, "new data confirm that there are large differences in plans to stay in teaching among first year teachers who felt well-prepared and those who felt poorly prepared in the key tasks of teaching when they entered the classroom" (Unraveling the "Teacher Shortage" Problem). The paper suggests that: "Since all routes to teaching lead to the front of the classroom, all teacher preparation programs must set and meet high standards. Short-term, quick-fix approaches to placing teachers in the classroom, fuel high teacher attrition rates and diminish teaching quality" (Unraveling the "Teacher Shortage" Problem, 2002).

Imig and Imig (2006) argued that a focus of teacher preparation programs needs to be on preparing teacher candidates to be prepared for what they will encounter upon completion of the teacher preparation program. They noted, "Education facilities that avoid addressing such questions and realities of working conditions fail to serve either the interests of their students or those who employ them in their early years of practice" (p. 2). They further reported that novice teachers should expect a full load of responsibilities their first year of practice. Novice teachers will more than likely have challenging students, more class preps than experienced teachers, and other demanding tasks related to teaching. Devastatingly, research shows that in general, teacher candidates are vastly under-prepared for their future roles as teachers (Darling-Hammond & Berry, 1999; Smylie, Bay, & Tozer, 1999).

According to published recommendations by the Association for Career and Technical Education (ACTE), there is a need to improve both pre-service and in-service training for career and technical education teachers" (Association for Career and Technical Education [ACTE], 2004). While some literature may suggest eliminating quick fix alternatives to licensure, elimination is not the answer, but, instead, a strong conceptual framework designed to provide strong pre-service training for educators. Furthermore, Ruhland and Bremer (2003) share that "research has indicated that adequate pre-service preparation and in-service support of novice teachers are important to improving both teaching quality and retention. Alternative certification programs vary widely in the amount of pre-service preparation provided; individuals with little pre-service preparation and no opportunity to engage in a supervised teaching experience may need higher levels of in-service support in order to be successful" (p. 290).

8.5 FUTURE TRENDS

The need for CTE teachers to integrate core academic and CTE content will continually shape the way teacher candidates study teaching, learning, and curriculum. Coupled with the NCLB legislation provision of increasing students' achievement on standardized assessments, CTE teachers will need to re-think how they teach their content and explicitly demonstrate the core academic skills that students are learning in the process. Thus, professional development regarding integrative

practices is necessary for CTE teacher candidates and practicing teachers. In addition to utilizing integrative curriculum strategies, CTE teachers will continually need to have an understanding of the contemporary workplace and the needs of business and industry.

Future research is warranted to examine the type of teacher preparation program (alternative v. traditional) teacher candidates are exposed to and their future performances in the classroom. Questions that still need to be answered include whether teacher candidates' levels of perceived competence in terms of pedagogy, pedagogical content, content, and professional knowledge, based on their teacher preparation programs. Research also is needed to understand the proficiencies that CTE teacher educators will need to fulfill their roles and responsibilities at the professoriate level. Last, a clearer conceptualization of alternative and traditional licensure should be established to enhance the ability to generalize findings from research on various licensure programs.

8.6 CONCLUSION

More attention is needed with regard to the development and vitality of CTE teacher preparation programs in the U.S, particularly due to the vast nature of retirements within the next decade. The pressing needs to adequately prepare CTE teachers to face the realities of teaching and to retain highly competent individuals still remain as two primary concerns in teacher licensure. Despite the controversy surrounding alternative teacher licensure, the prevalence of alternative licensure programs is rapidly increasing. For many CTE areas, alternative teacher licensure seems to be the only logical route to meet the demands of a differentiated curriculum to meet the interests and needs of current students. A discussion that is still needed is whether CTE teachers should indeed follow separate licensure requirements than their core academic teacher counterparts. With the increased accountability metrics for teachers, such as NCLB's Highly Qualified mandate, it may just be a matter of time before CTE teachers too will need to follow the same specifications of their core academic counterparts. Furthermore, a better understanding of the essential teacher knowledge base would help inform the needed curricula of appropriate teacher preparation programs.

REFERENCES

ACTE's recommendations for strengthening career and technical education through reauthorization of the Carl D. Perkins Vocational and Technical Education Act. (2004, January). Retrieved March 8, 2009, from www.acteonline.org/policy/legislative_issues/loader.cfm?url=/commonspot/security/getfile.cfm&PageID=13339

Alternative Teacher Certification. (2007). Retrieved April 18, 2009, from http://www2.edweek.org/rc/issues/alternative-teacher-certification

American Federation of Teachers. (2001). Beginning teacher induction: The essential bridge. *Educational Issues Policy Brief, 13,* 1–13.

Anderson, B. (1986). *The status of vocational teacher education in University Council for Vocational Education member institutions.* Fort Collins, CO: Colorado State University.

Andrews, S., Gilbert, L., & Martin, E. (2006). The first years of teaching: Disparities in perceptions of support. *Action in Teacher Education, 24*(4), 4–13.

Armstrong, W., & Stinnett, T. (1957). *A manual on certification requirements for school personnel in the United States.* Washington, DC: National Commission on Teacher Education and Professional Standards, National Education Association.

Bartlett, J. (2002). Preparing, licensing, and certifying postsecondary career and technical educators. *Journal of Vocational Education Research, 27*(1), 127–149.

Briggs, J. (2008). *Perceptions of career and technical education teachers about teacher mentoring and teacher retention.* Unpublished doctoral dissertation. The Ohio State University, Columbus, Ohio.

Bruening, T., Scanlon, D., Hodes, C., Dhital, P., Shao, X., & Liu, S. (2001a). *Characteristics of teacher educators in career and technical education.* Columbus, OH: The Ohio State University, National Dissemination Center for Career and Technical Education. Retrieved June 8, 2009, from http://nrccte.org/

Bruening, T., Scanlon, D., Hodes, C., Dhital, P., Shao, X., & Liu, S. (2001b). *The status of career and technical education teacher preparation programs.* Columbus, OH: The Ohio State University, National Dissemination Center for Career and Technical Education. Retrieved May 27, 2009, from http://nrccte.org/

Bullough, R., & Draper, R. (2004). Making sense of a failed triad: Mentors, university supervisors, and positioning theory. *Journal of Teacher Education, 55*(5), 407–420. doi:10.1177/0022487104269804

Carver, C., & Katz, D. (2004). Teaching at the boundary of acceptable practice. What is a new teacher mentor teacher to do? *Journal of Teacher Education, 55*(5), 449–462. doi:10.1177/0022487104269524

Cochran-Smith, M. (2004). Stayers, leavers, lovers, and dreamers. *Journal of Teacher Education, 55*(5), 387–392. doi:10.1177/0022487104270188

Cramer, K. (2004). *The vocational teacher pipeline: How academically well-prepared is the next generation of vocational teachers?* Washington, D.C.: U.S. Department of education, Office of the Deputy Secretary, Policy and Program Studies Service.

Darling-Hammond, L. (1996). The quiet revolution: Rethinking teacher development . *Educational Leadership, 53,* 4–10.

Darling-Hammond, L. (2002, September 6). Research and rhetoric on teacher certification: A response to "Teacher Certification Reconsidered," *Educational Policy Analysis Archives, 10*(36). Retrieved April 18, 2009, from http://epaa.asu.edu/epaa/v10n36.html

Darling-Hammond, L. (2003). Keeping good teachers: Why it matters what leaders can do. *Educational Leadership, 60*(8), 6–13.

Darling-Hammond, L., & Berry, B. (1999). Recruiting teachers for the 21st century: The foundation for educational equity. *The Journal of Negro Education, 68*(3), 254–279. doi:10.2307/2668100

Dove, M. (2004). Teacher attrition: A critical American and International education issue. *The Delta Kappa Gamma Bulletin, 71*(1), 8–30.

Educational Testing Service (ETS). (2009). *General frequently asked questions.* Retrieved April 30, 2009, from http://www.ets.org/portal/site/ets/

Feiman-Nemser, S. (2001). Helping novices learn to teach: Lessons from an exemplary support teacher. *Journal of Teacher Education, 52*(1), 17–30. doi:10.1177/0022487101052001003

Feiman-Nemser, S., Schwille, S., Carver, C., & Yusko, B. (1999). *A conceptual review of literature on new teacher induction. (National Partnership for Excellence and Accountability in Teaching).* College Park, MD: University of Maryland, Department of Education.

Gray, K. C., & Walter, R. A. (2001). *Reforming career and technical education licensure and preparation: A public policy synthesis.* Columbus, OH: The Ohio State University, National Dissemination Center for Career and Technical Education.

Guarino, C. M., Santibanez, L., & Daley, G. A. (2006). Teacher recruitment and retention: A review of the recent empirical literature. *Review of Educational Research, 76*(2), 173–208. doi:10.3102/00346543076002173

Hartley, N., Mantle-Bromley, C., & Cobb, R. B. (1996). A matter of respect. *Vocational Education Journal, 71*(1), 25.

Hawkey, K. (1997). Roles, responsibilities, and relationships in mentoring: A literature review and agenda for research. *Journal of Teacher Education, 48*(4), 325–335. doi:10.1177/0022487197048005002

Imig, D., & Imig, S. (2006). What do beginning teachers need to know? *Journal of Teacher Education, 57*(3), 1–6. doi:10.1177/0022487105285964

Ingersoll, R. (2002). The teacher shortage: A case of wrong diagnosis and wrong prescription. *NASSP Bulletin, 86*, 16–31. doi:10.1177/019263650208663103

Ingersoll, R. (2003). The teacher shortage: Myth or reality? *Educational Horizons, 81*(3), 146–152.

Ingersoll, R., & Smith, T. (2004). Do teacher induction and mentoring matter? *NASSP Bulletin, 88*, 28–40. doi:10.1177/019263650408863803

Jalongo, M., & Heider, K. (2006). Editorial teacher attrition: An issue of national concern. *Early Childhood Education Journal, 33*(6), 379–380. doi:10.1007/s10643-006-0122-y

Joerger, R., & Bremer, C. (2001). *Teacher induction programs: A strategy for improving the professional experience of beginning career and technical education teachers. (National Dissemination Center for Career and Technical Education).* Columbus, OH: The Ohio State University.

Kinney, L. (1964). *Certification in education.* Englewood Cliffs, NJ: Prentice-Hall.

Klehm, M. (1974). *The status of the certification requirements for trade & industrial teachers in the United States.* Unpublished doctoral dissertation, The Ohio State University, Columbus, Ohio.

Legler, R. (2002). Alternative certification: A review of theory and research. *North Central Regional Education Laboratory.* Retrieved April 18, 2009, from http://www.ncrel. org/policy/pubs/html/altcert/index.html

Lynch, R. (1991). *A national database on vocational teacher education.* Berkeley: University of California, Berkeley; National Center for Research in Vocational Education. (ERIC Document Reproduction Service No. ED329733).

Lynch, R. (1996). In search of vocational and technical teacher education. *Journal of Vocational and Technical Education, 13*(1), 5–16.

Lynch, R. (1997). *Designing vocational and technical teacher education for the 21st century: Implications from the reform literature.* Information Series No. 368. (ERIC Document Reproduction Service No. ED405499).

McCaslin, N., & Parks, D. (2002). Teacher education in career and technical education: Background and policy implications for the new millennium. *Journal of Vocational Education Research, 27*(1), 65–103.

McNergney, R., & Herbert, J. (1995). *Foundations of education.* Needham Heights, MA: Allyn & Bacon.

Miller, A. J. (1982). Certification: A question of validity. *VocEd, 57*(2), 27–29.

National Association of State Boards of Education. (2000). Teacher induction programs. *Policy Update, 8*(5), 1–2.

National Commission on Teaching and America's Future. (2002). Unraveling the "teacher shortage" problem: Teacher retention is the key. In *Symposium of The National Commission on Teaching and America's Future and NCTAF State Partners,* Washington, DC, (pp. 1-17). Retrieved November 11, 2006, from http://www.ncsu.edu/mentorjunction/text_files/teacher_retentionsymposium.pdf

Naylor, M. (1997). *Impacts of reform movements on vocational teacher education.* Columbus, OH: ERIC Clearinghouse on Adult Career and Vocational Education. (ERIC Document Reproduction Service No. ED 407572).

Odell, S., & Ferraro, D. (1992). Teacher mentoring and teacher retention. *Journal of Teacher Education, 43*(3), 200–204. doi:10.1177/0022487192043003006

Parks, D., & McCaslin, N. L. (2002). *Teacher education in career and technical education: Background and policy implications for the new millennium.* Columbus, OH: National Dissemination Center for Career and Technical Education. The Ohio State University (ERIC Document Reproduction Service No. ED 462546)

Pratzner, F., & Ryan, R. (1990). Vocational teacher education . In Houston, R. (Ed.), *Handbook of research on teacher education* (pp. 782–794). New York: Macmillan.

Ravitch, D. (2002). *A brief history of teacher professionalism.* Paper presented at the White House Conference on Preparing Tomorrow's Teachers, Washington, D.C.

Roehrig, G., & Luft, J. (2006). Does one size fit all? The induction experience of beginning science teachers from different teacher-preparation programs. *Journal of Research in Science Teaching, 43*(9), 963–985. doi:10.1002/tea.20103

Ruhland, S., & Bremer, C. (2002). *Alternative teacher certification procedures and professional development opportunities for career and technical education teachers*. Columbus, OH: National Dissemination Center for Career and Technical Education.

Ruhland, S., & Bremer, C. (2003). Perceptions of traditionally and alternatively certified career and technical education teachers. *Journal of Vocational Education Research*, *28*(3), 285–302.

Silverberg, M., Warner, E., Fong, M., & Goodwin, D. (2004). *National assessment of vocational education: Final report to Congress*. Washington, DC: U.S. Department of Education.

Smylie, M., Bay, M., & Tozer, S. (1999). Preparing teaches as agents of change . In Griffin, G. (Ed.), *The Education of Teachers* (pp. 29–62). Chicago: National Society for the Study of Education.

St. Arnauld, C. (2004). *The role of community colleges in preparing CTE teachers*. Retrieved September 27, 2008, from http://www.nccte.org/webcasts/description68c1.html

Strunk, K., & Robinson, J. (2006). Oh, won't you stay: A multilevel analysis of the difficulties in retaining qualified teachers. *Peabody Journal of Education*, *81*(4), 65–94. doi:10.1207/s15327930pje8104_4

Teacher attrition: A costly loss to the nation and to the states by Alliance for Excellent Education. (2005, August). Retrieved May 16, 2009, from http://www.all4ed.org/ publications/TeacherAttrition.pdf

Teacher retention is the key. (2002, August 20-22). *Symposium of the National Commission on Teaching and America's Future and NCTAF State Partners*. Retrieved November 10, 2008, from http://www.ncsu.edu/mentorjunction/text_files/teacher_retentionsymposium.pdf

Zirkle, C., Martin, L., & McCaslin, N. (2007). *Study of state certification/licensure requirements for secondary CTE teachers*. St. Paul, MN: National Dissemination Center for Career and Technical Education.

ENDNOTE

[1] For the purposes of this chapter "alternative licensure" will refer to these career-technical licenses granted based on work experience

Chapter 9
Prevalent Work Ethics in Career and Technical Education

Gregory C. Petty
University of Tennessee, USA

ABSTRACT

Career and technical education (CTE), has been defined as a series of classes and practical experiences that prepares students for future employment. A critical component of these components is the teaching of work ethics necessary for success in today's world of work. I believe it is important that the CTE teacher have a solid background of the genesis of the work ethic. This chapter is an exploration of the background of work ethic as developed by educators and philosophers. I have summarized the chapter by a presentation of a list of salient work ethic descriptors taken from my Occupational Work Ethic Inventory©.

9.1 INTRODUCTION

The history of the work ethic is most often introduced as beginning with the industrial revolution. The oft mentioned "Protestant work ethic" is tied to "toiling for God's will" as mentioned in the Bible and with religious leaders such as Martin Luther, dating to the 1500's (Brickman, 1983; Tilgher, 1965). It is my belief though, that working hard is an innate trait that exists in all of us. And like the natural instincts that are attributed to animals, we all want to work hard, to contribute,

to be part of the whole, a member of the team, in a word—accepted.

Acceptance is a need that is part of our culture, both societal and occupational. I often tell my students that we are the sons and daughters of the sons and daughters of the survivors—that is, those that were accepted. And it is here that the first rule of genetics kicks in, to wit—"if your parents did not have any children—chances are you won't either". Of course, I say this tongue in cheek but profoundly, it is true. We had to be accepted or we did not promulgate.

So if we accept that what I say is true then—where did this concept of work ethic begin? The

DOI: 10.4018/978-1-61520-747-3.ch009

obvious answer is that it began with survival. We toiled to survive and for the joy of relationships, family, and—acceptance by our peers. Work by definition was a daily part of our lives and one could say *was* our life. We didn't think twice about it

It was only when the first writers and philosophers had the time and the luxury to think about work that work became separate from life. It must be noted that the reason they had the time was that much of their work was done by others—usually slaves. These great men could literally sit back all day and just think about work. Now that's a luxury.

But for the rest of us, the so-called "working class", we worked to survive. Some suggest that the Protestant work ethic was invented to assure that a percentage of one's wages would be given to support the church. This took work beyond survival and gave it a higher purpose. "Serving God's will" became the reason to work (Tilgher, 1965).

The industrial revolution created an even greater dependence on the Protestant work ethic for worker acceptance since work was taken off of the farm and out of the household and into the factories in the city. The concept of hard work followed the young men and women reared on the simple farm values of hard work and diligence to duty, to the sterile, alien concept of working in a factory. Millions of workers migrated to the city and relied on their religion to carry them through the "drudgery of work" (Rodgers, 1979).

But what about the workers and cultures not part of the initial industrial revolution? This group includes what we today call third world countries such as the giants of India and China, and also the many smaller countries of Africa and South America. These countries are only now discovering the industrial revolution in their cultures. This is certainly a struggle for the governments of these developing nations but evidence of the rural work ethic is seen where these citizens immigrate to developed countries like the USA and form the basis of workers with a good work ethic.

In the USA many of these immigrants have come from Mexico and the Central American countries.

Between the world wars, an American educator, Bennett (1926) commented on the history of industrial (career and technical) education when he claimed that a stage of civilization was from savagery to barbarism. Earlier historians claimed that instruction became conscious but not necessarily organized (Davidson, 1901). Others pointed out that there has been no documented theory or system in the teaching of arts and crafts, even through the period of the ancient Egyptians (Maspero, 1985).

But, how can this be? How did workers in the world become so technologically literate? In the classic "how did we get here from there" question, an exploration of what ifs, and how dids might help us with some insight into not only our roots but our relevance and importance in the history and development of the world. Following is a treatise of these issues supported with historical reflections that offer to explain the logical development, success, and tragedies that have preceded the development of work ethics in career and technical education.

9.2 BACKGROUND

The work ethic in the United States is a construct of work that has a long history of evolution, with roots in religious concepts from Biblical times, Calvinist and Protestant asceticism, and the Industrial Revolution (Hill, 1996; Niles & Harris-Bowlsbey, 2004; Tilgher, 1965). Major theoretical changes in religious views of work and the impact of those changes on societal perspectives across decades have affected the attitudes people hold toward work and its value. In addition, the American work ethic continues to evolve as a result of current events and their socio-cultural impact. The goal of this chapter is to delineate paradigm shifts, especially recent ones, in the American work ethic as a means of discerning and understanding implications for work and life today, with special emphasis on how these considerations and implications affect the work of career counselors.

Evolution of the American work ethic may be viewed as a series of paradigm shifts or changes in the way people view work, beginning in biblical times and undergoing developmental changes affected by various historical and socio-cultural events. The roots of the work ethic belong to theological perspectives on work ranging from Scripture, most notably the Book of Genesis in the Bible through the Protestant Reformation and Calvinism. The modern, secularized view of the work ethic can be traced through Weber's (1958) contribution of the theory of the Protestant work ethic.

Americans' perceptions of the Protestant work ethic have been influenced by changes brought about by developments in capitalism and industrialization. In the last 100 years alone, the women's suffrage movement, desegregation, and an emphasis on cultural diversity represent "new" paradigm shifts that have certainly changed the perspective of work in the United States. Over time, work has increasingly become what Weber described as the compelling "ethos" in American culture and, arguably, in all human life (Weber, 1958). These paradigm shifts, ranging from religious perspectives on work to the secularization of work, have contributed to changing views of work over time, continue today, and will continue to have a profound impact on career and technical education. Time will tell if the events and aftermath of September 11, 2001, and recent corporate scandals lead to continued major shifts in the work ethic.

As a dominant social norm in the United States, the "traditional" work ethic of job commitment and achievement, of short-term pain for long-term gain, is often strongly held and highly valued. However, Brown (2000) noted that little direct research has emphasized the nature of the work ethic for members of cultural and social minority groups. Typically, research has focused on the work ethic as a cultural norm principally affected by formative socialization experiences during childhood and adolescence. A moral value is placed on the worth of work, and this attitude is internalized by children through experiencing and observing the attitudes and actions of family and peers at work (Brown, 2000; Hill, 1996; Hill & Petty, 1995).

Cultural values certainly have an impact on individual development, including career development (Super, 1957), however, because cultural values differ, the importance of work, among other life tasks, cannot be assumed universally to conform to the Protestant work ethic. Therefore, it is essential to consider whether the current concept of the work ethic can be accurately, uniformly applied to all individuals in the "salad bowl" of the United States today.

Modern ideas of the work ethic might be best conceptualized as a kind of uneasy compromise. Implicit in the understanding of the work ethic is what might be perceived as a social contract consisting of some key promises: the ability to afford necessities and luxuries, the idea that an individual's basic needs will be provided for, physical safety, economic gain, and psychological fulfillment. The compromise for individuals seems to be that, if they work hard, honestly, and well, these benefits will undoubtedly accrue (Rifkin, 1995). In other words, hard work pays off in the long term; however, in the United States, as well as in the rest of the world, economic turbulence, unemployment, underemployment, corporate downsizing, and scandals in accounting and management, such as those attributed to Enron, WorldCom, Tyco, and others in 2002, seem to at least threaten, if not invalidate, the old promises of the work ethic. Is the social contract dead?

9.3 WORK

To determine today's work ethic, it is helpful to analyze work from a systems approach. By this method, the history of the development of work and the work ethic has moved through three stages:

- Humans → Work.
- Humans → Work → Education.
- Humans → Education → Work.

These stages are simply that we worked to survive; then we developed knowledge (education) from our work; then we implemented education to foster work in our young. This progression has been for the purpose of survival of our species.

It can correctly be said that education for work has been the oldest and most important means of education. Today we are a bit more complex. Work provides us with:

- Survival.
- Economic means.
- Social satisfaction.
- Psychological needs.

One assumption many of us have about Career and Technical Education is that this structured, organized educational system helps people accept work. However, I would argue that the total educational system should be geared in the process of developing satisfying and productive work habits and a healthy work ethic. We work because we need to work. The need may be economic but even if this need is removed we still need to work. Work is that part of life that gives us status. Work constitutes the centrality of people's lives (Florida, 2002).

Work can be described as physical and/or mental effort directed toward some end or purpose. There are different view points toward work:

Figure 1. Play-burden continuum

Work:

- Is continuous and leads to additional activity.
- Is productive and produces goods and services.
- Requires physical and mental exertion.
- Has socio-psychological aspects.
- Performed on a regular or scheduled basis.
- Requires a degree of constraint.
- Performed for a personal purpose (intrinsic or extrinsic).

To distinguish between work and play we must define productive work. Productive work is performed when physical and mental efforts result in a product for common use. Productive work becomes our chief occupation or vocation when achieved for the purpose of making a living (Wirth, 1983).

The difference between work and play is not is the type of activity but its purpose. People can have a good work ethic for play, take football players for example, but not for the burden of work. Play is work done for its intrinsic values without the extrinsic rewards. Burden is work done for its extrinsic values without reaping intrinsic rewards.

This continuum is displayed in Figure 1.

9.4 RATIONALE OF CAREER AND TECHNICAL EDUCATION TOWARD WORK

Work is the foundation of life and work is the basic rationale of CTE. Work is the reason for the existence of CTE. CTE is *one* phase of the process of education for work. Evidence of the work of people gives us a history of people. People learn to work and CTE must play a vital role in instructing people *how* to work. An essential component of knowing how to work is to develop a good work ethic (Petty, 1995c).

The dynamics of education for work reveals that our primary and elementary schools do very little to entice young people to work. Yet we will spend 75% of our time in our lives working. And very little is known about the socio-psychological aspects of work. People need to appreciate the value of work and its value in their lives (Petty, 1995b).

9.5 THE MEANING OF WORK IN EARLY CIVILIZATIONS

9.5.1 Greeks

Homer has been a productive source of archaeological as well as sociological information concerning the early ancient Greek culture. He related that the gods hated mankind and out of spite condemned man to toil (Bennett, 1926; Mosse, 1969). To the ruling classes of ancient Greece, work was a curse. Tilgher (1965) quotes Xenophon as calling work the painful price that the gods charged mankind for living. In most cases, the meaning of work in early civilizations was derived primarily from two sources: social and religious.

The early Greeks, whose political organization was structured around the city-state, believed that the citizens should own businesses or supervise their own agricultural efforts. Farming, being a necessary factor for the survival of society, became exempt from the stigma attached to other forms of work (Borow, 1973). They deplored the mechanical arts as brutalizing the mind until the mind was unfit for the thinking of great truths or the practicing of virtue (Bennett, 1926; Mosse, 1969). Free artisans and craftsmen were scorned

and the mechanical and menial tasks were done by slaves. Slavery itself, in the classic civilization, was not regarded as wrong, morally or otherwise. In fact, slavery was a means of getting the bulk of the heavy, undesirable labor done (Dougherty & Kurke, 2003; Kazanas et al., 1973).

9.5.2 Romans

Cicero, a notable Roman philosopher and statesman, found two occupations worthy of a free man. The first was agriculture and the second was commerce, with all other pursuits being vulgar and dishonoring. Handcraft, the work of artisans, and the crafting of material goods were held in low esteem. As conquerors of the Greek civilization, they assimilated most of the Greeks' attitudes about the arts, science, and social values into their own culture (Tilgher, 1965).

9.5.3 Hebrews

The early Hebrews, as did the early Greeks, considered work as a painful drudgery. However, while the Greeks could see no reason why man should be condemned to labor other than at the whim of the Gods, the Hebrews felt that work was necessary to expiate the original sin committed by Adam and Eve in their earthly paradise (Petty & Brewer, 2008; Tilgher, 1965).

Since most early Christians were Jews, primitive Christianity followed the Jewish tradition and regarded work as a punishment imposed upon man by God because of man's original sin. However, to this negative doctrine of expiation was added one positive consideration. Not only was work necessary to provide expiation and the existence of many of the necessities, but it was a means for accumulating enough to share with one's fellow man (Borow, 1973). Upon work, then, was reflected some of the divine light that stems from charity. Riches shared with the poor were considered to bring God's blessing upon the giver (Tilgher, 1965).

To work and share the products of work with others (charity) was desirable. To eliminate the middleman and to allow the recipient of the sharing to share directly in the work was even more desirable. Thus, it became the duty of the Christian brotherhood to give work to the unemployed so that no man need remain in idleness. A refusal to work resulted in the offender being cast out of the community for the good of both the community and the offender (Kazanas et al., 1973; Tilgher, 1965). This early Christian doctrine recognized no separation between mental, bodily, or physical work. Despite these foundations, no intrinsic value was yet recognized in work. Therefore, work remained a means to a worthy end (Borow, 1973; Tilgher, 1965).

Early Christian leaders generally held a low opinion of physical labor. The artisans and craftsmen were not tied to the land; therefore, they were free to sell their services to the highest bidder. By keeping the processes and methods highly guarded secrets of their trade, they were able to control, to an extent, the commerce and the trades. Thus, greater diligence led to a degree of wealth that enabled a middle class to form about commerce and the trades (Mosse, 1969; Tilgher, 1965).

9.6 THE PROTESTANT ETHIC OF WORK

Tilgher (1965) cites Martin Luther, the first great Protestant reformer, as having held that work was both the universal base of society and the real distinction between social classes. Luther has been depicted as having little sympathy with commerce because it was a means of using work to pass from one social class to another. To rise in the social hierarchy was, to Luther, against God's laws (Borow, 1973). However, Luther's concept held that work was a form of serving God, and there was just one best way to serve God, and that was to do most perfectly the work of one's calling (Borow, 1973; Tilgher, 1965). To promote

this concept, Bennett (1926) portrays Luther as having promoted formal schooling in religious matters for all classes.

9.7 CALVINISM, PURITANISM AND THE PROTESTANT WORK ETHIC

Calvinism, as the next great Protestant movement, adopted a new attitude toward work. Borrowing from Luther's concept, Calvinism held that it was the will of God for all, including the rich and noble, to work. In addition, none should lust after the fruits of their labor—wealth, possessions, or luxurious living. However, all were obligated to God to extract the maximum amount of wealth from work. Therefore, the greater the profit, the more God was pleased and vice-versa (Tilgher, 1965). Eventually people experienced the paradox of profit. It was a paradox that ceaseless effort to acquire riches as opposed to ceaseless renunciation of the fruits of these efforts created profit (Nosow & Form, 1962).

Calvinism was the basis for most other Protestant movements but was also the foundation for the modern factory. Although the division of labor was not directly a result of the Protestant movement, the diligent application of human energy, regardless of the project upon which the efforts were spent, enabled the division of labor to occur within the Christian society (Tilgher, 1965).

Puritanism developed from Calvinism and evolved still further into the Protestant work ethic. It taught that one's duty was to extract the greatest possible gains from work, not from the love of money, nor to satisfy the thirst of pleasure, but so that an increased blessing would fall upon the head of the next needy person. Success, it was held, was most easily proven by profit. It was simply put that with the application of diligence and the choosing of occupation, God would reward you with greater profits. Puritanism opened to all the prospect of unlimited profit as a consecration of holy attributes (Tilgher, 1965).

Unlike Luther's concept of societal rigidity, both the Puritan and Calvinist form of Protestantism considered it no virtue to remain satisfied with the class or occupation into which one was born. On the contrary, it was a holy duty to seek the greatest possible return from one's life (Petty & Brewer, 2008; Tilgher, 1965).

9.8 THE PROTESTANT ETHIC OF WORK IN THE NEW WORLD

The New England colonies were settled by Puritans seeking religious and commercial freedom. The middle-Atlantic states were largely settled by Calvinists seeking both religious and economic advantages. As reported by Bennett (1926) although some colonies were founded by Catholics, most, including the southeastern states, were founded by various Protestant groups who were seeking not only wealth but freedom from persecution for their religious holdings (1926).

Certain religious obligations became matters of law as the colonies grew and prospered. Bennett (1926) gives examples of early laws which provided for the training of orphans and indigenous children, including Indians, at the public's expense. Bennett (1926) and Barlow (1967) both cite examples of laws requiring master craftsmen to provide certain types of training for their apprentices in reading, writing, and the arts in addition to mastery of their crafts. Thus began in the Americas the influence of the church on a Protestant work ethic.

In the western hemisphere, several conditions existed that were beneficial to the establishment and strengthening of the work ethic which became a powerful concept.. First, as reported by Weber (1958) strong feelings regarding the benefits of diligent work and prosperity were ingrained in both the moral and religious fiber of the colonists. The colonies were largely peopled by those who had everything to gain and comparatively little to lose. A third factor was the vast opportunity

in land and natural resources that could enable almost anyone to succeed who was willing to put forth the effort. Even the concept of indentured servitude was but a postponement of the probability of ultimate success. It provided a means of getting to the land where success was so probable (Barlow, 1967).

However, another factor entered into the evolving work ethic. This was the factor of education and training. Partly because of the availability of wealth, the established Protestant ethics, the ingrained social attitudes and regard for diligent work, and the social mobility possible in a culture without distinct and traditional cultural castes, many colonists wished for their sons and daughters better training and education than they had received (Bennett, 1926; Barlow, 1967). Colleges, universities, mechanics institutions and other forms of formal education appeared throughout the colonies (Bennett, 1926). Education and wealth were the means to social ascension (Barlow, 1967). This upward mobility was impossible in other societies, but was made possible in America. Therefore, the American working class achieved what no other working class had achieved in history. The working class became the middle class and the more they worked, the more and greater success and upward mobility they enjoyed (Nosow & Form, 1962; Petty & Brewer, 2008).

9.9 PESTALOZZI'S CLASS STRUCTURE, WORK ETHIC AND CAREER AND TECHNICAL EDUCATION

Johann Heinrich Pestalozzi (1746-1827) was an important figure because he linked the impact of education with the harsh class structure in Europe. In the latter 18th century financial wealth in most European nations established a man or woman's future life. Having wealth and title guaranteed access to higher education, preferment, and entry into higher paying professional fields. In the first decade of the nineteenth century, Napoleon initiated a short-lived reaction to traditional inclusive education by opening up French schools to any students who had the ambition and drive to enter a college or university, and graduate. Pestalozzi believed that education could level many of the disadvantages the poor had in life by providing them important job skills which would lead them out of poverty (Silber, 1973).

Pestalozzi believed that a child's innate faculties should be developed in accordance with nature. He believed that the work ethic, along with equal education, could be the key for the poor to advance in society. His teaching principles emphasized accurate observation of concrete objects, moving from the familiar to the new, and the creation of a loving and emotionally secure environment. These ideas, revolutionary in his day, subsequently influenced the development of progressive pedagogy in Europe and the United States (Silber, 1973).

9.10 THE INDUSTRIAL REVOLUTION AND THE WORK ETHIC

The accumulation of wealth led gradually to the establishment of large factories where labor could be divided so that semi-skilled individuals could perform repetitive elements of a job using apprentices. A working class was thereby initiated. With the advent of the industrial revolution and the vast flooding of the metropolitan areas with unemployed rural population, the old values, (such as the lord of the land exhibiting a degree of kindness and care) were eliminated. With the money economy, factory lords found a way to get around the traditional burden of responsibility through the payment of wages (Bennett, 1926; Tilgher, 1965).

The transition of serfs to workers was accomplished, thus creating a lower class composed largely of serfs and workers, middle class composed largely of artisans and merchants, and an upper class composed of the landed and titled nobility and the wealthy. This in itself was an innovation in that a person with luck and diligence could move, by virtue of accruing wealth, from the lowest class to within the limits of the upper class. This transition from feudal to industrial society, however, required several centuries (Bennett, 1926; Runes, 1951; Tilgher, 1965).

The industrial revolution was actually a result of several factors regarding the production of goods. These factors were the; division of labor; advent of power; increase in commerce; and modern transportation of goods:

- **Division of Labor.** The first was the concept of the division of labor which originated during the 14th and 15th centuries when semi-skilled workers repetitively worked on only one or two segments of the total assembly.
- **Advent of Power.** The second factor that promulgated the industrial revolution was the advent of power. Power, primarily in the form of water and steam power, enabled factories to spring up in places where the application of power could be made directly to endless numbers of machines devoted to the production of goods. The relative inefficiency of these 18th century machines by present day standards is academic; the fact which is important is that they enabled an industrial class to produce goods far beyond their ability to consume them, thus creating great surpluses leading to increased commerce and trade.
- **Increase in Commerce.** A third factor in the increase of commerce and industrialism was the innovation of interchangeable parts commonly attributed to the efforts of Eli Whitney in the early 19th century
- **Transportation.** The fourth factor in the industrial revolution was the use of power to move goods and pieces from one station to another, i.e. transportation. This reduced

human involvement and conserved effort in non-producing activities. The continuous processing of flour by Oliver Evans in the early 1800's and the assembly line of Henry Ford in the early 1900's are examples of the innovations brought about during the industrial revolution.

A number of authors have pointed out that one of the results which affected working during the industrial revolution was the intensification of the division of labor (Venn, 1964). The implications of the intense division of labor for the purpose of increasing production were to bring specific work processes to an ever increasing fragmentation. This removed the worker further and further from participating in the final product (Venn, 1964). This factor resulted in the change in work attitudes from those that existed in the sixteenth, seventeenth and eighteenth centuries to the emerging new work attitudes of today. Hoyt, (1972) reflected upon these changes as follows:

Ironically, those very changes that have increased our potential for work productivity—mass production, automation, cybernation and occupational technology—have resulted in making in the work ethic, in its classic form, less meaningful and seemingly less appropriate for the individual worker (p. 67).

9.11 BEGINNINGS OF THE EROSION OF THE WORK ETHIC

It is easily observed from a comparison of the production processes of the early seventeenth century and modern procedures that work had changed; however, the extent and the type of change in the work ethic is not as easily seen. Certain homilies such as "A task well done is its own reward," compared with the more recent, "Do unto others before they do unto you," reflect some of the changes in the work ethic. It is logical to

assume that as the work and society changed, the work ethic also changed (Petty & Brewer, 2008).

As the rate of production increased with industrial innovations in new production processes such as automation and fragmentation of labor, industries experienced increased profits. It was thought that the decreased manual labor and a reduction in the hours of work for the workers along with increased prosperity and freedom from toil would yield happier more satisfied workers. However, an unexpected twist happened. As industrial leaders deprived workers of involvement in the total production process as well as the possibility of self-realization through work, workers became more dissatisfied with work. This result has presented problems far beyond those imagined by the people who felt they were freeing humans for more honorable labors.

An earlier factor affecting the erosion of the traditional work ethic was the willingness of immigrants to provide cheap labor and to ultimately advance in a new society. Immigrants from countries undergoing political revolution, famine, or vast social pressures in the seventeenth, eighteenth and nineteenth centuries would literally sell themselves into servitude complete with their entire families for a period of time in order to move to the new world. These immigrants would gladly live in crowded tenements, work under less than desirable conditions and for substandard wages in order to provide themselves with a means of transportation to the new world and a basic amount with which to start once their condition of servitude was finished (Kazanas et al., 1973).

However, a historical discussion of the development of the work ethic is only part of the discussion of prevalent work ethics. Just as important is the individual's development. Some say that we are born with a strong work ethic and that it is in the genes (Weber, 1958). A more practical conclusion is to look at the process of human development as a source for developing our own work ethic and that of our students.

9.12 PSYCHO-SOCIAL DEVELOPMENT

Erik Erikson (1964) published a seminal paper on learning by stages. Erikson argued that children undergo eight stages (or ages) of psycho-social development and that these changes reflect psychological factors and subsequently their work ethic. Like Piaget, Erikson's division was based upon specific developmental concerns (Coyhis, 1997; Erikson, 1997; Neysmith-Roy, & Kleisinger, 1997; Romero et al., 1990).

Erikson's Eight Stages of Development are:

- **Stage 1:** Trust versus Mistrust (Birth to 18th Months). In this stage, children develop levels of trust based upon their growing experience with their environment. Material dependency is important to this stage because most of an infant's direct needs are based upon the mother's attention toward the child.
- **Stage 2:** Autonomy versus Shame and Doubt (18 months to 3 Years). The "terrible twos" is an appropriate term for this period because young toddler seek to establish their independence, to grab or hold onto things, and to come and go as they please.
- **Stage 3:** Initiative versus Guilt (3 to 6 Years). In this stage, children begin to develop more advanced motor and language abilities. Interaction with other family members is very important during this stage. Through that contact, the child develops attitudes and belief systems.
- **Stage 4:** Industry versus Inferiority (6 to 12 Years). Teachers and peers become more important to students than immediate family as children enter school and to develop peer friendships and other relationships.
- **Stage 5:** Identity versus Role Conclusion (12 to 18 Years). In this period of self-exploration, teenagers grope with confusion about sexual identity and the future. Teens remain confused about roles.
- **Stage 6:** Identity versus Isolation (Young Adult). Young men or women develop a desire to establish personal relations with others (especially of the opposite sex). Erikson noted that failure to establish such relationship resulted in feelings of inadequacy, insecurity, etc.
- **Stage 7:** Generativity versus Stagnation (Middle Adulthood). Men or women begin to think about having children, being able to afford them, and giving them a good life. Adults unable to work through these issues tend to become self-absorbed.
- **Stage 8:** Integrity versus Despair (Late Adulthood). In this stage, men and women reconsider their lives and consider their mortality. Those satisfied with their lives tend to feel positively and those dissatisfied are depressed with feelings of despair.

Erikson (1964) based his system on personal, subjective experiences. Hence, there may be questions about the validity of each stage. However, Erikson's Eight Stages do offer some perspectives about the emotional issues of teenagers and adults which are relevant to the development of a work ethic. Career and technical education can play a significant, direct role in helping men and women with emotional concerns resolve problem issues. For example, concern about career development and success in Stage Seven may be resolved with career and technical training and preparation. Teachers can use Erikson to identify potential crises in their students' lives.

9.13 FIVE BEHAVIORAL STAGES OF HUMAN DEVELOPMENT

The study of human development was refined to explore the entire human life cycle (Whitney, 1979). Several researchers including Erikson himself (1980) sought to further explain learning and psychological development by exploring thought and behavioral processes within a chronological system. Additionally, researchers such as Benjamin Bloom (1956) and Erik Erikson (1980) linked behavior to age cycles. Each divided the life cycle into periods of development based upon the correlation of behavior or physical characteristics and cognitive and affective development. The five stages of life suggested below demonstrate how a chronology of life in years reflects specific changes in men and women.

- **Stage 1: Growth (birth-14)**
  - Infancy (birth-3). Child makes transition from sensory and tactile perception.
  - Fantasy (4-10). Child begins to explore his/her place in the world as senses mature and child begins basic reasoning.
  - Interest (11-12). Child's identity is established; the child explores interests related to future career potential.
  - Capacity (13-14). Child develops adult motor skills and critical thinking skills.
- **Stage 2: Exploration (15-24)**
  - Tentative (15-17). Psycho-sexual identity matures as young man/woman develops goals and career objects.
  - Transition (18-21). Early adulthood, man/woman develops work ethic and pursues career objectives; period of psycho-sexual development.
  - Trial (22-24). Career development begins, man/ woman explores relationships.
- **Stage 3: Establishment (25-44)**
  - Trial (25-30). This represents a period of domestication and settling down; man/woman begin planning

for future, retirement, and long-term needs/goals.
  - Advancement (31-44). This is a period of career advancement, change, and renewal; continued planning and long-term goal assessment.
- **Stage 4: Maintenance (45-64)**
  - Achievement (45-55). This is the apex of worker achievement; family development in flux (if children are involved).
  - Plateau (56-61). Workforce advancement is stifled; some anxieties from aging process.
  - Anxiety (62-64). Pre-retirement and income reduction concerns; identity problems for.
  - Workers in transition from work to retirement.
- **Stage 5: Decline (65-on)**
  - Deceleration (65-70). This is a period of worker retirement, financial and health concerns, some quality of life disruption.
  - Retirement (70-on). Anxiety over health issues, family dislocation, and mortality.

9.14 PROCESS OF PSYCHOLOGICAL DEVELOPMENT

Psychological development is a determining factor in the success or failure of students in career and technical training. Bloom's (1956) Taxonomy of Educational Objectives identified three psycho-social factors to human behavior:

- Cognitive Domain.
- Psychomotor Domain.
- Affective Domain.

9.15 COGNITIVE DOMAIN

Bloom (1956) divided the cognitive domain into six component areas, each rising in terms of complexity.

- **Knowledge Ability** to recall information (i.e., memorization of facts, formulate, conjugation).
- **Comprehension Ability** to interpret and translate knowledge (i.e., can understand and use information).
- **Application Ability** to use information to solve problems (i.e., can apply information to form conclusions).
- **Analysis Ability** to break down information and relationships into parts and understand them (i.e. understanding a short story or the difference between related information).
- **Synthesis Ability** to use information to create or develop additional approaches or analyses (i.e., writing a novel or conducting experiments).
- **Evaluation Ability** to compare, contrast, and evaluate information against a specific or given, criterion (i.e., comparing A, B, C, D, F and Pass/Fail grading systems on ACT and SAT scores).

9.16 PSYCHOMOTOR DOMAIN

The Psychomotor Domain deals mainly with the physical, those who are primarily motor coordinated. It is concerned with levels of movement, sensory and tactile development, and physical growth and maturity. Psychomotor functions include basic mobility, physical maturity, and reflexibility (Bloom, 1956).

9.17 AFFECTIVE DOMAIN

The Affective Domain deals with sending and receiving emotions. Students listen, reason with their thoughts, and express their feelings. In discussing the affective domain, educators usually refer to intrinsic and extrinsic reactions to outside stimuli. The response is in the form of an emotion like anger, hatred, love, fear, etc. Emotional maturity and ability to handle problems is a necessary learning skill (Bloom, 1956; Krathwohl, Bloom, & Masia, 1964).

9.18 DEWEY'S INFLUENCE ON THE DEVELOPMENT OF THE WORK ETHIC

An individual's career and technical development consists of sequential patterns largely irreversible, for all who develop normally. Because it is skill based with values competency and skill mastery, career and technical development can be measured in terms of how successfully workers can achieve new skill masteries and update newer skills to remain current. The foundations of career and technical education that are the basis of today's career and technical education can be linked to many influential educators. However, the individual who has probably been the most influential was John Dewey.

John Dewey (1849-1952) was an American philosopher, educator, and psychologist. An 1879 graduate of the University of Vermont, he received his Ph.D. from Johns Hopkins University in 1884. His teachers were G. Stanley Hall, a founder of experimental psychology, and Charles S. Pierce. Dewey was particularly disposed to German philosophic thought, especially the unifying, organic characteristic of the idealism of Hegel, in contrast to British empiricism (Thayer, 1990). Dewey is probably best remembered for four specific contributions: (a) as president of the University of Chicago, he withdrew Chicago from the Big Ten athletic conference; (b) he propagated an Aristotelian teaching/learning approach which emphasized hands-on practical experience (trial and error; direct observation) called "learning by 'Dewy-ing'" or "learning by doing"; (c) he connected chronological human development to the organization of schools by grade and age levels; and (d) he advocated involvement in and elevated importance of the community public school.

9.19 HOW THE WORK ETHIC AND CAREER AND TECHNICAL EDUCATION CONNECT TO THE WORLD

Career and technical education is the study of the nature of people interacting in the arenas of education, work, and society. Philosophical study of career and technical education naturally requires that humankind consider the nature and ontology of existence and humankind's place in the cosmos. To understand order and the need of humankind and to find purpose in life and in work represent the ends of this philosophy (Kazanas et al., 1973; Kneller, 1971).

Four basic points exist:

- To exist: nature of humans.
- To know: nature of education.
- To value: nature of work.
- To inquire: nature of society.

Some components of these systemic ways are: (a) prescriptive style, and (b) analytical style.

Prescriptive Style. Prescriptive evaluation is the act of evaluating actions and events on some common scale or standard. Based on the results, an assessment or interpretation is offered in response. The prescriptive style has six basic components:

- Identifying what something ought to be (must); seeks to establish a basis for establishing standards.
- Assessing value.
- Judging conduct.
- Appraising act.
- Determining qualities that are worthwhile and why.
- Stating the ends that career and technical education ought to follow and the general means it must use to obtain them (Kneller, 1971).

Analytical Style. Analytical evaluation is concerned with causal analysis and comparison or contrast. It attempts to prove given information and facts by close analysis of gaps in what is and is not known. The analytical style focuses on words and meanings by examining concepts such as:

- Cause and effect relationships.
- Mind and cognitive relationships.
- Equality of opportunity.
- Academic freedom.
- Qualify known data.
- Identifying inconsistencies between beliefs and actions (Kneller, 1971).

9.20 THE LINK OF VALUES TO WORK ETHIC AND CAREER AND TECHNICAL EDUCATION

Career and technical education is linked to values in a variety of ways. Axiology concerns objective and subjective values that are relative to personal desires. To be valuable is to be valued by somebody. Therefore, whatever is valuable is so because individuals assign a certain value to it. Some values are absolute and external, constant, never changing. For example, charity is a value that is good for people anytime. Values are relative to people's desires. Some say there is a fixed hierarchy of values—spiritual on top, material on bottom. Others say there is no fixed hierarchy of values.

9.21 VALUE TYPES

There are four value types. Each type, a definition and its characteristics are listed below:

*   **Idealism**—values and ethics are absolute. They are:
    a.   Not made by people.
    b.   Part of the universe.
    c.   Fundamental and do not change.
*   **Realism**—that there is a universal moral law that is:
    a.   Basically permanent and reliable.
    b.   Established by God (religious).
    c.   Established by nature (scientific).
    d.   Timeless, unchangeable, and universal.
*   **Pragmatic**—values are relative to the situation and time (Kneller, 1971). They state that:
    a.   People must be flexible and willing to change their values based on consequences.
    b.   Ethics are not permanent but must change.
*   **Existentialistic**—views are individualistic and lack clear-cut patterns:
    a.   Not to choose is a choice; and one must choose.
    b.   Do not look for the way, look for your way.

9.22 THE LINK OF ETHICS AND LOGIC TO WORK ETHIC

Ethics. Ethics is the philosophic study of moral values. The study of ethics deals with the value question "How ought one to behave?" This question was primarily linked to religions in the past,

derived from the authoritative wording of sacred writings. In recent years, ethics have become secular—naturalistic or relativistic—as a result of separation of church and state. Eliminating the teaching of religion in schools has eliminated a basic source of society's moral values. A search for substitutes has been based on the intuitivism theory and naturalistic theory.

Intuitivistic values are apprehended immediately as an inborn moral sense. Naturalistic values are derived from people's needs, desires, and indirect needs. Therefore, values should be determined on the basis of consequences (Kneller, 1971).

9.23 LOGIC AND EDUCATION

Psychology helps people to learn and understand the process of thinking, but they must study logic as well. Psychology deals with the nature of thinking, whereas logic deals with the nature of orderly thinking.

9.24 TWO FORMS OF LOGIC

Deductive Reasoning. Deductive reasoning is the process whereby conclusions are derived from exterior evidence (general to specific). Students reach conclusions by piecing information together.

Inductive Reasoning. Inductive reasoning is the process of examining conclusions by figuring out the evidence for those conclusions. An example of inductive reasoning would be trying to figure out why something happened by breaking the event down and rechecking everything (specific to general).

9.25 CONCLUSION

Surely, global competition has created a lot of pressure for establishing and sustaining a positive work ethic. Traditionally, a person's work ethic was related to production and historically has been established during the post industrial revolution period and the change from an agrarian society to an industrial society. Workers in developed countries were engaged in the making of something of value and learned to develop their work ethic from this basis. Increasingly though production work has been "outsourced" to developing countries where labor is cheaper, leaving the preponderance of jobs to a more educated, technologically skilled workforce. This global transfer has created new fields of work which are not directly related to production (Petty & Brewer, 2005).

The great rise of service workers in such fields as teaching, police and fire protection, medical assistance, and many others, not only have a recognized place in our society but have become specialized at a rate consistent with the industrial advancements made through the use of modern technology. In addition, the services of these workers have been extended to include the areas of convenience, leisure and entertainment. This has been a result of the increased productivity of the American worker along with an increased standard of living and pay rate. However, these increases in the worker's manner of living have also been brought about in part by the decrease of his personal involvement in his way of earning a living. Thus, the situation has been established to gradually erode the traditional work ethic by lessening the personal involvement and commitment to work. Work, then becomes more and more a means of financing entertainment, a high standard of living and other non-work activities.

The white collar worker generally has been held in higher regard as to status and prestige than the blue collar worker, partly because his is associated with the wealthy and partly because of the work he is called upon to do. The application of earlier Christian ethics to this meant that the white collar worker was therefore more successful and his job more desirable than that of his blue collar counterpart. In addition, the necessity of increased education to deal with complexities of nonproduction work such as machine design, resource management, planning, marketing, and other factors involved in modern commerce have helped to establish the desirability of the white collar job over that of the blue collar job in the minds of many people (Kazanas et al., 1973).

On the other hand, the rise in the cost for skilled labor prepared the way for the rise in the per unit production cost which in turn made it necessary to have more automated production facilities, more efficient management and greater efficiency from those workers retained in the production sequences. This makes separating today's blue collar workers from white collar workers more and more difficult.

The traditional work ethic, however, is undergoing a radical transformation, especially in the minds of young workers. Changing attitudes of young people in conjunction with changing economic times and conditions are presenting greater demands for change. Herzberg supported the concept of change but comments that for industrial workers in our world of work, where work is a means of providing the way of life rather than the thing desired in itself, the traditional work ethic is being replaced by an avoidance ethic (Herzberg, Mausner, & Snyderman, 1959). Hoyt (1972) believed that work ethic will be replaced by the concept of "work values."

Still another variable affecting the work ethic as a result of our modern industrial society is the choice between the work ethic that built this nation and the characteristics that could cause the American character to weaken. Although the middle class is the working class in America, poverty is a persistent problem. An increasing number of people are being added to welfare budgets which have been growing at a rate that threatens to bankrupt state and federal budgets. However this notion is refuted by authors such as Rodgers (1979) who argued that the work ethic was a value that Americans refused to reject during the industrial revolution. Indeed the work ethic poisoned all efforts to render industrial toil more humane (p. 10).

Rodgers (1979) hails the efforts of the beginning worker who embraces hard work as a generous and prosperous system. And yet there are those who feel we should spend more money for meeting increasing needs and providing greater services to help those in need. Goodwin (1973) reported that this is contrasted with those who feel that too much is presently being spent and most of what is spent is going to support people who receive more money from welfare than from any form of employment. While there are questions relating to the interpretation of work and the desire to work on the part of some Americans, Goodwin (1973) went on to state that the work ethic is strong among the poor and also among welfare recipients.

Indications are that the work ethic is changing and is being challenged by several forces of modern society. America appears to reject the notion that work is good in itself and has intrinsic value to the individual worker. More and more people are retiring early in both the blue collar and white collar categories. The work week has been reduced so that more emphasis is placed upon non-work or leisure activities. The increased rates in standards of living have promoted a new hedonism from one facet of the population and anti-materialistic reactions from other groups. These factors, in conjunction with factors developed from automation and the elimination of jobs, are jeopardizing the heritage of the traditional work ethic which states that work in itself is important and has value (Csikszentmihalyi, 2003).

9.26 SUMMARY

In 1991 I attempted to consolidate the factors of work ethic that affect students of career and technical education (Petty, 1993). From this effort I developed the Occupational Work Ethic Inventory© (OWEI©). This instrument has been used in several studies and continues to be a critical tool for use by educators to identify work habits, skills and attitudes necessary for successful work, i.e. the work ethic. Though this chapter does not allow for a full and thorough explanation of the OWEI development, I want to present a summary of the most recent salient factors revealed by our research.

To summarize prevalent work ethics in career and technical education, I have compiled the following list of items from an analysis of recent data collected from my Occupational Work Ethic Inventory© (OWEI©). A factor analysis of data revealed items loaded on four factors: Actively Caring; Workplace Resilience; Organizational Commitment; and Workplace Resistance. This analysis was from data collected from workers and their supervisors and reflected their perceptions of exhibiting a good work ethic (Petty & Hill, 2005). There is no fee for use of the inventory and to date I have not sold the rights to a proprietary agent for their sole use. To use the OWEI for your research or to enhance classroom skills, please contact me at gpetty@utk.edu.

9.27 OCCUPATIONAL WORK ETHIC INVENTORY FACTORS

- Actively Care
  - courteous
  - friendly
  - cheerful
  - considerate
  - pleasant
  - cooperative
  - helpful
  - likeable
  - devoted
  - loyal
  - well groomed
  - patient
  - appreciative
  - hard working

- modest
- emotionally stable
- stubborn
- Workplace Resilience
  - perceptive
  - productive
  - resourceful
  - initiating
  - ambitious
  - efficient
  - effective
  - enthusiastic
  - dedicated
  - persistent
  - accurate
  - conscientious
  - independent
  - adaptable
  - persevering
  - orderly
- Organizational Commitment
  - following directions
  - following regulations
  - dependable
  - reliable
  - careful
  - honest
  - punctual
- Workplace Resistance
  - rude
  - selfish
  - devious
  - irresponsible
  - careless
  - negligent
  - depressed
  - tardy
  - apathetic

REFERENCES

Barlow, M. L. (1967). *History of industrial education in the United States*. Peoria, Illinois: Chas. A. Bennett.

Bennett, C. A. (1926). *History of manual and industrial education up to 1870*. Illinois: Chas. A. Bennett Co., Inc.

Bloom, B. S. (1956). *Taxonomy of educational objectives: The classification of educational goals. Handbook 1: The cognitive domain*. New York: David McKay Co., Inc.

Borow, H. (Ed.). (1973). *Career guidance for a new age*. Boston: Houghton Mifflin.

Brickman, W. W. (1983). The educational evangelist of Eisleben: Martin Luther (1483-1546). *Western European Education, 15*(3), 3–35.

Brown, D. (2000). The role of work and cultural values in occupational choice, satisfaction, and success: A theoretical statement. *Journal of Counseling and Development, 80*, 48–56.

Coyhis, D. (1997). The developmental cycle: Teachings on the eight stages of growth of a human being. *Winds of Change, 12*(4), 114–119.

Csikszentmihalyi, M. (2003). The Evolving nature of work. *NAMTA Journal, 28*(2), 87–107.

Davidson, T. (1901). *A history of education*. New York: Charles Scribner's Sons.

Dougherty, C., & Kurke, L. (Eds.). (2003). *The cultures within ancient Greek culture: Contact, conflict, collaboration. Cambridge, UK*. New York: Cambridge University Press.

Erikson, E. H. (1964). *Childhood and society*. New York: Norton.

Erikson, E. H. (1977). *Eight ages of man: Childhood and society*. London: Paladin.

Erikson, E. H. (1980). *Identity and the life cycle.* New York: W. W. Norton & Company.

Erikson, E. H. (1997). *The life cycle completed: Extended version with new chapters on the ninth stage of development by Joan M. Erikson.* Retrieved May 25, 2009, from http://www.csa.com

Florida, R. (2002). *The rise of the creative class.* New York: Basic Books.

Goodwin, L. (1973). Middle-class misperceptions of the high life aspirations and strong work ethic held by the welfare poor. *The American Journal of Orthopsychiatry, 43*(4), 554–564.

Herzberg, F., Mausner, B., & Snyderman, B. B. (1959). *The motivation to work.* New York: Wiley.

Hill, R. B. (1996). Historical context of the work ethic. Retrieved March 10, 2007, from http://www.coe.uga.edu/~rhill/workethic/hist/htm

Hill, R. B., & Petty, G. C. (1995). A new look at selected employability skills: A factor analysis of the occupational work ethic. *Journal of Vocational Education Research, 20*(4), 59–73.

Hollingsworth, C., Brewer, E. B., & Petty, G. C. (2002). Leadership characteristics and work ethic of extension family and consumer science educators. *Journal of Family and Consumer Sciences, 94*(3), 46–55.

Hoyt, K. B. (1972). *Career education: what it is and how to do it.* Salt Lake City. Olympus Publishing Co. (ED 062573).

Kazanas, H. C. (1977). Relationship of job satisfaction and productivity to work values of vocational education graduates. *Journal of Vocational Behavior, 2*(1), 1–10.

Kazanas, H. C., Baker, G. E., Miller, F. M., & Hannah, L. D. 1973. *The meaning and value of work.* Information Series No. 71. Columbus, OH: The Center for Vocational Education, (ED 091 504).

Kneller, G. F. (1971). *Introduction to the philosophy of education.* New York: John Wiley and Sons.

Krathwohl, D. R., Bloom, B. S., & Masia, B. B. (1964). *Taxonomy of educational objectives, handbook II: Affective domain.* New York: David McKay Co., Inc.

Lipset, S. M. (1992). The work ethic, then and now. *Journal of Labor Research, 13*(1), 45–54. doi:10.1007/BF02685449

Maspero, G. C. C. (1985). *Manual of Egyptian archaeology* (Edwards, A. B., Trans.). New York: G. P. Putnam's Sons.

McCortney, A. L., & Engels, D. W. (2003). Revisiting the work ethic in America. *The Career Development Quarterly, 52*(2), 132–140.

Mirels, H. L., & Garrett, J. B. (1971). The protestant work ethic as a personality variable. *Journal of Consulting and Clinical Psychology, 36*(1), 40–44. doi:10.1037/h0030477

Mosse, C. (1969). *Le Travail en Grece et a Rome, English Title: The ancient world at work* (Lloyd, J., Trans.). New York: Norton.

Neysmith-Roy, J. M., & Kleisinger, C. L. (1997). Using biographies of adults over 65 years of age to understand life-span developmental psychology. *Teaching of Psychology, 24*(2), 116–118. doi:10.1207/s15328023top2402_6

Niles, S. G., & Harris-Bowlsbey, J. (2004). *Career Development Interventions in the 21st Century* (2nd ed.). Prentice-Hall.

Nosow, S., & Form, W. H. (1962). *Man, work, and society: A reader in the sociology of occupations.* New York: Basic Books.

Petty, G., Lim, D. H., Yoon, S. W., & Fontan, J. (2008). The effect of self-directed work teams on work ethic. *Performance Improvement Quarterly, 21*(2), 49–63. doi:10.1002/piq.20022

Petty, G. C. (1993). *Development of the occupational work ethic inventory*. Paper presented at the American Vocational Association Conference, Nashville, Tennessee.

Petty, G. C. (1995). Adults in the work force and the occupational work ethic. *Journal of Studies in Technical Careers, 15*(3), 133–140.

Petty, G. C. (1995b). Education and the occupational work ethic. *SAEOPP Journal, 14*(2), 47–58.

Petty, G. C. (1995c). Vocational-technical education and the occupational work ethic. *Journal of Industrial Teacher Education, 32*(3), 45–58.

Petty, G. C. (2009). Psychometric methods for work ethic research: Factor analysis and structural equation modeling . In Wang, V. C. X. (Ed.), *Handbook of research on E-learning applications for career and technical education: Technologies for vocational Training* (pp. 589–602). Hershey, PA: Information Science Reference.

Petty, G. C., & Brewer, E. B. (2005). Perspectives of a health work ethic in a 21st-Century international community. *International Journal of Vocational Education and Training, 13*(1), 93–104.

Petty, G. C., & Brewer, E. B. (2008). Perspectives of a healthy work ethic in a 21st-century international community . In Wang, V. C. X., & King, K. P. (Eds.), *Innovations in career and technical education: Strategic approaches towards workforce competencies around the globe* (pp. 119–131). Charlotte, NC: Information Age Publishing.

Petty, G. C., & Hill, R. B. (1994). Are men and women different? A study of the occupational work ethic. *Journal of Vocational Education Research, 19*(1), 71–89.

Petty, G. C., & Hill, R. B. (2005). Work ethic characteristics: Perceived work ethics of supervisors and workers. *Journal of Industrial Teacher Education, 42*(2), 5–20.

Petty, G. C., & Kazanas, H. C., & Eastman. (1981). Affective work competencies of workers, supervisors, and vocational educators. *Journal of Vocational Education Research, 6*(2), 55–71.

Rifkin, J. (1995). *End of work: Decline of the global labor force and the dawn of the post-market era*. New York: Putnam.

Rodgers, D. T. (1979). *The work ethic in industrial America, 1850-1920*. Chicago, London: University of Chicago Press.

Romero, F., & Others. (1990). Aspects of adult development, the Rossman adult learning inventory: Creating awareness of adult development. *New Directions for Adult and Continuing Education, 45*(1), 3–26. doi:10.1002/ace.36719904503

Runes, D. D. (1951). *The Hebrew impact on Western civilization*. New York: Philosophical Library.

Silber, K. (1973). *Pestalozzi: The man and his work*. New York: Schocken Books Inc. (ED088078)

Super, D. E. (1953). Theory of vocational development. *The American Psychologist, 8*(5), 185–190. doi:10.1037/h0056046

Super, D. E. (1957). *The psychology of careers*. New York: Harper & Row.

Thayer, H. S. (1990). Dewey and the theory of knowledge. *Transactions of the Charles S. Peirce Society, 26*(4), 443–463.

Tilgher, A. (1965). *Homo faber: Work through the ages* (Fisher, D. C., Trans.). Chicago: Regnery.

Venn, G. (1964). *Man, education, and work: Post secondary vocational and technical education*. Washington, D.C.: American Council on Education.

Weber, M. (1958). *The Protestant ethic and the spirit of capitalism* (Parsons, T., Trans.). New York: Scribner's. (Original work published 1904)

Whitney, R. (1979). Beyond Erikson's eight stages. [from http://www.csa.com]. *Counseling and Values*, *23*(3), 174–183. Retrieved May 25, 2009.

Wirth, A. G. (1983). Productive work and learning—In industry and schools. *Teachers College Record*, *85*(1), 43–56.

Chapter 10
Examining the Impact of Tracking on Long-Term Student Outcomes

Edward C. Fletcher Jr.
Illinois State University, USA

Chris Zirkle
Ohio State University, USA

ABSTRACT

The focus of this chapter is to review the literature dealing with the impact of tracking on long-term student outcomes, such as postsecondary education attainment and earnings potential. As a result, this chapter will examine whether the goals of the Carl D. Perkins Vocational and Applied Technology Education Act of 1990 have been met: that is, preparing CTE students for the workforce as well as for postsecondary education. This particular legislative initiative is critical since it was the first endeavor to expand the historical goal of preparing students solely for the workforce. The discussion ends with an articulation of future trends for practice and research.

10.1 INTRODUCTION

Vocational education and academic education has traditionally constituted two separate trajectories stratifying students with low academic promise into vocational education and students with strong academic promise into academic education, along with administering distinct curricula (Castellano, Stringfield, & Stone, 2003; Gordon, 2008; Lewis, 1998; Lynch, 2000; Plank, 2001; Scott & Sarkees-Wircenski, 2008). As a result, vocational education and academic education had separate funding sources and had different objectives (Bragg, 1999; Castellano et al., 2003; Gordon, 2008; Gray, 1999; Gray & Herr, 1998; Lynch, 2000; Plank, 2001; Scott & Sarkees-Wircenski, 2008). According to Lewis (1998):

The practice of dividing the curriculum into academic and vocational aspects, and treating the latter as a default for and those deemed to be ill-suited to the former, has been an enduring staple of educational systems across the globe...those who pursue the vocational route thereby effectively forfeit the opportunity to go on to university and then on to high-status jobs. (p. 284-5)

DOI: 10.4018/978-1-61520-747-3.ch010

However, current educational legislation and comprehensive school reform (CSR) efforts are attempting to re-structure entire schools to promote an increasingly integrated system of CTE and traditional academic education (Castellano et al, 2003; DeLuca, Plank, & Estacion, 2006; Gordon, 2008; Hudson & Hurst, 1999; Scott & Sarkees-Wircenski, 2008). As a result, the objectives of CTE (formerly known as vocational education) have transformed to not only preparing students for the workforce, but for postsecondary education attainment as well (Association for Career and Technical Education [ACTE], 2006; DeLuca et. al, 2006; Gordon, 2008; Hudson & Hurst, 1999; Scott & Sarkees-Wircenski, 2008; Stone & Aliaga, 2005). Despite this recent phenomenon, little research has been rendered examining CTE's impact on students' educational outcomes (Fletcher, 2009; Kulik, 1998). Kulik (1998) indicated the pressing need that exists to study CTE student outcomes by stating, "To decide whether vocational education shortchanges students, we must first know what its results are and whether they differ from results of other programs." (p. 7)

The objectives of this chapter are first to provide a background discussion of federal legislation leading up to the current Carl D. Perkins Career and Technical Education Improvement Act of 2006 that has and continues to shape the goals and direction of CTE. Second, this chapter reviews the literature regarding tracking and long-term student outcomes. Third, this chapter articulates future trends related to tracking, as well as implications for further research.

10.2 BACKGROUND

With the establishment of public schools in the last quarter of the nineteenth century (during the industrial age), philosophical debates proliferated around the issue of classical and practical education programs (Gordon, 2008; Scott & Sarkees-

Wircenski, 2008). Soon after, the enactment of the Smith-Hughes Act of 1917 was instituted. This legislation was the first time the federal government supported and provided funding for vocational education (Jacobs & Grubb, 2003; Stasz & Bodilly, 2004) and marked the initiation of ongoing involvement in its programs. It called for the separation of vocational education from all other curricula in comprehensive high schools. Accordingly, the legislation mandated that vocational education have a separate state board distinguished from the State Board of Education. According to Gordon (2008), "The impact of this separation has been felt through subsequent decades in the development of separate training programs, separate teacher organizations, and separate student organizations" (p. 88). In addition, the objective of vocational education was to prepare youth and adults for the workforce.

The federal government has had a tremendous role in enacting educational legislation since the 1950s (Umpstead, 2008). During the 1950s, legislative initiatives centered around the issue of providing all students with educational opportunities regardless of race, ability, or gender (Hardman & Dawson, 2008). In fact, the 1954 *Brown v. Board of Education* Supreme Court case was pivotal in setting the precedent for equal educational rights for all citizens, and marked the end of segregated schools (Blanchett, Mumford, & Beachum, 2005); therefore, this case overturned the *Plessy v. Ferguson* separate but equal policy. During this time, the Civil Rights movement was occurring. In 1965, the Elementary and Secondary Education Act (ESEA) was enacted to encourage states and local school districts to provide supplemental educational services to schools with large enrollments of economically and educationally disadvantaged students (McDonnell, 2005). In addition, the Individuals with Disabilities Education Act (IDEA) of 1997 mandated that all students have access to the general education curriculum (Courtade & Ludlow, 2008).

Legislation for vocational education, in the 1960s, responded to societal concerns as well. In 1963, the Vocational Education Act was passed. This piece of legislation was in alignment with the ESEA of 1965, in that it designated programs for economically and educationally disadvantaged students (Scott & Sarkees-Wircenski, 2008). The objective of the legislation was to ensure that individuals of all ages and of all backgrounds would have access to workforce preparation.

In response to the lack of quality in education, a number of reports and educational legislation initiatives have been implemented since the 1980s. *A Nation at Risk*, a report written by The National Commission on Excellence in Education (NCEE, 1983), was written to address the heightened concern for educational quality and articulated the need for transformation in education (Hardman & Dawson, 2008). Concomitantly, the U.S. was experiencing increased pressure due to high unemployment, high inflation, and concern for international competitiveness (Harris & Herrington, 2006). As a result, the NCEE (1983) recommended that: (a) schools increase graduation requirements; (b) that schools administer more rigorous and measurable standards with heightened expectations for student performance and conduct; (c) that schools spend more time with students to learn the basics; (d) that postsecondary education institutions improve the preparation of teachers; and (e) that teachers and elected officials ensure the implementation of the new standards.

Meanwhile, the Carl D. Perkins Vocational and Applied Technology Education Act of 1990 was enacted ([an amendment to the Carl D. Perkins Vocational Act of 1984], Gordon, 2008). This name change was significant in that it was the first legislation that emphasized the integration of traditional academic and vocational content needed to equip students with the skills to compete in a technologically advanced global society (Jacobs & Grubb, 2003; King, Schexnayder, &

Gourgey, 2005; Lewis & Cheng, 2006; Silverberg, Warner, Fong, & Goodman, 2004). Thus, the Carl D. Perkins Vocational and Applied Technology Education Act had a new vision that promoted CTE as a vehicle that not only equipped students with the skills to enter the workforce, but also provided academic rigor to prepare them for postsecondary education (Hudson & Hurst, 1999; Rojewski, 2002).

The recommendations of the NCEE led to fundamental changes in the educational arena with many efforts to reform education. The most recent and comprehensive reform initiative is the NCLB legislation signed into effect by President George W. Bush in 2001, which is an eighth amendment to the earlier ESEA of 1965 (Fletcher, 2006; Fletcher & Zirkle, 2009; NCLB, 2001). The main objectives of the legislation were to increase academic achievement of all students and to close the achievement gap between students of all races, socioeconomic statuses (SES), and backgrounds (Fletcher, 2006; Mantel, 2005; NCLB, 2001).

Current CTE legislation objectives coincide with the accountability era for education. President George W. Bush reauthorized the Carl D. Perkins Vocational and Technical Education Act of 1998 (which historically was the Vocational Education Act of 1963) and named it the Carl D. Perkins Career and Technical Education Improvement Act of 2006 (Gordon, 2008; Scott & Sarkees-Wircenski, 2008). Accordingly, the new legislation reflected the name transformation from vocational education to CTE. In addition, it communicated the new goals of CTE as a vehicle for preparing students for the workforce and for postsecondary education attainment. The primary new provisions included the following: (a) accountability and continued improvement of CTE programs; (b) a more seamless transition between secondary and postsecondary education for students; (c) and an increased focus on the knowledge, skills, and dispositions expected from business and industry.

10.3 ISSUES, CONTROVERSIES, AND PROBLEMS

10.3.1 The Separation of Academic and Vocational Education

In the latter 1800's, schools were primarily focused on the core academic areas. However, many believed that vocational education was a way to establish more equality in the schools due to the few opportunities afforded for students to pursue postsecondary degrees. Two influential Black educational philosophers, Booker T. Washington and W.E.B. Du Bois, debated the purposes of education, particularly for Blacks. Washington believed in the pedagogical concept of learning by doing. On the contrary, W.E.B. Du Bois argued for a more academic education for Blacks to release them from the oppressive social and economic inequalities of pursuing a more vocationally focused education (Gordon, 2008). According to Gordon (2008), "Washington and Du Bois were trailblazers for the pattern of philosophical distinction between vocational and academic education" (p. 25).

In the early twentieth century, a newer philosophical approach was emerging that was concerned with students' interests. The philosophy of idealism was moving towards pragmatism and experimentalism. The educational leaders of this philosophy were John Dewey and Charles Prosser. The ideas of Charles Prosser merged into the creation of the Smith-Hughes Act of 1917. Similar to the debates of Washington and Du Bois, Dewey and Prosser also had distinct views of vocational and academic education. Prosser emphasized the need for students to gain practical experiences and have financial rewards. He also believed that the learning space be highly similar to the workplace. John Dewey, on the other hand, proclaimed that education be democratic. Dewey wanted education to include vocational exploration to assist students in gaining more practical knowledge. Thus, he supported the integration of vocational

and academic content. He advocated for vocational education as a means for transforming the social inequalities that existed (Gordon, 2008).

Dewey's vision of academic and vocational integration was transcendental. In fact, the Carl D. Perkins Vocational and Applied Technology Education Act of 1990 was the first time federal legislation stressed the need to integrate academic and vocational content. This legislation was transformational and set out new objectives for vocational education. These new objectives included the charge for vocational education to prepare students not only for the demands of the workplace, but also to pursue postsecondary degrees. However, individuals' perspectives regarding the purposes and nature of vocational education have been difficult to change. The difficulty of transforming perspectives may be closely related to the historical nature of vocational education and its separation from the core academic curriculum that had been in place since the Smith-Hughes Act of 1917.

American high schools structure educational opportunities for students by providing them with differentiated curricular programs based on their purported interests and talents (Gamoran, 1987; Gamoran & Weinstein, 1998; Hallinan, 1994). This sorting process results in stratified learning opportunities of students within the same school. Thus, the learning opportunities and instruction that schools expose students to (for i.e., advanced placement courses) often set the boundaries for student experiences and achievement (Gamoran, 1987; Gamoran & Nystrand, 1991).

A wealth of long-standing knowledge and research has matriculated within the last few decades based on the phenomenon of tracking in U.S. schools, which has been well-documented in the literature (Gamoran, 1989; Lewis, 2007; Oakes & Guiton, 1995) and highly contentious (Hallinan, 1994) among educators, administrators, researchers, and parents. Tracking, which is the separation of students into distinct curricula tracks based on perceived or measured cognitive ability, has been cited as a vehicle that provides students with an unequal education (Alvarez & Mehan, 2007; Hallinan, 1991, 1994; Rubin, 2006); long-term social inequalities (Arum & Shavit, 1995; Ayalon & Gamoran, 2000; Biafora, & Ansalone, 2008; Gamoran, 1989; Gamoran & Mare, 1989; Kelly, 2007; Page, 1990; Rojewski, 1997; Rubin, 2006); unequal status attainment (Ayalon & Gamoran, 2000; LeTendre, Hofer, & Shimizu, 2003; Lewis, 2007; Oakes & Guiton, 1995; Rubin, 2006; Vanfossen, Jones, & Spade, 1987); and lower self-esteem, motivation to learn, and academic status (Hallinan, 1994). Researchers have also indicated that ability (Alexander & Mc-Dill, 1976; Biafora & Ansalone, 2008; Gamoran & Mare, 1989; Hallinan, 1991; Kelly, 2007; Lee & Bryk, 1988; Vanfossen et al., 1987; Yonezawa, Wells, & Serna, 2002), past performance/achievement (Gamoran, 1989; Lee & Byrk, 1988; Rubin, 2006), teacher and counselor recommendations (Hallinan, 1991), college and career aspirations (Akos et al., 2007; Gamoran, 1989; Lee & Byrk, 1988; Rojewski, 1997; Vanfossen et al., 1987), interests (Lee & Bryk, 1988), race/ethnicity (Akos et al., 2007; Alvarez & Mehan, 2007; Burris, & Welner, 2005; Hallinan, 1991; Kelly, 2007; Lee & Byrk, 1988; Lewis, 2007; Lewis & Cheng, 2006; Oakes & Guiton, 1995; Rubin, 2006; Welner & Oakes, 1996; Yonezawa et al., 2002), SES (Akos et al., 2007; Alvarez & Mehan, 2007; Gamoran, 1989; Kelly, 2007; Kilgore, 1991; Lee & Byrk, 1988; Lewis, 2007; Lewis & Cheng, 2006; Oakes & Guiton, 1995; Rojewski, 1997; Rubin, 2006; Vanfossen et al., 1987; Yonezawa et al., 2002), structural/institutional constraints (Gamoran, 1986; Oakes & Guiton, 1995), and family backgrounds (Kelly, 2007) are all determinants in the placement of students in different curriculum tracks. Thus, research examining, and explanations describing the antecedents and effects of tracking are quite complex (Oakes & Guiton, 1995).

The distinct curricula tracks include: (a) a college preparatory curriculum; (b) a CTE curriculum; and (c) a general curriculum. However, recent initiatives have developed an integrated curriculum combining college preparatory and CTE coursework. This new phenomenon has been referred to as the new vocationalism and includes programs such as Tech- Prep, Career Academies, and HSTW. These curriculum reform models have attempted to increase college preparatory coursework in CTE programs as well as provide pathways for postsecondary education participation. In addition, tracking in schools may also take the form of differentiated levels of courses such as "advanced placement, honors, regular, and basic" (Hallinan, 1994, p. 1). Thus, the conceptualization of separate tracks is widely varied among American schools (McPartland & Schneider, 1996).

The phenomenon of tracking students may be traced back as early as 1940 (Mayer, 2008). Tracking has been shown to be a mechanism that strongly influences students' perceptions of the types of post-high school opportunities that are available (Akos et al., 2007). In fact, tracking has been a source of much litigation and has been contested in many court cases (Welner & Oakes, 1996). Research on the effects of tracking has shown to lead to long-term negative outcomes such as an academic achievement gap between college preparatory and non-college preparatory students. Despite the negative long-term effects of tracking, the primary rationale for tracking in schools is pedagogical, in that, students vary greatly in their academic ambitions, prior knowledge, and the environment in which learning is optimal (Gamoran & Mare, 1989; Lucas & Berends, 2002; McPartland & Schneider, 1996), and tracking provides teachers with an opportunity to tailor their instruction in order to meet the varied student learning needs (Gamoran, Nystrand, Berends, & LePore, 1995; Hallinan, 1991; Page, 1990). Nevertheless, research has shown that high-ability tracks often engage in much higher quality discourse than their low-tracked counterparts, which typically involves the emphasis of lower-order cognitive skills (Lee & Byrk, 1988).

10.3.2 Research on Tracking

Akos et al. (2007) studied 522 eighth grade students from four middle schools in North Carolina to determine the relationship between curriculum track choices and achievement indicators such as G.P.A., behavior, attendance, ability classification, as well as student characteristics such as gender, SES, and race. The researchers found statistically significant positive relationships between students choosing a college and university track as well as a career track. Achievement indicators were also found to be significant with track and G.P.A. Additional significant negative relationships were found between curriculum track choices and attendance and behavior referrals. Therefore, students that chose a college and university track had fewer absences and behavior referrals than those students that were in a College-Tech track. Lastly, a statistically significant difference was found in curriculum track choices and ability classifications. More special education students chose the Career and Occupational track; more gifted students chose the College and University track; and, students in regular education chose College-Tech. The researchers contended that approximately 95% of students in North Carolina may be prepared for postsecondary education. They also discussed the instrumentality of tracking on students' career and educational aspirations, as well as pointed out the need for school counselors to advocate against curriculum tracking.

In a study investigating the perceptions of 272 principals of New York City schools regarding tracking, Biafora and Ansalone (2008) found that 56.5% believed that their teachers were supportive of tracking in their schools. Further analyses revealed that principals in lower SES schools were more favorable of tracking. In addition, 65.5% agreed to the statement that tracking promotes inequalities. Principals in higher SES schools (70.7%) agreed with this statement at a statistically significant higher rate than their lower SES counterparts (50.5%). Furthermore, 64.9% of principals in higher SES schools supported the eradication of tracking. The researchers concluded that principals' perceptions of tracking were strongly influenced by political, SES, and academic concerns.

Lewis and Cheng (2006) explored the perceptions of 665 high school principals on whether race and SES were contributing factors influencing tracking. Findings demonstrated that a statistically significant difference was found in the percentage of free/reduced priced lunches to determine whether a CTE track or college preparatory track was predominant. In addition, principals' expectations of students' likelihood of attending a four-year college or university compared to directly pursuing work was statistically significant with income and free/reduced priced lunches. Similar to the self-fulfilling prophecy, the researchers contended that principals' expectations of students' status attainment may significantly influence school policies and the occurrence of tracking in their schools.

Oakes and Guiton (1995) conducted qualitative and quantitative analyses of three high schools to determine how teachers conceive of tracking. Findings demonstrated that teachers utilized junior high school teachers' opinions of students' abilities and motivation to determine their track placements. Second, teachers believed that students' track placements were accommodations that were in alignment with students' abilities and motivation and they did not attempt to alter students' abilities or motivation. Third, race/ethnicity and social class were determining factors for track placements. Fourth, structural issues (such as policies regulating course offerings) impacted curriculum decisions, as well as reduced resources and transformations in demographics. In addition, students in high-status curriculum tracks were more positively benefited when structural changes, resources, and shifting demographics occurred. Correspondingly, the researchers suggested that a complex interplay of structural, cultural, and political dynamics accounted for decision-making in the placement of students in differentiated tracks.

To determine how tracking was administered, Kelly (2007) analyzed curriculum guides of 92 North Carolina high schools from 1997 to 1998. He found that all of the North Carolina high schools in the study had the same course requirements for graduation. However, course-taking in English and mathematics courses were highly differentiated. The findings indicated that most students were tracked based on ability and age. Kelly (2007) further stated that tracking was intensified by school policies such as co-requisite regulations that link placements in academic courses. This, he described as, "Track placements in English and math often determine placement in social studies and science respectively" (Kelly, 2007, p. 29).

Vanfossen et al. (1987) utilized the High School and Beyond (HS&B) dataset to assess the influence of curriculum tracking over a two-year period. They found that one-third of students participated in a college preparatory curriculum, approximately one-half were in the general track, and one-fifth were in a CTE track. Students scoring in the upper quartile were in the college preparatory track. Findings also indicated that students that were in the college preparatory and general tracks were statistically significant predictors of postsecondary education attainment. The researchers concluded that students in general and CTE tracks are not given adequate opportunities to increase their academic performance as well as educational and occupational aspirations.

10.4 SOLUTIONS AND RECOMMENDATIONS

An earlier summarization of findings resulting from tracking studies was rendered by Kulik's (1998) review entitled, *Curricular tracks and high school vocational education*. Kulik (1998) concluded that ethnographic studies on tracking have demonstrated that there are varying degrees of time on-task between upper- and lower-tracks, differences in teachers, in student-teacher relationships, and instruction. In addition, Kulik (1998) reported that the majority of regression studies have explored factors influencing students' decisions to enroll in particular tracks as well as how the different tracks impact students. The majority of findings pointed to students' personal preferences as the primary factor influencing their decisions to enroll in a curriculum track. Whereas, factors such as gender, race, and SES show inferior roles in students' placement in tracks. Moreover, the overwhelming majority of studies have shown that students in college-preparatory tracks enroll in postsecondary education, subsequent to high school, at a higher rate than any other curriculum track. Studies' findings are inconclusive regarding students track placement and student achievement (i.e., test scores). Lastly, Kulik (1998) concluded that experimental studies have shown that students of different ability groups that are placed in the same curriculum track achieve at a lower rate than those students tracked according to their ability levels. Students in the lower tracks suffer from much lower self-esteem.

Kulik (1998) further commented that tracking studies typically do not examine academic and vocational tracks, leaving little insight to vocational constituents. In addition, little attention has been given to comparing student outcomes of general and vocational tracks. In fact, according to Kulik (1998),

The overwhelming impression that one gets from literature reviews on grouping and tracking, in fact, is neglect of vocational education. Reviewers of survey research usually fail to distinguish between general and vocational tracks. Instead, they lump general and vocational classes together into a single category of nonacademic classes. Reviewers of ethnographic studies examine instruction in upper- and lower-track academic classes, but not in vocational courses. Reviewers of the experimental literature cite relatively few studies of ability grouping at the senior-high level and seldom mention the topic of vocational education. (p. 58)

Based on the literature on tracking, findings have demonstrated that tracking has a negative impact on achievement in the CTE and general tracks (Akos et al., 2007). In addition, tracking has been shown to be influenced by ability (Kelly, 2007), age (Kelly, 2007), and institutional factors of the school (Kelly, 2007). Furthermore, tracking has been associated with impacting students' postsecondary education attainment (Vanfossen et al., 1987).

Similarly, teachers' perceptions of tracking have shown that SES, race, ethnicity, perceptions of students, institutional factors, and school resources are factors associated with the placement of students in tracks. In regards to perceptions of principals, principals' perceptions of students have been found to influence tracking placements (Lewis & Cheng, 2006). In addition, research findings have indicated that tracking has had a negative impact on low SES students (Biafora & Ansalone, 2008), which has been shown to promote social inequalities (Biafora & Ansalone, 2008). Thus, many researchers have called for the abolishment of tracking (Biafora & Ansalone, 2008).

10.4.1 De-tracking

Within the last decade, some schools in the U.S. have been implementing reform initiatives to "detrack" curricula in an attempt to fix the negative effects associated with tracking (Alvarez & Mehan, 2007; Rubin, 2006) and improve the likelihood of underserved students participating in postsecondary education (Alvarez & Mehan, 2007). These schools use academic and racially heterogeneous grouping (Rubin, 2003, 2006) and place *all* students in a college preparatory program regardless of ability level (Lewis, 2007); this new unified curriculum is deemed to be highly challenging with increasing standards (McPartland &

Schneider, 1996). However, some scholars argue for an integrated curriculum for all students that includes study in the core academic areas as well as in CTE (Lewis, 1998; Lewis & Cheng, 2006). This perspective of schooling is the primary objective and result of the new vocationalism, making CTE more attractive and relevant to students. To illustrate, Rubin (2006) described the wide spectrum of school structural reform efforts as follows:

Schools and school districts have taken widely divergent approaches to de-tracking. Of one end of the spectrum are deep restructuring efforts, such as the complete elimination of ability grouping in all subject areas throughout an entire school district. On the other end are changes that do not directly affect a school's track structure, such as providing more access to high-track classes for students formerly in lower tracks. (p. 7)

Despite the attempts to improve the academic achievement of all students, de-tracking reform efforts have been quite controversial (Rubin, 2003). The implementation of de-tracking in schools have been fraught with challenges and tremendously complex, not only with the logistics, but particularly with the attempt to transform parents' and students' long-held, deeply-ingrained dispositions regarding the acquisition of intelligence and privilege that is rooted in years of tracking (Oakes, Wells, Jones, & Datnow, 1997). In addition, the varying conceptualizations of de-tracking in different schools makes the evaluation of these efforts difficult and quite problematic (Rubin, 2003, 2006). Thus, findings of quantitative and qualitative research that have been conducted on de-tracking are inconclusive (Rubin, 2003, 2006; Yonezawa et al., 2002), with some studies showing positive outcomes (Alvarez & Mehan, 2007; Cohen & Lotan, 1995) and others showing little to no gains (Gamoran & Weinstein, 1998; Yonezawa et al., 2002).

In a qualitative study of four middle schools and six high schools, Yonzawa et al. (2002) found that schools engaged in implementing de-tracking were ineffective at enabling students to have "freedom of choice" in the selection of course-taking (p. 38). It is important to note that the schools had varied conceptualizations of de-tracking, in that, some schools enabled their students to choose honors courses, while other schools permitted students to select courses across curricula. The researchers suggested that these schools were unsuccessful primarily due to long-standing, imbedded school structures and cultural dynamics of schools and student relationships. The researchers found three main themes in their study. These themes included institutional barriers, tracked aspirations, and choosing respect. Institutional barriers such as the amount of information that was provided to some students were limited, having an impact on students' known options in regards to course-taking. Tracked aspiration was an important factor because students held on to long-standing aspirations and identities of prior schooling experiences and reduced the likelihood of choosing alternative courses. Lastly, "choosing respect" referred to the phenomenon of low to middle income students choosing lower tracks based on supportive environments with courses that was comprised of many students of similar races, and peers and teachers that valued their cultures.

In another qualitative research study utilizing focus group interviews from 12 schools, Yonezawa and Jones (2006) found that students perceived tracking as unjust. They described instances in which their friends and relatives were placed in inappropriate tracks based on prior performance/ achievement and work habits, as well as how those students were viewed as unintelligent by their teachers. These students believed that education should be equitable and enable *all* students to gain equal access to a rigorous curriculum. The researchers concluded that educational constituents should follow the same reasoning of the students when implementing de-tracking in their schools.

10.4.2 Factors Influencing Postsecondary Education Attainment for CTE Students

The pathways of CTE concentrators and college-preparatory concentrators are markedly different (Kulik, 1998). Kulik (1998) estimated that 75% of college-preparatory students do indeed continue on to pursue postsecondary educational opportunities; however, only 20% of CTE students decide to further their education subsequent to earning their high school diplomas. Several research studies have examined the influence of students participating in CTE on postsecondary education aspirations (Alfeld, Hansen, Aragon, & Stone, 2006; Harnish & Lynch, 2005; Rojewski, 1997; Stone & Aliaga, 2005), attainment (Silverberg et al., 2004), and degree completion (Esters, 2007).

Findings from the 2004 *National Assessment of Vocational Education* (NAVE) indicated that CTE concentrators have increasingly higher postsecondary education participation rates (Silverberg et al., 2004). However, these students still enroll in postsecondary education at a much lower rate than other students. Nevertheless, CTE students were much more likely to earn an associate's degree or complete a certificate program than a bachelor's degree.

In comparison to students with a curriculum specialization in CTE solely, Hudson and Hurst (1999) reported that 1992 high school graduates that participated in CTE and college preparatory courses enrolled in college at a higher rate two years subsequent to graduating high school and were almost as likely to enroll compared to their college preparatory counterparts. The researchers suggested that the findings indicated that students with a curriculum specialization in CTE and college preparatory are benefiting from the increased integration of CTE and academic concepts in their courses

Stone and Aliaga (2005) utilized the 1997 National Longitudinal Survey of Youth (NLSY) dataset to investigate participation rates of CTE concentrators, career majors, tech prep, cooperative education, job shadowing, mentoring, school-based enterprises, and internship and apprenticeships. In addition, they described students' characteristics in terms of family background, community, and school achievement. Lastly, the researchers examined the relationship among curriculum participation, students' characteristics, indicators of academic rigor, and college aspirations. As a result of their analyses, the researchers found that 6.6% of students nationwide indicated that they were CTE concentrators. A third of students reported to have chosen a career major at some point in their education; a fifth indicated they participated in job shadowing; and, a fourth stated they participated in cooperative education or an internship or apprenticeship. Parents' educational levels had a statistically significant negative relationship with a student being a CTE concentrator. Nevertheless, CTE concentrators completed high school at a higher rate than general education concentrators. However, CTE concentrators had the lowest college aspirations and had a tremendously lower (71%) likelihood of completing high school in comparison with academic concentrators. The researchers concluded that CTE accounts for a large portion of students' high school experiences; while, race, gender, ethnicity, and SES are strong influencers of CTE concentration.

Esters (2007), utilizing discriminant analysis, examined factors that influenced 88 agricultural education urban high school graduates' decisions of enrolling in postsecondary education. These graduates were from a school in the Midwest and earned their high school diplomas between the years of 1992 and 1995. Fifty-four percent of the participants were Caucasian, 40% were African-American, 4% were Hispanic, and 2% indicated "other". The respondents who had completed bachelors' degrees were as follows: (a) eight percent were in agricultural; (b) seven percent were in the liberal arts; and (c) five percent were in education. The researchers did not report the percentage of students earning masters' degrees;

however, they did indicate that students completed masters' degrees in agriculture, education, and liberal arts. None of the respondents had earned a doctoral degree.

In addition, respondents reported that their mothers or female guardians had the most impact (M=4.07) on their decisions to pursue a postsecondary degree. The second highest influence came from their fathers (M=3.64). Further, respondents indicated that their interest in agriculture was the most significant factor in deciding to enroll in postsecondary education. Students' high school grade point averages (GPA) and mothers' or female guardians' influence only explained eight percent of the variance in their decisions' to enroll in postsecondary education. The researchers cautioned readers when interpreting their findings because of the small sample size and because of the utilization of only one school. They recommended that parents and/or guardians should be encouraged to be involved in students' college decision processes. The researchers further stated that there are many contributing factors in students' decisions to enroll in postsecondary education.

In a four group pre-test/post-test, longitudinal research design, Alfeld et al. (2006) utilized hierarchical linear modeling to examine whether students' participation in career and technical student organizations (CTSOs) affected outcomes such as achievement, transition to postsecondary education and training, and employability. Their study included a sample of 1,797 high school students in general classes, CTE classes, and CTE classes with CTSOs. When comparing students in CTE classes and students in CTE classes with CTSOs, findings revealed that students in CTE classes with CTSOs had significantly higher academic motivation, academic engagement, civic engagement, and career self-efficacy initially. However, students in CTE courses had gained higher increases than students in CTE classes with CTSOs. When comparing CTE classes with CTSOs and general classes, findings indicated that CTE classes with CTSOs initially had significantly higher career self-efficacy. However, general classes had a more substantial and significant increase in career self-efficacy. Additional findings concluded that the amount of CTSO participation did not significantly impact any of the dependent variables. The researchers concluded that CTSOs are of value to students' high school experiences. They further mentioned that despite the finding that students in CTE classes have less college aspirations than students in the general classes, they still aspire to earn bachelors' and masters' degrees.

One approach utilized to increase the likelihood of high school students to pursue postsecondary education is through dual enrollment programs. Dual enrollment programs enable students to earn college credit by taking high school courses. In a longitudinal mixed methods study of Georgia's dual enrollment programs, Harnish and Lynch (2005) explored students' transitions from high school to technical colleges. By analyzing focus group interviews of 43 high school students from six different schools, the researchers found two major incentives for participating in dual enrollment courses; these incentives included gaining college credit and increasing their earning potential. The high school students reported that friends were the most significant factor influencing their decisions to enroll in dual credit courses. A barrier identified as inhibiting enrollment in dual credit classes was the admission test. Dual enrollment students also reported that benefits to participating included exposure to college, increased options, and helping them to make choices regarding their careers. Lastly, administrators reported that enrollment increased by 10% as a result of more students participating in dual enrollment. The researchers suggested that administrators should attempt to focus on those students that are not intending on pursuing college immediately following high school.

Rojewski (1997) utilized the 1988 to 1994 NELS dataset to investigate disadvantaged high school CTE students' participation rates in CTE, work experiences, and postsecondary aspirations.

He found that the CTE rate of participation for disadvantaged students was more than twice that of non-disadvantaged students. Students that enrolled in a CTE program had higher employment rates regardless of disadvantaged status. One-third of students reported working at fast food restaurants, particularly for disadvantaged students. On the contrary, many of the non-disadvantaged students worked in sales-related occupations. CTE students were more likely to work in mechanical or general repair occupations. Three-fourths of all students reported earning slightly above the minimum wage (which was $4.25 at the time). Unexpectedly, the more disadvantaged students that were involved in CTE, the higher the likelihood of them receiving less than minimum wage. In regards to educational and occupational aspirations, CTE students had the lowest educational and occupational aspirations regardless of disadvantaged status. The researcher concluded that CTE practitioners should attempt to deal with concerns of tracking disadvantaged youth into CTE programs. Rojewski (1997) further indicated that more research should determine whether CTE students participate because of their own decisions or because of systemic approaches.

Novel (2009) used the 1997 NLSY dataset to investigate degree attainment of students in different curriculum tracks. She found that participating in a college preparatory or a CTE + curriculum were positive and significant predictors of degree attainment. She encouraged states to develop policies and structures for promoting collaboration between K-12 schools and colleges and universities. She further recommended that educational constituents ensure that students in CTE take a rigorous course of study.

Fletcher (2009), utilizing the 1997 NLSY dataset, examined degree attainment and occupational earnings of 6,064 former high school students based on their various curriculum tracks. He found that postsecondary degree attainment was not related to participating in the CTE track. However, those in the college preparatory track were much more likely to earn high school diplomas, associates, bachelors, and graduate degrees. Those in the dual track were much more likely to earn associates and graduate degrees. In terms of earnings, those in the CTE track were more likely to earn more than their general, college preparatory, and dual counterparts. Fletcher recommended that the general track be eliminated, and suggested that educational constituents encourage students to participate in the college preparatory or dual tracks.

10.4.3 Labor Market Outcomes

Despite the acknowledgement that obtaining a bachelor's degree has many benefits and provides access to increased opportunities, according to the Bureau of Labor Statistics data, projections of job opportunities for individuals without a bachelor's degree indicated that approximately 42 million positions will be available between 2002 and 2012 (Moncarz & Crosby, 2004). This projection outweighs the number of expected positions available for those with bachelor's degrees by three-fold.

10.4.4 School-to-Work Transitions

The school-to-work network includes collaborative relationships among three parties, including students, employers, and schools (Rosenbaum, Kariya, Settersten, & Maier, 1990). This relationship is often problematic: in that, the needs of the workforce are constantly transforming while communication oftentimes is lacking between the employers and schools. Further, schools sometimes fail to adapt to the dynamic needs of the workforce. This sometimes is due to the lack of communication and other times might be due to lack of resources or teachers' professional development.

Unlike college graduates whom might have more insight into the labor market within their disciplines and have gained greater field relevant knowledge and skills, adolescents that do not participate in postsecondary education encoun-

ter varied experiences in their transitions from school to the workforce with some employed in several jobs as contingent workers, some landing permanent long-term careers, and others finding themselves unemployed (Yates, 2005). Educators and policymakers share varied perspectives in relation to the phenomenon of adolescents working in multiple jobs. One perspective is that these individuals, by experiencing and accumulating a wide variety of work opportunities, gain valuable work experience in the process: work experience that might be substantially valuable to increasing their knowledge, skills, and interests as well as increasing their prospects of earning a higher wage. On the contrary, another perspective is that the unnecessary time these adolescents take by transitioning into multiple jobs is unproductive and increases their opportunity costs (Rosenbaum et al., 1990).

Yet another group of adolescents do not earn a high school diploma and are oftentimes disadvantaged in comparison with their high school graduate counterparts. Yates (2005) described their likely outlook: "they lack both general and job-specific skills, and they face employers who have low expectations and little incentive to invest in their matches" (p. 21). Kulik (1998) estimated the number of students dropping out of high school to be an astounding 450,000 in non-academic curricula tracks. This large number of students dropping out of high school tends to be equated with high societal costs in terms of placing these individuals in social welfare programs for housing, healthcare, and employment (Kulik, 1998). Furthermore, it is unfortunate that the majority of individuals that comprise this category are minorities and economically disadvantaged. Proponents of CTE have long perceived CTE to be a preventative component in students dropping out of high school due to students' interest in the curriculum, relevance to students, and because students find it rewarding (Kulik, 1998). And, researchers have supported this assertion (Kulik, 1998; Rasinski & Pedlow, 1998). Thus, students' educational experiences are strongly associated with employment prospects – for that is the time where students should learn about hard (i.e., literacy and mathematical) and soft (i.e., employability) skills (Yates, 2005).

Utilizing the 1979 NLSY dataset, Yates (2005) investigated the school-to-work transitions of high school graduates of the period in which they graduated to the time they reached 35 years of age. She found that 17% of students dropped out of high school approximately at the age of 17; 55% graduated, but did not attend college; 22% graduated from high school and went to college, but did not earn a bachelor's degree; and 11% earned a college degree. In regards to demographics, men were both more likely to drop out of high school as well as earn a college degree; whites were more likely than students of color to earn a high school diploma as well as a college degree.

Further, Yates (2005) found that high school student dropouts' employment was not stable. In fact, these students, on average, had positions lasting no longer than two years in duration. Yates (2005) noted,

At age 20, 14 percent of dropouts have never held a job and 58 percent had yet to hold a job for more than one year…Only 36 percent of high school dropouts had held a job for 5 years or more by age 35. (p. 24)

Those findings are in stark contrast to college-goers whom by age 30, approximately 86% held positions for at least two years and 82% of college degree holders held a job for at least two years. The percentage increased to 95% by age 35. Lastly, Yates found that college graduates had steady, long-lasting employment relationships in contrast to high school dropouts whom had multiple short-term positions 15 years subsequent to leaving high school. Therefore, Yates concluded that increases in education positively impacts school-to-work transitions.

In a review of research findings, Kulik (1998) concluded that CTE students were more satisfied with their jobs than students in the general education track (44% of CTE students compared to 37% of general students). However, he further stated that future studies should explore what may account for attributions of students' job satisfaction.

10.4.5 The Impact of CTE on Long-Term Earnings

Meer (2007) contested the research that demonstrated lower earnings potential for CTE students because of the contextual factors that are omitted from the findings. He commented,

After all, it is just as plausible that these students earn less because of unobservable characteristics that are correlated with track choice as it is that vocational education is somehow diminishing their earnings potential. Simply because those who are currently on the academic or general track earn more than vocational students does not mean that shifting vocational students to those tracks would increase their income (p. 560).

Therefore, based on analyzing NELS 1988 dataset, Meer (2007) examined students in the general, academic, technical, and business tracks instead of the more common three-track system (general, academic, and CTE) that is often studied. They found that students in the technical track are not more likely to have higher incomes if they had chosen another track. Those individuals in a general track were more likely to have benefited from a technical track. Further, those individuals that were in a technical or an academic track benefited greatly from their choices in terms of earnings potential. Unexpectedly, those individuals in the business track were more likely to have gained from choosing a general track. The researcher concluded that CTE has been wrongly stigmatized as an inferior curriculum track and encourages

CTE constituents to prepare its students for the current high-technology workforce.

Mane (1999) utilized the NLSY of 1972, the HS&B survey of 1980, and the NELS of 1988 to examine the short and medium term outcomes of non-college bound students in academic and CTE high school courses. He found that non-college bound students in CTE earned a higher wage than their academic counterparts for those graduating in 1980 and 1992, but not graduates of 1972. The researcher concluded that the findings argue against those that propose closing CTE programs. He further supported the advancement of articulation agreements with institutes of higher education, stating "While the return to high school vocational education is substantial, the return to post secondary study is larger still. Consequently, high school students should always be encouraged to plan on getting further education after high school" (Mane, 1999, p. 434).

Based on the studies reviewed, the majority of studies provide evidence for the assertion that increasing the attainment of higher education credentials is positively related to earnings and employment (Bailey, Kienzl, & Marcotte, 2004; Liming & Wolf, 2008). Therefore, the argument for increasing students' opportunities for postsecondary education attainment is warranted.

Further, important factors influencing students' postsecondary education decision-making are family influence (Legutko, 2008), parents' educational levels (Hossler & Stage, 1992), and gender (Hossler & Stage, 1992). In regards to students' participation in specific types of high school curricula, research findings have found that CTE concentrators are more likely to be disadvantaged (Rojewski, 1997), have the lowest college aspirations (Rojewski, 1997; Stone & Aliaga, 2005) and have the lowest occupational aspirations (Rojewski, 1997) compared to their college preparatory concentrating counterparts. Nevertheless, CTE concentrators have demonstrated higher employment rates (Rojewski, 1997). In terms of the dual track, recent research has demonstrated positive postsecondary outcomes (Fletcher, 2009; Novel, 2009) and occupational earnings (Fletcher, 2009) for those students.

10.5 FUTURE TRENDS

Research findings from tracking studies clearly points to the need to eradicate the general track. This track does not enhance students' probabilities to gain postsecondary education credentials, nor does it contribute to increased labor market outcomes for its students. For those students that may not be suited or have an interest in the college preparatory curriculum, the dual and CTE tracks are much more promising in terms of long-term student outcomes. In fact, school districts are increasingly eliminating the general track altogether.

In fact, new research has suggested that the outcomes of students participating in the dual track, in terms of degree attainment and earnings, are much more hopeful than the general track. Further, comprehensive high school reform has increasingly focused on the integration of CTE and core academic concepts with the goal of increasing students' opportunities to participate in postsecondary educational opportunities and providing them with skills for the workforce. Thus, reform initiatives such as High Schools That Work (HSTW), career academics, and Tech Prep programs seem to be on the right track in affording students more optimistic long-term trajectories.

With the increased accountability of schools through federal legislative initiatives such as the No Child Left Behind (NCLB) legislation and the Carl D. Perkins Career and Technical Education Improvement Act of 2006, future CTE legislation may seek for stronger accountability measures for states and local school districts in determining long-term student outcomes. Furthermore, the need for students to gain postsecondary education credentials seems to be growing in importance for the future.

As indicated in the review of literature on de-tracking, much of the research demonstrates that de-tracking efforts have not resulted in substantial gains. However, more research is needed to understand the long-term benefits or disadvantages of de-tracking efforts. Further, more qualitative research might investigate the reasons why de-tracking attempts are successful or not.

10.6 CONCLUSION

As a result of an extensive review of the literature on the factors influencing students' long-term student outcomes, it is evident that the type of high school curriculum a student participates in significantly impacts their long-term opportunities. Coupled with the changing nature of the workplace, the unstable economy, and the growing awareness of the need for postsecondary education credentials, more research is needed on the relationship between the type of high school curriculum a student is exposed to and their actual long-term outcomes. This need is further explicated in the new Carl D. Perkins Career and Technical Education Improvement Act of 2006 guiding the objectives of CTE. In fact, CTE too has recognized the need for the changing needs of its students and in 1990 incited the charge for CTE programs to ensure their students are not only prepared for the workforce, but are also prepared to pursue postsecondary educational experiences. The pressing nature of research investigating CTE student long-term outcomes is explicated in the following quote:

The neglect of vocational education in research reviews is distressing because important questions are being raised today about the effectiveness of vocational education. Are disproportionate numbers of minorities and poor children shunted into the vocational track? Do these students receive an inferior education there? Are they taught low-status subjects from low-status teachers?

Would everyone's needs be better met in one-track schools? These questions need to be answered, and the answers to the questions need to be based on careful analyses of evidence not hearsay and stereotyping. (Gamoran, Kulik, Lynch, Rasinski, & Pedlow, 1998, p. 2).

REFERENCES

Akos, P., Lambie, G., Milsom, A., & Gilbert, K. (2007). Early adolescents' aspirations and academic tracking: An exploratory investigation. *Professional School Counseling, 11*(1), 57–64.

Alexander, K., & McDill, E. (1976). Selection and allocation within schools: Some causes and consequences of curriculum placement. *American Sociological Review, 41*(6), 963–980. doi:10.2307/2094797

Alfeld, C., Hansen, D., Aragon, S., & Stone, J. (2006). Inside the black box: Exploring the value added by career and technical student organizations to students' high school experience. *Career and Technical Education Research, 31*(3), 121–155.

Alvarez, D., & Mehan, H. (2007). Whole school de-tracking: A strategy for equity and excellence. *Theory into Practice, 45*(1), 82–89. doi:10.1207/s15430421tip4501_11

Arum, R., & Shavit, Y. (1995). Secondary vocational education and the transition from school to work. *Sociology of Education, 68*(3), 187–204. doi:10.2307/2112684

Ayalon, H., & Gamoran, A. (2000). Stratification in academic secondary programs and educational inequality in Israel and the United States. *Comparative Education Review, 44*(1), 54–80. doi:10.1086/447591

Bailey, T., Kienzl, G., & Marcotte, D. (2004). *The return to a sub-baccalaureate education: The effects of schooling, credentials, and program of study on economic outcomes.* Washington, DC: U.S. Department of Education.

Biafora, F., & Ansalone, G. (2008). Perceptions and attitudes of school principals towards school tracking: Structural considerations of personal beliefs. *Education, 128*(4), 588–602.

Blanchett, W., Mumford, W., & Beachum, F. (2005). Urban school failure and disproportionality in a post-Brown era: Benign neglect of the constitutional rights of students of color. *Remedial and Special Education, 26*(2), 70–81. doi:10.117 7/07419325050260020201

Bragg, D. (1999). Reclaiming a lost legacy: Integration of academic and vocational education . In Pautler, A. J. (Ed.), *Workforce education: Issues for the new century* (pp. 181–196). Ann Arbor, MI: Prakken.

Burris, C., & Welner, K. (2005). Closing the achievement gap by de-tracking. *Phi Delta Kappan, 86*(8), 594–598.

Castellano, M., Stringfield, S., & Stone, J. (2003). Secondary career and technical education and comprehensive school reform: Implications for research and practice. *Journal of Vocational Education Research, 73*(2), 231–272.

Cohen, E., & Lotan, R. (1995). Producing equal-status interaction in the heterogeneous classroom. *American Educational Research Journal, 32*(1), 99–120.

Courtade, G., & Ludlow, B. (2008). Ethical issues and severe disabilities: Programming for students and preparation for teachers. *Rural Special Education Quarterly, 27*(1/2), 36–42.

DeLuca, S., Plank, S., & Estacion, A. (2006, February). *Does career and technical education affect college enrollment?* Columbus, OH: National Dissemination Center for Career and Technical Education. Retrieved on July 18, 2008, http://www.nccte.org/publications/infosynthesis/r&dreport/DoesCTEAffectCollegeEnrollment/DoesCTEAffectCollegeEnrollment.html

Esters, L. (2007). Factors influencing postsecondary education enrollment behaviors of urban agricultural education students. *Career and Technical Education Research, 32*(2), 79–98.

Fletcher, E. (2006). No curriculum left behind: The effects of the No Child Left Behind Legislation on career and technical education. *Career and Technical Education Research, 31*(3), 157–174.

Fletcher, E. (2009). *The relationship of high school curriculum tracks to degree attainment and occupational earnings.* (Unpublished Dissertation).

Fletcher, E., & Zirkle, C. (2009). Career and technical education in light of the No Child Left Behind legislation . In Wang, V. (Ed.), *The Handbook of Research on E-Learning Applications for Career and Technical Education: Technologies for Vocational Training* (pp. 495–507). Hershey, PA: Information Science Reference.

Gamoran, A. (1987). The stratification of high school learning opportunities. *Sociology of Education, 60*(3), 135–155. doi:10.2307/2112271

Gamoran, A. (1989). Measuring curriculum differentiation. *American Journal of Education, 97*(2), 129–143. doi:10.1086/443918

Gamoran, A., Kulik, J., Lynch, R., Rasinski, K., & Pedlow, S. (1998). *The quality of vocational education: Background papers from the 1994 national assessment of vocational education.* Retrieved on January 22, 2009, from http://www.ed.gov/pubs/VoEd/index.html

Gamoran, A., & Mare, R. (1989). Secondary school tracking and educational inequality: Compensation, reinforcement, or neutrality. *American Journal of Sociology, 94*(5), 1146–1183. doi:10.1086/229114

Gamoran, A., & Nystrand, M. (1991). Background and instructional effects on achievement in eight-grade English and social studies. *Journal of Research on Adolescence, 1*(3), 277–300. doi:10.1207/s15327795jra0103_5

Gamoran, A., Nystrand, M., Berends, M., & LePore, P. (1995). An organizational analysis of the effects of ability grouping. *American Educational Research Journal, 32*(4), 687–715.

Gamoran, A., & Weinstein, M. (1998). Differentiation and opportunity in restructured schools. *American Journal of Education, 106*(3), 385–415. doi:10.1086/444189

Gordon, H. (2008). *The history and growth of career and technical education in America* (3rd ed.). Long Grove, IL: Waveland Press.

Gray, K. (1999). High school vocational education: Facing and uncertain future . In Pautler, A. J. (Ed.), *Workforce education: Issues for the new century* (pp. 159–169). Ann Arbor, MI: Prakken.

Gray, K. C., & Herr, E. L. (1998). *Workforce education: The basics.* Needham Heights, MA: Viacom.

Hallinan, M. (1991). School differences in tracking structures and track assignments. *Journal of Research on Adolescence, 1*(3), 251–275. doi:10.1207/s15327795jra0103_4

Hallinan, M. (1994). School differences in tracking effects on achievement. *Social Forces, 72*(3), 799–821. doi:10.2307/2579781

Hardman, M., & Dawson, S. (2008). The impact of federal public policy on curriculum and instruction for students with disabilities in the general classroom. *Preventing School Failure, 52*(2), 5–11. doi:10.3200/PSFL.52.2.5-11

Harnish, D., & Lynch, R. (2005). Secondary to postsecondary technical education transitions: An exploratory study of dual enrollment in Georgia. *Career and Technical Education Research, 30*(3), 169–188.

Harris, D., & Herrington, C. (2006). Accountability, standards, and the growing achievement gap: Lessons from the past half-century. *American Journal of Education, 112*, 209–238. doi:10.1086/498995

Hossler, D., & Stage, F. (1992). Family and high school experience influences on the postsecondary educational plans of ninth-grade students. *American Educational Research Journal, 29*(2), 425–451.

Hudson, L., & Hurst, D. (1999). *Students who prepare for college and a vocation* (National Center for Education Statistics Rep. No. 1999-072). Washington, DC.

Jacobs, J., & Grubb, W. (2003). The federal role in vocational-technical education. *Community College Research Center Brief, 18*, 1–4.

Kelly, S. (2007). The contours of tracking in North Carolina. *High School Journal, 90*(4), 15–31. doi:10.1353/hsj.2007.0016

Kilgore, S. (1991). The organizational context of tracking in schools. *American Sociological Review, 56*(2), 189–203. doi:10.2307/2095779

King, C., Schexnayder, D., & Gourgey, H. (2005). *Beyond the numbers: Improving postsecondary success through a central Texas high school data center.* University of Texas at Austin: The LBJ School of Public Affairs.

Kulik, J. (1998). Curricular tracks and high school vocational education. In A. Gamoran & H. Himmelfarb (Eds.), *The quality of vocational education: Background paper from the 1994 national assessment of vocational education.* Washington, DC: U.S. Department of Education. Retrieved on November 11, 2008, from http://www.ed.gov/pubs/ VoEd/Chapter3/Part2.html

Lee, V., & Byrk, S. (1988). Curriculum tracking as mediating the social distribution of high school achievement. *Sociology of Education, 61*(3), 78–94. doi:10.2307/2112266

Legutko, R. (2005). A decade's difference: Research revisited on family influence of rural high school students' postsecondary decisions. *Rural Educator, 29*(2), 4–7.

LeTendre, G., Hofer, B., & Shimizu, H. (2003). What is tracking? Cultural expectations in the United States, Germany, and Japan. *American Educational Research Journal, 40*(1), 43–89. doi:10.3102/00028312040001043

Lewis, T. (1998). Vocational education as general education. *Curriculum Inquiry, 28*(3), 283–309. doi:10.1111/0362-6784.00092

Lewis, T. (2007). Social inequality in education: A constraint on an American high-skills future. *Curriculum Inquiry, 37*(4), 329–349.

Lewis, T., & Cheng, S. (2006). Tracking, expectations, and the transformation of vocational education. *American Journal of Education, 113*(1), 67–99. doi:10.1086/506494

Liming, D., & Wolf, M. (2008). Job outlook by education, 2006-16. *Occupational Outlook Quarterly, 3*(52), 2–29.

Lucas, S., & Berends, M. (2002). Sociodemographic diversity, correlated achievement, and de facto tracking. *Sociology of Education, 75*(4), 306–327. doi:10.2307/3090282

Lynch, R. (2000). High school career and technical education for the first decade of the 21st Century. *Journal of Vocational Education Research, 25*(2), 155–198.

Mane, F. (1999). Trends in the payoff to academic and occupation-specific skills: The short and medium run returns to academic and vocational high school courses for non-college-bound students. *Economics of Education Review, 18*(4), 417–437. doi:10.1016/S0272-7757(99)00019-9

Mantel, B. (2005, May 27). No Child Left Behind: Is the law improving student performance? *The CQ Researcher, 15*(20), 469–492.

Mayer, A. (2008). Understanding how U.S. schools sort students for instructional purposes: Are all students being served equally? *American Secondary Education, 36*(2), 7–25.

McDonnell, L. (2005). No Child Left Behind and the federal role in education: Evolution or revolution? *Peabody Journal of Education, 80*(2), 19–38. doi:10.1207/S15327930pje8002_2

McPartland, J., & Schneider, B. (1996). Opportunities to learn and student diversity" Prospects and pitfalls of a common core curriculum. *Sociology of Education, extra issue, 69*(2), 66-81.

Meer, J. (2007). Evidence on the returns to secondary vocational education. *Economics of Education Review, 26*(5), 559–573. doi:10.1016/j.econedurev.2006.04.002

Moncarz, R., & Crosby, O. (2004). Job outlook for people who don't have a bachelor's degree. *Occupational Outlook Quarterly, 48*(4), 3–13.

National Commission on Excellence in Education. (1983). *A Nation at Risk: The imperative for educational reform.* Retrieved July 18, 2008, from http://www.ed.gov/pubs/ NatAtRisk/index.html

No Child Left Behind Act. (2001). 115 U.S.C. § 1425.

Novel, J. (2009). *Implementation of the Carl D. Perkins Career and Technical Education Reforms of the 1990s: Postsecondary education outcomes of students taking an enhanced vocational curriculum.* (Unpublished Dissertation).

Oakes, J., & Guiton, G. (1995). Matchmaking: The dynamics of high school tracking decisions. *American Educational Research Journal, 32*(1), 3–33.

Oakes, J., Wells, A., Jones, M., & Datnow, A. (1997). De-tracking: The social construction of ability, cultural politics and resistance to reform. *Teachers College Record, 98,* 482–510.

Page, R. (1990). Games of chance: The lower-track curriculum in a college-preparatory high school. *Curriculum Inquiry, 20*(3), 249–281. doi:10.2307/1180226

Plank, S. (2001). A question of balance: CTE, academic courses, high school perspective, and student achievement. *Journal of Vocational Education Research, 26*(3), 279–327.

Rasinski, K., & Pedlow, S. (1998) The effect of high school vocational education on academic achievement gain and high school persistence: Evidence from NELS:88. In A. Gamoran, & H. Himmelfarb (Eds.), *The quality of vocational education: Background paper from the 1994 national assessment of vocational education.* Washington, DC: U.S. Department of Education. Retrieved on November 11, 2008, from http://www.ed. gov/pubs/VoEd/Chapter5/index.html

Rojewski, J. (1997). Effects of economic disadvantaged status and secondary vocational education on adolescent work experience and postsecondary aspirations. *Journal of Vocational and Technical Education, 14*(1). Retrieved October 22, 2008, from http://scholar.lib.vt.edu/ejournals/JVTE/v14n1/JVTE-4.html

Rojewski, J. (2002). Preparing the workforce of tomorrow: A conceptual framework for career and technical education. *Journal of Vocational Education Research, 27*(1), 7–35.

Rosenbaum, J., Kariya, T., Settersen, R., & Maier, T. (1990). Market and network theories of the transition from high school to work: Their application to industrialized societies. *Annual Review of Sociology, 16,* 263–299. doi:10.1146/annurev.so.16.080190.001403

Rubin, B. (2003). Unpacking de-tracking: When progressive pedagogy meets students' social worlds. *American Educational Research Journal, 40*(2), 539–573. doi:10.3102/00028312040002539

Rubin, B. (2006). Tracking and de-tracking: debates, evidence, and best practices for a heterogeneous world. *Theory into Practice, 45*(1), 4–14. doi:10.1207/s15430421tip4501_2

Scott, J., & Sarkees-Wircenski, M. (2008). *Overview of career and technical education* (4th ed.). Homewood, IL: American Technical Publishers.

Silverberg, M., Warner, E., Fong, M., & Goodwin, D. (2004). *National assessment of vocational education: Final report to Congress.* Washington, DC: U.S. Department of Education.

Stasz, C., & Bodilly, S. (2004). *Efforts to improve the quality of vocational education in secondary schools: Impact of federal and state policies.* Washington, DC: U.S. Department of Education.

Stone, J., & Aliaga, O. (2005). Career and technical education and school-to-work at the end of the 20th century: Participation and outcomes. *Career and Technical Education Research, 30*(2), 125–144.

Umpstead, R. (2008). The No Child Left Behind Act: Is it an unfunded mandate or a promotion of federal educational ideas? *Journal of Law & Education, 37*(2), 193–229.

Vanfossen, B., Jones, J., & Spade, J. (1987). Curriculum tracking and status maintenance. *Sociology of Education, 60*(2), 104–122. doi:10.2307/2112586

Welner, K., & Oakes, J. (1996). Li(ability grouping): The new susceptibility of school tracking systems to legal challenges. *Harvard Educational Review, 66*(3), 451–470.

Yates, J. (2005). The transition from school to work. *Monthly Labor Review, 128*(2), 21–32.

Yonezawa, S., & Jones, M. (2006). Students' perspectives on tracking and de-tracking. *Theory into Practice, 45*(1), 15–23. doi:10.1207/s15430421tip4501_3

Yonezawa, S., Wells, A., & Serna, I. (2002). Choosing tracks: "Freedom of choice" in de-tracking schools. *American Educational Research Journal, 39*(1), 37–67. doi:10.3102/00028312039001037

Chapter 11

Adult Learning and CTE:
A Shared History Influenced by Technology

Judith Parker
Teachers College/Columbia University, USA

ABSTRACT

While the fields of adult learning and career and technical education began in isolated silos, as the fields emerged, their histories became entwined and technology had a profound influence on their growth and direction. This chapter will begin by exploring the beginnings of adult learning and CTE as two fields developing in parallel paths and serving two different audiences. However, as the fields developed, there is evidence of their entwinement in both the literature and programs within organizations. In addition, from the Gutenberg printing press to today's Web 2.0, technology has played an important part in the development and direction of both of these fields. This chapter will examine this history of silos and connections and continue to explore the role of technology in the future growth and meshing of these fields to generate even more effective and efficient learning.

11.1 INTRODUCTION

The fields of adult learning and career and technical education (CTE) began in isolated silos. Adult learning traces its history to philosophical roots in ancient civilizations while career and technical education cites the importance of work as the motivation for its being. But as the fields emerged, their histories became entwined and technology has had a profound influence on their growth and direction.

This chapter will begin by exploring the emergence of adult learning and CTE as two fields developing in parallel paths and serving two different audiences. This represents a dichotomy of the thinkers and the doers or the philosophers and the pragmatists. These separate histories will be explored in detail in the following background section. However a few significant milestones

DOI: 10.4018/978-1-61520-747-3.ch011

will be considered here. Vocational focused programs such as the Workers Education Movement in Great Britain, and apprenticeships and Agricultural Societies in the U.S. emerged in the post-Renaissance era. The Land Grant Act of 1862 established colleges for "research and study in the agricultural and mechanical arts" followed by the 20th century Vocational education act in the U.S.

Adult education was considered to emerge as an academic field with the establishment of the American Association of Adult Education in the early 20th century. However, there is evidence of their entwinement soon after that. Malcolm Knowles, credited with popularizing adult learning theory, titled a chapter in his autobiography as "Landmarks and Heroes in Adult Education". Yet it includes examples of vocational as well as adult learning landmarks and heroes. Donald Schon (1983) discusses reflection-in-action and reflection-on-action in his book "The Reflective Practitioner" whose title alone suggests a merging of the philosopher and pragmatist roles.

Technology has played an important part in the development and direction of both fields of adult learning and CTE. While the Gutenberg printing press is often credited as the beginning of the influence of technology on learning, all early advances in transportation and communication have had an influence on adult education and CTE. Any technology before and since Gutenberg that has facilitated the coming together of individuals and knowledge whether by transporting the individuals to a common place or by communicating the information to the individual has influenced adult learning and CTE. This chapter will continue this thread of meshing by exploring the role of today's Web 2.0 technology in today's learning and the future growth and meshing of these fields to generate even more effective and efficient learning. Mazarr (1999) notes that "the knowledge era is an interdisciplinary time" (p. 11) and that the "new sciences of complexity remind us that boundaries between problems and disciplines are less important than the threads that connect them" (p. 12).

11.2 BACKGROUND

To understand the development of each of the three components of this chapter, the history of adult learning, career and technical education and technology will each be explored individually. By approaching it this way, readers will have a clear understanding of how the fields of adult learning and career and technical education began in isolated silos, then emerged as inseparable fields and later became profoundly influenced by technology.

11.2.1 History of Adult Learning

While the field of adult learning is often synonymous with the name Malcolm Knowles, adult learning as an academic field has its roots in the early 1900s with earlier foundational ideas. Knowles (1989) describes himself as being "part of a long and significant historical movement" (p. 72) and credits great teachers of ancient China, Rome and Greece with the role of adult educators. He suggests that because of their experience with adults, they "perceived learning to be a process of active inquiry, not passive reception of transmitted content" and therefore "invented techniques for engaging learners in active inquiry" (p. 61). He credits the Chinese and Hebrews with the "case method or critical incident" and the Greeks with the "Socratic dialogue" in which a dilemma was posed to the group who would pool their knowledge and experience to develop a solution. The Roman methodology involved forcing the students to state positions and to defend them.

Knowles (1989) notes a gap in the literature on adult education between the fall of Rome and the Renaissance but also indicates that during that period the "institutionalization of education for children" (p. 62) developed. Following the Renaissance, several adult education institutions developed in Europe: "the folk high schools in Germany, the Netherlands, and the Scandinavian countries; the workers' education movement in Great Britain; and study circles of a variety of types in many countries. Knowles (1989) suggests that Benjamin Franklin might have been the first American role model for adult learning. Franklin founded the "Junto, a discussion club ... to explore such intellectual challenges as morals, politics, and natural philosophy" (p. 63) which became a model for other discussion groups and study circles. Knowles (1989) continues to note the importance of adult education throughout and on history citing examples in the citizen involvement initiatives in the American colonies and during the Civil War and the "compulsion for knowledge" (p. 64) instigated by the industrial revolution.

In his autobiography, Knowles (1989) begins his list of influential adult educators with John Dewey and Edward Thorndike. Dewey's notion that practice is superior to theory was in direct conflict with the theories of Aristotle and Plato who espoused the superiority of theory. Dewey's ideas are associated with pragmatism and progressive thought (Elias & Merriam, 2005). This influenced education by implying that the experiences of the learners were at the heart of the educational process thus impacting the role of the instructor in the classroom and that curriculum should be expanded to include practical knowledge. Edward Thorndike's ideas are connected with the behaviorist movement with a focus on performance and an emphasis on the scientific method and experimentation to arrive at truth. Thorndike's 1928 publication, *Adult Learning* is considered the first major report of research on learning with adults. He reported that adults could be expected to learn at the same rate as younger students and that the best time to learn was just prior to using the knowledge (Elias & Merriam, 2005). Both Dewey and Thorndike seemed to be building a bridge between theory and practice.

As early as the 1920's, The American Association of Adult Education, the forerunner of today's Association of Adult and Continuing Education, began to sponsor studies in the field. In 1934, this Association published the first *Handbook of Adult and Continuing Education* that "met the chief function of the Association as a clearinghouse for information about adult education" (Wilson & Hayes, p. 7). This Handbook and its next edition in 1936 were a directory of both national organizations and local initiatives of national significance in adult education including descriptions of the activities of the organizations such as "agricultural extension, workers education, and Americanization programs" (Wilson & Hayes, p 7). Wilson and Hayes (2000) explain that the "first attempts to define the field were to show its institutional and programmatic manifestations throughout society" and the "relation of knowledge and practice" (p. 7). The formalization of graduate programs in adult education began in the late 1920's and early 1930's with the first doctorates awarded in 1935 (Rowden, 1934).

While the next edition of the handbook in 1948 reflected the influence of World War II, it continued the tradition of informing the reader about how people "in the conduct of their daily lives go about the business of informing and educating themselves" (Cartwright, p. xi). This seems like a clear connection to what Knowles later terms "self-directness". This edition also demonstrated a connection to academia as it was published by the Institute of Adult Education at Teachers College, Columbia University where the first graduate program of adult education was established. Wilson and Hayes (2000) reflect that this handbook demonstrated that "the field was beginning to develop a sense of its professional identity first through study of its practices and now through developing a body of knowledge to inform that practice" (p. 8).

The next edition in 1960, edited by Malcolm Knowles, was the first to include individual essays by adult educators in order to "provide an overview description of the current nature, characteristics, and trends in the field of adult education" (p. xii). It was during this period that icons in the field of adult learning emerged. In 1961, Cyril Houle's "The Inquiring Mind" and his 1972 book *Design of Education* laid the foundation for Tough's "Learning Without a Teacher" and "The Adult's Learning Projects". These introduced the concept of self-directed learning and later influenced Knowles. Tough's (1979) research indicated that adults were more successful learners if they were aware of the benefits of their learning and the negative consequences of not learning. This became one of Knowles assumptions about adult learners.

Knowles (2005) early contributions to the field also included the articulation of his 6 core andragogical principles as "the learner's need to know, self-directed learning, prior experience of the learner, readiness to learn, orientation to learning and problem solving, and motivation to learn" (p. 183). While a great deal of discussion around these principles continues in the field of adult learning, they provide a foundation for new theories and a guide for practice. These principles will be examined with regard to their connection with CTE and the influence of technology later in this chapter.

While the 1970 edition of the handbook has new editors, Knowles makes a significant contribution in his prologue to the volume. He summarizes the themes of the earlier handbooks as focusing on topical issues such as "educating the public, collecting information, the elimination of 'profit makers', the debate between cultural and vocational adult education, and the tensions between self-actualization and educating a democratic citizenry" (Wilson and Hayes, p. 9). Wilson and Hayes describe the focus of the 1970's and 1980's handbooks as reflecting the "dominance of scientifically defined professional practice" (p. 12) of those decades.

Knowles 1970 text *The Modern Practice of Adult Education* and his 1973 *The Adult Learner: A Neglected Species* introduced to the term "andragogy" in the United States. Knowles learned the term from a European colleague who defined it as the "art and science of helping adults learn" (Merriam, Caffarella, & Baumgartner, 2007, p. 84). By the 1980's he had delineated several assumptions about adult learners. He characterized them as self-directed, having experience that was a resource for learning, needing to be ready to learn and needing to have an immediate application for the new knowledge (Merriam, Caffarella, & Baumgartner, 2007). By 1984 Knowles titled his new book *Andragogy in Action: Applying Modern Principles of Adult Learning* (Merriam, Cararella & Baumgarten, 2007, p. 473).

Knowles ideas drew commentary from a number of noted adult educators, among them Stephen Brookfield. Brookfield (1986) questioned Knowles ideas of self-directedness, his assumption of relating learning to particular social roles and his focus on the need of adult's for immediate application while developing his own ideas on critical thinking and critical theory. Critical thinking or critical reflection is "reflecting on the assumptions underlying our and others' ideas and actions, and contemplating alternative ways of thinking and living" (Brookfield, 1986, p. x). Brookfield (2005) further suggests that critical theory and critical reflection on assumptions were distinctive characteristic both of adult learning and of adult education practice.

Mezirow continues the discussion by introducing his own transformative learning theory which he defines as a process by which our taken-for-granted frames of references are transformed by making them more "inclusive, discriminating, open, emotionally capable of change, and reflective" (Merriam, 2007, p. 255). Transformational learning has had a longstanding impact on adult education. As Sharan Merriam (2008) reviewed three updates of *New Directions for Adult and Continuing Education* she noticed, she cites a chapter on transformational learning as the only constant across the updates. She does however note important differences in emphasis across the 15 years that these chapters span. The 1993 edition was mostly descriptive while by 2001 the chapter focused on empirical research. While the empirical research emphasis continued in the 2008 update, it was enhanced by diverse theoretical perspectives.

Illeris (2004) introduced a Danish perspective, on Brookfield's and Mezirow's ideas on critical reflection but also developed his own theory of the three dimensions of adult learning: cognitive, emotional and social. His model consisted of an inverted triangle with the two psychological poles, Piaget's cognition and Freud's emotion, at the two corners at the top and society at the lower vertex. However, he stressed that "all three dimensions are always integrated parts of the learning process and in practice do not exist as separate functions" (p. 20).

As editors of the 2000 edition of the *Handbook of Adult and Continuing Education*, Wilson and Hayes had the challenge of creating a text with the theme of seeing "adult education as a social practice of practical and prudent action, not just as an applied technical science" (p. 12). They claim that this series of handbooks "represent an unchanging epistemology for understanding the relationship between theory and practice" (p. 17).

11.2.2 History of Career and Technical Education

This relationship between theory and practice continues to be present in the exploration of the history of CTE. As noted in the introduction, many elements of the history of career and technical education are delineated by Malcolm Knowles (1989) in the "Landmarks and Heroes in Adult Education" chapter. He mentions that "ancient teachers were following their intuitions rather than some prescribed doctrine such as pedagogy" (p. 61). One might imagine that much of what was taught was very pragmatic life skills passed on from experts or from generation to generation. He includes the workers' education movement in Great Britain in his list of post Renaissance edu-

cational movements. Knowles (1989) also makes note of the emergence of apprenticeships, private vocational schools and agricultural societies during the colonial period in America. Elias and Merriam suggest that it was during the colonial period in the U.S. that a struggle between two educational philosophies developed. They compare the "elitist-classical education" that was transplanted from primarily France and England to American educational institutions, notably Harvard with Benjamin Franklin's efforts to establish a more "utilitarian democratic-vocational preparation" (p. 21) for the young colonies. Franklin's ideas here might be compared to his efforts of establishing an elitist Junta mentioned earlier in this chapter in the section on the history of adult education. He seemed to be an advocate for both the more theoretical as well as the practical education.

Knowles (1989) suggests that the adult education movement during the early 1800s "that had the greatest impact on the quality of life in this country is agricultural education" and cites local and regional agricultural societies and fairs as locations for farmers to learn new practices to improve productivity on their farms. He credits organizations such as the Grange, Farmers' Union, and the American Farm Bureau Federation in the last quarter of the 1800s with educating the farmers. The Land Grant Act of 1862 was especially significant in that it set aside land in every state for a "land-grant college for research and study in the agricultural and mechanical arts by average students" (Knowles, 1989, p. 65). After the Civil War, the new industrial society brought vocational education into the limelight again and the secondary education "curriculum expanded to include vocational and life-related subjects (Elias & Merriam, 2005, p. 23).

The progressive education movement that was prevalent at the beginning of the 1900s included "vocational education, university extension and cooperative extension, settlement houses for new immigrants and Americanization education" (Elias & Merriam, 2005, p. 58). Agricultural and industrial training were an important part of the movement. While Dewey is noted in the previous section on adult education, he played an important role in the development of vocational education during this progressive era. He argued that "education appropriate for American society must include both the liberal and the practical, both education for work and education for leisure" (Elias & Merriam, 2005, p. 62). This was a digression from the earlier thinkers that primarily liberally educated leaders were required for the growth of America.

While James Watson is credited with founding behaviorism in the 1920's, (Elias & Merriam, p. 83), the focus on changing behavior to optimize performance must have been a part of the everyday life of individuals from ancient times. Elias and Merriam (2005) state that "behaviorism grounds vocational education or what is now more commonly called career and technical education" (p. 99). They note that career and technical education is concerned with the outcomes rather than the process of learning and with criterion-referenced evaluation that compares the learner's progress with a fixed criterion of mastery. The competencies that the learner is expected to master are derived by the analysis of worker roles.

The period between the Civil War and World War I is credited with the emergence of numerous organizations focused on practical adult education. The creation of the Cooperative Extension Service and the passage of the Smith-Hughes Vocational Education Act began the formation of vocational schools open to adults across the country (Knowles, 1989).

Elias and Merriam (2005) note that by the mid-1990s the competency idea that was the backbone of vocational education was replaced by skill standards that were established by the National Skills Standards Board (NSSB). The NSSB's mission is to "develop skills standards in each of the 15 industry sectors and to establish assessment and certification systems (p. 100). But the implementation of these standards as well as

other aspects of adult learning and CTE could not avoid the impact of technology.

11.2.3 History of Technology

While today the term technology seems to be synonymous with computers it is important to consider that technology in many forms has been impacting educational practice for centuries. Lesgold (2000) reminds us that "prior to the 15th century, codified knowledge was extremely rare" and that "direct discussion with a wise person was the primary way of gaining knowledge" (p. 399). Books were not easily replicated so where expensive and rare. Even with the development of printing, only certain key books were reproduced widely. Knowles (1989) credits the invention of the printing press as having a great "impact on the advancement of adult education" (p. 62).

But between the printing press of the mid 1400s and today's computers is a history filled with technological innovations. Therefore it is useful to reflect on the development of these technological advances and the influences they have had on teaching and learning. In the courses that the author teaches at Teachers College/Columbia University, she often divides the class into groups and assigns each group a period in history. She then presents the scenario that the students have just been invited to attend a workshop on the latest technology in teaching and learning in their field of practice. They are asked to identify what technologies they will expect to be presented at the workshop and how those technologies likely impacted educational practice at that time. With so much focus on computers and learning it is always informative for students to realize that this is not the first time that educators have had to adapt to technological changes in their practice. Whether it was the printing press, telephone, copying machine, or computer, educators have always been challenged to use new technology for effective teaching and learning.

Shea-Schultz and Fogarty (2002) note that it wasn't until the late 1960's when the U.S. Department of Defense initiated a project (Advanced Research Projects Agency Network: ARPANET) to create a nation-wide computer network using phone lines. Over the next two decades, the network became the "province of academic institutions, scientists, and government employees engaged in research and communications" (p. 7) because it allowed them to share data by connecting to each others' computers. Lack of standards was a problem and it wasn't until 1989 when "Tim Berners-Lee led a team at Switzerland's European Particle Physics Laboratory (CERN) in developing what he dubbed World Wide Web standards" (p. 8). By 1991, scientists at CERN had conceptualized the World Wide Web (WWW) with the sole purpose of making research findings and scientific materials available to the academic and scientific community on a global network (Lau, 2000, p. i).

Shea-Schultz and Fogarty (2002) note 1992 as the next "great innovation for the Web" when programmers at the National Center for Supercomputing Applications (NCSA) at the University of Illinois developed the Mosaic browser which displayed embedded graphic elements as well as text (p. 8). Also noteworthy in 1992 was the U.S. government's decision to "bail out of network management" freeing the web for commercial use (p. 9). The expanded use of the internet was fueled by a parallel advancement in the "rise of increasingly powerful, yet reasonably priced, personal computers fueled by silicon microchip processors" (p. 9). At this point one is tempted to add the cliché that the rest is history. However history in this case has become a quickly moving target. Wiki's and blogs have become a part of our everyday vocabulary, and Web 2.0 surfaces in discussions as online social networks become more commonplace. It becomes ever more important that we take the advice of Kasworm and Londoner (2000) "to accept and embrace the possibilities of technology" (p. 225).

However reviewing these separate histories leads to the discovery that they are not in fact individual silos but the development of each was very influential to the others. Reviewing these separate histories further confirm that career and technical education and adult education have been inseparable fields. No wonder many land-grant universities in the United States have a department of career and technical education and adult education or vice versa.

11.3 EVIDENCE AND CONSEQUENCES OF CONNECTIONS BETWEEN ANDRAGOGY, CTE, TECHNOLOGY

Not only did they influence each other but in fact they all developed as a result of societal influences and in turn had an impact on that very society. The interconnections and cross influences become apparent in several instances of how they connect in real world examples. This chapter will provide several case studies in connections in academic and business venues.

11.3.1 Adult Learning and CTE Intertwined

Using the traditional 80-20 rule, traditional adult learning would seem to be 80% adult learning and 20% CTE while traditional CTE courses would be the reverse, 80% CTE and 20% adult learning. But real examples produce a more even split between the two; nearer to 70-30 or even 60-40. Elias and Merriam (2005) articulate the need for theory as a foundation of practice. "Theory without practice leads to empty idealism and action without philosophical reflection leads to a mindless activism" (p. 4). Much of the work of the theorists has been developed through the lens of the practitioner. As theories developed, practice changed. As practice changed, new theories developed. Malcolm Knowles (2005), in his classic text "The Adult Learner", provides the historical development of learning theories in a summary of propounders and interpreters. His list includes 61 propounders and 33 interpreters who have influenced the development of learning theories over the past 130 years by their complimentary roles of putting forward new ideas for consideration and interpreting those ideas in light of practice. This list begins with Thorndike and Dewey of the early 1900s to Brookfield and Mezirow today. Dewey believed that experience was always the starting point of an educational process, not the end result. Thorndike believed that 3 laws governed the learning of animals and human beings: the law of readiness for learning, the law of exercise which connects learning to practice, the law of effect which is dependent on the consequences of learning. This theory-practice duality continues in Knowles' andragogical principles: "the learner's need to know, self-directed learning, prior experience of the learner, readiness to learn, orientation to learning and problem solving, and motivation to learn" (2005, p. 183).

11.3.2 Technicians Advancing Their Careers

Several of Knowles' principles of adult learning, especially self-directedness and the connection between experience and learning, are evident in the next example. Knowles indicated that adult learners had experience that could be a resource for their learning, needed to feel ready to learn, and saw an immediate application for their new knowledge. These needs were evident in the experiences of the technical employees who participated in the program described below. Over a period of time, a large multinational corporation had employed a number of technically trained individuals for its laboratories. As employment needs changes, the company realized that it needed more individuals with a broader perspective and desired to have more technical employees with a

baccalaureate degree. Similarly many of the technicians who had completed a two-year vocational degree were feeling the need to advance in their careers, a move that only would happen if they had a four-year degree. The company partnered with several local academic institutions to provide courses on the company site so that employees who wished to pursue a bachelor degree would have the opportunity to do so. The initiative valued the prior experience of the learners as employees as well as the knowledge that they had acquired in their vocational training. The employees were self-directed in their commitment to earn a B.S. degree and motivated to do so by the possibility of a promotion. This arrangement not only provided a convenient venue for the classes but enhanced the learning by providing out of class opportunities for collaboration. As Palloff and Pratt (1999) suggest, "key to the learning process are the interactions among students themselves, the interactions between faculty and students, and the collaboration in learning that results from these interactions" (p. 5).

11.3.3 Action Learning Example of Reflection and Action

Rag Ravens (1982) pioneered action learning as a way of combining working on real work opportunities, problems, tasks and projects with thoughtful reflection. It encompasses a learning cycle of action, reflection, theorization and application. While the three essential components of action learning: action, critical reflection, and the building of one's own theories were delineated by Mezirow (2000), numerous practitioners and theorists have added their comments on the process over the decades. For example, Mumford (1997) notes that learners are expected to try out new behaviors, to reflect critically on their experiences, to distil some generalizable principles and to try out the results in other similar contexts. He cites "recognized ignorance not programmed knowledge is the key to Action Learning; people start to learn with and from each other only when they discover that no one knows the answer but all are obliged to find it" (p. 3). Marsick (1999) describes action learning as a process in which "people take action while they are learning, and bring the results of their experiments to the group for discussion, as would happen in an action research project. Unlike action research, however, equal (and sometimes more) attention is paid to the personal learning than to problem solving" (p. 120). All of these authors position action learning in the intersection of thinking and doing.

The venue for this example of action learning was a Fortune 500 company founded in Minnesota over 100 years ago and currently operating in 63 countries worldwide. The issue surfaced as a result of the rapid growth in business in the Asia region. This resulted in the need for effective leadership among the country nationals managing the technical centers in their home country. A learning forum was established with twelve technical managers who headed technical centers and laboratories in the Mainland, Hong Kong and Taiwan of China, India, Philippines, Singapore, Republic of Korea, Thailand and the regional technical managers from the regional headquarters of 3M in Asia. The function of these technical laboratories was to support the business plans at the country and regional levels. Geographically, the participants and facilitators were separately located in three continents, 10 countries and 5 time zones. While the participants represented culturally diverse groups they had very similar problems in their quickly growing technical centers. The objective of the learning process was to enhance management and leadership competencies of the technical managerial team in the Asia region in order to enhance their performance and their careers. Because of the rapid business growth, these academically trained engineers and scientists had the opportunity to move quickly from the individual contributor to the leadership role in their technical center. Their academic background had prepared them for the individual contributor role but not for

their new leadership role. They were still functioning as 80% technical and 20% management/adult learners. The task of this training program was to provide them with the knowledge and skills to be comfortable and competent in their new roles which required them to function at 20% technical and 80% management/adult learners.

It was important to consider that while training is one of the often-used solutions for rapidly strengthening management capacities within local subsidiaries, to carry out traditional training in a non-western context could have inherent difficulties. Transfer of management know-how to a non-western business environment has proven to be difficult by numerous studies (Hofstede, 2001; Kanungo & Mendonca, 1996; Saner & Yiu, 1994). This type of organization learning requires changes of mental models and behavioral responses (Senge, 2006). Edmondson & Moingeorn (1998) suggest that innovation and organization learning have to be an on-going process that requires individual cognition and supports organizational adaptiveness.

In the context of this Asia Technical Managers' Learning Forum (ATMLF), the linkages between action and reflection were explicit. Managers were asked to work in 2 peer groups. One task oriented group worked on a real management related project with the objective of formulating recommendations based on research and data analysis (action research). The other group shared reflections on the process itself. The entire development, delivery, and management of the learning experience took 3 months to prepare and 15 months to implement through an onsite workshop and online activities. The entire learning process consisted of outlining the activities in line with Raven's action-learning model, identifying issues and sites for the projects, involving participants in self-assessments, managing the process of online activities, compiling project reports for discussion and general dissemination, and commencing a virtual graduation ceremony. The instructors continually emphasized that the learning was to be both informational and experiential so they would be able to learn new skills and practice them on a real life issue. Yiu and Parker (2005) provided a strategic model which integrated numerous distance learning elements such as electronic forums, video/phone conference meetings, email and a virtual graduation into an action learning program on leadership.

11.3.4 From Engineer to Trainer

Growth in the Asia region resulted in a second project. This one involved the technical service engineers in the country technical centers. Each country technical center had a large numbers of recent college science and engineering graduates in their centers functioning as technical service engineers. A large part of the job of technical service is to train customers, sales/marketing people, etc on the technical aspects of new products. These highly trained technical employees however, had no knowledge or experience in developing and delivering successful training. These employees are located throughout the Asia region from as far north as China and the Democratic People's Republic of Korea to as far south as Singapore and Malaysia with most traveling only in their own country.

While other options were considered, the decision was made to develop sustainable expertise to deliver a train-the-trainer course within the technical community itself in each country. This would establish a master trainer in each country who would be available to conduct future courses and provide continuing support for the technical service engineers themselves. The regional technical manager selected a group of experienced technical service professionals from countries across the region to be trained to deliver the course. A course was designed to accomplish these goals.

An onsite learning experience in Singapore was the focal point of the training. For the first ½ of the first week of onsite training the two co-instructors taught the theory and its applications to the new trainers. During the second ½ of that

week they taught the methodology of how to teach the course that they had just participated in. During the second week, actual classes of employees at the Singapore technical center were scheduled. The new trainers were grouped to co-train these classes under the supervision of the two instructors. An hour feedback session was scheduled at the end of each day for new trainers to receive feedback from their peer trainers and the instructors who observed the class. This also provided an opportunity for the new trainers to critically reflect on their previous assumptions about training and their new role as a trainer. Since the participants had been selected for this training as a tribute to their experience and the confidence that their country technical manager had in them, there was a high level of motivation to succeed. They were then encouraged to adapt or integrate any country/culture specific activities as they prepared to deliver the course in their home country. Upon returning to their home technical center, the new trainers scheduled their own classes. After completing their first training, the new trainers either video-conferenced or audio-conferenced their follow-up session with one of the instructors. This included both questions on the content and the opportunity for reflection on the process. Only at the completion of all the steps were they awarded a plaque as a certified instructor.

11.3.5 From Nurse to Nurse Educator

Another example of the confluence of CTE and adult learning exists in the author's experience as an instructor in a cohort masters program for practicing nurses who are aspiring to become nurse educators either in a medical or academic setting. Several of these nurses began their careers as vocationally trained health care workers, eventually earned a B.S. in nursing and now are enrolled in a program to earn an academic masters degree. Their previous training and experience gained over usually a decade or more seem to be the perfect foundation for their new role in education. As subject matter experts in their nursing specialty they are eager to learn training techniques but also the foundational adult learning theories behind these educational practices. Because many of them are already recognized as subject matter experts within their organizations, they have often been given mentorship and training responsibilities with no guidance for their new role. They are eager to review the literature and study the empirical research behind teaching and learning. They exhibit the qualities of an adult learner that Knowles delineates. They are self-directed, motivated to learn, feel the need to know and are utilizing their prior experience.

11.3.6 The Influence of Technology on Adult Learning and CTE

Malcolm Knowles (2005) sees technology as providing learning opportunities in the "andragogical tradition" (p. 237) and as consistent with the adult learning idea of self-directedness. Lesgold (2000) suggests that just as the book "removed some of the need for memorization as a force for knowledge distribution, so the computer removes some of the need for overlearning of routine information processing procedures, since these can be accomplished by computers" (p. 401). He cites the example of whether or not students need to know how to perform complex algebraic calculations if they can be done by computer or calculator.

11.3.7 Technology Integrated Into Classroom Learning

Some essentials exist for effective learning with or without technology. Nilson (2003) observed that students learn best when they are actively engaged, when learning evokes emotional not just intellectual involvement. This is consistent with Illeris's three dimensions of learning. Cranton (2006) emphasizes the importance of empowering the student by interactions in the learning environment and being aware of power relationships.

"The creation of a learning community supports and encourages knowledge acquisition. It creates a sense of excitement about learning together and renews the passion involved with exploring new realms in education" (Palloff & Pratt, 1999, p. 163). But introducing technology includes an added dimension. Loader (1998) announces that "the emergence of the new information and communications technologies such as the Internet are said to herald the coming of the "information society": a new social and economic paradigm restructuring the traditional dimensions of time and space within which we live, work, and interact" (p. 3)

The following example illustrates some of these ideas. When the author teaches on campus courses in staff development and adult learning and leadership, there is always an online assignment to provide students with the experience of learning online. Using technology in an education course offers a unique advantage. In most courses technology is utilized as a course delivery system. In an education course, the course objectives facilitate the inclusion of an analysis of the effectiveness of the use of technology. Students are continually required to reflect on and discuss the learning advantages and disadvantages of technology as they participate in the learning. Course assignments that utilize technology enhance this learning.

The use of the asynchronous Discussion Board where students post their own ideas and comments then reply to other students' ideas was seen to facilitate critical reflection. On assignment requires students to read a journal article of their choosing related to staff development. They are then to summarize their article and post their reflection on it. They must then read several other student postings and comment on them. Following are a few representative student comments on this assignment:

- "The discussion conducted here is very involving; everybody could get a chance to express his own ideas. Moreover, the discussion board online gives us a further opportunity to share ideas with all of the class. It has been developed into a real learning forum. Everybody chose their favorite articles about learning and training in their fields, and then shared their own ideas on the "blackboard", thus evokes a real open discussion. This learning style makes me feel that I can learn anytime anywhere from so many people of diverse fields. By posting, reading, and replying online, our learning location has burst out of the limited classroom and lecture time boundary, thus it has given us an authentic flexibility and motivation to learn."

- "It is a medium that does promote student engagement in discourse without the normal bias of face-to-face communication (because our appearance is reduced to letters in a computer screen). And although we have the opportunity to influence and suggest tone, etc. by the use of color, sizes, etc. the initial barriers to traditional communication are somehow diminished. The use of discussion boards allows for a lot of reflection prior to committing to opinions. The student has the time and the resources to build a message that will convey every idea that s/he wants to communicate".

- "The process of responding to skilled questions posed by co-group members allowed me to consider and deeply reflect on my actions with respect to learning and how it is applied at workplace."

- "The conversations were not superficial interactions but purposeful, focused and useful. The instructions allowed all group members an equal opportunity to have their "voices" heard.

It was interesting to see words like discourse, critical reflection and community as part of the student reflections on the online experience. In the chapter, "The Passion of Pluralism", Maxine Greene (1995) comments about community: "We are in search of what John Dewey called 'the Great Community" but at the same time, we are challenged as never before to confront plurality and multiplicity" (p. 155). "To open up our experience to existential possibilities of multiple kinds is to extend and deepen what each of us thinks of when he or she speaks of a community" (p. 161). Elements of adult learning theory in action are evidenced in the comments and actions of participants in technology enhanced learning cited above.

11.3.8 Distance Education and Online Learning

Knowles (1989) credits William Harper with offering the first distance education course. Harper was a professor at Yale but taught courses during the summer at Chautauqua in western New York. As an outgrowth of his Chautauqua experience he developed a course in the format of a correspondence course in 1879. This grew into more formalized home study programs. When Harper became president of the University of Chicago in 1892 he established an extension department with a correspondence division there.

Distance education has taken many forms over the decades, always leveraging the newest technology for its benefit. Yermish (2000) defines a "passing of remoteness" as a "phenomenon of the rise of the Internet and other distance-shrinking technologies" (p. 208) and reminds us that "ever since the advent of television, educators have wrestled with the viability of using this technology to reach wider audiences. Educational television facilitated the distribution of high-quality program content in a one-directional fashion"(p. 208). Lau (2000) suggests that "Distance learning was pioneered at Stanford University" in 1970's "to meet the increasing demand for high-tech engineers and computer scientists at Silicon Valley" (p. i).

These virtual classrooms are modeled after the familiar on campus classroom. For example, in physical dimensions, the virtual classroom is really thousands of miles wide by thousands of miles long by thousands of miles high. The physical distance is further amplified by time difference. The challenge is how to foster a sense of "community" among the participants without the comfort of physical proximity. The traditional whiteboard and flip charts are replaced by fax machines, computer files, email, telephones, and video conferencing facilities. The instantaneous feedback between a teacher and a student are broken when using any asynchronous communication medium. The challenge is to sustain the individual learners willingness to participate. With competing personal and professional priorities participants' attention is often diverted from the learning process. Conditions can also differ from location to location in terms of communication infrastructure. The challenges are to present the information in an engaging manner and to accommodate the logistical constraints faced by different participants.

Sitting in the classroom is replaced by typing on a computer keyboard, reading a computer screen, listening to voices on the phone, or watching a monitor. Instead of feeling the presence of other learners, participants are learning in front of their monitors and hence are often distracted by other more pressing daily tasks. With the exception of pre-arranged synchronous activities, the participants need to direct their own learning just as they would in regard to their day-to-day responsibility. The teacher's communications are limited to writing and reading, but much less speaking; facilitating and group maintaining become essential skills. In cyberspace, individual actors move on their own orbit in the pursuit of learning.

The adaptation to this new environment provides a new idea of space and society. Loader (1998) reminds us that numerous social scientists share the notion that "society is being transformed by a revolution in information technology which is creating an entirely new social structure" (p. 4). Hakken (1999) suggests that the @ symbol used to indicate an electronic domain in an email address, is also an indication of the social space to which one is connected. Yiu and Parker (2005) provided a strategic model which integrated numerous distance learning elements (electronic forums, video/phone conference meetings, email, and even a virtual graduation) into an action learning model program on leadership. Jochems, Merrienboer and Koper (2004) stress the importance of addressing the pedagogical, technological and organizational aspects in order for online learning to be successful (p.199). Adams and Freeman (2000) suggest that "a primary determinant of the success of an online distance learning program is its ability to develop a sense of community among its online participants" (p. 157). While many of the student quotes cited earlier would seem to disagree with this, Web 2.0 technologies promise to improve social networks. Hakken (1999) advises that "we must come to terms…with an accelerated decoupling of space from place (p. 215). White and Bridwell (2004) concur by suggesting that new technology is "significantly altering the social role of learning" and that distance learning is only an intermediate step toward a "telelearning environment" in which distance and location become arbitrary" (p. 287).

11.4 FUTURE DIRECTIONS

Merriam (2008) suggests that as we begin the twenty-first century, we should consider the past shifts in the focus of adult learning in order to prepare for those of the future. She identifies two main shifts in this focus of adult learning. One shift is from the individual learner to the learner within the various contexts in which learning takes place. This new perspective considers "learning as part of the system's cultural and historical norms… (and) how physical space and spatiality encourages or inhibits learning" (p. 94). The second shift is from learning as a purely cognitive activity to one that is multidimensional in nature. This might be considered to be a more holistic approach in which "learning is construed as a much broader activity involving the body, the emotions, and the spirit as well as the mind" (p. 95). This seems consistent with Illeris' three dimensions of learning mentioned earlier: cognitive, emotional, social. Mazarr (1999) suggests similar ideas by noting that "knowledge-era learning" must become more "holistic" and "high-tech"; must "emphasize creativity and participation" and be "characterized by more choice and competition" (p. 285).

Fenwick (2008) lists 4 emerging trends in adult learning: areas of definitions, an increased emphasis on practice-based learning, the importance of identity and literacy and power and politics. He defines learning not as an outcome but as a process that is "understood to involve not just human change but interconnections of humans and their actions with rules, tools and texts, cultural, and material environments" (p. 19). The emphasis on practice-based learning is consistent with Merriam's note on the increasing emphasis on the contexts in which learning takes place. Its importance is also evident in Senge's (2006) concept of the learning organization that he proposed in the early 1990's and Wenger's (1998) communities of practice model that emerged in the late 1990's. This was also evidenced by the growing popularity of Ravens (1982) Action Learning methodology which was discussed in more detail in an earlier case study. Fenwick (2008) suggests that "people's sense of their own knowledge in work and the knowledge valued by the group to which they see themselves belonging form a critical element of their sense of identity" (p. 22) and there are "fundamental tensions related to what knowledge counts most and who says so (p. 24). Finally, the traditional organizational power and politics are taking new forms in the virtual organizations and transnational work sites.

Further future predictions follow two themes. The first cautions that emerging new technologies will not replace the old. Valmont (2003) reminds us that "oral storytelling did not die when Gutenberg

created the printing press" and "novels did not go away when films became popular. Literacies simply evolve" (p. 298). Nilson (2003) agrees and adds that she expects the low-tech instructional tools such as the black or white board or overhead projector to be around for years while the high tech tools will become obsolete very quickly. The second theme challenges us to envision the impact of new technologies on learning. In his predictions for the future, Mazarr (1999) delineates "three specific categories of technologies: biotechnology, renewable energy, and information technology" (p. 73). Under information technology he notes the "Pervasive Knowledge Network" and "nanotechnology" (pp. 82-83). Bray (2009) summarizes this by reminding us that "Career and technical education is always about the future" because its focus is on preparing "lifelong learners who are able to transition today's knowledge to the needs of tomorrow" (p. 6).

The author's predictions might be a future with even more connections, more blurring of boundaries; a future that values personal philosophies but shared experiences and goals. With opportunities for more attention to individual needs and learning styles, Shea-Schultz and Fogarty (2002) might say it best with their chapter heading "The Student Rules" (p. 14). Maxine Greene (2001) challenges us to see the future as an opportunity for "thinking of things as if they could be otherwise" (Greene, 2001, p. 127).

11.5 CONCLUSION

Adult learning. Career and technical education. History. Technology. Each of these represents a discipline in its own right and as such, they are often studied individually as if they existed in a silo without any influence from the other three or even the social context in which they develop. Yet, in reality, it is impossible to isolate one from the others. The author's physics background has led to a familiarity with a video series called "The Mechanical Universe". The videos are significant because they show scientists as individuals in a societal context with their daily struggles and controversies. One of these videos provides insights into the contributions of the Greek mathematicians and philosophers. The narrator discusses the golden age of Greece and suggests that it was so because they focused on the questions more than the answers. He suggests that it was the continuous questioning that moved them forward. It is an opportunity for the author to remind the students that they are expected to leave class with more questions than they had when they started the class. So it might be fitting that after viewing the past history of adult learning and CTE and technology to consider some questions as a guide into the future. How can Web 2.0 enhance out teaching and learning? Should there be more of an intentional meshing of adult learning with career and technical education? If so, how? Could Guttenberg ever have imagined what he had started by connecting information with people at a distance and connecting authors of information with readers who were previously total strangers?

REFERENCES

Adams, E., & Freeman, C. (2000). Commuting the distance of distance learning: the Pepperdine story . In Lau, L. (Ed.), *Distance learning technologies: issues, trends and opportunities* (pp. 157–165). Hershey, PA: Idea Group Publishing.

Bray, J. (2009). Embrace the future now! *Techniques, 84*(5), 6.

Brookfield, S. (1986). *Understanding and facilitating adult learning.* San Francisco:Jossey-Bass.

Brookfield, S. (2005). *The power of critical theory: liberating adult learning and teaching.* San Francisco: Jossey-Bass.

Cartwright, M. (1948). Preface . In Ely, M. (Ed.), *Handbook of adult education* (pp. xi–xii). New York: Institute of Adult Education, Teachers College, Columbia University.

Cranton, P. (2006). *Understanding and promoting transformative learning.* San Francisco: John Wiley & Sons.

Edmondson, A., & Moingeon, B. (1998). From Organizational Learning to the Learning Organisation. *Management Learning, 29*(1), 5–20. doi:10.1177/1350507698291001

Elias, J. L., & Merriam, S. B. (2005). *Philosophical foundations of adult education.* Malabar, FL: Krieger Publishing Company.

Fenwick, T. (Fall 2008). Workplace learning: emerging trends and new perspectives in *New directions for adult and continuing education No. 119* (pp. 17-26). San Francisco: Jossey-Bass.

Greene, M. (1995). *Releasing the imagination.* San Francisco: Jossey-Bass.

Greene, M. (2001). *Variations on a blue guitar.* New York: Teachers College Press.

Hakken, D. (1999). *Cyborgs@cyberspace.* New York: Routledge.

Hofstede, G. (2001). *Culture's consequence: Comparing values, behaviors, institutions and organizations across nations.* Beverly Hills, CA: Sage Publication.

Houle, C. O. (1961). *The Inquiring Mind.* Madison, WI: University of Wisconsin Press.

Illeris, K. (2004). *The three dimensions of learning.* Malabar, FL: Krieger.

Jochems, W., von Merrienboer, J., & Koper, R. (2004). *Integrated e-learning: Implications for pedagogy, technology and organization.* New York: RoutledgeFalmer.

Kanungo, R. N., & Mendonca, M. (1996). Cultural contingencies and leadership in developing countries . In Banberger, P. A., Erez, M., & Bacharach, S. B. (Eds.), *Research in the Sociology of Organizations* (pp. 263–295). Greenwich, CT: Jai Press.

Kasworm, C. D., & Londoner, C. A. (2000). Adult learning and technology . In Wilson, A. L., & Hayes, E. (Eds.), *Handbook of adult and continuing education* (pp. 224–242). San Francisco: John Wiley & Sons.

Knowles, M. (1960). *Handbook of adult education.* Chicago: Adult Education Association.

Knowles, M. (1989). *The making of an adult educator.* San Francisco: Jossey-Bass.

Knowles, M., Holton, E., & Swanson, R. (2005). *The adult learner.* Burlington, MA: Elsevier.

Lau, L. (2000). *Distance learning technologies: Issues, trends and opportunities.* Hershey, PA: Idea Group Publishing.

Lesgold, A. (2000). What are the tools for? Revolutionary change does not follow the usual norms . In Lajoie, S. (Ed.), *Computers as cognitive tools* (pp. 399–408). Mahwah, NJ: Lawrence Erlbaum Associates.

Loader, B. (1998). *Cyberspace divide: Equality, agency, and policy in the information society.* New York: Routledge. doi:10.4324/9780203169537

Marsick, V., & Watkins, K. (1999). *Facilitating learning organizations.* Brookfield, VT: Gower.

Mazarr, M. (1999). *Global trends 2005: An owner's manual for the next decade.* New York: St. Martin's Press.

Merriam, S., Caffarella, R., & Baumgartner, L. (2007). *Learning in adulthood: A comprehensive guide.* San Francisco: John Wiley & Sons.

Merriam, S. B. (Fall 2008). Adult learning theory for the twenty-first century in *New directions for adult and continuing education* (pp. 93-98). San Francisco: Jossey-Bass.

Mezirow, J. (2000). *Learning as transformation.* San Francisco: Jossey- Bass.

Mumford, A. (1997). Action learning as a vehicle for learning . In Mumford, A. (Ed.), *Action learning at work* (pp. 3–24). Hampshire, UK: Gower.

Nilson, L. B. (2003). *Teaching at its best.* San Francisco, CA: Anker Publishing.

Palloff, R., & Pratt, K. (1999). *Building learning communities in cyberspace.* San Francisco, CA: Jossey-Bass.

Ravens, R. (1982). *The origin and growth of action learning.* London: Chartwell Bratt.

Rowden, D. (Ed.). (1934). *Handbook of adult education.* New York: American Association for Adult Education.

Schon, D. (1983). *The reflective practitioner.* New York: Basic Books.

Senge, P. M. (2006). *The fifth discipline: The art and practice of the learning organization.* New York: Doubleday Currency.

Shea-Schultz, H., & Fogarty, J. (2002). *Online learning today: Strategies that work.* San Francisco: Berrett-Koehler Publishers.

Tough, A. (1967). *Learning without a teacher.* Toronto: Institute for Studies in Education.

Tough, A. (1979). *The adult's learning project.* Toronto: Institute for Studies in Education.

Valmont, W. (2003). *Technology for literacy teaching and learning.* New York: Houghton Mifflin.

White, B. A., & Bridwell, C. (2004). Distance learning techniques . In Galbraith, M. (Ed.), *Adult learning methods: A guide for effective instruction* (pp. 273–288). Malabar, FL: Krieger.

Wilson, A. L., & Hayes, A. R. (2000). *Handbook of adult and continuing education.* San Francisco: Jossey-Bass.

Yermish, I. (2000). A case for case studies via video-conferencing . In Lau, L. (Ed.), *Distance learning technologies: Issues, trends and opportunities* (pp. 208–217). Hershey, PA: Idea Group Publishing.

Yiu, L., & Parker, J. (2005). Cyber action learning and virtual project teams for leadership and management development . In Jacobs, R. L., & Osman-Gani, A. M. (Eds.), *Workplace training & learning: Cases from cross-cultural perspectives* (pp. 1–14). New York: Pearson/Prentice Hall.

Chapter 12
Challenges and Opportunities in Career and Technical Education

Leane B. Skinner
Auburn University, USA

Maria M. Witte
Auburn University, USA

James E. Witte
Auburn University, USA

ABSTRACT

Career and Technical Education (CTE) is no longer just a training program for workers. CTE today prepares students for employment, industry credentialing, postsecondary education, and lifelong learning. This change, stimulated by demand and federal legislation, has brought many new challenges and opportunities for CTE. Federal legislation, CTE image, and decrease in secondary enrollment and in teacher education programs have created challenges and opportunities for all CTE stakeholders. In 2008, a National Career and Technical Education Research Agenda were approved by the Association of Career and Technical Education (ACTE). This agenda will be the framework for future research relating to the critical issues and concerns in CTE. This chapter addresses the challenges and opportunities for CTE as well as future trends.

12.1 INTRODUCTION

Federal support for Career and Technical Education (CTE), previously called Vocational Education, began with the Smith-Hughes Vocational Act of 1917. Historically, CTE provided job-specific training to non-college bound students. Today, required work skills include problem-solving, reasoning, flexibility, interpersonal skills, and

technological skills. These skills cannot be obtained by simple job-specific training. In addition to cognitive skills, many jobs require postsecondary education (Rojewski, 2002). As CTE has strong ties to the workforce, changes in employer demands, economic conditions, educational philosophies, and funding support, have tremendously impacted even the definition and name of the field. The most recent reauthorization of the Carl D. Perkins Career and Technical Education Act of 2006 defines CTE as:

DOI: 10.4018/978-1-61520-747-3.ch012

Organized educational activities that offer a sequence of courses that provides individuals with coherent and rigorous content aligned with challenging academic standards and relevant technical knowledge and skills needed to prepare for further education and careers in current or emerging professions; provides technical skills proficiency, an industry-recognized credential, a certificate, or an associate degree; and may include prerequisite courses that meet the requirements of this subparagraph; and include competency-based applied learning that contributes to the academic knowledge, higher-order reasoning and problem-solving skills, work attitudes, general employability skills, technical skills, and occupation-specific skills, and knowledge of all aspects of an industry, including entrepreneurship, of an individual. (p. 4)

Unlike some academic areas, CTE must be in a constant state of change to serve all the stakeholders. Changes in labor market should drive constant and ongoing change in CTE. Attention must be paid to changes in the labor market and career-focused education must be redefined in response to emerging trends (Kazis, 2005). Abel (2006) discusses the book, *The Jobs Revolution: Changing How America Works*, and states that students should be equipped with concepts that relate to all problems, rather than specific job related problems. Just as we have witnessed tremendous changes in the labor market since 1917, so have we experienced tremendous changes in CTE. These changes provide new challenges and opportunities for CTE.

The purpose of this chapter is to address the challenges facing CTE, as well as the opportunities that may thrive from the challenges. This chapter is organized using the following sections: background, challenges and opportunities, future trends, and a conclusion. The challenges include meeting the requirements of legislation, CTE image, and decline of CTE enrollment and teacher education.

12.2 BACKGROUND

Early in the history of CTE, there was a need to prepare additional blue-collar workers for the nation's farms and factories (Lynch, 2000). Today there are CTE academies that are viewed as a passage way to Ivy League schools. These academies may offer programs such as science and technology, engineering, medicine, business, telecommunications and computer science, culinary and hotel administration, and the arts (Hu, 2009). The years from 1982-1994 reflected a steep decline in CTE programs and enrollment. Programs were not viewed as meeting the needs of the students, employers, and communities. In addition, CTE programs were not considered an option for the college-bound students and the curriculum was judged as being weak. There was a perception that CTE would inhibit rather than enhance a student's future (Catri, 1998). The goal of CTE today is to prepare students for employment, industry credentialing, postsecondary education, and lifelong learning.

Bill Gates said the following on March 9, 2007 at a U.S. Senate Committee Hearing:

Our current expectations for what our students should learn in school were set fifty years ago to meet the needs of an economy based on manufacturing and agriculture. We now have an economy based on knowledge and technology. Despite the best efforts of many committed educators and administrators, our high schools have simply failed to adapt to this change. As any parent knows, however, our children have not—they are fully immersed in digital culture. As a result, while most students enter high school wanting to succeed, too many end up bored, unchallenged and disengaged from the high school curriculum—'digital natives' caught up in an industrial-age learning model. Many high school students today either drop out or simply try to get by. For those who graduate, many lack the skills they need to attend college or to find a job that can support a family. Until we transform the American high school for the 21st century, we will continue limiting the lives of millions of Americans each year. The cost of inaction substantially increases each year that we fail to act. (p. 4)

If there is one thing all can agree on, it is that the world around has changed and that in order to keep up, CTE must also change. Toffler (Partnership for 21st Century Skills, 2003), a futuristic writer said, "The illiterate of the 21st century will not be those who cannot read and write, but those who cannot learn, unlearn, and relearn" (p. 4). In a video by Fisch (2008), "Shift Happens," former U.S. Secretary of Education is quoted as saying that the top 10 jobs in 2010 will not have existed 2004. A knowledge and technology economy has emerged. Google supports 31 billion searches each month. Technical information is doubling every two years (Fisch). How does CTE prepare students for jobs and technologies that may not yet exist?

12.3 CHALLENGES AND OPPORTUNITIES

Competing in the global economy is an absolute necessity for survival of the American way of life. Education, especially CTE education, has been endorsed for years as a means of providing career opportunities. President Barack Obama stated the following in his February 24, 2009 State of the Union address:

In a global economy where the most valuable skill you can sell is your knowledge, a good education is no longer just a pathway to opportunity—it is a pre-requisite. (p. 63)

Right now, three-quarters of the fastest-growing occupations require more than a high school diploma. And yet, just over half of our citizens have that level of education. We have one of the highest high school dropout rates of any industrialized

nation. And half of the students who begin college never finish. (p. 64)

And so tonight, I ask every American to commit to at least one year or more of higher education or career training. This can be community college or a four-year school; vocational training or an apprenticeship. But whatever the training may be, every American will need to get more than a high school diploma. And dropping out of high school is no longer an option. It's not just quitting on yourself, it's quitting on your country—and this country needs and values the talents of every American. That is why we will provide the support necessary for you to complete college and meet a new goal: by 2020, America will once again have the highest proportion of college graduates in the world. (p. 68)

A quality career/technical program can reduce a school's dropout rate by as much as six percent (Southern Regional Education Board [SREB], n.d.). In a Gates Foundation report, *The Silent Epidemic* (Bridgeland, Dilulio, & Morison, 2006), almost half of the high school dropouts stated that a major reason for dropping out was that classes were not interesting. The report recommends improving curricula to make schools more relevant and to improve the connection between school and work. Eighty-one percent (81%) of the dropouts surveyed said there should be more real world learning. This is the call for CTE. Lynch (2000) found that there is support for a "13th and 14th year as a minimum education benchmark for the next generation of American students" (p. 10).

CTE has survived many threatening hurricanes, but still may have many storms to face. As we work through some of the challenges that have created the framework for change, CTE educators must be innovative and creative. Career and Technical Education programs in the U.S. exist because of federal legislation. Federal government has been an influence in determining the direction of career and technical education, especially secondary

(Rowjeski, 2002). Economic development has also had an influence on the direction and content of CTE Since inception.

12.3.1 Challenge and Opportunities I: Meeting the Requirements of Legislation

From the initial stages of CTE, legislation has played a role in the development. The next section will cover recent legislation and the challenges and opportunities associated with each. The re-authorization of the Carl D. Perkins Act of 2006 and No Child Left Behind will be reviewed.

12.3.2 Carl D. Perkins Act of 2006

The Carl D. Perkins Vocational and Technical Education Act was first authorized by the federal government in 1984 and reauthorized in 1998. The act aims to increase the quality of technical education. On August 12, 2006 President George W. Bush signed into law the reauthorization of the Act of 1998. The new law, the Carl D. Perkins Career and Technical Education Improvement Act of 2006, was passed almost unanimously by Congress in late July, 2006.

The reauthorization of the Carl D. Perkins Act of 2006 establishes specific criteria that must be a part of all CTE programs. In order to receive funds, a CTE program must offer at least one program of study (POS) that must include (Lewis & Kosine, 2008):

Coherent and rigorous content aligned with challenging academic standards and relevant CTE content. This content must be delivered in a co-ordinated, non-duplicative progression of courses that align secondary education with postsecondary education and lead to an industry-recognized credential or certificate at the postsecondary level or an associate or BS degree. Programs must include opportunities for postsecondary credit through dual or concurrent enrollment. (p. vi)

Several pioneer initiatives have led to the inclusion of programs of study in the legislation. These initiatives include: (a) Tech Prep, (b) Career Clusters, and (c) Dual Enrollment. Each initiative will be discussed.

Tech Prep was an early attempt to connect secondary with postsecondary. Dale Parnell is known as the father of Tech Prep based on his discussion in his 1984 text *Neglected Majority* (Lynch, 2000). Included is an articulation agreement between one or more secondary and post-secondary institutions. The idea was supported initially in the 1990 reauthorization of the Carl D. Perkins Act which authorized funds to support Tech Prep. There is very little difference between Tech Prep and POS.

Career Clusters were released by the Office of Vocational and Adult Education in 1999. There are 16 career clusters and occupational areas with industry-validated knowledge and skill statements that identify what students need to know and be able to do in order to be successful in a particular field. The clusters have pathways or programs of study associated with each. Courses are sequenced and may began in the 9th grade and proceed through higher-levels of education. Some states are requiring students to develop an electronic comprehensive portfolio based on their chosen cluster/pathway. The 16 clusters are presented in Table 1.

The Carl D. Perkins Act (2006) states that a POS may include opportunities for students to participate in dual or concurrent enrollment to earn credit. Dual enrollment provides the student with an opportunity to receive both high school and college credit for the same course. Dual enrollment courses must be taught by college qualified instructors. In a dual enrollment program, the secondary student may attend classes at a local college, the college instructor may come to the high school, or the high school instructor may be a qualified college instructor.

As we continue to move forward in CTE, developing new creative and innovative programs

Table 1. The 16 career clusters

Agriculture, Food, and Natural Resources	Architecture and Construction	Arts, AV and Communications	Business, Management, and Administration
Education and Training	Finance	Government and Public Administration	Health Science
Hospitality and Tourism	Human Services	Information Technology	Law, Public Safety, Corrections, and Security
Manufacturing	Marketing, Sales, and Service	Science, Technology, Engineering, and Mathematics	Transportation, Distribution and Logistics

of study will be a necessity. "It does not require much imagination or insight to read the handwriting on the wall for education: Support the emerging knowledge economy by adding to or reengineering your services or face the threat of obsolescence" (Harkins, 2002, p. 13).

The seamless linkage between secondary, postsecondary, and the workplace that is demanded, is possible via programs of study. Programs of study demand collaboration among CTE educators at all levels, as there must be an alignment of standards. A continuum is developed that designs a complete program that may include career awareness at the elementary level, exploration of careers at the middle school level, preparation for work at the high school level, credentialing at the postsecondary level, and life-long learning (Stone, 2008). Ongoing reputable rigorous research is going to be the tool that guides the development of effective CTE programs of study.

12.3.3 No Child Left Behind

No Child Left Behind (NCLB) has been one of the most controversial pieces of educational legislation. NCLB requires each teacher to be highly qualified; however this definition does not apply to CTE teachers. Scientifically-based research, accountability, and support for teachers and professional staff are among the recommendations in NCLB. In the next section, each of the above NCLB recommendations will be discussed in relation to improvement of the CTE image.

12.3.4 Challenge and Opportunities II: CTE Image

It has been well known for years that CTE suffers an image issue. In 2006, President Bush proposed to zero out all dedicated federal funding for CTE through the Perkins Act in order to add resources to a new high school reform initiative (Kazis, 2005). What does this say about CTE image? Despite efforts including a name change, the reality is that most parents still view CTE as a program for someone else's child, the child not going to college. Between 1987 and 1997 the American Vocational Association (now ACTE) dedicated three journal issues to the topic of CTE image. These issues were December 1987, January 1993, and September 1997.

A recent story in *The New York Times* (Hu, 2009) describes the possibilities for CTE. James M. Carroll, chairman of the Bergen County Board of Freeholders, said "This isn't the N.B.A.; we're not taking anybody. We don't go out and recruit, the students come to us" (p. 2). This is in response to an uproar from superintendents who claim CTE programs have "strayed from their original mission and are poaching many of New Jersey's best and brightest" (p. 1). In New Jersey, 27,766 students are enrolled in the 21 county-run vocational school systems. About 17% of the class of 2008 were accepted at Ivy League colleges. The average SAT score in 2008 was well above the statewide averages. All 110 teachers have master's degrees, and some have a doctorate. The average class size is 18, and the school day is about 90 minutes longer than the typical day. The admission process is rigorous and admission is seen as an honor. Nearly all graduates go on to a 4 year college. Bergen Academies include seven career-based academies in: (a) science and technology, (b) engineering, (c) medicine, (d) business, (e) telecommunications, (f) computer science, and, (g) culinary and hotel administration and the arts. When Daniel Jaye was recruited in 2006 to become principal at one of the academies, his first reaction was "I heard 'vocational school,' and in my mind I'm conjuring up a prison setting where they're doing plumbing and license plates like the typical vo-tech school" (p. 1). What he found was math and science magnets that often function as a stepping stone for students to attend elite universities.

As part of the drive to reform high schools, some states have taken a lead by realizing that school reform includes CTE. Virginia and New York State have introduced innovations that include an incentive for CTE students to pursue industry certification and a career readiness certificate that indicates competencies in writing, reading, math, and communications. Other states are looking at setting up a competitive innovation fund for CTE programs to modernize (Kazis, 2005).

Part of the CTE image problem stems from an identity crisis. In the past CTE only prepared students for the workplace, now students are prepared for both the workplace and higher education. Over the years CTE has been referred to as vocational education, applied studies, technical education, applied technology education, workforce education, human resource education, and career and professional education (Lynch, 2000). In December 1998, the American Vocational Association changed to the Association for Career and Technical Education. The University Council on Vocational Education became the University Council for Workforce and Human Resource Education. The Carl D. Perkins Act of 2006 changed the verbiage of Vocational Education to Career and Technical Education. While name changes may be necessary to keep up with a changing world, this provides the possibility of an identity crisis as various interpretations are considered. For example, Rojewski (2002) advocated that school reform, legislation, and changes in the workplace provide a need to move some CTE programs to workforce education. Lazaros and Roger (2006) identified the number two problem in Technical Education to be loss of identity.

A positive image begins with outstanding programs that meet the needs of students, employers, and the community. CTE stakeholders must be willing to work hard to build outstanding programs, and then promote the programs. We must demonstrate the importance of the life and workplace skills taught in CTE through well-respected quality research and dissemination. Daggett (2008) argues that CTE utilizes the best instructional methodology to teach rigor and relevance. The term rigor and relevance was first developed as a framework by the International Center for Leadership in Education. Later in 2005, Bill Gates popularized the term in a speech given to the National Governors' Association entitled, "America's High Schools are Obsolete." Gates added a third "R" for relationship. We cannot just sustain our CTE programs, we must recreate them. The image of CTE begins with the attitude of CTE educators. It will take an abundance of positive attitude and hard work to turn around the image issues in CTE. In the next section, there will be a discussion of some specific ways to improve the image of CTE.

12.3.5 Teacher Quality

Improving teacher quality is an opportunity to improve the image of CTE. The challenge of teacher quality starts with teacher education. "Unfortunately, higher education, for the most part, has failed to invest in career and technical education personnel, productivity tools, and physical facilities to support quality teacher education programs" (McCaslin & Parks, 2002, p. 11). It is recommended that college presidents and deans should place additional emphasis on quality CTE programs in order to recruit the brightest students. Universities need to re-evaluate promotion and tenure criteria to include recognition for state and accreditation requirements. Rewards should be offered to teacher education faculty for spending time in secondary classrooms.

Camp and Heath-Camp (2007) reported the following:

A study conducted for the National Center for Research in Vocational Education reported that the nation's CTE teacher education programs were declining quickly, and a shortage of well-prepared CTE teachers was the result. Quoted in a Techniques article eight years later, the study's author R.L. Lynch said, 'If I were to do another study like the one I did in the early 1990s, I'll probably wind up repeating myself... What we need to do now is re-conceptualize the whole arena of [career and technical] teacher education.' He continued later, 'I do believe that if we don't have some sort of reinvention of CTE teacher education, I'm afraid it will just peter out.' (p. 18)

In 2001, teacher education programs had reduced by another 11% within 10 years. It also reported that teacher preparation programs remained traditional both in structure and delivery with two exceptions. There was more emphasis placed on the integration of academic and technical education, and it was planned to double the growth of distance education courses. Studies indicate that a reinvention of teacher education has not taken place since Lynch's original study in 1991 (Camp & Heath-Camp, 2007). "It does not require much imagination or insight to read the handwriting on the wall for education: Support the emerging knowledge economy by adding to or reengineering your services or face the threat of obsolescence" (Harkins, 2002, p. 13).

In the past, more emphasis was placed on student outcome than teacher preparation and professional development. Silverberg, Warner, Fong, and Goodwin (2004) reported that CTE teachers are less likely to hold a minimum of a bachelor's degree and prospective CTE teachers scored lower on reading and writing on the praxis than elementary teachers. The first order of business must be to make certain that teacher education programs are high standard quality programs. Even though NCLB does not require CTE teachers to meet the standards of "highly qualified", if CTE teacher education wants to be given the same respect as other academic areas, we must be willing to meet the same standards.

Carl D. Perkins Act (2006) states that each POS must contain coherent and rigorous content aligned with challenging academic standards and relevant CTE content. The purpose of the Act was to develop more fully the academic and career and technical skills of secondary and postsecondary education students. A common theme exist to promote the development of activities which integrate academic and career and technical instruction in order to prepare students for high-skill high-wage occupations. Integration of academics in CTE curriculum not only has the ability to help students succeed on the state assessment tests which align directly with the NCLB legislation, but also prepares them for the world of work (Threeton, 2007).

We live in a new technology and knowledge economy with different skill demands. In the past, CTE taught job-specific skills, now workers need to possess a broad set of skills that include both technical and interpersonal communication skills. Higher order thinking skills such as decision making and problem solving, as well as flexibility, creative thinking, conflict resolution, managing information and resources, reading, math, critical thinking, technological literacy, and the capacity for reflection will also be expected from workers of the future (Rojewski, 2002). If CTE educators are going to be called upon to teach this range of skills and academics, then teacher education programs have to verify that graduates have the proper preparation. Academics must prepare educators for change.

Internship, or student teaching, has long been seen as a vital part of all teacher education programs. However, teacher education programs must take tremendous care when making internship placements. If internship placements are with ineffective CTE educators, the result will be the development of more ineffective CTE educators. Teacher education programs typically have well thought out and researched methods courses available. What is covered in a methods course can be very quickly erased by an ineffective internship experience.

During 1996 and 1997, several groups came together to discuss preparing CTE teachers for the 21st Century through teacher education programs. The National Association of State Directors of Vocational Technical Education Consortium and the University Council for Workforce and Human Resource Education (previously called The University Council on Vocational Education) created task forces and frameworks for revising CTE teacher education. After reviewing various documents, Lynch (1997) compiled the following recommendations from the collaboration:

- Creation of a new vision for career and technical education.
- Increase in funding for teacher education.
- Greater collaboration between all stakeholders.
- Authentically access teacher education candidates.
- Improve academic preparation of career and technical education teachers.
- High standards for teacher education.
- Increase the supply and academic quality of CTE teacher education graduates.
- All CTE educators should have a minimum of a baccalaureate degree.

- Each state (or region) needs to establish a commission on professional development.
- Create a culture of lifelong learning (pp. 71-72)

As stated in Number nine above, professional development for CTE educators is important. It must be effective and ongoing. New technologies and distance learning allows for just-in-time professional development. Medrich (2005) supports contextual teaching as an effective method of teaching, but emphasizes that contextual teaching can be very difficult to master. According to the contextual learning theory, learning occurs when students process new information or knowledge in a way that it makes sense to them in their own frames of reference. Connecting previous knowledge to current information helps to connect the dots. Students must understand why they are learning what they are learning. According to Daggett (2008), only 39.8% of students surveyed stated that their classes help them understand what is going on in their everyday life. Only 58.8% of the students surveyed stated that they are encouraged to be creative. Educators may not provide the type of learning needed, not because they do not want to, but because they may not know how. Professional development is the model by which teachers keep current and motivated. Effective ongoing professional development may be a method of reinforcing effective teaching methods.

Career/Technical teachers who participated in the 2000 High Schools That Work Teacher Survey revealed the following (SREB, n.d.):

- 70% received no staff development in getting career-oriented students to master complex content in algebra, geometry and statistics.
- 64% received no staff development in teaching science in an applied or occupational context.
- 88% received less than 20 hours of staff development in integrating reading, writ-

ing and communication skills into curriculum and instruction. (p. 8)

Teacher education should include how to deal with diversity, students in crisis, and leadership (Rojewski, 2002). In addition, CTE teacher education programs should include knowledge and skills on current topics such as integration of academic and technical skills, career clusters, career academies, accountability and assessment, career development, and the development of new CTE programs (McCaslin & Parks, 2002). Teacher education candidates must be able to manage and create a classroom environment that fosters the development of those students preparing for postsecondary education and the workplace. There is a need for core academic knowledge and pedagogy mastery (Bottoms, 2005). Teacher candidates should thoroughly understand authentic assessment.

Teacher education programs, postsecondary, and secondary CTE programs must be forward-thinking, innovative, and creative to attract and keep the best students. All educators must be divergent thinkers instead of convergent thinkers. Divergent thinking refers to creativity, problem-solving, and brainstorming, whereas, convergent thinking means one is capable of giving the correct answer to a standard question (memorization). Willard Daggett shows a video titled "the broken elevator" in his 2008 ACTE presentation. The video depicts two people "trapped" on an escalator. The escalator stops while riders are half way up; the two sit and wait for help to come. This is a great demonstration of the need for problem-solving skills in contrast to convergent thinking. CTE educators at all levels must think outside the box.

In order to develop innovative creative CTE educators, educator empowerment must take place. Empowerment happens by providing the educator adequate time, ownership of the program, the intentional opportunity to share best practices, and allowing faculty driven program changes.

Tough economic times make it even more difficult for educator collaboration and sharing of best practices. However, new technologies available on Web 2.0 and via distance learning are a solution. In addition, standard based instruction must not lead to teaching to the test.

Recent legislation, many credentialing organizations, and school administrations now mandate program accountability. With the requirement of data-driven accountability, another challenge for teacher education programs is to graduate teachers with the knowledge, to develop, implement, and maintain accountability systems (Rojewski, 2002).

12.3.6 Accountability

Meeting federal legislation through accountability is another vehicle for improving the image of CTE. Meaningful accountability requires meaningful data (Wiener, 2005). Determining meaningful data will require additional training and professional development for CTE educators. The issue of accountability has been around for a long time. The First Vocational Act of 1963 mandated evaluation of CTE programs (McCaslin & Parks, 2002). Additional legislation has continued to reinforce accountability. CTE educators will have to decide the most effective method of collecting, analyzing, and reporting data.

Accountability may include CTE student graduation rates, impact of CTE courses, proficiency of CTE students on standardized tests, tracking of CTE student employment and earnings, and technical skill assessment. The National Assessment of Vocational Education (NAVE) indicates there are considerable inconsistencies of measurement of accountability across and within states, and may not be tied to outcomes (NAVE, 2004). Measuring student outcomes should be data-driven and is the key to improvement.

The Carl D. Perkins Act of 2006 states that CTE content may lead to an industry-recognized credential. At Auburn University in Alabama, business/marketing teacher education students are required to take and pass the Microsoft Certified Application Specialist (MCAS) exams for Word, Excel, Access, and PowerPoint prior to internship. This assures future employers (schools) that graduates have mastered certain specific computer applications at the industry level. The state of Virginia has an initiative that provides students with the opportunity to acquire industry credentials. The initiative also establishes teacher training academies to increase the number of secondary teachers with industry certification (Bottoms, 2005). Texas has a goal to develop or identify assessments so that by 2013, all secondary CTE concentrators will have a means to validate technical skills. Over 16,000 secondary CTE students annually earn industry-recognized certifications. The top three certifications earned are Information Technology, Health Services, and Cosmetology (Association of Career and Technical Education [ACTE], 2009, April). The Cisco Networking Academy program is designed to teach high school students and college students to design, build, and maintain computer networks. These certifications are based on student mastery of industry standards through computer-based demonstrations and internships (Lynch, 2000). More than 5,000 network academies have trained more than 750,000 students to work as IT network administrators, and provided a foundation for postsecondary study in engineering and computer science. These are just a few examples of authentic assessments that are being advocated by CTE educators and included in accountability reports.

CTE educators who design secondary or postsecondary industry certification programs may face significant challenges. Haimson and VanHoy (2004) identified a couple of the major challenges: (1) balancing certification preparation with other vocational and academic standards, and (2) the substantial investment required for equipment and teacher professional development. They found "The average equipment expenditure was about $16,000 among case study high schools and $67,000 among colleges" (p. xii). These figures were based on 2004 costs for seven high schools and six colleges. Current costs would certainly exceed these estimates. IT certification programs tend to be more prevalent in postsecondary than secondary CTE. However, some states are pushing for secondary educators to get certified and then develop programs for their students. Many students who have the opportunity to complete an industry certification continue their education. Accountability and record keeping will be an important aspect of continuous improvement in industry certification programs. Follow-up information is needed on student outcomes.

As we consider the development of accountability data, it is important to weigh the advantages and disadvantages. Educators need availability of time to be creative and innovative. Burying educators in unnecessary paperwork may not only be a waste of valuable time, but may also affect the retention rate of CTE educators. We may lose great educators to paper bureaucracy.

Just as it is recommended that teacher education candidates are authentically assessed, so should all CTE students be authentically assessed. Authentic assessment includes multiple assessments and may include portfolios, demonstrations, oral or written presentations, work-based activities, student productions, student critiques, observations, paper and pencil tests, cases analysis, and reflection. Assessments should represent learning over a period of time (Lynch, 2000).

12.3.7 High Schools That Work

High Schools That Work (HSTW) is the oldest and largest school improvement initiative administered by the Southern Regional Education Board (SREB). Following the framework of HSTW is another route to improving the image of CTE by increased standards. A set of strategies are designed to raise the academic achievement of high school students by combining college prep work with career and technical education. More than 1,200 sites follow the framework. The SREB specifies the following as key practices to become affiliated with High Schools That Work (Lynch, 2000):

- High expectations for student learning.
- Rigorous career and technical courses.
- More required academic courses.
- Learning in work environments.
- Collaboration among academic and career and technical teachers.
- An individualized advising system.
- Active encouragement of students' interests.
- Extra help outside of school and in the summer.
- Use of assessment and evaluation data to improve students' learning. (School Reform section, p. 8)

High Schools That Work (HSTW) deserves increased attention by career and technical educators (Lynch, 1997). It is based on much of the research on school reform and is targeted toward CTE students. More than 60% of career/technical graduates at HSTW sites pursue further education (SREB, n.d.).

12.3.8 Career Academies

Career Academies offer another opportunity for CTE to engage students in higher academic achievement, successful employment, college preparation, and lifelong learning. The Association for Career and Technical Education recently (2009, March) released a brief, *The Role of Career Academies in Education Improvement*. Career Academies are "schools with in schools" that bring together a team of teachers and a cohort of students based around a college and career preparation cluster. Career academies provide a program that creates a link among secondary CTE, strong academics and postsecondary education.

Career Academies were developed over 30 years ago by business and community leaders. Today these academies are learning communities that integrate college prep, rigorous academics, and practical application as students and educators work as a team. It is estimated that over 2,500 Career Academies operate around the country. Kemple and Willner (2008) stated that "Career Academies are one of the few youth-focused interventions that have been found to improve the labor market prospects of young men" (p. iii). Business and industry engagement is another important aspect of Career Academies.

12.3.9 Quality Research

NCLB requires that instruction be based on scientifically-based research. Quality research is another mechanism by which CTE can gain respect, support, and improve image. Rojewski (2002) concluded there is a need for relevant and rigorous research in CTE. Little is known about what makes a good CTE teacher and what constitutes an effective teacher education program (McCaslin & Parks, 2002). The ultimate goal of researchers in CTE should be to relate our work to a larger research and theoretical community. "Systematically, ignoring larger issues at the level of grand theory, as we are so often tempted to do for the sake of expediency, will only delay the time when our profession can began to address its larger issues and solve its larger problems" (Camp, 2001, p. 13).

Creating a national CTE research agenda was vital to the alignment of CTE with federal legislation. On July 21, 2008, the ACTE Board of Directors approved a national research agenda for CTE. The agenda was developed by researchers, practitioners, and business leaders. The purpose of the research agenda is to guide students, professors, and researchers as they select research projects. There are five broad areas of the agenda (Lambeth, Elliot, & Joerger, 2008):

- **Knowledge Base for Teaching and Learning**
  a. Instructional strategies (critical thinking and problem solving, higher order thinking, quality of instruction, teacher-learner interaction, work-based learning).
  b. Professional preparation (teacher competence, CTE teacher education, CTE leader preparation).
  c. Leadership and organizational development (career and technical education student organizations, teacher professional organizations, CTE administrator professional organizations).
- **Curricula and Program Planning**
  d. Academic infusion/integration (infusion of communications and language, infusion of mathematics and science, integration of basic skills, literacy).
  e. Curricula designs (needs of future workforce, work-based learning).
  f. Future CTE content (employment-supply-demand and nature of workforce, entrepreneurship and free enterprise, global market demands).
- **Delivery Methods**
  g. Best practices (CTE teacher preparation, ESL/ELL learners in CTE, marketing for rigor and relevance, educational methods, CTE student organizations, parent and student perceptions-satisfaction and retention).
  h. Integration of technology (innovative instructional technologies, distance education and technology).
  i. Transition to postsecondary education (alignment of secondary and postsecondary education standards, articulation of programs between secondary, postsecondary and higher education, dual enrollment, programs of study).

- **Accountability**
  j. Assessment (CTE student graduation rate, end of program assessment, impact of CTE courses on student achievement, levels of performance, proficiency of CTE students on standardized tests, technical skill assessment).
  k. Economic impact of CTE (impact of CTE in community development, high skill-high wage or high demand occupations, return on investment by state for CTE).
  l. Quality of teachers (teacher standards, teacher education).
- **Program Relevance and Effectiveness**
  m. Faculty and staff development (recruitment and retention of alternatively certified teachers, recruitment and retention of teachers, professional development of teachers, recruitment and retention of CTE administrators/local directors).
  n. Policy development (alignment with economic development, alignment with federal education policy, workforce investment).
  o. Relevance of workforce standards (follow-up program completers, industry credentials for program completers, impacts of external program standards and accreditation).

The dissemination of rigorous and relevant CTE research is another method of strengthening the image of CTE. In 2004, the name of the American Vocational Education Research Association was changed to the Association for Career and Technical Education Research (ACTER). ACTER has four purposes that are critical to our future and some may say more critical today than ever before. The purposes are to (Jackman, 2006):

- Stimulate research and development activities related to career and technical education;
- Stimulate the development of training programs designed to prepare persons for responsibilities in research in career and technical education;
- Foster a cooperative effort in research and development activities within the total program of career and technical education, with other areas of education and with other disciplines; and
- Facilitate the dissemination of research findings and the diffusion of knowledge.

It was determined that obviously a purpose did exist; there was just a need for better dissemination. In 2005, ACTER planned a successful research preconference at ACTE.

NCLB calls for scientifically-based research in education. Gemici and Rojewski (2007) evaluated recent issues of CTER 2001-2005. The majority of the articles were descriptive or qualitative. Only 6% were quasi-experimental. This does not indicate that there is a lack of quality CTE research, but it does differ from the governmental definition of scientifically-based research. To meet the NCLB definition of "scientifically based," research must (The National Institute for Literacy, 2005):

a. Employ systematic, empirical methods that draw on observation or experiment.
b. Involve rigorous data analyses that are adequate to test the stated hypotheses and justify the general conclusions.
c. Rely on measurements or observational methods that provide valid data across evaluators and observers, and across multiple measurements and observations; and
d. Be accepted by a peer-reviewed journal or approved by a panel of independent experts through a comparatively rigorous, objective, and scientific review.

This definition of scientifically-based research encourages quantitative research. In more recent years, the definition has expanded to include additional methods of research including qualitative; however, the major emphasis is still on quantitative research.

As suggested previously, universities may need to consider the criteria for promotion and tenure of CTE teacher education faculty. The current system requires faculty to have a proven record of scholarly publications. Given the tremendous pressure to publish; faculty may prefer descriptive and qualitative articles that can in most cases be completed in a more timely fashion. Experimental studies may seem counter-productive, and can also be more cost consuming. In most promotion and tenure systems, quantity is more prestigious than quality (Gemici & Rojewski, 2007). Exemplary teacher education programs get their students involved in research (Bruening et al., 2002) at all levels.

12.3.10 Challenge and Opportunities III: Decline in CTE Enrollment and Teacher Education

According to a new National Center for Education Statistics [NCES] study (2009), ninety-five percent of all public high school graduates in 2005 earned credit in career and technical education; however, only twenty-one percent completed 3 or more credits in a single occupational area. Fifty-eight percent (58%) earned credits in more than one area. During the past 15 years, universities have downsized the number of CTE teacher education programs. According to Lynch, Hartley, and Wentling (1996), in 1991 only 100 U.S. colleges offered four or more CTE teacher education programs. Teachers who enter education from business and industry may have extensive work experience, but no pedagogical training (SREB, n.d.). Continuous discussion should take place on how to best prepare those entering the field of education from business and industry.

In 2002, the most common occupational programs at the high school level were business, health care, and computer science. More credits were earned at the secondary level in business services and computer technology than any other area. At the postsecondary level more students majored in business and marketing and health care than any other career area (NCES, 2008).

Secondary students who graduate with a CTE concentration are 2 ½ times more likely to be employed while pursuing postsecondary education than are students in college prep (SREB). Students employed around 12-15 hours a week while in college tend to be better students.

As baby-boomers retire, there will be a challenge to fill the CTE teacher positions. "More than 1.7 million teachers—53% of our nation's teaching workforce, and an even greater percentage of our principals are baby-boomers. Their retirement could open the way for new teaching models to emerge, but this opportunity could become a crisis" (The Governor's Commission on Quality Teaching, 2008). In addition, the number of CTE teacher education programs has declined at least 11% during the 1990s (Bruening et al., 2001). Research indicates that over the next decade there will be an increase in secondary students, which should also impact CTE. Camp, Case, Dean, and Fannon (1998) found in a study that has been supported by the Agricultural Education Division of the American Vocational Association and completed each year since 1965, the number of newly qualified Agriculture educators has declined from 1660 in 1975 to 625 in 1995. "Our nation's colleges and universities have greatly diminished their capacity to prepare teachers for vocational and technical education programs. Enrollments in teacher education have declined (significantly in some subject areas), large numbers of programs have been eliminated" (Lynch, 1996, Conclusions section, p. 2). Most of the studies relating to declines in CTE enrollment or CTE teacher education are from the 1990s. There is a need for more current research to reveal the current status

of the supply and demand of CTE educators and CTE teacher education programs.

12.4 FUTURE TRENDS

In his address to the U.S. Senate Committee on strengthening American competitiveness in March 7, 2007, Bill Gates stressed the importance of the business community being an advocate for high-quality education. He suggests that the business community will be a leader in workforce training. Innovative ways of using online training and skills testing should be utilized by educational institutions and the business community. Web 2.0 and now Web 3.0 will definitely widen the opportunities for effective online training. Who better to design and deliver this training than CTE educators?

As distance learning becomes increasingly important to the field of CTE, teacher education programs will need to not only offer additional distance learning programs, but also include the design and delivery of distance learning in the methods course. Pritchett, White, and Skinner (2006) surveyed Alabama secondary business educators and found that 98.5% of respondents had not taught a distance learning class; however, the majority (81.8%) expressed a willingness to teach distance learning courses with training or professional development. In 2005, Alabama Governor Riley proposed an initiative for Alabama Connecting Classrooms, Educators and Students Statewide (ACCESS). ACCESS provides the opportunity for Alabama secondary students to take advanced placement courses, foreign language courses, and other courses via distance learning that may not be offered onsite at their school. By the school year 2009-2010, every Alabama high school will have ACCESS. As the trend to offer distance learning at the secondary level increases, teacher education programs must include the instruction needed to teacher candidates. Although distance learning offers many opportunities for

CTE, it is imperative that rigor and quality be maintained.

Distance learning and online technologies may be the answer to providing advanced degrees and ongoing professional development to CTE educators. With current economic conditions, it is more difficult for CTE educators to take advanced courses, participate in workshops, or attend professional conferences. Collaboration among professionals in the CTE field is an important factor in the future success of the field. "In 21st century schools our teachers need continuous opportunities to collaborate with their colleagues as they develop the knowledge and skill to facilitate the acquisition of competencies in their students. It is time to recognize that quality teaching is not an individual accomplishment" (The Governor's Commission on Quality Teaching, 2008, p. 6). Pritchett, White, and Skinner (2006) reported 84.7% of Alabama business educators who responded to a survey had not participated in distance learning to obtain an advance degree or credential; however, 63.3% expressed an interest in participating in a distance learning program to obtain an advanced degree or professional development. In 2002, Auburn University began offering graduate business/marketing education programs via distance learning. The programs offered include alternative masters, traditional masters, and educational specialist. These programs have placed outstanding educators in CTE classrooms, and provided the opportunity for current business/marketing educators to obtain advanced degrees and professional development.

"Just as the "Agricultural-Era" and the "Industrial-Age" were named for their dominant modes of work, the 21st century will become known as the "Learning-Age" (The Governor's Commission on Quality Teaching, 2008). As baby-boomers begin to retire there will be many opportunities, but also a loss of knowledge. In an effort to recognize and reward the various career stages of an educator, Alabama released a report to Governor Bob Riley in December, 2008 outlining a plan for continuous learning not only for students, but also

for educators. The plan outlines a vision for improving teacher quality and student achievement in Alabama. The plan has the following goals:

- High quality teaching for all students.
- A school culture that supports adult learning: There is recognition that time and resources are available for teacher inquiry and collaboration.
- Recruitment and retention of talented individuals: There is recognition that life-long learning and teacher ownership are important.
- Teacher-driven process.

The plan recommends five teacher pathways:

- **Apprentice teacher:** prospective teachers.
- **Classroom teacher:** focus on student learning.
- **Professional teacher:** most of time is spent in classroom, but may take on some leadership roles.
- **Master teacher:** assume more complex roles. May teach larger number of students or distance learning.
- **Learning designer:** professional teacher interested in system design.

As states re-evaluate how to handle teacher shortages and re-creation of effective learning systems to meet the needs of today's employers, systems that recognize and reward educators will be essential to the success. There is a need to recruit the brightest and best into CTE education and then give incentives for them to stay in the profession.

12.5 CONCLUSION

For CTE to thrive in the ever-changing world, all stakeholders will need to work together. "The continuous deconstruction and construction of jobs, driven by continuous innovation, offers a current opportunity for CTE leadership" (Harkins, 2002, p. 8). Albert Einstein said "We can't solve problems by using the same kind of thinking we used when we created them."

As CTE stakeholders work together to meet the challenges by turning them into opportunities, the CTE image issue will take care of itself. The Association for Career and Technical Education has a website which includes CTE profiles for each state (http://www.acteonline.org/StateProfiles.aspx). This is an excellent resource for researching the innovation and creativity taking place in the states.

The National Career and Technical Education Research Agenda (Lambeth, Elliot, & Joerger, 2008) is the framework that should guide CTE research in order to overcome the challenges and to prosper from the opportunities. CTE teacher education programs must encourage and promote high academic standards and student involvement in research. As more experienced CTE educators retire, it is very important to recruit the brightest and best into the field and equip them with the skills necessary for success in the 21st century.

REFERENCES

Abel, B. (2006, Winter). The new frontier—the world. *The Magazine of Marquette University*. Retrieved May 1, 2009, from http://www.marquette.edu/magazine/winter06/fro ntier.shtml

Association for Career and Technical Education. (2009, April). Texas state CTE profile. Retrieved May 1, 2009, from http://www.acteonline.org/content.aspx?id=2074

Association for Career and Technical Education. (2009, March). *The role of career academies in education improvement*. Retrieved May 1, 2009, from http://www.acteonline. org/uploadedFiles/Publications_and_Online_Media/files/Career_academies.pdf

Bottoms, G. (2005, April). The SREB model: Academic rigor, technical relevance, and a head start on a career. In Kazis, R. (Ed.), *Remaking career and technical education for the 21st century: What role for high school programs* (pp. 35–37). Boston, MA: Jobs for the Future/Aspen Institute.

Bridgeland, J., Dilulio, J., & Morison, K. (2006, March). *The silent epidemic: Perspectives of high school dropouts*. Civic Enterprises in association with Peter D. Hart Research Associates for the Bill and Melinda Gates Association.

Bruening, T., Scanlon, D., Hodes, C., Dhital, P., Shao, X., & Liu, S. (2001). Characteristics of teacher educators in career and technical education. National Research Center for Career and Technical Education. Retrieved May 1, 2009, from http://www.eric. ed.gov/ERICDocs/data/ericdocs2sql/content_storage_01/0000019b/80/19/61/ee.pdf

Bruening, T., Scanlon, D., Hoover, T., Hodes, C., Shao, X., Dhital, P., & Zolotov, A. (2002, December). Attributes and characteristics of exemplary, leading, and innovative, career and technical education teacher preparation programs. National Research Center for Career and Technical Education Retrieved May 1, 2009, from http://www.acteonline. org/uploadedFiles/About_CTE/files/Attributes%20and%20Characteristics%20of%20Exemplary%20CTE.pdf

Camp, W., Case, R., Dean, A., & Fannon, C. (1998, August). National study of the supply and demand for teachers of agricultural education in 1995. Retrieved May 2, 2009, http://www.eric.ed.gov/ERICDocs/data/ericdocs2sql/content_storage_01/0000019b/80/16/fd/36.pdf

Camp, W., & Heath-Camp, B. (2007, September) *The status of CTE teacher education today: The old models for CTE teacher preparation are no longer producing adequate numbers of well-prepared teachers as they once did. Techniques*. Retrieved May 1, 2009, from http://www.acteonline.org/uploadedFiles/Publications_and_E-Media/files/files-tec hniques-2007/Sept07_Thm1.pdf

Camp. W. (2001). Formulating and evaluating theoretical frameworks for career and technical education research. *Journal of Vocational Education Research*. Retrieved May 1, 2009, from http://scholar.lib.vt.edu/ejournals/JVER/v26n1/camp.html

Carl, D. Perkins Career and Technical Education Act of 2006. Retrieved May 1, 2009, from http://www.ed.gov/policy/sectech/leg/perkins/index.html

Catri, D. (1998). *Vocational education's image for the 21st century*. Retrieved May 1, 2009, from http://www.ericdigests.org/1999-2/21st.htm

Daggett, B. (2008). Presentation to ACTE. International Center for Leadership in Education. Retrieved May 1, 2009, from http://www.acteonline.org/conventionsessions08. aspx

Fisch, K. (2008). Shift happens. Retrieved May 1, 2009, from http://shifthappens.wikis paces.com/

Gates, B. (2007, March 7). U.S. Senate committee hearing. Retrieved May 1, 2009, from http://www.gatesfoundation.org/speeches-commentary/Pages/bill-gates-2007-senate-hea ring.aspx.

Gemici, S., & Rojewski, J. (2007). Evaluating research in career and technical education using scientifically-based research standards. *Career and Technical Education Research, 32*(3), 143-159. Retrieved May 1, 2009, from http://scholar.lib.vt.edu/ejournals/CTER/ v32n3/

Haimson, J., & VanNoy, M. (2004, September). *Certification programs, participants and outcomes in high schools and two-year colleges*. Retrieved May 1, 2009, from http://www.acteonline.org/uploadedFiles/About_CTE/files/MPR_IT_Workforce_Certification_Programs_Participants_Outcomes_High_School_Two-Year_Colleges_Sep2004. pdf

Harkins, A. (2002). *The futures of career and technical education in a continuous innovation society. Journal of Vocational Education Research*. Retrieved on May 1, 2009, from http://scholar.lib.vt.edu/ejournals/JVER/v27n1/harkins.html

Hu, W. (2009, March 3). Vo-Techs are new elite, local districts complain. *The New York Times*. Retrieved May 1, 2009, from http://www.nytimes.com/2009/03/03/education/ 03vocational.html?sq=career%20and%20technical%20education%20and%20wood%20shop&st=cse&scp=9 &pagewanted=print

Jackman, D. (2006). 2005 Presidential address: Our future is what we collectively determine. *ACTER Career and Technical Education Research, 31*(2), 75-78. Retrieved May 1, 2009, from http://scholar.lib.vt.edu/ejournals/CTER/v31n2/pdf/jackman.pdf

Kazis, R. (2005, April). *Remaking career and technical education in the 21st century: What roles for high schools programs*. Retrieved May 1, 2009, from http://www.jff. org/Documents/RemakingCTE.pdf

Kemple, J., & Willner, C. (2008, June). *Career academies: Long term impacts on labor market outcomes, educational attainment, and transitions to adulthood*. Retrieved May 1, 2009, from http://www.mdrc.org/publications/482/full.pdf

Lambeth, J., Elliot, J., & Joerger, R. (2008, October). The national career and technical education research agenda. *Techniques*. Retrieved May 1, 2009, from http://www.acteonline.org/uploadedFiles/Publications_and_Online_Media/files/ResearchReport.pdf

Lazaros, E., & Roger, G. (2006, Summer). *Critical problems facing technology education: Perceptions of Indiana teachers. Journal of Industrial Teacher Education*. Retrieved May 1, 2009, from http://scholar.lib.vt.edu/ejournals/JITE/v43n2/lazaros.html

Lewis, M. V., & Kosine, R. (2008, October). *What will be the impact of programs of study? A preliminary assessment based on similar previous initiatives, state plans for implementation, and career development theory.* Washington, D.C.: National Research Center for Career and Technical Education. Retrieved May 1, 2009, from http://136.165.122.102/UserFiles/File/pubs/POS_Study_Morgan.pdf

Lynch, R. (2000). High school career and technical education for the first decade of the 21st century. *Journal of Vocational Education Research.* Retrieved May 1, 2009, from http://scholar.lib.vt.edu/ejournals/JVER/v25n2/lynch.html

Lynch, R., Hartley, N., & Wentling, T. (1996). *Beyond tradition: Preparing the teachers of tomorrow's workforce.* Columbia, Missouri: University Council for Vocational Education.

Lynch, R. L. (1996, Fall). In search of vocational and technical teacher education. *Journal of Vocational and Technical Education.* Retrieved May 1, 2009, from http://scholar.lib.vt.edu/ejournals/JVTE/v13n1/lynch.html

Lynch, R. L. (1997). *Designing vocational and technical teacher education for the 21st Century. Implications from the reform literature.* Retrieved May 1, 2009, from http://www.eric.ed.gov/ERICDocs/data/ericdocs2sql/content_storage_01/0000019b/80/16/61/27.pdf

McCaslin, N., & Parks, D. (2002). *Teacher education in career and technical education: Background and policy implications for the new millennium.* Retrieved May 1, 2009, from http://scholar.lib.vt.edu/ejournals/JVER/v27n1/special.html

Medrich, E. A. (2005). Change or die: The challenge facing career and technical education today. In Kazis, R. (Ed.), *Remaking career and technical education for the 21st century: What role for high school programs* (pp. 23–25). Boston, MA: Jobs for the Future/Aspen Institute.

National Assessment of Vocational Education (NAVE). (2004, June). *Earning, learning, and choice: Career and Technical Education works for students and employers.* Retrieved May 1, 2009, from http://www.ed.gov/rschstat/eval/sectech/nave/naveiap.pdf

National Center for Education Statistics (NCES). (2009). *Career and technical education (CTE) statistics.* Retrieved May 1, 2009, from http://nces.ed.gov/surveys/ctes/highlights.asp

National Center for Education Statistics [NCES]. (2008, July). Career and technical education in the United States: 1990 to 2005. Retrieved May 1, 2009, from http://nces.ed.gov/pubs2008/2008035.pdf

National Institute for Literacy. (2005). *What is scientifically based research? A guide for teachers.* Retrieved May 1, 2009, from http://www.nifl.gov/partnershipforreading/publications/html/science/stanovich.html

Obama, B. (2009, February, 24). Remarks of President Barack Obama -- Address to Joint Session of Congress. Retrieved May 1, 2009, from http://www.whitehouse.gov/the_press_office/remarks-of-president-barack-obama-address-to-joint-session-of-congress/

Partnership for 21st Century Skills, (2003), *Learning for the 21st Century: A Report and Mile Guide for 21st Century Skills.* Retrieved May 1, 2009 from http://www.21stcentury skills.org/images/stories/otherdocs/p21up_Report.pdf

Pritchett, C., White, B., & Skinner, L. (2006, Winter). The use of distance learning technology by business teachers for credentialing and instruction. *Delta Pi Epsilon Journal, 48*(1), 4–18.

Rojewski, J. (2002). *Preparing the workforce of tomorrow: A conceptual framework for career and technical education. Journal of Vocational Education Research.* Retrieved May 1, 2009, from http://scholar.lib.vt.edu/ejournals/JVER/v27n1/rojewski.html

Silverberg, M., Warner, E., Fong, M., & Goodwin, D. (2004). *National assessment of vocational education: Final report to congress.* Retrieved May 1, 2009, from http://www. ed.gov/rschstat/ eval/sectech/nave/navefinal.pdf

Southern Regional Education Board (SREB). (n.d.). *Facts about high school career and technical education studies.* Retrieved May 1, 2009, from http://www.sreb.org/programs/hstw/career/ facts_about_hs_career.pdf

Stone, J. R., III. (2008, December). *Programs of study: Issues and approaches.* powerpoint presentation made at the 2008 ACTE Convention, Charlotte, NC.

The Governor's Commission on Quality Education. (2008, December). Innovations in teaching: Creating professional pathways for Alabama teachers. Retrieved May 1, 2009, from http:// www.governorpress.alabama.gov/documents/ InnovationsinTeachingRpt.pdf

Threeton, M. (2007, Spring). The Carl D. Perkins career and technical education (CTE) Act of 2006 and the roles and responsibilities of CTE teachers and faculty members. *Journal of Industrial Teacher Education.* Retrieved May 1, 2009, from http://scholar. lib.vt.edu/ejournals/JITE/v44n1/ threeton.html

Wiener, R. (2005, April). How the federal government could promote academically rigorous career and technical education. In R. Kazis (Ed.), *Remaking career and technical education for the 21st century: What role for high school programs* (pp. 32-34). Boston, MA: Jobs for the Future/Aspen Institute. Retrieved May 1, 2009, from http:// www. eric.ed.gov/ERICDocs/data/ericdocs2sql/ content_storage_01/0000019b/80/30/b1/d6.pdf

Chapter 13

Career and Technical Education Technology:
Three Decades in Review and Technological Trends in the Future

Lesley Farmer
California State University, Long Beach, USA

ABSTRACT

In the last three decades, the nature of technology incorporation into career and technical education (CTE) training has changed. Technology used in the field has been supplemented by technology used in training per se. Technology has increasingly infiltrated into today's social arena, workplace, and education. In response, the use of technology in CTE reflects both educational philosophy and societal context. Teaching about technology differs from teaching with technology; the former focuses on content, and the latter focuses on process. The nature of CTE, instruction as a whole, and technology in particular, have shaped how CTE faculty teach with technology over the past three decades. In this period, technology-enhanced CTE instruction has moved from top-down to broad-based, from one-directional to two- and multi-directional communication, from static to dynamic, from programmer-dependent to content-dependent, and from administrative- to learning-oriented. Representative practices and a model of CTE technology-enhanced instruction are discussed.

13.1 INTRODUCTION

By its nature, career and technical education (CTE) has incorporated technology from its inception. Apprenticeships illustrate the basic premise of seeing, doing under supervision, and performing independently. Only in the last century has CTE become more theoretical and less hands-on, due to scale as factories and other large companies have emerged, increasing sophistication of the career field's skill set, and advanced knowledge and growing theoretical underpinnings that impact problem-solving. Having one teacher train a room full of CTE students in basic processes, such as reading and producing blueprints, for instance, enables employers to provide targeted on-the-job training rather than starting from scratch.

DOI: 10.4018/978-1-61520-747-3.ch013

In the last three decades, instruction about specific technology tools has been complemented with instruction to support generic technology competency. The basic notion is that the entire workforce needs to be able to select and apply technology for specific tasks (U.S. Department of Labor, 1991).

As training has expanded in scale and format, the nature of technology incorporation into CTE training has also changed. Technology used in the field has been supplemented by technology used in training per se. For example, a PowerPoint might never be used in daily work, but CTE instructors might routinely incorporate such a presentation tool in preparation courses.

This chapter examines the trends in technology-enhanced CTE instruction in the late 20th century and early 21st century. As such, it notes the conditions for technology incorporation, and explains representative practices.

13.2 TECHNOLOGY TRENDS

In the last 30 years, the work force in general has come to routinely use technology. A brief history of significant technology advances offers an overview of technology's infiltration into today's workplace, education, and social arena (Shelly, Cashman, Gunter, & Gunter., 2007).

13.2.1 Technology Inventions

By the late 1970s, micro processor chips, desktop computers, and the Ethernet had been invented. In 1979 the spreadsheet program VisiCalc was introduced; its acceptance by business heralded the start of personal computers on a large scale. In the same year, the first public information service, CompuServe and the Source, enabled people to connect with each other via remote servers and agreed upon protocols.

In 1980 two inventions made the personal computer more useable by the general public:

the MS-DOS operating system developed for IBM's forthcoming personal computer, and the Winchester hard drive for storage. Building on IBM's computer reputation in the business world, its 1981 introduction of their desktop computer led to immediate acceptance by corporations; within a year the number of computers sold doubled.

In 1982 the introduction of the Hayes 300 bps modem signaled the ability for individuals to telecommunicate, sharing digital documents efficiently. It was no surprise that Time magazine named the computer as Machine of the Year, displacing any influential people.

Lotus 1-2-3 constituted the first "suite" of productivity program applications (spreadsheet, database, and graphics), which became a best-seller for IBM personal computers (PC) in 1983. Hewlett-Packard's LaserJet printer, introduced the following year, enabled users to produce professional looking documents. Not to be outdone by IBM, Apple released the Macintosh in the same year, which had the significance of using an intuitive graphical user interface. This approach to computing was readily accepted by graphics and multimedia industries.

By 1987 the Intel 80386 microprocessor enabled personal computers to perform as well as large computer systems. Perl, a general high-level dynamic programming language, was invented to facilitate report processing.

The next significant step occurred in 1989 when Tim Berners-Lee created an Internet-based hypermedia information sharing innovation called the World Wide Web (WWW). It leveraged graphical interfaces so that users did not have to type sequential instructions in order to transfer information. Three years later, Microsoft's Windows 3.1 operating system joined the graphical interface bandwagon. In 1993, Marc Andreessen's graphic Web browser Mosaic, which led to Netscape's Navigator WWW browser in 1994, completed the graphical computer "picture."

Sun Microsystem launched the object-oriented programming language Java in 1995. This breakthrough product enable programmers to write one application that could cross computer platforms, thus helping to break down the wall between IBM-type and Apple PCs.

Although Apple had introduced the Newton "tablet" in 1993, it did not take off like U. S. Robotic's handheld PalmPilot of 1996, largely because the latter was easier to use and much cheaper. The Telecommunications Act of 1996 required that schools and libraries receive low-cost telecommunication service, which facilitated the incorporation of the Internet for CTE.

Multimedia got a boost in 1997 when the Intel Pentium II process was able to support multimedia applications efficiently. DVDs (digital video disc) were also introduced, which enabled computer, audio and video data to be stored in a single format that approximated studio-quality output.

E-commerce reached the tipping point in 1998 as marketing enterprises such as Amazon, Dell, and E*TRADE facilitated online shopping. Traditional companies quickly incorporated online buying options in order to expand their market spread. Part of e-commerce success was due to the introduction of PayPal, which facilitated convenient, secure online payments. The search engine Google was launched, which used a sophisticated algorithm to rank hits. Blogging software was also introduced.

Microsoft's Office2000 suite enabled users to save documents directly onto the Web. RSS feeds, introduced in 1999 as well, enabled users to aggregate online information into a single Web-based interface. However, that same year found businesses and governments anxious because older programs might confuse 2000 dates with 1900 dates; Y2K compliant programming efforts cost over $500 billion.

The year 2000 was a year of contrasts. While Internet traffic grew more than 700 percent in one year, and e-commerce sales exceeded $100 billion, Internet-based companies (dot-coms) crashed at a rate of one a day because they were overextended.

2001 was a brighter year. AOL and Time Warner merged, signaling the convergence of

telecommunications and entertainment industries. Another technology, wireless (wifi), also reached market penetration to support an increasing mobile workforce; the introduction of ebooks further encouraged portable technologies. Likewise, satellite and video conferencing matured with robotics and virtual environments so that remote training and operations could be supported. Apple launched its storage/playing device in 2001.

In response to Apple, in 2002 Handspring marketed the first all-in-one device that combined a cell phone, Web browser and email. Microsoft's Pocket PC 2002 software allowed handheld devices to interface with PCs and MS software. In the same year, video editing equipment, software and storage devices facilitated professional-looking video productions by the general public. Social networking sites were also starting to appear.

In 2003 wifi became commonplace, and Bluetooth standards were also supported. These technologies supported free phone calling, Skype being the most popular application. Intel finally integrated its computing technology for wireless notebook PCs, and phones with embedded cameras were launched. Additionally, Delicious popularized social bookmarking and tagging. The first World Summit on the Information Society convened, globally recognizing the role of information technology.

By 2004 iTunes and other online music stores were in full swing; Podcasting and photo sharing (via Flickr) expanded document sharing to multimedia formats. Flat LCD monitor screens were overtaking bulky CRTs. China surpassed the U.S. in exporting information and communication technology hardware.

YouTube was launched in 2005, starting an avalanche of video sharing. The Blu-Ray optic disc is introduced, becoming the standard for the high definition disc format. Interactive Web 2.0 was launched, available due to asynchronous Javascript and XML programming.

Video venues expanded in 2006: on cell phones, on computers (VOIP), on vlogs, on TV on demand.

Leveraging quick and easy, microblogging via Twitter connected people's daily lives. Likewise, integrated digital media systems became a household staple. Multi-core processors were starting to be produced widely.

Apple introduced its iPhone in 2007. This device helped expand m-commerce (mobile). Twitter was also introduced, enabling individuals to share short messages, mainly on mobile devices.

Green technology became widespread in 2008. With the expansion of bandwidth and high definition, video networking grew to support public demand. Growing affinity social networking provided targeted audiences.

13.2.2 Major Societal Workplace Trends and Technology

Technology in CTE exists within the larger frameworks of the workplace and society at large. As such, societal trends in the last three decades have demonstrated an ongoing recognition of technologies' important roles. These social technological trends are well captured by seminal futurists writing about their contemporary culture and predicting about the culture to be. The following works encapsulate recent decades' attitudes about technology in the workplace.

In his book *The Third Wave,* Toffler (1980) asserted that the U.S. was transitioning from an industrial society to a super- or post-industrial society. He noted the accelerated change of pace and people's sense of information overload. He thought that people saw themselves as consumers and producers, helping themselves to improve.

Naisbett's (1982) book *Megatrends: Ten New Directions Transforming Our Lives,* likewise asserted that the nation was becoming an information society. He also thought that technology advanced would require "high touch"; that is, technology could be harnessed to improve people's daily lives and provide value-added service. Naisbette predicted a flattened social hierarchy, from representative democracy to participatory democracy built on human connections.

A decade later, Toffler's (1991) book *Powershift,* emphasized value-added networks and mass democracy. He asserted that power would flow to those sectors that regulated corporate information, and considered the knowledge worker to be the social working core. Technology and information flowed together.

Writing about the early 21st century in his book *The World is Flat,* Friedman (2005) intertwined technology and industry. Technology served as a catalyst for globalization, facilitating outsourcing and supply-chaining to streamline operations. Online collaboration and sharing has become ubiquitous at all levels, from convergent corporations to individuals using personal digital devices such as cell phones and iPods.

In the same year, Pink's (2005) book *A Whole New Mind* "spun" the trends of globalization and automation to push for creativity. Technology could engage the senses and help people find deeper meaning and values.

13.2.3 Education and Workforce Technology

As technologies have advanced in the public arena, so too have the technology needs of the workforce increased.

Noting the importance of technology in society, the U.S. Department of Education (1983) report *A Nation at Risk* contended that

The people of the United States need to know that individuals in our society who do not possess the levels of skill, literacy and training essential to this new era will be effectively disenfranchised, not simply from the material rewards that accompany competent performance, but also from the chance to participate fully in our national life (p. 6).

The SCANS (Secretary's Commission on Achieving Necessary Skills) Report of the U.S.

Department of Labor (1991) recommended five overarching competencies for the entire workforce: resource management, interpersonal skills, information use, systems understanding, and technology use. Specifically, workers should be able to select equipment and tools, apply technology appropriately to specific tasks, and maintain and troubleshoot equipment.

The U.S. Department of Education developed a national technology plan in 2004, asserting that "The technology that has so dramatically changed the world outside our schools is now changing the learning and teaching environment within them" (p. 6).

At this point, each industry sector has developed technology standards, based on its internal needs and external factors. For example, transportation has made great technology advances within the industry, and has been significantly influenced by political energy agendas.

13.2.4 Federal Acts

Concurrently, several federal acts mandated technology-based efforts that have impacted CTE. In some cases, legislation has focused on funding targeted programs, serving as an incentive for CTE faculty to develop relevant curriculum. In other cases, the laws have served as an administrative function to coordinate or monitor CTE efforts (Scott & Sarkees-Wircenski, 1996).

In 1978 the Comprehensive Employment and Training Act (CETA) Amendments linked manpower legislation and other work-preparation programs, including vocational education. The services for individuals with disabilities needed to be identified in training plans of prime sponsors.

In 1982 the Job Training Partnership Act (JPTA) signaled significant collaborations between the private sector and vocational education in terms of job training and related services. Regional services delivery areas (SDAs) were funded to work with private industry councils (PICs) to assess and meet training needs (70

percent of funding had to be directed to training). Special summer youth employment programs were established.

In 1983 the Education Handicapped Act Amendments supported education and service programs to help relevant youth transition from secondary education to post-secondary education or employment. The Rehabilitation Act Amendments of the same year underwrote demonstration projects to help youth with disabilities to address problems transitioning from school to work; 1986 amendments expanded transition programs.

The main vocational education legislation has been the Perkins Act of 1984, which focused on preparing adults of job opportunities and improving workforce skills, and insuring equal opportunities therein. Disadvantaged and handicapped individuals were targeted service populations. The 2000 amendment was wide-ranging, allocating funds for research and development, bilingual vocational training, career guidance programs, partnerships with business, and the development of CTE data systems. Other amendments have addressed linkages between secondary and post-secondary education (1998), non-traditional training and employment (1999), and technology preparation programs and native populations (2006).

Disabilities were targeted during this time. The 1988 Technology-Related Assistance for Individuals with Disabilities Act helped states develop technology-related assistance programs for individuals with disabilities and their families. The 1990 Education of the Handicapped Amendments, also known as the Individuals with Disabilities Education Act (IDEA), was groundbreaking legislation for educating disabled youth. Schools were required to provide assistive devices to help these youth function, and special transition programs were required.

Several acts linked school and CTE. The School-to-Work Opportunities Act of 1994 supported career exploration and counseling, and on-the-job training linked with school-based learning. The Personal Responsibility and Work Opportunity Reconciliation Act of 1996 encouraged training that helped people on welfare enter the workplace economy. The Telecommunications Act of 1996 required that schools and libraries receive low-cost telecommunication service, which facilitated the incorporation of the Internet for CTE. The Adult Education and Family Literacy Act, Title II of the Workforce Investment Act of 1998 was intended to provide a unified, one-step delivery system for workforce investment and education efforts for youth and adults.

The 21st century continued to see legislation that impacted CTE. The No Child Left Behind Act of 2001 addressed secondary education, calling for more local control and flexibility, greater accountability, and scientifically-based decision making. The 2008 Higher Education Opportunity Act extended the Higher Education Act of 1965. Seeing the impact of globalization in the marketplace, the law promoted world language and international education. Business education was especially targeted, particularly addressing the needs of part-time and mid-career learners. The American Recovery and Reinvestment Act of 2009 supported funding for educational technology and job training, including targeted vocational education for the disabled.

In the last three decades the federal government has also legislated several programs in support of CTE, usually focusing on a specific, underserved population. Examples include rehabilitation programs, the farmworker program, the Appalachian Regional program, and services for the blind and disabled.

Legislation that addresses technology and CTE also exists on the state level. The most recent example is California State's Executive Order S-06-09. On May 28, 2009, California Governor Schwarzenegger authorized a California Action Plan for ICT (Information and Communications Technology) Digital Literacy. One of the steps of the plan mandates strategies and actions for incorporating Digital Literacy into workforce training.

The order asserts that ICT digital literacy skills are "vital to California's ability to compete successfully in a global information and knowledge economy" (p. 1). The policy specifically supports the administration's goal to "expand the skilled workforce, and increase competitiveness in sciences, technology, engineering and math industries and careers" (p. 2). The policy also supports digital literacy standards and accountability for assessing the success of training programs. As part of this order, the state's Workforce Investment Board is mandated to develop a technology literacy plan that supports technology training into workforce preparation, and expands CTE opportunities in community colleges. This executive order signals state governmental legitimization of and pro-active involvement in technology education, with explicit attention to CTE.

13.3 CTE INSTRUCTIONAL USE OF TECHNOLOGY

The use of technology in CTE reflects both educational philosophy and societal context. The instructional use of technology has encompassed: 1) variations on demonstration and practice of technology tools to be used in the field, and 2) technology that facilitates instruction itself but differs from the technology used in the profession. In both cases, technology can serve management functions such as overseeing personnel and operation, instructional systems administration (such as resources, equipment, and infrastructure), and instructional design functions.

Over the past three decades, CTE philosophy about technology education has evolved. As the definition and implementation of industrial arts was changing in the 1980s, CTE educators held differing views about technology. DeVore and his followers considered technology as the basis of industrial arts, Maley encouraged a student-centered approach, and Ohio State University Industrial Arts Curriculum Project staff favored an industry focus (Kirkwood, Foster & Bartow, 1994). In the 1990s, the influence of industry clearly marked CTE as education in general was under great scrutiny, and technological advances were making formal educational methods look seriously out of step with the marketplace. Business consultant Chafy (1997) contended that

Teachers of technology education, in both secondary and higher levels, are in a unique position to directly influence administration, peer, and student perceptions of the role technology in contemporary society. Technology education must seek to go beyond the transmission of the most effective and economic usage of "tools" in modern society to include critical investigations of the social purpose of technology (p. 9).

In the face of decreasing number of students enrolling in CTE, curriculum sought to incorporate rigorous academic standards and prepare students for employment in general (Lynch, 2000). In the 21st century, high school career awareness and exploration reconfigured itself into small learning academies whereby core academic course curricula aligned with career clusters such as health or business. In the process, employers linked with schools, and students understood the practical reasons for learning subject matter (ACTE, 2009). Students were more actively engaged in their learning, and less likely to drop. Thus, over the recent years, CTE has changed from a marginalized curriculum to a broad-based platform for workplace readiness. In the process, technology education itself has transcended CTE to become a basic literacy.

13.3.1 Learning Using Professional Technology Tools

In the traditional apprentice model, the learner would watch the yeoman at work using the associated technology. The yeoman would guide the apprentice's initial efforts with the technology, providing support as needed, until the apprentice could operate the technology independently. The yeoman served as a mentor, providing individualized instruction based on ongoing assessment and feedback.

This type of instruction continues to the present in the same way, but many variations now exist. For instance, factories and corporations may be structured into very specialized functions so that the learner has to operate just one machine or do a single set of actions. The extent of training depends on the complexity of the task and associated technology. Trainers and supervisors should explain how the learner's function contributes to the overall process and product. Increasingly, industry promotes cross-function training so that employees can back up each other in emergencies; this practice also fosters mutual appreciation and interdependence.

In contrast, a job might use just a handful of technologies, but each tool enables one to perform many complex tasks. Computer-aided design and chemical engineering exemplify fields that require the employee to manipulate specialized tools to solve sophisticated problems. For such training, tool use is just one aspect of education; learners must gain deep knowledge and develop complex schemas in order to ascertain which strategy to use for a particular situation. While an apprenticeship might be useful, it is more likely that formal academic courses will provide such in-depth preparation.

Laboratories enable a class of learners to practice similar tasks using the same tools simultaneously, which facilitates supervision and feedback. In the best case scenario, industry and academia partner to provide the same technology in both settings. If academic conducts advanced research, they may be testing technology that is unavailable on the market. However, chances are unlikely that an entire lab can be equipped with such ground-breaking technology. Usually, industry's technology level surpasses the educational world's, so that CTE training enables students to practice using baseline technology, but state-of-the-art advanced technology is more likely to be learned on the job. Part of the reason for this technology time lag is due to educators' own lack of current training and experience with cutting edge technology.

Specific and standardized, repetitive tasks lend themselves well to technology-aided learning aids, often as a self-paced training. The function can be broken down into its requisite steps and variations, with each step being documented in text, image, sound, video or multimedia format. The steps are then sequenced in order. If the function includes decision points with different options, then the reference document needs to provide "branching" so that the learner can follow the consequences of each decision. Instructions can also include troubleshooting tips if a step does not work. The final product can be duplicated and reused, and scaled to the extent that the task is standardized and performed. For instance, fast food chains routinely use videos as a training tool because of that format's ease of use and duplication.

The choice of technology format for such self-contained learning aids depends on several factors:

- Match with the task's communication channel (data input lends itself to text reference sheet or screen "dump" tutorial; wood lathe work is better captured in video).
- Match with the task's sequence (linear works with video; decision tree works with simulation).
- Existing equipment (and connectivity) and facilities must be available to support the document.
- The type of audience impacts choice; for example, podcasts and vidcasts are good for individual use; PowerPoints can be used with large groups.
- The instructional style fits the format; presentations support lectures while simulations foster student-centered learning, as examples.
- Cost is often the bottom line.

13.3.2 Conditions for Teaching with Technology

Teaching *about* technology differs from teaching with technology; the former focuses on content, and the latter focuses on process. The Panel on Undergraduate Engineering Education (1986) discussed several factors that influence the extent to which individual CT educators incorporate technology in their instruction.

Educational philosophy. Pragmatists favor structured hands-on learning, perennialists emphasize enduring principles and theories, constructivists provide resources and a learning environment in which students explore possibilities.

Instructional strategies. CTE naturally supports project-based learning, particularly in developing skills and supporting applications. Students are likely to be engaged with technology tools, but might not be engaged with their peers unless technology access is structured for small group coordination. Contextual instruction enables learners to see the big picture, and facilitates effective communication skills.

Instructional delivery. CTE instruction may be located in a lecture hall, computer lab, traditional lab, or at the work site. The delivery mode may be face-to-face, online, or broadcast (such as video, audio, television). Each of the setting can support technology, depending on the setting's infrastructure and available equipment.

Educational institutions. Instructors find it difficult to incorporate technology that is incompatible with the educational system. CTE is particularly vulnerable to this issue because industries can acquire technology at a scale that makes sufficient return on the investment. Educational systems, in contrast, tend to be smaller and decentralized so that mass adoption and standardized coordination are seldom feasible. Academic money is usually spent on faculty rather than on instructional system. Nor do most CTE faculty share their syllabi and course activities, even when technology comprises a significant part of instruction content matter.

Knowledge. Instructor knowledge about teaching methods, specifically incorporating technology, vary greatly. Some CTE instructors have a strong functional skill set but might not have much andragological training. Particularly since courses about technology-enhanced teaching have changed radically in the past three decades, if existing instructors have not continued to develop their teaching strategies, they are likely to use the same instructional approaches year after year. Up until most recently, academic faculty were not given incentives to gain technology expertise, or were they rewarded for technology incorporation. Just keeping current in the field can be a time-consuming effort, so carving out additional time to learn instructional technologies may seem daunting.

Availability. Some institutions might have productivity technology but neglect to think about instructional technology such as web-based course management systems and grading programs. Cost for equipment acquisitions and maintenance can also preclude use. On a more basic level, CTE software has been slow to develop. Few CTE faculty have been involved in commercial software development, partly due to their lack of knowledge of computers. In the early 1980s, a non-print university consortium established a national clearinghouse for microcomputer-based instructional materials for engineers. That practice has grown to the present situation where several educational repositories exist: by campus, profession, or organization (Panel on Undergraduate Engineering Education, 1986).

Culture. In some cultures, the teacher is all-knowing, and students are expected to recite back what they learned, and not question the expert. In other cultures, active inquiry and critical thinking are encouraged; the instructor serves as a facilitator for student learning. Because technology tends to be content-neutral, it usually serves as a learning tool rather than an end itself. Even if the instructor provides the content matter, students need to manipulate that information in order to take advantage of technology features such as editing, repurposing, and combining with other media. Students have more control and responsibility so the instructor's role changes to that of a coordinator or "orchestrator," which can conflict with static knowledge and transmission of that knowledge.

13.3.3 Technology-Enhanced Instruction

The nature of CTE, instruction as a whole, and technology in particular have shaped how CTE faculty teach with technology over the past three decades. Already by 1980 technical training was shifting from a skill-transmission model to a competency-development model (Knowles, 1978). In this period, technology-enhanced CTE instruction has moved from top-down to broad-based, from one-directional to two- and multi-directional communication, from static to dynamic, from programmer-dependent to content-dependent, and from administrative- to learning-oriented. As early as 1960, it was predicted that teachers and even the school system could be eliminated and replaced by educational technology developed alternative institutions. Such predictions have largely fallen by the wayside, but in 1979 the Association of Educational Communications and Technology did contend that educational technology affected the organizational structure of education at the curricular level such that an array of facilitated learning could exist in a variety of institutions. Instructional design, delivery and assessment could change dramatically because of educational technology.

13.3.4 Emerging Practices in the 1980s

Even in 1980 computers were acknowledged as contributing to effective teaching. The Panel on Undergraduate Engineering Programs asserted that computers helped students focus on central problems rather than on routine calculations, and that its main benefit was individualized learning. Typical uses of computer technology included programming language, computer modeling and simulations, and drill and practice. Engineering students used interactive graphics for computer-aided design and manufacturing design applications. Considering computers as an alternative to experimental laboratory work, educators noted that computer-aided data collection could be easier and more precise, and it could be less costly or dangerous than working with actual products; nevertheless, computer simulations were considered supplementary to "live" lab work. Computers were also used to access library network data, but at that time, the cost could run up to hundreds of dollars per hour for each search.

Computer-based training had become attractive to large corporations with multiple remote sites. The following benefits were cited: faster learning, more timely training (not counting the time needed to develop the training), the ability for self-pacing, and standardization. However, few products were readily available, and in-house product development was costly (Craig, 1987).

Another emerging technology of the time was video, which was produced in tape and disc format. Videotapes were attractive for distance learning because lectures could be recorded, duplicated, and disseminated at relatively low cost. The size of an LP record (an even older technology), videodiscs could hold 30-60 minutes of full-motion video or other information, and supported random access. Television constituted another venue for instructional delivery. Older visual media, 8- and 33mm film, continued to be used to explain CTE processes.

Other low-tech instructional tools included audiocassettes, overhead projectors and lap-dissolve projection (i.e., two slide projectors). Instructors were expected to produce content that could be displayed with the appropriate equipment. Similarly, instructors developed content and used authoring languages to communicate with the student. Coding was a challenge (Chambers, 1982).

Faculty use of technology was uneven, and called for financial and administrative support. Faculty needed research to back claims of technology's contribution to learning, and faculty were encouraged to participate in educational technology development. It was posited that technology industry advertising and student video gaming would spur the incorporation of technology into CTE (Panel on Undergraduate Engineering Education, 1986).

13.3.5 Coordinated Practices in the 1990s

Coordinated technology-enhanced CTE instruction was a central motif in the 1990s. The term "learning organization" emerged, reflecting the need for organizations as a whole to develop skills and manage knowledge systematically. CTE used technology to build information systems for recording and assessing training. Employers could track professional development efforts, and monitor performance; trainers could align curriculum with business goals, coordinate instruction, and monitor system performance.

Instructional design systems development examined an enterprise's inputs, outputs, throughputs, feedback, and control elements to develop a set of performance objectives that would determine a sequence of aligned instruction. Technology-enhanced media could be chosen based on the learning task (Calder & McCollum, 1998).

Instructional technology became more integrated in the 1990s, with desktop computers being able to connect peripherals such as CDs and link to the Internet. The goal was a one-stop training support system that could deliver voice, data, images, and motion. This goal was implemented in the form of electronic performance support systems (EPSS), which could be described as a database of job aids that provided information, explained procedures, and aided in decision-making. The supporting documents typically consisted of directions, worksheets, spreadsheets, decision tables, flowcharts, and checklists. Online help and expert systems provided just-in-time help. EPSS adoption was spotty, despite its promise, because many settings did not have the required infrastructure or coordination capacity. Furthermore, trainers and users were not skilled in EPSS use or resisted this training innovation (Craig, 1996).

The 1990s witnessed a huge expansion in open and flexible CTE instructional delivery that facilitated greater instructor-student interaction, through digital forms of synchronous conferencing and asynchronous communication. Course management systems appeared, which provided for a coordinated approach to course content, communication, and management (Rossett, 2002). These systems were usually Web-based, which enabled users to communicate across computer platforms.

13.3.6 21ˢᵗ Century Trends

The Internet constituted the main technology content vehicle for CTE. As speed and bandwidth improved, the learning community could access information in a wide variety of formats online from around the world. Developing instructional content also became easier with "natural" programming language and templates, robust productivity applications, and lower-cost equipment such as digital cameras and camcorders. Uploading and sharing content was also facilitated by the Web's graphical interface. As a result, more applicable learning aids such as tutorials and interactive simulations were available, feeding the production and training cycle.

In general, instructional technology has become a more mature tool. Instructional design aligns outcomes with student needs, resources, learning activities, and assessment. Course and training delivery ranges from one-time workshops anywhere/anytime to permanent learning communities. Courses may incorporate technology in class or online, with hybrid delivery systems constituting the preferable stance. The underlying

instructional question is: how does technology enhance CTE teaching and learning? CTE learners also make more choices as to their form and source of learning, often creating a collage of educational venues provided by a variety of CTE "vendors."

More innovative technology-based tools have been considered for CTE, blending industry, education and public use. Probably the highest profile technology form under discussion has been games, be they console or computer-based. This medium actively engages students, provides both textual and visual cues, often requires collaboration in order to accomplish a task, often demands clear communication, facilitates problem-solving skills, provides immediate feedback, and fosters attention to detail (Gros, 2003). On the other hand, existing games seldom support the curriculum and content standards, and many involve violence. A feasible theoretical model to employ when examining the educational potential of games is Activity Theory (Engeström, 1987). It focuses on subject (i.e., students) manipulation (that is, a learning task) of objects (e.g., concepts, artifacts) to achieve a desired outcome (i.e., meet a standard). This process is impacted by the rules, the tools used (e.g., resources), and community (including division of labor). As CTE instructors select games into their curriculum, they need to look at the underlying concepts being addressed, the educational value of the tools, and the pedagogical "fit" of the sequence of tasks. Nevertheless, games have not yet been broadly accepted in CTE because few games focus on CTE content, and easy yet robust gaming authoring tools have not appeared in the educational marketplace. Nor are some faculty comfortable with the underlying concept of gaming for CTE purposes.

13.4 TRENDS

Probably the most influential change in teaching with technology within CTE currently has been the introduction and increasing acceptance of interactive Web 2.0. Knowledge is collaboratively built and shared. Whereas earlier decades focused more on instructor-produced content, which could involve high-level technical expertise, Web 2.0 tools are often easy to use so that content can regain intellectual focus. Adding this broadbased authoring set of tools to the educational concept of constructivism results in student-centered curriculum. Johnson (2009) suggests several Web 2.0 tools that work well for CTE learning across the curriculum.

- **Audio files.** Audacity (http://audacity. sourceforge.net) is an open source application for recording and editing sound. Instructors can record lectures and shorter tutorials, and learners can listen to the audio files at their convenience for as many times as they wish.
- **Blogs**. 21classes (http://www.21classes. com) enables instructors to develop a class blog portal. For a fee, access can be restricted, and each student can upload up to 25 MB of content. This software also supports subject "tagging" and full-text searching. Class Blogmeister (http://class-blogmeister.com) is a free product that enables instructors to set up and monitor student blog accounts.
- **Graphic organizers**. Bubbl.us (http://bubbl.us) is a visual brainstorming and concept mapping tool. Conceptshare (http://www. conceptshare.com) is an online design collaboration tool that allows comments. Gliffy (http://www.gliffy. com) provides a variety of diagrams and other graphic organizer templates.
- **Image sharing**. Bubbleshare (http://www. bubbleshare.com) permits individuals to upload photos and other images with unlimited storage. Audio and video captions can be added to "albums." Flickr (http://www.flickr.com) is a free photograph management system that operates on sev-

eral digital platforms, including mobile devices. Individuals can also "push" photos through feeds and other alert systems.

- **Multimedia**. Voicethread (http://www. voicethread.com) is a free (or low-cost) program that enables users to develop and share online "albums" of mixed media; viewers can comment in several ways. Zoho (http://zoho.com) is a free online collaborative environment that supports group projects in a variety of formats.
- **Networking**. Ning (http://www.ning.com) is a free online social networking environment that supports links, groups, and sharing of documents such as videos. LinkedIn (http://www.linkedin.com) facilitates business and professional connections, so lends itself to mentoring opportunities.
- **Presentations**. Slideshare (http://www. slideshare.net) is a free site that allows users to upload and share PowerPoint/ OpenOffice/pdf presentations and documents. Audio can also be incorporated. Spresent (http://www.spresent.com) is a free web-based application that enables users to create and disseminate Flash presentations.
- **Video**. Viddler (http://www.viddler.com) supports uploading and share of video within a browser. Vimeo (http://www. vimeo.com) provides 500 MG of video storage and sharing capacity. YouTube (http://www.youtube.com) is a free online video streaming service that allows users to upload and share videos.
- **Virtual environments.** Second Life (http:// www.secondlife.com) is an object-oriented online environment in which to interact with artifacts and avatars (personalities). University of Illinois at Chicago's School of Public Health is using this environment to prepare students for health-related response planning. Microsoft and VMware have introduced virtual "machine" soft-

ware that creates a "sandbox" for technical students to explore hardware without harming it. ALIVE (Advanced Learning and Immersive Virtual Environment) laboratory in Queensland is developing simple tools to enable educators to teach with ready-made or customized embedded three-dimensional applications (de Byl, 2009).

- **Wikis**. PB Wiki (http://www.pbwiki.com) is a free webpage creator application that can be used collaboratively. Alternatively, individuals can make comments on peer pages. Wiki creators, such as instructors, can customize access options. WikiSpaces (http://www.wikispaces.com) is another site that can be secured; K-12 educators can establish a free account.

- **Group writing**. Google Docs (http://docs.google.com) allows learners to share and edit documents using a suite of productivity tools. Google Notebook (http://www.google.com/notebook) organizes text, images and links that can be sharing, even from cell phones. Whiteboard (http://www.whiteboard.com) facilitates collaborative writing, and saves earlier versions.

Another major trend is the use of learning objects. These digital documents are building blocks for instructional design. They can consist of presentations, simulations, case studies, tutorials, assessments, or even readings (which might well be considered a traditional learning object). Each learning object can be embedded into an existing instructional session or learning activity to provide a variety of ways to experience a concept or deepen understanding. Learning objects are usually found in federated repositories that index them, and facilitate their retrieval. Representative CTE repositories include: (a) MERLOT (http://www.merlot.org): Multimedia Educational Resource for Learning and Online Teaching; (b) Vocational Information Center (http://www.khake.com/); (c)

Learning Object Repository Network (http://lorn.flexiblelearning.net.au/) for Australian vocational educators; (d) LeOb (http://www.poriakk.fi/leob/): Learning Objects for Vocational Adult Education; and (e) GLOBE (http://www.globe-info.org): Global Learning Objects Brokered Exchange

On a more philosophical level, the issue of professional learning communities and advancement of knowledge has clashed with traditional copyright issues. On one hand, intellectual property and proprietary information has become an industry nightmare as employees shift from company to company, taking their brain power and corporate knowledge with them. Exit clearance often involves signing non-disclosure agreements to prevent corporate piracy. On the other hand, copyright restrictions can seriously slow down and impede technological advancements. Scientists in particular are adopting open source publication venues to speed up peer review and communication. Creative Commons (http://creativecommons.org) allows creators and licensors more latitude in intellectual rights management. CTE instructors and learners can build on other's knowledge, and contribute to the field, more openly in the Creative Commons.

13.5 INSTRUCTIONAL TECHNOLOGY FUTURE

With the speed of technology, predicting its use in CTE is foolhardy. However, the speed of CTE instruction has not always kept up with that speed. Each career cluster has its own technology standard in practice and preparation, and instructors within each domain exhibit a wide range of expertise and interest in incorporating technology into their instruction. Particularly since CTE institutions tend to act autonomously, widespread practices are unlikely even though they could be cost-effective. More likely, CTE learners will shop around for a widening variety of learning opportunities that best meet their needs.

A model of technology-enhanced CTE may serve as a more useful way to look at future scenarios. The modified model may be represented as a three-dimensional learning environment: rather like a spherical cell representing the learning environment.

One dimension consists of the learners: students (less expert learners) and instructor (more expert learners) with an extension to encompass the best practitioners and experts in the field. Thus, the continuum along this dimension is expertise; by the end of an instructional term, all should become more expert. Typically, traditional CTE instructors maintain the locus of control relative to learning within the course "sphere," and over time share that control with their students and the profession; thus, the locus of control tends to move towards a learning community model over time.

The second dimension is defined by the resources. As with the first dimension, the continuum of resources ranges from uninformed pre-conceptions to expert knowledge. The first dimension intersects, or interacts, with this continuum; the degree of interaction ranging from "consuming" pre-existing sources created by experts in the field to generating/producing new knowledge. The instructor usually controls that interaction by selecting and organizing resources for inclusion in the course, as well as controlling the students' access to–and contributions to–that dimension via learning activities and assignments. If the first dimension holds that learners become more expert, then in this dimension learner's products, (i.e. the resource that they generate), should become more expert as well. With technology, instructors tend to share access "rights" to that dimension; the locus of control shifts to the students as they migrate from the role of resource consumers to resource producers.

The third dimension may be defined as the learning environment or space itself. The continuum here ranges from entirely face-to-face to entirely online or virtual space. Instructors tend to use technology first as a supplement to their training, using features that resemble current instructional practice. With experience, CTE instructors use technology to complement other forms of instruction, and may eventually replace seat time entirely with virtual learning (anytime, anywhere). In the process, decision-making about appropriate technology use becomes less a factor of the format and more a factor of optimal learning. In other words, the intersection of the population and the resources impacts the shape of the learning environment. Over time the instructor tends to share that control with students and practitioners. Again, the locus of control drifts towards practitioner-centered learning. Unlike the other two dimensions where the goal is towards one end of the spectrum, towards expertise, the goal here is optimal learning (which is most likely to consist of a mixed environment). However, the move to expertise is consistent in its application relative to this dimension; the choice of learning environment becomes more expertly determined.

Connections among the three dimensions then constitute interaction. One may visualize these as "strings" or vectors if accomplished along the same dimension (such as student-teacher interaction face-to-face), as a plane if accomplished between two dimensions (i.e., student-resource interaction online), or as a 3D shape if accomplished among all dimensions (i.e., group project done on an industry's intranet).

The fourth dimension in this model is time, which has as its continuum locus of control. As illustrated in light of other dimensions, the trend over time goes from faculty to shared control with students and practitioners. This trend is activated through assessment. Over time, the learning community becomes more critical thinkers. Faculty assess students, resources, and the learning environment (i.e., coursework and its delivery) more explicitly and closely. Students too become more critical of their own work as well as their peers'. Through this process, outcomes can be judged more objectively, which also facilitates sharing control since there is agreement about standards and related indicators of quality.

One might also state that over time, the walls or surface of the course becomes more porous as the three dimensions (learners, resources, learning environment) interact with professional community at large. Then true CTE exists: a mindset that can change the world. As seen here, technology can become a catalyst in this change process.

13.6 CONCLUSION

Technology has permeated society in general, and major government and economic stakeholders have recognized the importance of incorporating technology throughout education in order to prepare a competitive workforce in a global economy. In the last three decades, CTE instruction about specific technology tools has been complemented with instruction to support generic technology competency. The nature of CTE, instruction as a whole, and technology in particular have shaped how CTE faculty teach with technology over the past three decades. Pre-conditions that impact CTE incorporation of technology include educational philosophy, instructional strategies and delivery, technical and educational knowledge, institutional capacity and support, and cultural norms. In the last thirty years, technology-enhanced CTE training has shifted from a top-down to broad-based basis, from one-directional to two- and multi-directional communication, from static to dynamic content, from programmer-dependent to content-dependent resources, and from administrative- to learning-oriented focus. With the advent of Web 2.0's interactivity, the conditions for a true learning community involving CTE instructors, students and practitioners can emerge. The future will depend on each stakeholder's expertise and support.

REFERENCES

Association for Career and Technical Education. (2009). The Role of career academies in school improvement. *Issue Briefs* (March).

Association for Educational Communications and Technology. (1979). *The definition of educational technology*. Alexandria, VA: Association for Educational Communications and Technology.

Calder, J., & McCollum, A. (1998). *Open and flexible learning in vocational education and training*. London: Kogan Page.

California. Office of the Governor. (2009). *Executive Order S-06-09*. Sacramento: California State.

Chafy, R. (1997). Exploring the intellectual foundation of technology education: From Condorcet to Dewey. *Journal of Technology Education, 9*(1). Retrieved June 23, 2009, from http://scholar.lib.vt.edu/ejournals/JTE/v9n1/chafy.html

Chambers, G. (1982). A model for the development of technical instructors. *Master Abstracts International*, *20*(4), 342.

Craig, R. (Ed.). (1987). *Training and development handbook* (3rd ed.). New York: McGraw-Hill.

Craig, R. (Ed.). (1996). *Training and development handbook* (4th ed.). New York: McGraw-Hill.

De Byl, P. (2009). Making web3D less scary. *Innovate, 5*(4). Retrieved from http://innovateonline.info/

Engeström, Y. (1987). *Learning by expanding: An activity-theoretical approach to developmental research*. Helsinki, Finland: Orienta-Konsultit Oy.

Friedman, T. (2005). *The world is flat*. New York: Farrar, Straus and Giroux.

Gros, B. (2003). The impact of digital games in education. *First Monday, 8*(7). Retrieved from http://first monday.org/issues/issue8_7/gros/index.html.

Johnson, M. (2009). *Primary source teaching the Web 2.0 way K-12*. Columbus, OH: Linworth.

Kirkwood, J., Foster, P., & Bartow, S. (1994). Historical leaders in technology education philosophy. *Journal of Industrial Teacher Education, 32*(1). Retrieved May 24, 2009, from http://scholar.lib. vt.edu/ ejournals/JITE/v32n1/Kirkwood.html.

Knowles, M. (1978). Gearing up for the eighties. *Training & Development, 32*(July), 12–14.

Lynch, R. (2000). High school career and technical education for the first decade of the 21st century. *Journal of Vocational Education Research, 25*(2). Retrieved June 25, 2009, from http://scholar.lib. vt.edu/ ejournals/JVER/v25n2/lynch.html

Naisbett, J. (1982). *Megatrends: Ten new directions transforming our lives*. New York: Warner.

National Commission on Excellence in Education. (1983). *A nation at risk*. Washington, DC: U.S. Department of Education.

Panel on Undergraduate Engineering Education. et al. (1986). *Engineering undergraduate education*. Washington, DC: National Academy Press.

Pink, D. (2005). *A whole new mind*. New York: Riverhead. Rossett, A. (Ed.). *ASTD e-learning handbook*. New York: McGraw-Hill.

Scott, J., & Sarkees-Wircenski, M. (1996). *Overview of vocational and applied technology education*. Homewood, IL: American Technical Publishers.

Shelly, G., Cashman, T., Gunter, R., & Gunter, G. (2007). *Teachers discovering computers: Integrating technology in the classroom* (4th ed.). Boston: Thomson.

Toffler, A. (1980). *The third wave*. New York: Bantam Books.

Toffler, A. (1991). *Powershift*. New York: Bantam.

U.S. Department of Education. (1983). *A nation at risk*. Washington, DC: Government Printing Office.

U.S. Department of Labor. (1991). *Secretary's Commission on Achieving Necessary Skills*. Washington, DC: Government Printing Office.

Compilation of References

Abel, B. (2006, Winter). The new frontier—the world. *The Magazine of Marquette University.* Retrieved May 1, 2009, from http://www.marquette.edu/magazine/winter06/fro ntier.shtml

Abell, S., Boone, W., Arbaugh, F., Lannin, J., Beilfuss, M., Volkmann, M., & White, S. (2006). Recruiting future science and mathematics teachers into alternative certification programs: Strategies tried and lessons learned. *Journal of Science Teacher Education, 17,* 165–183. doi:10.1007/s10972-005-9001-4

ACTE. (2002). A new age of technology. *Techniques, 77*(2), 38–43.

ACTE. (2002). An association is reborn. *Techniques, 77*(2), 44–45.

ACTE. (2006). Career and technical education's role in American competitiveness. [from http://www.acteonline.org/uploadedFiles/Publications_and_Online_Media/files/Competitiveness.pdf]. *Issue Brief,* (October): 2006. Retrieved May 20, 2009.

Adams, D. (Ed.). (1995). *Health issues for women of color: A cultural diversity perspective.* Thousand Oaks, CA: Sage.

Adams, E., & Freeman, C. (2000). Commuting the distance of distance learning: the Pepperdine story . In Lau, L. (Ed.), *Distance learning technologies: issues, trends and opportunities* (pp. 157–165). Hershey, PA: Idea Group Publishing.

Adams, E., Liston, J., & Hall, H. (2005). Preparing accomplished career and technical education teachers. *Proceedings of the Association for Career and Technical Education Research Conference,* 141-155.

Adult Learning in Focus. *National and State-by-State Data.* (2008). Council for adult and experiential learning (CAEL) in Partnership with NCHEMS. Retrieved August 25, 2008, from http://www.cael.org/pdf/State_Indicators_Monograph.pdf

Alabama Course of Study. *Career and technical education.* (2007). Retrieved on May 15, 2009, from ftp://ftp.alsde.edu/documents/54/3-CTE%20Clusters%20Pathways%20and% 20Courses.doc

Alliman-Brissett, A., & Turner, S. (2005). Supporting the career aspirations of American Indian Youth. *CURA Reporter* (Spring).

Allison, H. E. (2004). *Kant's transcendental idealism.* New Haven, CT: Yale University Press.

Alternative Teacher Certification. (2007). Retrieved April 18, 2009, from http://www2.edweek.org/rc/issues/alternative-teacher-certification

American Educational Research Association. (2005). *Teaching teachers: Professional deve-lopment to improve student achievement.* Retrieved November 13, 2007, from http://www.aera.net/uploadedFiles/Journals_and_Publications/Research_Points/RPSummer05.pdf

American Federation of Teachers. (2001). Beginning teacher induction: The essential bridge. *Educational Issues Policy Brief, 13,* 1–13.

American Society for Training and Development. (2008). *About us.* Retrieved May 17, 2009, from http://www.astd.org/ASTD/aboutus/

Anderson, B. (1986). *The status of vocational teacher education in University Council for Vocational Education member institutions.* Fort Collins, CO: Colorado State University.

Andrews, S., Gilbert, L., & Martin, E. (2006). The first years of teaching: Disparities in perceptions of support. *Action in Teacher Education, 24*(4), 4–13.

Armstrong, W., & Stinnett, T. (1957). *A manual on certification requirements for school personnel in the United States.* Washington, DC: National Commission on Teacher Education and Professional Standards, National Education Association.

Association for Career and Technical Education (ACTE). (2008). *Issue brief: Career and technical education's role in workforce readiness credentials.* Retrieved May 15, 2009, from http://www.acteonline.org/uploadedFiles/Publications_and_Online_Media/files/Wo rkReadinessCredentials.pdf

Association for Career and Technical Education. (2009). The Role of career academies in school improvement. *Issue Briefs* (March).

Association for Career and Technical Education. (2009, April). Texas state CTE profile. Retrieved May 1, 2009, from http://www.acteonline.org/content.aspx?id=2074

Association for Educational Communications and Technology. (1979). *The definition of educational technology.* Alexandria, VA: Association for Educational Communications and Technology.

Ausburn, L. J., & Brown, D. (2006). Learning strategy patterns and instructional preferences of career and technical education students. *Journal of Industrial Teacher Education, 43*(4), 6–39.

Baldacchino, J. (2008). The power to develop dispositions: Revisiting John Dewey's democratic claims for education. *Journal of Philosophy of Education, 42*(1), 149-163. Retrieved June 5, 2009, from http://dx.doi.org/10.1111/j.1467-9752.2008.00602.x

Ball, D. L. (2000). Bridging practices: Intertwining content and pedagogy in teaching and learning to teach. *Journal of Teacher Education, 51*(3), 241–247. doi:10.1177/0022487100051003013

Barlow, M. (1976). 200 years of vocational education: 1776-1976: The awakening, 1776-1826. *American Vocational Journal, 51*(5), 23–28.

Barlow, M. (1976). 200 years of vocational education: 1776-1976: Independent Action, 1826-1876. *American Vocational Journal, 51*(5), 31–40.

Barlow, M. (1976). 200 years of vocational education: 1776-1976: The vocational education age emerges, 1876-1926. *American Vocational Journal, 51*(5), 45–58.

Barriers to Implementing College and Workforce Readiness Initiatives in Texas. (2009). Texas association of school boards. Retrieved March 24, 2009, from http://www.tasb. org/issues/resource_center/college_readiness/index.aspx

Bartlett, J. (2002). Preparing, licensing, and certifying postsecondary career and technical educators. *Journal of Vocational Education Research, 27*(1), 127–149.

Beck, J. K., & Biggs, B. T. (2009). Serving rural communities using blended technology . In Wang, V. C. X. (Ed.), *Handbook of research on E-learning applications for career and technical education: Technologies for vocational training* (pp. 681–694). Hershey, PA: Information Science Reference.

Benson, A. D. (2003). Assessing participant learning in online environments. In S. Aragon (Ed.), *Facilitating learning in only environments* (pp. 69-77). New Directions for Adult and Continuing Education, No. 100. San Francisco: Jossey-Bass.

Benson, A., Johnson, S., Taylor, G., Treat, T., Shinkareva, O., & Duncan, J. (2004). *Distance learning in postsecondary career and technical education: A comparison of achievement in online vs. on-campus CTE courses.* St. Paul, MN: National Research Center for Career and Technical Education.

Bergen, D. (1981). *The dialogue of metaphysics and empirics: Librarianship as platonic and Aristotelian.* Retrieved May 24, 2009, from http://www.csa.com

Berliner, D. C., & Biddle, B. J. (1996). In defense of schools. *Vocational Educational Journal, 71*(3), 36–38.

Biggs, J. (2003). *Teaching for quality learning at university.* New York: Society for Research into Education & Open University Press.

Blank, W. (1982). *Handbook for developing competency-based training programs.* Engle- wood Cliffs. NJ: Prentice-Hall.

Boshier, R. (1991). Psychometric properties of the alternative form of the education participation scale. *Adult Education Journal, 41*(3), 150–167. doi:10.1177/0001848191041003002

Boston, C. (2002). *The concept of formative assessment.* College Park, MD: ERIC Clearinghouse on Assessment and Evaluation. (ERIC Reproduction Service No. ED470206). Retrieved May 20, 2009, from http://www.ericdigests.org/2003-3/concept. htm

Bottoms, G. (2005, April). The SREB model: Academic rigor, technical relevance, and a head start on a career . In Kazis, R. (Ed.), *Remaking career and technical education for the 21st century: What role for high school programs* (pp. 35–37). Boston, MA: Jobs for the Future/ Aspen Institute.

Bray, J. (2009). Embrace the future now! *Techniques, 84*(5), 6.

Bremer, T. (2006). Teacher preparation solutions: Rumbling for quality just won't do. *Studies in Art Education, 47*(3), 269–285. doi:10.2307/25475785

Brewer, E. W., Campbell, A. C., & Petty, G. C. (2000). *Foundations of workforce education: Historical, philosophical, and theoretical applications.* Dubuque, IA: Kendall/Hunt Publishing Co.

Bridgeland, J., Dilulio, J., & Morison, K. (2006, March). *The silent epidemic: Perspectives of high school dropouts.* Civic Enterprises in association with Peter D. Hart Research Associates for the Bill and Melinda Gates Association.

Bridgeland, J., Dilulio, J., Jr., & Morrison, K. B. (2006). *The silent epidemic.* Washington, D.C.: Civic Enterprises, LLC.

Briggs, J. (2008). *Perceptions of career and technical education teachers about teacher mentoring and teacher retention.* Unpublished doctoral dissertation. The Ohio State University, Columbus, Ohio.

Brookfield, S. (1986). *Understanding and facilitating adult learning.* San Francisco:Jossey-Bass.

Brookfield, S. (2005). *The power of critical theory: liberating adult learning and teaching.* San Francisco: Jossey-Bass.

Brubacher, J. S. (1939). *Modern philosophies of education.* New York: McGraw-Hill.

Bruell, C. (1999). *On the socratic education: An introduction to the shorter platonic dialogues.* Lanham, MD: Rowman & Littlefield Publishers Inc.

Bruening, T., Scanlon, D., Hodes, C., Dhital, P., Shao, X., & Liu, S. (2001). Characteristics of teacher educators in career and technical education. National Research Center for Career and Technical Education. Retrieved May 1, 2009, from http://www.eric. ed.gov/ERICDocs/data/eric-docs2sql/content_storage_01/0000019b/80/19/61/ee.pdf

Bruening, T., Scanlon, D., Hodes, C., Dhital, P., Shao, X., & Liu, S. (2001a). *Characteristics of teacher educators in career and technical education.* Columbus, OH: The Ohio State University, National Dissemination Center for Career and Technical Education. Retrieved June 8, 2009, from http://nrccte.org/

Bruening, T., Scanlon, D., Hodes, C., Dhital, P., Shao, X., & Liu, S. (2001b). *The status of career and technical education teacher preparation programs*. Columbus, OH: The Ohio State University, National Dissemination Center for Career and Technical Education. Retrieved May 27, 2009, from http://nrccte.org/

Bruening, T., Scanlon, D., Hoover, T., Hodes, C., Shao, X., Dhital, P., & Zolotov, A. (2002, December). Attributes and characteristics of exemplary, leading, and innovative, career and technical education teacher preparation programs. National Research Center for Career and Technical Education Retrieved May 1, 2009, from http://www.acteonline. org/uploadedFiles/About_CTE/files/Attributes%20and%20Characteristics%20of%20Exemplary%20CTE.pdf

Buford, T. O. (1969). *Toward a philosophy of education.* New York: Holt, Rinehart & Winston, Inc.

Bullough, R., & Draper, R. (2004). Making sense of a failed triad: Mentors, university supervisors, and positioning theory. *Journal of Teacher Education, 55*(5), 407–420. doi:10.1177/0022487104269804

Burstow, B. (1983). Sartre: A possible foundation for educational theory. [from http://www.csa. com]. *Journal of Philosophy of Education, 17*(2), 171–185. Retrieved April 24, 2009. doi:10.1111/j.1467-9752.1983.tb00028.x

Burstow, B. (1984). Adult education: A Sartrean-based perspective. [from http://www.csa. com]. *International Journal of Lifelong Education, 3*(3), 193–202. Retrieved May 26, 2009. doi:10.1080/0260137840030303

Butler, J. D. (1969). *Four philosophies and their practice in education and religion* (3rd ed.). New York: Harper and Row.

Bybee, R., & Starkweather, K. (2006). The twenty-first century workforce: A contemporary challenge for technology education. *Technology Teacher, 65*(8), 27–32.

Calder, J., & McCollum, A. (1998). *Open and flexible learning in vocational education and training*. London: Kogan Page.

California. Office of the Governor. (2009). *Executive Order S-06-09*. Sacramento: California State.

Camp, W., & Heath-Camp, B. (2007, September) *The status of CTE teacher education today: The old models for CTE teacher preparation are no longer producing adequate numbers of well-prepared teachers as they once did. Techniques.* Retrieved May 1, 2009, from http://www.acteonline.org/uploadedFiles/Publications_and_E-Media/files/files-tec hniques-2007/Sept07_Thm1.pdf

Camp, W., Case, R., Dean, A., & Fannon, C. (1998, August). National study of the supply and demand for teachers of agricultural education in 1995. Retrieved May 2, 2009, http://www.eric.ed.gov/ERICDocs/data/ericdocs2sql/content_storage_01/0000019b/80/16/fd/36.pdf

Camp. W. (2001). Formulating and evaluating theoretical frameworks for career and technical education research. *Journal of Vocational Education Research*. Retrieved May 1, 2009, from http://scholar.lib.vt.edu/ejournals/JVER/v26n1/camp.html

Career and Technical Education Administration. (2006). *Section A*. Retrieved May 1, 2009, from http://www.michigan.gov/documents/Section_A_CTE_Administrators_-_Admin_ Guide_169117_7.doc

Carl, D. *Perkins Career and Technical Education Improvement Act*. (2006). Retrieved May 13, 2008, from http://frwebgate.access.gpo.gov/cgi-bin/getdoc.cgi?dbname=109_cong_ bills&docid=f:s250enr.txt.pdf

Cartwright, M. (1948). Preface . In Ely, M. (Ed.), *Handbook of adult education* (pp. xi–xii). New York: Institute of Adult Education, Teachers College, Columbia University.

Carver, C., & Katz, D. (2004). Teaching at the boundary of acceptable practice. What is a new teacher mentor teacher to do? *Journal of Teacher Education, 55*(5), 449–462. doi:10.1177/0022487104269524

Catri, D. (1998). *Vocational education's image for the 21st century*. Retrieved May 1, 2009, from http://www.ericdigests.org/1999-2/21st.htm

Chafy, R. (1997). Exploring the intellectual foundation of technology education: From Condorcet to Dewey. *Journal of Technology Education, 9*(1). Retrieved June 23, 2009, from http://scholar.lib.vt.edu/ejournals/JTE/v9n1/chafy.html

Chambers, G. (1982). A model for the development of technical instructors. *Master Abstracts International, 20*(4), 342.

Cherwitz, R. A., & Hikins, J. W. (1979). John Stuart mill's "on liberty": Implications for the epistemology of the new rhetoric. *The Quarterly Journal of Speech, 65*(1), 12–24. doi:10.1080/00335637909383455

Chin, E., & Young, J. (2007). A person-oriented approach to characterizing beginning teachers on alternative certification programs. *Educational Researcher, 36*(2), 74–83. doi:10.3102/0013189X07299192

Christie, K. (2009). Stateline: Anticipating 2009's top 10. *Phi Delta Kappan, 90*(5), 317–319.

Clark, M. C., & Caffarella, R. S. (Eds.). (2000). *An update on adult development theory: New ways of thinking about the life course. New Directions for Adult and Continuing Education, No. 84.* San Francisco: Jossey-Bass.

Cochran-Smith, M. (2004). Stayers, leavers, lovers, and dreamers. *Journal of Teacher Education, 55*(5), 387–392. doi:10.1177/0022487104270188

Coffield, F., Moseley, D., Hall, E., & Ecclestone, K. (2004). *Learning styles and pedagogy in post-16 learning: A systematic and critical review.* Retrieved May 20, 2009, from http://www.lsda.org.uk/files/PDF/1543.pdf

Cohen, M. (2008). *Philosophical tales.* Oxford: Wiley Blackwell. doi:10.1002/9781444301045

Compton, J., Cox, E., & Laanan, F. (2006). Adult learners in transition. *New Directions for Student Services, 114*, 73–80. doi:10.1002/ss.208

Constantino, R. (Ed.). (1998). *Literacy, access, and libraries among the language minority population.* Lanham, MD: Scarecrow Press.

Conti, G. J., & Kolody, R. C. (1999). The relationship of learning strategy preference and personality type. In A. Rose (Ed.), *Proceedings of the Adult Education Research Conference* (pp. 86-90). Dekalb, IL: Northern Illinois University. Retrieved May 18, 2009, from http://www.adulterc.org/Proceedings/1999/99conti.htm

Conti, G. J., & Kolody, R. C. (2004). Guidelines for selecting methods and techniques . In Galbraith, M. W. (Ed.), *Adult learning methods: A guide for effective instruction* (3rd ed., pp. 181–192). Malabar, FL: Kreiger Publishing Company.

Cornett, L. (1990). Alternative certification: State policies in the SREB states. *Peabody Journal of Education, 67*(3), 55–83. doi:10.1080/01619569009538692

Council for Adult and Experiential Learning (CAEL) and National Council of Higher Education Management Systems (NCHEMS). (2008). *Adult learning in focus: National and state-by-state data.*

Craig, R. (Ed.). (1996). *ASTD training and development handbook.* New York: McGraw- Hill.

Cramer, K. (2004). *The vocational teacher pipeline: How academically well-prepared is the next generation of vocational teachers?* Washington, D.C.: U.S. Department of education, Office of the Deputy Secretary, Policy and Program Studies Service.

Cranton, P. (2006). *Understanding and promoting transformative learning.* San Francisco: John Wiley & Sons.

Cross, T., Bazron, B., Dennis, K., & Isaacs, M. (1989). *Towards a culturally competent system of care: A monograph on effective services for minority children who are severely emotionally disturbed (Vol. 1).* Washington, DC: Georgetown University Child Development Center.

Crowe, J. (2000). Evaluation of adult learners: Ethical issues. *New Horizons in Adult Education, 14*(3). Retrieved May 20, 2009, from http://www.nova.edu/~aed/horizons/vol14 n3.html

Cruickshank, D. R., & Associates. (1996). *General studies, content studies, and professional education* (pp. 4-28). Preparing America's Teachers. Bloomington, IN: Phi Delta Kappa Educational Foundation.

Daggett, B. (2008). Presentation to ACTE. International Center for Leadership in Education. Retrieved May 1, 2009, from http://www.acteonline.org/conventionsessions08. aspx

Dai, C., Sindelar, P., Denslow, D., Dewey, J., & Rosenberg, M. (2007). Economic analysis and the design of alternative-route teacher education programs. *Journal of Teacher Education, 58*(5), 422–439. doi:10.1177/0022487107306395

Daniels, D., & Shumow, L. (2003). Child development and classroom teaching: A review of the literature and implications for educating teachers. *Applied Developmental Psychology, 23*, 495–526. doi:10.1016/S0193-3973(02)00139-9

Darkenwald, G. G., & Valentine, T. (1985). Factor structure of deterrents to public participation in adult education. *Adult Education Quarterly, 35*(40), 177–193. doi:10.1177/0001848185035004001

Darling-Hammond, L. (1990). Teaching and knowledge: Policy issues posed by alternative certification for teachers. *Peabody Journal of Education, 67*(3), 123–154. doi:10.1080/01619569009538694

Darling-Hammond, L. (1996). The quiet revolution: Rethinking teacher development . *Educational Leadership, 53*, 4–10.

Darling-Hammond, L. (2000). Teacher quality and student achievement: A review of state policy evidence. *Education Policy Analysis Archives, 8*(1). Retrieved October 7, 2007, from http://epaa.asu.edu/epaa/v8n1/

Darling-Hammond, L. (2001). Standard setting in teaching: Changes in licensing, certification, and assessment . In Richardson, V. (Ed.), *Handbook of research on teaching* (pp. 751–776). Washington, DC: American Educational Research Association.

Darling-Hammond, L. (2002, September 6). Research and rhetoric on teacher certification: A response to "Teacher Certification Reconsidered," *Educational Policy Analysis Archives, 10*(36). Retrieved April 18, 2009, from http://epaa.asu.edu/epaa/v10n36.html

Darling-Hammond, L. (2003). Keeping good teachers: Why it matters what leaders can do. *Educational Leadership, 60*(8), 6–13.

Darling-Hammond, L., & Berry, B. (1999). Recruiting teachers for the 21st century: The foundation for educational equity. *The Journal of Negro Education, 68*(3), 254–279. doi:10.2307/2668100

Davis, S. M., & Franklin, S. V. (2003). Assessing the impact of student learning style preferences. *Proceedings of the 2003 American Association of Physics Teachers Physics Education Research Conference*. Retrieved May 20, 2009, from http://arxiv.org/ PS_cache/physics/pdf/0608/0608296v1.pdf

De Byl, P. (2009). Making web3D less scary. *Innovate, 5*(4). Retrieved from http://innovateonline.info/

Deal, C. (2005). Training across cultures: Designing training for participants from China, India, and Mexico. *Dissertation Abstracts International, 65*(08), 2836.

Dembo, M. H., & Howard, K. (2007). Advice about the use of learning styles: A major myth in education. *Journal of College Reading and Learning, 37*(2), 101–108.

Dial, M., & Stevens, C. (1993). Introduction: The context of alternative certification. *Education and Urban Society, 26*(1), 4–17. doi:10.1177/0013124593026001002

Dill, V. (1996). Alternative teacher certification . In Sikula, J. (Ed.), *Handbook of research on teacher education* (pp. 932–960). New York: Macmillan.

Dove, M. (2004). Teacher attrition: A critical American and International education issue. *The Delta Kappa Gamma Bulletin, 71*(1), 8–30.

Dunn, R. (2000). Learning styles: Theory, research, and practice. *National Forum of Applied Educational Research Journal, 13*(1), 3–22.

Dunn, R., & Dunn, K. (1998). *Practical approaches to individualizing staff development for adults.* Westport, CT: Praeger.

Dupuis, A. M. (1996). *Philosophy of education in historical perspective* (2nd ed.). Lanham, MD: Rowman & Littlefield Publishers Inc.

Earning, Learning, and Choice: Career and Technical Education works for students and em- ployers. (2004). Report of the national assessment of vocational education (NAVE), Independent Advisory Panel. Retrieved September 21, 2008, from http://www.ed.gov/ rschstat/ eval/sectech/nave/index.html

Eaton, T. H. (1926). *Education and vocations: Principles and problems of vocational education.* New York: John Wiley & Sons.

Echevarria, J., & Vogt, M. (2004). *Making content comprehensive to English language learners: the SIOP model* (2nd ed.). Boston: Allyn & Bacon.

Edmondson, A., & Moingeon, B. (1998). From Organizational Learning to the Learning Organisation. *Management Learning, 29*(1), 5–20. doi:10.1177/1350507698291001

Education and workforce issues: Public attitudes and awareness. (1997). *Washington State Workforce Training and Education Board.* Olympia, WA: WSWTEB.

Educational Testing Service (ETS). (2009). *General frequently asked questions.* Retrieved April 30, 2009, from http://www.ets.org/portal/site/ets/

Educational Testing Services. (2004). *Where we stand on teacher quality: An issue paper from ETS.* Retrieved December 3, 2007, from http://www.ets.org/Media/ News_and_ Media/position_paper.pdf

Effectiveness Fact Sheet. (2009). ACTE home website. Retrieved May 1, 2009, from http://www.acteonline.org

Elias, J. L., & Merriam, S. B. (2005). *Philosophical foundations of adult education.* Malabar, FL: Krieger Publishing Company.

Engeström, Y. (1987). *Learning by expanding: An activity-theoretical approach to developmental research.* Helsinki, Finland: Orienta-Konsultit Oy.

English, L. M., & Gillen, M. A. (Eds.). (2000). *Addressing the spiritual dimensions of adult learning: What educators can do. New Directions for Adult and Continuing Education, No. 85.* San Francisco: Jossey-Bass.

Evan, R. N. (1971). *Foundations of vocational education.* Columbus, OH: Charles E. Merrill.

Ewing, A. C. (Ed.). (1957). *The idealist tradition: From Berkeley to Blanshard.* London: Free Press.

Feathers, J. (2007). The development, implementation, and process evaluation of the REACH Detroit Partnership's diabetes lifestyle intervention. *The Diabetes Educator, 33*(3), 509–520. doi:10.1177/0145721707301371

Feiman-Nemser, S. (2001). Helping novices learn to teach: Lessons from an exemplary support teacher. *Journal of Teacher Education, 52*(1), 17–30. doi:10.1177/0022487101052001003

Feiman-Nemser, S., Schwille, S., Carver, C., & Yusko, B. (1999). *A conceptual review of literature on new teacher induction. (National Partnership for Excellence and Accountability in Teaching).* College Park, MD: University of Maryland, Department of Education.

Feistritzer, C. (1993). National overview of alternative certification. *Education and Urban Society, 26*(1), 18–28. doi:10.1177/0013124593026001003

Feistritzer, C. (2005). *Alternative routes to teacher certification: An overview.* Washington, DC: National Center for Education Information.

Fenstermacher, G. (1990). The place of alternative certification in the education of teachers. *Peabody Journal of Education, 67*(3), 155–185. doi:10.1080/01619569009538695

Fenwick, T. (Fall 2008). Workplace learning: emerging trends and new perspectives in *New directions for adult and continuing education No. 119* (pp. 17-26). San Francisco: Jossey-Bass.

Ferraro, J. (1998). I already have a bachelor's degree, how can I obtain a teaching license? *ERIC Clearinghouse on Teaching and Teacher Education: Washington, DC.* Retrieved December 21, 2007, from http://www.ericdigests.org/1999-3/degree.htm

Fisch, K. (2008). Shift happens. Retrieved May 1, 2009, from http://shifthappens.wikis paces.com/

Fletcher, E. (2006). No curriculum left behind: The effects of the No Child Left Behind legislation on career and technical education. *Career and Technical Education Research, 31*(3), 157–174.

Fletcher, E., & Zirkle, C. (2009). Career and technical education in light of the No Child Left Behind legislation . In Wang, V. (Ed.), *Handbook of esearch on E-learning applications for career and technical education: Technologies for vocational training* (pp. 495–507). Hershey, PA: Information Science Reference.

Fortune, J., & Blecharczyk, S. (1983). The effect of setting-culture interaction on the vocational education of American Indians. *Rural Educator, 2*(1), 1–2.

Foster, J., Kiker, J., Ruffing, K., & Kelley, P. (2006). *Preparing tomorrow's skilled workforce: NOCTI outcomes demonstrate consistent improvements in secondary career and technical education.* Retrieved May 3, 2009, from http://whitenergroups.net/PDFs/Pre paring%20Tomorrows%20Skilled%20Workforce.pdf

Freeman, D. (2002). The hidden side of the work: Teacher knowledge and learning to teach. *Language Teaching, 35*, 1–13. doi:10.1017/S0261444801001720

Friedel, J. (2006). The role of career and technical education in Iowa community colleges. *Community College Journal of Research and Practice, 30*, 293–310. doi:10.1080/10668920500479184

Friedman, T. (2006). *The world is flat: A brief history of the twenty-first century.* New York: Farrar, Straus and Giroux.

Fujita-Starck, P. (1996). Validity, factor structure and reliability of Boshier's education participation scale. *Adult Education Quarterly, 47*(1), 29–40. doi:10.1177/074171369604700103

Galbraith, M. W. (2004). The teacher of adults . In Galbraith, M. W. (Ed.), *Adult learning methods: A guide for effective instruction* (3rd ed., pp. 3–22). Malabar, FL: Kreiger Publishing Company.

Gates, B. (2007, March 7). U.S. Senate committee hearing. Retrieved May 1, 2009, from http://www.gatesfoundation.org/speeches-commentary/Pages/bill-gates-2007-senate-hea ring.aspx.

Gemici, S., & Rojewski, J. (2007). Evaluating research in career and technical education using scientifically-based research standards. *Career and Technical Education Research, 32*(3), 143-159. Retrieved May 1, 2009, from http://scholar.lib.vt.edu/ejournals/CTER/ v32n3/

Gordon, H. (2003). *The history and growth of vocational education in America* (2nd ed.). Long Grove, IL: Waveland Press.

Gordon, R. D. (n.d.). *History of vocational and technical education-Current trends, preparation of teachers, international context.* Retrieved May 28, 2009, from http://education. stateuniversity.com/pages/2536/Vocational-Technical-Education.html

Gray, K. C. (1997). The gatekeepers. *Techniques, 71*(9), 24–27.

Gray, K. C., & Walter, R. A. (2001). *Reforming career and technical education licensure and preparation: A public policy synthesis.* Columbus, OH: The Ohio State University, National Dissemination Center for Career and Technical Education.

Gray, K., & Herr, E. (1998). *Workforce education: The basics.* Boston: Allyn and Bacon.

Gray, K., & Walter, K. (2001). *Reforming career and technical education teacher licensure and preparation: A public policy synthesis.* Columbus, OH: National Dissemination Center for Career and Technical Education.

Green, J. (2004). Critique, contextualism and consensus. *Journal of Philosophy of Education, 38*(3), 511-525. Retrieved June 24, 2009, from http://dx.doi.org/10.1111/j.0309- 8249.2004.00401.x.

Greene, M. (1995). *Releasing the imagination.* San Francisco: Jossey-Bass.

Greene, M. (2001). *Variations on a blue guitar.* New York: Teachers College Press.

Gros, B. (2003). The impact of digital games in education. *First Monday, 8*(7). Retrieved from http://first monday.org/issues/issue8_7/gros/index.html.

Grossman, P., Schoenfeld, A., & Lee, C. (2005). Teaching subject matter . In Darling-Hammond, L., & Bransford, J. (Eds.), *Preparing teachers for a changing world: What teachers should learn and be able to do* (pp. 201–231). San Francisco, CA: Jossey-Bass.

Guarino, C. M., Santibanez, L., & Daley, G. A. (2006). Teacher recruitment and retention: A review of the recent empirical literature. *Review of Educational Research, 76*(2), 173–208. doi:10.3102/00346543076002173

Haimson, J., & VanNoy, M. (2004, September). *Certification programs, participants and outcomes in high schools and two-year colleges.* Retrieved May 1, 2009, from http://www.acteonline.org/uploadedFiles/About_CTE/files/MPR_IT_Workforce_Certification_Programs_Participants_Outcomes_High_School_Two-Year_Colleges_Sep2004. pdf

Hakken, D. (1999). *Cyborgs@cyberspace.* New York: Routledge.

Hammerness, K., Darling-Hammond, L., Bransford, J., Berliner, D., Cochran-Smith, M., McDonald, M., & Zeichner, K. (2005). How teachers learn and develop . In Darling-Hammond, L., & Bransford, J. (Eds.), *Preparing teachers for a changing world: What teachers should learn and be able to do* (pp. 232–274). San Francisco: Jossey-Bass.

Hansen, F. T. (2005). The existential dimension in training and vocational guidance—when guidance counselling becomes a philosophical practice. *European Journal of Vocational Training, 34*(1), 49–62.

Harkins, A. (2002). *The futures of career and technical education in a continuous innovation society. Journal of Vocational Education Research.* Retrieved on May 1, 2009, from http://scholar.lib.vt.edu/ejournals/JVER/v27n1/harkins.html

Hart, P. D. (2006). *Report findings based on a survey among California ninth and tenth graders.* Research Associates Inc. Retrieved May 5, 2009, from http://www.connected california.org/downloads/irvine

Hartley, N., Mantle-Bromley, C., & Cobb, R. B. (1996). A matter of respect. *Vocational Education Journal, 71*(1), 25.

Haveman, R., Wolfe, B., & Spaulding, J. (2001). Childhood events and circumstances influencing high school completion. *Demography, 28*(1), 133–157. doi:10.2307/2061340

Hawkey, K. (1997). Roles, responsibilities, and relationships in mentoring: A literature review and agenda for research. *Journal of Teacher Education, 48*(4), 325–335. doi:10.1177/0022487197048005002

Hawley, W. (1990). The theory and practice of alternative certification: Implications for the improvement of teaching. *Peabody Journal of Education, 67*(3), 3–34. doi:10.1080/01619569009538690

Heinrich, G., Jordan, K., & Smalley, A. (2005). Prepare students for technical careers. *Quality Progress, 38*(10), 33–38.

Henke, R., Chen, X., Geis, S., & Knepper, P. (2000). *Progress through the teacher pipeline: 1992-93 college graduates and elementary/secondary school teaching as of 1997 (NCES 2000-152).* Washington, DC: National Center for Education Statistics.

Henke, R., Choy, S., Chen, X., Geis, S., Alt, M., & Broughman, S. (1997). *America's Teachers: Profile of a Profession, 1993-94 (NCES 97-460).* Washington, DC: U.S. Department of Education, National Center for Education Statistics.

Heo, M. (2009). Design considerations for today's online learners. *International Journal on E-Learning, 8*(3), 293–311.

Hiebert, J., Gallimore, R., & Stigler, J. (2002). A knowledge base for the teaching profession: What would it look like and how can we get one? *Educational Researcher, 31*(5), 3–15. doi:10.3102/0013189X031005003

Hoerner, J., & Wehrley, J. (1995). *Work-based learning: The key to school-to-work transition. New York.* Glencoe: McGraw-Hill.

Hofstede, G. (2001). *Culture's consequences, comparing values, behaviors, institutions, and organizations across nations.* Thousand Oaks, CA: Sage Publications.

Hogan, T., Rabinowitz, M., & Craven, J. A. (2003). Representation in teaching: Inferences from research to expert and novice teachers. *Educational Psychologist, 38*(4), 235–247. doi:10.1207/S15326985EP3804_3

Honigsfeld, A., & Dunn, R. (2006). Learning-style characteristics of adult learners. *The Delta Kappa Gamma Bulletin, 72*(2), 14-17, 31.

Houle, C. O. (1961). *The Inquiring Mind.* Madison, WI: University of Wisconsin Press.

Houser, N. (2008). Cultural plunge. *Race, Ethnicity and Education, 11*(4), 465–482. doi:10.1080/13613320802479034

Houston, W., Marshall, F., & McDavid, T. (1993). Problems of traditionally and prepared and alternatively certified first-year teachers. *Education and Urban Society, 26*(1), 78–89. doi:10.1177/0013124593026001007

Hu, W. (2009, March 3). Vo-Techs are new elite, local districts complain. *The New York Times.* Retrieved May 1, 2009, from http://www.nytimes.com/2009/03/03/education/ 03vocational.html?sq=career%20and%20technical%20education%20and%20wood%20shop&st=cse&scp=9&pagewanted=print

Huang, Y. C. (2006). E-portfolios: Their impact on self-directed learning and computer technology skills on preservice teachers. (Doctoral dissertation, University of Missouri - Saint Louis, 2006). *Dissertation Abstracts International, 133,* AAT 3298785.

Humphrey, D., & Wechsler, M. (2007). Insights into alternative certification: Initial findings from a national study. *Teachers College Record, 109*(3), 483–530.

Husain, D. D. (1999). Good news on the horizon. *Techniques, 74*(3), 14–17.

Hyslop-Margison, E. J. (2002). Liberalizing career education: An aristotelian approach. *The Alberta Journal of Educational Research, 48*(4), 350–363.

Illeris, K. (2004). *The three dimensions of learning.* Malabar, FL: Krieger.

Ilmer, S., Elliott, S., Snyder, J., Nahan, N., & Colombo, M. (2005). Analysis of urban teachers' 1st year experiences in an alternative certification program. *Action in Teacher Education, 27*(1), 3–14.

Imig, D., & Imig, S. (2006). What do beginning teachers need to know? *Journal of Teacher Education, 57*(3), 1–6. doi:10.1177/0022487105285964

Ingersoll, R. (2002). The teacher shortage: A case of wrong diagnosis and wrong prescription. *NASSP Bulletin, 86,* 16–31. doi:10.1177/019263650208663103

Ingersoll, R. (2003). The teacher shortage: Myth or reality? *Educational Horizons, 81*(3), 146–152.

Ingersoll, R., & Smith, T. (2004). Do teacher induction and mentoring matter? *NASSP Bulletin, 88,* 28–40. doi:10.1177/019263650408863803

Isaac, E. P., Guy, T., & Valentine, T. (2001). Understanding African American adult learners' motivations to learn in church-based adult education. *Adult Education Quarterly, 52*(1), 23–38. doi:10.1177/07417130122087377

Isaacs, M., & Benjamin, M. (1991). *Towards a culturally competent system of care: programs which utilize culturally competent principles* (Vol. 2). Washington, DC: Georgetown University Child Development Center, CASSP Technical Assistance Center.

Jackman, D. (2006). 2005 Presidential address: Our future is what we collectively determine. *ACTER Career and Technical Education Research, 31*(2), 75-78. Retrieved May 1, 2009, from http://scholar.lib.vt.edu/ejournals/CTER/v31n2/pdf/jackman.pdf

Jackson, B., & Hardiman, R. (1981). *Organizational stages of multi-cultural awareness.* Amherst, MA: New Perspectives.

Jalongo, M., & Heider, K. (2006). Editorial teacher attrition: An issue of national concern. *Early Childhood Education Journal, 33*(6), 379–380. doi:10.1007/s10643-006-0122-y

Jelmberg, J. (1996). College-based teacher education versus state-sponsored alternative programs. *Journal of Teacher Education, 47*(1), 60–67. doi:10.1177/0022487196047001010

Jervis, K., & Montag, C. (Eds.). (1995). *Progressive education for the 1990's: Transforming practice.* New York: Teachers College Press.

Jochems, W., von Merrienboer, J., & Koper, R. (2004). *Integrated e-learning: Implications for pedagogy, technology and organization.* New York: RoutledgeFalmer.

Joerger, R., & Bremer, C. (2001). *Teacher induction programs: A strategy for improving the professional experience of beginning career and technical education teachers. (National Dissemination Center for Career and Technical Education).* Columbus, OH: The Ohio State University.

Johnson, M. (2009). *Primary source teaching the Web 2.0 way K-12.* Columbus, OH: Linworth.

Jokinen, B. (2009). *Negative perception still surrounds career tech education.* Retrieved May 18, 2009, from http://www.limaohio.com/news/career-37483-education-technical.html

Jones, E., Voorhees, R., & Paulson, K. (2002). *Defining and assessing learning: Exploring competency-based initiatives.* National Postsecondary Education Cooperative Working Group in Competency-Based Initiatives, National Center for Education Statistics (NCES). Retrieved May 2, 2009, from http://nces.ed.gov/pubs2002/2002159.pdf

Jordan, K. (2006). A case study: How a disaster mental health volunteer provided spiritually, culturally, and historically sensitive trauma training to teacher-counselors and other mental health professionals in Sri Lanka, 4 weeks after the tsunami. *Brief Treatment and Crisis Intervention, 6*(4), 316–325. doi:10.1093/brief-treatment/mhl012

Jorissen, K. (2003). Successful career transitions: Lessons from urban alternate route teachers who stayed. *High School Journal, 86*(3), 41–51. doi:10.1353/hsj.2003.0003

Kankkunen, M. (2001). Concept mapping and Peirce's semiotic paradigm meet in the classroom environment. *Learning Environments Research, 4*(3), 287–324. doi:10.1023/A:1014438905784

Kanungo, R. N., & Mendonca, M. (1996). Cultural contingencies and leadership in developing countries . In Banberger, P. A., Erez, M., & Bacharach, S. B. (Eds.), *Research in the Sociology of Organizations* (pp. 263–295). Greenwich, CT: Jai Press.

Kasworm, C. D., & Londoner, C. A. (2000). Adult learning and technology . In Wilson, A. L., & Hayes, E. (Eds.), *Handbook of adult and continuing education* (pp. 224–242). San Francisco: John Wiley & Sons.

Kazanas, H. C., Harris, J. N., & Lomons, D. (1973). *The philosophy and foundations of vocational education.* New York: MSS Information Corporation.

Kazis, R. (2005, April). *Remaking career and technical education in the 21ˢᵗ century: What roles for high schools programs.* Retrieved May 1, 2009, from http://www.jff.org/Documents/RemakingCTE.pdf

Kellogg Commission on the Future of State and Land-Grant Universities. (1998). *Student access: Data related to change* (Second working paper). Washington, DC: National Association of State Universities and Land-Grant Colleges, Office of Public Affairs.

Kemple, J. (2001, December). Career academies: Impacts on students' initial transitions to post-secondary education and employment. *Manpower Demonstration Research Corporation.* Retrieved May 22, 2009, from http://www.mdrc.org/publications/105/execsum.html

Kemple, J., & Willner, C. (2008, June). *Career academies: Long term impacts on labor market outcomes, educational attainment, and transitions to adulthood.* Retrieved May 1, 2009, from http://www.mdrc.org/publications/482/full.pdf

Kerka, S. (2000). *Health and adult education.* Columbus, OH: ERIC Clearinghouse on Adult, Career, and Vocational Education.

Kincheloe, J. L. (2008). *Critical pedagogy* (2nd ed.). New York: Peter Lang. doi:10.1007/978-1-4020-8224-5

Kinney, L. (1964). *Certification in education.* Englewood Cliffs, NJ: Prentice-Hall.

Kirkwood, J., Foster, P., & Bartow, S. (1994). Historical leaders in technology education philosophy. *Journal of Industrial Teacher Education, 32*(1). Retrieved May 24, 2009, from http://scholar.lib.vt.edu/ ejournals/JITE/v32n1/ Kirkwood.html.

Klehm, M. (1974). *The status of the certification requirements for trade & industrial teachers in the United States.* Unpublished doctoral dissertation, The Ohio State University, Columbus, Ohio.

Knaak, W. C. (1983). *Learning styles: Applications in vocational education.* Columbus, OH: National Center Publications, The Ohio State University. (ERIC Reproduction Service No. ED229 573).

Kneller, G. F. (1971). *Introduction to the philosophy of education.* New York: John Wiley & Sons.

Knowles, M. (1960). *Handbook of adult education.* Chicago: Adult Education Association.

Knowles, M. (1978). Gearing up for the eighties. *Training & Development, 32*(July), 12–14.

Knowles, M. (1989). *The making of an adult educator.* San Francisco: Jossey-Bass.

Knowles, M. S. (1975). *Self-directed learning.* New York: Association Press.

Knowles, M. S. (1980). *The modern practice of adult education: From pedagogy to andragogy* (2nd ed.). New York: Cambridge Books.

Knowles, M., Holton, E., & Swanson, R. (2005). *The adult learner.* Burlington, MA: Elsevier.

Koballa, T., Glynn, S., Upson, L., & Coleman, D. (2005). Conceptions of Science Teacher Education. *Journal of Science Teacher Education, 16,* 287–308. doi:10.1007/ s10972-005-0192-5

Kofman, S. (1998). *Socrates: Fictions of a philosopher.* New York: Cornell University Press.

Kolb, A. Y., & Kolb, D. A. (2005). *The Kolb learning style inventory. Version 3.1: 2005 Technical specifications.* Boston: Hay Group. Retrieved May 20, 2009, from http://www.learningfromexperience.com/images/ uploads/Tech_spec_LSI.pdf

Kolb, D. A. (1976). *Learning style inventory.* Boston: McBer & Co.

Kolb, D. A. (1985). *Learning style inventory: Self-scoring inventory and interpretation booklet.* Boston: McBer & Co.

Kostovich, C. T., Poradizisz, M., Wood, K., & O'Brien, K. L. (2007). Learning style preference and student aptitude for concept maps. *The Journal of Nursing Education, 46*(5), 225–231.

Kuhajda, M. (2006). Training community health workers to reduce health disparities in Alabama's black belt. *Family & Community Health, 29*(2), 89–102.

Kymes, N. (2004). The no child left behind act: A look at provisions, philosophies, and compromises. *Journal of Industrial Teacher Education, 41*(2), 58–68.

Lambeth, J., Elliot, J., & Joerger, R. (2008, October). The national career and technical education research agenda. *Techniques.* Retrieved May 1, 2009, from http://www. acteonline.org/uploadedFiles/Publications_and_Online_Media/files/ResearchReport.pdf

Laroche, L. (2003). *Managing cultural diversity in technical professions.* Boston: Butterworth Heinemann.

Lau, L. (2000). *Distance learning technologies: Issues, trends and opportunities.* Hershey, PA: Idea Group Publishing.

Law, C. J., Jr. (1975). *A search for a philosophy of vocational education.* (Report: ED126368).

Lazaros, E., & Roger, G. (2006, Summer). *Critical problems facing technology education: Perceptions of Indiana teachers. Journal of Industrial Teacher Education.* Retrieved May 1, 2009, from http://scholar.lib.vt.edu/ejournals/JITE/v43n2/lazaros.html

Legler, R. (2002). Alternative certification: A review of theory and research. *North Central Regional Education Laboratory.* Retrieved April 18, 2009, from http://www.ncrel. org/policy/pubs/html/altcert/index.html

Legler, R. (2002, November). The impact of alternative certification in the Midwest. *NCREL Policy Issues, 12,* 1–16.

Lemire, D. (2000). Research report--A comparison of learning styles scores: A question of concurrent validity. *Journal of College Reading and Learning, 31*(1), 109–116.

Lesgold, A. (2000). What are the tools for? Revolutionary change does not follow the usual norms . In Lajoie, S. (Ed.), *Computers as cognitive tools* (pp. 399–408). Mahwah, NJ: Lawrence Erlbaum Associates.

Levesque, K., Laird, J., Hensley, E., Choy, S. P., Cataldi, E. F., & Hudson, L. (2008). *Career/technical education in the United States: 1990 to 2005. (NCES 2008-035). National Center for Education Statistics, Institute of Education Sciences, U.* Washington, D.C.: S. Department of Education.

Lewis, M. V., & Kosine, R. (2008, October). *What will be the impact of programs of study? A preliminary assessment based on similar previous initiatives, state plans for implementation, and career development theory.* Washington, D.C.: National Research Center for Career and Technical Education. Retrieved May 1, 2009, from http://136.165.122. 102/UserFiles/File/pubs/POS_Study_Morgan.pdf

Li, B., Caniano, D., & Comer, R. (1998). A cultural diversity curriculum: Combining didactic, problem-solving, and simulated experiences. *Journal of the American Medical Women's Association, 53*(3), 127–129.

Liaw, S. (2006). E-learning and the development of intercultural competence. *Language Learning & Technology, 10*(3), 49–64.

Livingstone, D. W. (1999). Exploring the icebergs of adult learning: Findings of the first Canadian survey of informal learning practices. *Canadian Journal for the Study of Adult Education, 13*(2), 49–72.

Loader, B. (1998). *Cyberspace divide: Equality, agency, and policy in the information society.* New York: Routledge. doi:10.4324/9780203169537

Long, H. B. (1985). Critical foundations for lifelong learning/lifelong education . In Long, H. B., Apps, J. W., & Hiemstra, R. (Eds.), *Philosophical and other views on lifelong learning* (pp. 63–92). Athens, GA: University of Georgia.

Long, H. B. (2004). Understanding adult learners . In Galbraith, M. W. (Ed.), *Adult learning methods: A guide for effective instruction* (3rd ed., pp. 181–192). Malabar, FL: Kreiger Publishing Company.

Loo, R. (2004). Kolb's learning styles and learning preferences: Is there a linkage? *Educational Psychology, 24*(1), 99–108. doi:10.1080/0144341032000146476

Lowenstein, K. (2009). The work of multicultural teacher education: Reconceptualizing white teacher candidates as learners. *Review of Educational Research, 79*(10), 163–196. doi:10.3102/0034654308326161

Lucas, C. J. (1969). *What is the philosophy of education?* New York: Macmillan Co.

Lynch, R. (1991). *A national database on vocational teacher education*. Berkeley: University of California, Berkeley; National Center for Research in Vocational Education. (ERIC Document Reproduction Service No. ED329733).

Lynch, R. (1996). In search of vocational and technical teacher education. *Journal of Vocational and Technical Education, 13*(1), 5–16.

Lynch, R. (1996). Vocational teacher education: At a crossroads. *Vocational . Education Journal, 71*(1), 22–24.

Lynch, R. (1997). *Designing vocational and technical teacher education for the 21ˢᵗ century: Implications from the reform literature*. Information Series No. 368. (ERIC Document Reproduction Service No. ED405499).

Lynch, R. (1997). *Designing vocational and technical teacher education for the 21ˢᵗ century: Implications from the reform literature. (ERIC Clearinghouse on Adult, Career, and Vocational Education).* Columbus, OH: U.S. Department of Education.

Lynch, R. (1998). Vocational teacher education in U.S. colleges and universities, and its responsiveness to Carl D. Perkins Vocational and Applied Technology Education Act of 1990 . In Gamoran, A., & Himmelfarb, H. (Eds.), *The quality of vocational education: Background papers from 1994 National Assessment of Vocational Education* (pp. 15–43). Washington, DC: U.S. Department of Education.

Lynch, R. (2000). High school career and technical education for the first decade of the 21ˢᵗ century. *Journal of Vocational Education Research, 25*(2). Retrieved June 25, 2009, from http://scholar.lib.vt.edu/ ejournals/JVER/v25n2/lynch.html

Lynch, R. L. (1996, Fall). In search of vocational and technical teacher education. *Journal of Vocational and Technical Education*. Retrieved May 1, 2009, from http:// scholar. lib.vt.edu/ejournals/JVTE/v13n1/lynch.html

Lynch, R. L. (1997). *Designing vocational and technical teacher education for the 21st Century. Implications from the reform literature.* Retrieved May 1, 2009, from http://www.eric.ed.gov/ERICDocs/data/ericdocs2sql/ content_storage_01/0000019b/80/16/61/27.pdf

Lynch, R. L. (1997). *Designing vocational and technical teacher education for the 21st century: Implications from the reform literature. Information Series No. 368 Publications.* Columbus, OH: Center on Education and Training for Employment.

Lynch, R., Hartley, N., & Wentling, T. (1996). *Beyond tradition: Preparing the teachers of tomorrow's workforce.* Columbia, Missouri: University Council for Vocational Education.

Marenbon, J. (1999). *The philosophy of Peter Abelard.* West Nyack, NY: Cambridge University Press.

Marsick, V., & Watkins, K. (1999). *Facilitating learning organizations.* Brookfield, VT: Gower.

May, H. (2000). *On Socrates.* Belmont, CA: Wadsworth.

Mayes, C. (1998). The Holmes reports: Perils and possibilities. *Teaching and Teacher Education, 14*(8), 775–792. doi:10.1016/S0742-051X(98)00029-8

Mazarr, M. (1999). *Global trends 2005: An owner's manual for the next decade.* New York: St. Martin's Press.

McAllister, G., & Irvine, J. (2002). The role of empathy in teaching culturally diverse students: A qualitative study of teachers' beliefs. *Journal of Teacher Education, 53*(5), 433–443. doi:10.1177/002248702237397

McCaslin, N., & Parks, D. (2001). *Teacher education in career and technical education: Background and policy implications for the new millennium. (National Dissemination Center for Career and Technical Education).* Columbus, OH: U.S. Department of Education.

McCaslin, N., & Parks, D. (2002). *Teacher education in career and technical education: Background and policy implications for the new millennium.* Retrieved May 1, 2009, from http://scholar.lib.vt.edu/ejournals/JVER/ v27n1/special.html

McCaslin, N., & Parks, D. (2002). Teacher education in career and technical education: Background and policy implications for the new millennium. *Journal of Vocational Education Research, 27*(1), 65–103.

McKinney, J., & Kurtz-Ross, S. (2000). *Culture, health and literacy: A guide to health education materials for adults with limited English literacy skills.* Boston: World Education.

McMahon, C., & Bruce, C. (2002). Information literacy needs of local staff in cross-cul-tural development projects. *Journal of International Development, 14*(1), 113–137. doi:10.1002/jid.864

McNergney, R., & Herbert, J. (1995). *Foundations of education.* Needham Heights, MA: Allyn & Bacon.

Medrich, E. A. (2005). Change or die: The challenge facing career and technical education today . In Kazis, R. (Ed.), *Remaking career and technical education for the 21st century: What role for high school programs* (pp. 23–25). Boston, MA: Jobs for the Future/Aspen Institute.

Merriam, S. B. (2001). Andragogy and self-directed learning: Pillars of adult learning theory. In S. B. Merriam (Ed.), *The new update on adult learning theory* (pp. 3-13). New Directions for Adult and Continuing Education, No. 89. San Francisco: Jossey-Bass Publishers.

Merriam, S. B. (Fall 2008). Adult learning theory for the twenty-first century in *New directions for adult and continuing education* (pp. 93-98). San Francisco: Jossey-Bass.

Merriam, S. B., & Caffarella, R. S. (1999). *Learning in adulthood: A comprehensive guide* (2nd ed.). San Francisco: Jossey-Bass.

Merriam, S. B., Caffarella, R. S., & Baumgartner, L. M. (2007). *Learning in adulthood: A comprehensive guide* (3rd ed.). San Francisco: Jossey-Bass.

Merriam, S. B., Courtenay, B. C., & Cervero, R. M. (Eds.). (2006). *Global issues and adult education.* San Francisco: Jossey-Bass.

Merriam, S., Caffarella, R., & Baumgartner, L. (2007). *Learning in adulthood: A comprehensive guide.* San Francisco: John Wiley & Sons.

Mezirow, J. (1978). Perspective transformation. *Adult Education, 28*(2), 100–110. doi:10.1177/074171367802800202

Mezirow, J. (2000). *Learning as transformation.* San Francisco: Jossey- Bass.

Miao, C. (2000). Transformative learning and social transformation: A cross-cultural perspective. *Masters Abstracts International, 36*(06), 1415. (AAT MZ50488).

Miller, A. J. (1982). Certification: A question of validity. *VocEd, 57*(2), 27–29.

Miller, J., McKenna, M., & McKenna, B. (1998). A comparison of alternatively and traditionally prepared teachers. *Journal of Teacher Education, 49*, 165–176. doi:10.1177/0022487198049003002

Miller, M. D. (1984). *Principles and philosophy for vocational education. Special publication series No. 48.* Columbus: Ohio: Center for Research in Vocational Education. (ERIC Document Reproduction Service No. ED 250 497).

Mises, L. (2006). *Human action: A treatise on economics* (4th ed.). Indianapolis, IN: Liberty Fund, Inc.

Misko, J. (1994). *Review of research 2: Learning styles.* Adelaide, Australia: National Centre for Vocational Education Research.

Mohr, C. (2008). Aligning classroom instruction with workplace skills: Equipping CTE students with the math skills necessary for entry-level carpentry. *Techniques: Connecting Education and Careers, 83*(8), 34–38.

Moran, J. J. (1997). *Assessing adult learning: A guide for practitioners.* Malabar, FL: Krieger.

Morton, A. (2002). *A guide through the theory of knowledge* (3rd ed.). Oxford, UK: Blackwell Publishing.

Mündel, K., & Schugurenksy, D. (2008). Community based learning and civic engagement: Informal learning among adult volunteers in community organizations. In S. C. Reed & C. Marienau (Eds.), *Linking adults with community: Promoting civic engagement through community based learning* (pp. 49-58). New Directions for Adult and Continuing Education, No. 118. San Francisco: Jossey-Bass.

Mullens, J., Murname, R., & Willett, J. (1996). The contribution of training and subject matter knowledge to teaching effectiveness: A multilevel analysis of longitudinal evidence from Belize. *Comparative Education Review, 40*, 139–157. doi:10.1086/447369

Mullock, B. (2006). The pedagogical knowledge base of four TESOL teachers. *Modern Language Journal, 90*(1), 48–66. doi:10.1111/j.1540-4781.2006.00384.x

Mumford, A. (1997). Action learning as a vehicle for learning. In Mumford, A. (Ed.), *Action learning at work* (pp. 3–24). Hampshire, UK: Gower.

Naisbett, J. (1982). *Megatrends: Ten new directions transforming our lives.* New York: Warner.

Nakiboglu, C., & Karakoc, O. (2005). The fourth knowledge domain teachers should have: The pedagogical content knowledge. *Educational Sciences: Theory and Practice, 5*(1), 201–206.

Nash, P. (1966). *Authority and freedom in education: An introduction to the philosophy of education.* New York: Wiley.

National Assessment of Vocational Education (NAVE). (2004, June). *Earning, learning, and choice: Career and Technical Education works for students and employers.* Retrieved May 1, 2009, from http://www.ed.gov/rschstat/eval/sectech/nave/naveiap.pdf

National Assessment of Vocational Education Independent Advisory Panel. (n.d.). *Earning, learning, and choice: Career and technical education works for students and employers.* Retrieved May 2, 2009, from http://www.ed.gov/rschstat/eval/sectech/nave/ naveiap.pdf

National Association of State Boards of Education. (2000). Teacher induction programs. *Policy Update, 8*(5), 1–2.

National Center for Alternative Certification. (2007). *Alternative teacher certification: A state by state analysis.* Retrieved December 19, 2007, from http://www.teach-now.org/ overview.cfm

National Center for Education Statistics (NCES). (2009). *Career and technical education (CTE) statistics.* Retrieved May 1, 2009, from http://nces.ed.gov/surveys/ctes/highlights.asp

National Center for Education Statistics [NCES]. (2008, July). Career and technical education in the United States: 1990 to 2005. Retrieved May 1, 2009, from http://nces.ed.gov/pubs2008/2008035.pdf

National Center for Education Statistics. (1994). *Public secondary school teacher survey on vocational education.* Retrieved August 11, 2008, from http://nces.ed.gov/pubs94/ 94409.pdf

National Commission on Adult Literacy. (2008). *Reach Higher, America: Overcoming crisis in the U.S. workforce.* Retrieved April 30, 2009, from http://www.nationalcomm issiononadultliteracy.org/report.html

National Commission on Excellence in Education. (1983). *A nation at risk.* Washington, DC: U.S. Department of Education.

National Commission on Teaching and America's Future. (2002). Unraveling the "teacher shortage" problem: Teacher retention is the key. In *Symposium of The National Commission on Teaching and America's Future and NCTAF State Partners,* Washington, DC, (pp. 1-17). Retrieved November 11, 2006, from http://www.ncsu.edu/mentorjunction/text_files/teacher_retentionsymposium.pdf

National Council for Accreditation of Teacher Education. (2006). *Professional Standards for the Accreditation of Schools, Colleges, and Departments of Education.* Retrieved November 6, 2006, from http://www.ncate.org/documents/standards/unit_stnds_2006. pdf

National Council for Accreditation of Teacher Education. (2007). *What makes a teacher effective?* Retrieved December 3, 2007, from http://www.ncate.org/documents/resources/ teacherEffective.pdf

National Dropout Prevention Center/Network. (n.d.). *Effective strategies for dropout prevention.* Retrieved May 6, 2009, from http://www.dropoutprevention.org/effstrat/default.htm

National Institute for Literacy. (2005). *What is scientifically based research? A guide for teachers.* Retrieved May 1, 2009, from http://www.nifl.gov/partnershipforreading/publications/html/science/stanovich.html

Natriello, G., & Zumwalt, K. (1993). New teachers for urban schools? The contribution of the provisional teacher program in New Jersey. *Education and Urban Society, 26*(1), 49–62. doi:10.1177/0013124593026001005

Naylor, M. (1997). *Impacts of reform movements on vocational teacher education.* Columbus, OH: ERIC Clearinghouse on Adult Career and Vocational Education. (ERIC Document Reproduction Service No. ED 407572).

Nebraska Student Competencies in Technology. (n.d.). *Guidelines for essential learnings in technology, Nebraska Department of Education.* Retrieved May 10, 2009, from http://www.nde.state.ne.us/techcen/documents/student_essential.pdf

Nielsen. (2009). *Global faces and networked places.* New York: Nielsen. Retrieved June 25, 2009, from http://blog.nielsen.com/nielsenwire/wp-content/uploads/2009/03/nielsen_globalfaces_mar09.pdf

Nilson, L. B. (2003). *Teaching at its best.* San Francisco, CA: Anker Publishing.

Norvack, G. E. (1975). *Pragmatism versus Marxism: An appraisal of John Dewey's philosophy.* New York: Pathfinder Press.

Obama, B. (2009, February, 24). Remarks of President Barack Obama -- Address to Joint Session of Congress. Retrieved May 1, 2009, from http://www.whitehouse.gov/the_ press_office/remarks-of-president-barack-obama-address-to-joint-session-of-congress/

Odell, S., & Ferraro, D. (1992). Teacher mentoring and teacher retention. *Journal of Teacher Education, 43*(3), 200–204. doi:10.1177/0022487192043003006

Osborn, M., Thomas, E., & Hartnack, D. (2005). An evolving model of knowledge management in education and the South African reality . In Lee, S. (Eds.), *Information leadership in a culture of change: IASL reports* (pp. 1–15). Erie, PA: International Association of School Librarianship.

Ozmon, H. A., & Craver, S. M. (2007). *Philosophical foundations of education* (8th ed.). Columbus, OH: Prentice Hall.

Palloff, R., & Pratt, K. (1999). *Building learning communities in cyberspace.* San Francisco, CA: Jossey-Bass.

Panel on Undergraduate Engineering Education. et al. (1986). *Engineering undergraduate education.* Washington, DC: National Academy Press.

Parks, D., & McCaslin, N. L. (2002). *Teacher education in career and technical education: Background and policy implications for the new millennium.* Columbus, OH: National Dissemination Center for Career and Technical Education. The Ohio State University (ERIC Document Reproduction Service No. ED 462546)

Parnell, D. (1995). *Why do I have to learn this? Teaching the way people learn best.* Waco, TX: Cord Communications.

Partnership for 21st Century Skills, (2003), *Learning for the 21st Century: A Report and Mile Guide for 21st Century Skills.* Retrieved May 1, 2009 from http://www.21stcentury skills.org/images/stories/otherdocs/p21up_Report.pdf

Paulson, K. (2001). Using competencies to connect to workplace and postsecondary education. *New Directions for Institutional Research, 110,* 41–54. doi:10.1002/ir.10

Peckman, S. (2006). Technically speaking. *Tech Directions, 66*(5), 5–6.

Perrone, V., & Traver, R. (1996). Secondary Education . In Sikula, J. (Ed.), *Handbook of Research on Teacher Education* (pp. 392–409). New York: Macmillan Library Reference.

Peters, R. S. (1966). *Ethics and education.* Australia: Allen and Unwin Pty., Limited.

Peters, S. J. (2008, Summer). The promise of career/tech. *ASCD educational leadership.* Retrieved September 15, 2008, from http://www.ascd.org/portal

Petty, G. C. (1983). Affective work competencies of workers and supervisors from metalworking, building and construction, and maintenance/repair industries. *Journal of Industrial Teacher Education, 21*(1), 28–36.

Petty, G. C. (1993). Technical education delivery systems . In Campbell, C. P., & Armstrong, R. (Eds.), *Workforce development in the Federal Republic of Germany* (pp. 122–138). Pittsburg, KS: Press International.

Petty, G. C. (1995). Adults in the work force and the occupational work ethic. *Journal of Studies in Technical Careers, 15*(3), 133–140.

Petty, G. C. (1995). Education and the occupational work ethic. *SAEOPP Journal, 14*(2), 47–58.

Petty, G. C. (1995). Vocational-technical education and the occupational work ethic. *Journal of Industrial Teacher Education, 32*(3), 45–58.

Petty, G. C. (1997). Employability skills . In Campbell, C. P. (Ed.), *Best practices in workforce development* (pp. 144–164). Lancaster, PA: Technomic Publishing, Co.

Pink, D. (2005). *A whole new mind.* New York: Riverhead. Rossett, A. (Ed.). *ASTD e-learning handbook.* New York: McGraw-Hill.

Pitts, J. (2009). Identifying and using a teacher-friendly learning-styles instrument. *Clearing House (Menasha, Wis.), 82*(5), 225–331. doi:10.3200/TCHS.82.5.225-232

Plank, S. (2001). *Career and technical education in the balance: An analysis of high school persistence, academic achievement, and postsecondary destinations.* National Research Center for Career and Technical Education. Retrieved April 6, 2009, from http://www.nccte.org/publications/infosynthesis/r&dreport/CTE%20in%20Blnce_Plank. pdf

Pratzner, F., & Ryan, R. (1990). Vocational teacher education . In Houston, R. (Ed.), *Handbook of research on teacher education* (pp. 782–794). New York: Macmillan.

Pritchett, C., White, B., & Skinner, L. (2006, Winter). The use of distance learning technology by business teachers for credentialing and instruction. *Delta Pi Epsilon Journal, 48*(1), 4–18.

Pushkin, D. (2001). *Professional development / professional disillusionment. Contemporary education issues: Teacher training a reference handbook.* Santa Barbara, CA: ABC CLIO.

Rapoport, A. (2008). The impact of international programs on pedagogical practices of their participants. *Teachers and Teaching: Theory and Practice, 14*(3), 225–238.

Ravens, R. (1982). *The origin and growth of action learning.* London: Chartwell Bratt.

Ravitch, D. (2002). *A brief history of teacher professionalism.* Paper presented at the White House Conference on Preparing Tomorrow's Teachers, Washington, D.C.

Ready or not. (2009). *A teachers resource for r u ready? and Career Education.* Richmond, VA: Virginia Department of Education.

Reese, S. (2004). The highly qualified teacher under NCLB. *Techniques, 79*(8), 33–35.

Reeves, T. C. (2000). Alternative assessment approaches for online learning environments in higher education. *Journal of Educational Computing Research, 23*(1), 101–111. doi:10.2190/GYMQ-78FA-WMTX-J06C

Rochford, R. A. (2003). Assessing learning styles to improve the quality of performance of community college students in a developmental writing program: A pilot study. *Community College Journal of Research and Practice, 27*(8), 665–677. doi:10.1080/713838240

Roehrig, G., & Luft, J. (2006). Does one size fit all? The induction experience of beginning science teachers from different teacher-preparation programs. *Journal of Research in Science Teaching, 43*(9), 963–985. doi:10.1002/tea.20103

Rogov, K. (2009). *HR.com: Workforce readiness skills gap issues.* Retrieved June 23, 2009, from http://www.hr.com/sfs?t=/contentManager/onStory&e=UTF-8&i=1116423256281 &l=0&ParentID=1119278152254 &StoryID=1236102662055&highlight=1&keys=work force+%2Breadiness+%2Bskills+%2Bgap+%2Bissue &lang=0&active=no

Rojewski, J. (2002). *Preparing the workforce of tomorrow: A conceptual framework for career and technical education. Journal of Vocational Education Research.* Retrieved May 1, 2009, from http://scholar.lib.vt.edu/ejournals/JVER/v27n1/rojewski.html

Rosiek, J., & Atkinson, B. (2005). Bridging the divides: The need for a pragmatic semiotics of teacher knowledge research. *Educational Theory, 55*(4), 421–442. doi:10.1111/j.1741-5446.2005.00004.x

Rothwell, W., & Sredl, H. (2000). *The ASTD reference guide to workplace learning and performance: Present and future roles and competencies* (3rd ed.). Amherst, MA: HRD Press.

Rouse, C. (2005, October). *Labor market consequences of an inadequate education.* Paper presented at the Colombia University Teacher College Symposium on the Social Cost of Inadequate Education, NY.

Rowden, D. (Ed.). (1934). *Handbook of adult education.* New York: American Association for Adult Education.

Ruffing, K. (n.d.). *The history of career clusters.* Retrieved May 17, 2009, from http://www. careerclusters. org/resources/publications/TheHistoryofCareerClusters2006.pdf

Ruhland, S., & Bremer, C. (2002). *Alternative teacher certification procedures and professional development opportunities for career and technical education teachers.* Columbus, OH: National Dissemination Center for Career and Technical Education.

Ruhland, S., & Bremer, C. (2003). Perceptions of traditionally and alternatively certified career and technical education teachers. *Journal of Vocational Education Research, 28*(3), 285–302.

Salopek, J. (2007). Education for work and life. *Training & Development, 61*(2), 22–24.

Salopek, J. (2009). The power of the pyramid: ASTD unveils world-class sales competency model. *Training & Development, 63*(5), 70–75.

Schirmer, J. (2004). A collaborative needs assessment and work plan in behavioral medicine curriculum development in Vietnam. *Families, Systems & Health, 22*(4), 410–418. doi:10.1037/1091-7527.22.4.410

Schoen, L., & Fusarelli, L. (2008). Innovation, NCLB, and the fear factor: The challenge of leading 21st-century schools in an era of accountability. *Educational Policy, 22*(1), 181–203. doi:10.1177/0895904807311291

Schon, D. (1983). *The reflective practitioner.* New York: Basic Books.

Scott, J., & Sarkees-Wircenski, M. (1996). *Overview of vocational and applied technology education.* Homewood, IL: American Technical Publishers.

Scott, J., & Sarkees-Wircenski, M. (2008). *Overview of career and technical education* (4th ed.). American Technical Publishers.

Segall, A. (2004). Revisiting pedagogical content knowledge: The pedagogy of content/the content of pedagogy. *Teaching and Teacher Education, 20,* 489–504. doi:10.1016/j.tate.2004.04.006

Selke, M., & Fero, G. (2005). A collaborative alternative-path program for career-changing mathematics and science professionals: Context, design, and replication. *Action in Teacher Education, 27*(1), 26–35.

Senge, P. M. (2006). *The fifth discipline: The art and practice of the learning organization*. New York: Doubleday Currency.

Shea-Schultz, H., & Fogarty, J. (2002). *Online learning today: Strategies that work*. San Francisco: Berrett-Koehler Publishers.

Shelly, G., Cashman, T., Gunter, R., & Gunter, G. (2007). *Teachers discovering computers: Integrating technology in the classroom* (4th ed.). Boston: Thomson.

Shen, J. (1997). Has the alternative certification policy materialized its promise? A comparison between traditionally and alternatively certified teachers in public schools. *Educational Evaluation and Policy Analysis*, *19*(3), 276–283.

Shrestha, M., Wilson, S., & Singh, M. (2008). Knowledge networking: A dilemma in building social capital through nonformal education. *Adult Education Quarterly*, *58*(2), 129–150. doi:10.1177/0741713607310149

Shulman, L. S. (2005). Pedagogies. *Liberal Education*, *91*(2), 18–25.

Sieber, V. (2009). Diagnostic online assessment of basic IT skills in 1st-year undergraduates in the Medical Sciences Division, University of Oxford. *British Journal of Educational Technology*, *40*(2), 215–226. doi:10.1111/j.1467-8535.2008.00926.x

Silverberg, M., Warner, E., Fong, M., & Goodwin, D. (2004). *National assessment of vocational education: Final report to congress*. Retrieved May 1, 2009, from http://www.ed.gov/rschstat/eval/sectech/nave/navefinal.pdf

Smeyers, P. (2008). Child-rearing: On government intervention and the discourse of experts. *Educational Philosophy and Theory*, *40*(6), 719–738. doi:10.1111/j.1469-5812.2008.00465.x

Smith, P., & Dalton, P. (2005). *Accommodating learning styles: Relevance and good practice in vocational education and training*. Australia: Australian National Training Authority.

Smylie, M., Bay, M., & Tozer, S. (1999). Preparing teaches as agents of change . In Griffin, G. (Ed.), *The Education of Teachers* (pp. 29–62). Chicago: National Society for the Study of Education.

Sokal, L., Smith, D., & Mowat, H. (2003). Alternative certification teachers' attitudes toward classroom management. *High School Journal*, *86*(3), 8–16. doi:10.1353/hsj.2003.0004

Southern Regional Education Board (SREB). (n.d.). *Facts about high school career and technical education studies*. Retrieved May 1, 2009, from http://www.sreb.org/programs/hstw/career/facts_about_hs_career.pdf

St. Arnauld, C. (2004). *The role of community colleges in preparing CTE teachers*. Retrieved September 27, 2008, from http://www.nccte.org/webcasts/description68c1.html

Stanage, S. M. (1994). Charles Sanders Peirce's pragmaticism and praxis of adult learning theory: Signs, interpretation, and learning how to learn in the post-modern age. *Thresholds in Education*, *20*(2-3), 10–17.

States' Career Clusters Initiative. (2009). Retrieved on April 13, 2009, from http://www. careerclusters.org

Steadman, S., & Simmons, J. (2007). The cost of mentoring non-university-certified teachers: Who pays the price? *Phi Delta Kappan*, *88*(5), 364–367.

Stoddart, T. (1993). Who is prepared to teach in urban schools? *Education and Urban Society*, *26*(1), 29–48. doi:10.1177/0013124593026001004

Stoddart, T., & Floden, R. (1995). *Traditional and alternate routes to teacher certification: Issues, assumptions, and misconceptions*. East Lansing, MI: National Center for Research on Teacher Learning.

Stone, J. (2009). A Perkins challenge: Assessing technical skills in CTE. *Techniques*, *84*(2), 21–23.

Stone, J. R., III. (2008, December). *Programs of study: Issues and approaches*. powerpoint presentation made at the 2008 ACTE Convention, Charlotte, NC.

Stone, M. (2007). E-Learning applications for career and technical education. *Techniques, 82*(5), 44–48.

Strunk, K., & Robinson, J. (2006). Oh, won't you stay: A multilevel analysis of the difficulties in retaining qualified teachers. *Peabody Journal of Education, 81*(4), 65–94. doi:10.1207/s15327930pje8104_4

Suefert, S. (2002). Cultural perspectives . In Adelsberg, H., Collis, B., & Pawlowski, J. (Eds.), *Handbook on information technology for education and training* (pp. 411–424). Munich, Germany: Springer-Verlag.

Suell, J., & Piotrowski, C. (2006). Efficacy of alternative teacher certification programs: A study of the Florida Model. *Education, 127*(2), 310–315.

Sullivan, D., Ford, B., & Murphree, T. (n.d.). *Educational competencies for marine science and technology occupations.* Marine Advanced Technology Education Center (MATE). Retrieved May 15, 2009, from http://www.marinetech.org/marineworkforce/pdf/educational_comps.pdf

Taylor, C. C. W. (2001). *Socrates: A very short introduction.* Oxford, UK: Oxford University Press.

Taylor, C. C. W., Hare, R. M., & Barnes, J. (1998). *Greek philosophers—Socrates, Plato, and Aristotle.* New York: Oxford University Press.

Teacher retention is the key. (2002, August 20-22). *Symposium of the National Commission on Teaching and America's Future and NCTAF State Partners.* Retrieved November 10, 2008, from http://www.ncsu.edu/mentorjunction/text_files/teacher_retentionsymposium.pdf

Teacher attrition: A costly loss to the nation and to the states by Alliance for Excellent Education. (2005, August). Retrieved May 16, 2009, from http://www.all4ed.org/ publications/TeacherAttrition.pdf

Texas Department of Health, National Maternal and Child Health Resource Center on Cultural Competency. (1997). *Journey towards cultural competency: Lessons learned.* Vienna, VA: Maternal and Children's Health Bureau Clearinghouse.

Thayer-Bacon, B. (2003). Pragmatism and feminism as qualified relativism. [from http://www.csa. com]. *Studies in Philosophy and Education, 22*(6), 417–438. Retrieved June 22, 2009. doi:10.1023/A:1025735417682

The changing world of international students. (2006). *NEA Higher Education ADVOCATE* (December), 6-8.

The Education Trust. (2003). *Telling the whole truth (or not) about high school graduation.* Retrieved May 20, 2009, from http://www2.edtrust.org/NR/rdonlyres/4DE8F2E0-4D08-B3B0-013F6DC3865D/0/tellingthetruthgraduates.pdf

The Governor's Commission on Quality Education. (2008, December). Innovations in teaching: Creating professional pathways for Alabama teachers. Retrieved May 1, 2009, from http://www.governorpress.alabama.gov/documents/InnovationsinTeachingRpt.pdf

Thompson, L. H. (1973). *Foundations of vocational education: Social and philosophical concepts.* Englewood Cliffs, NJ: Prentice Hall.

Threeton, M. D. (2007). The Carl D. Perkins Career and Technical Education (CTE) Act of 2006 and the roles and responsibilities of CTE teachers and faculty members. *Journal of Industrial Education, 44*(1). Retrieved May 24, 2009, from http://scholar.lbo.vt.edu/ejournals/JITE/v44n1/threeton.html

Tisdell, E. J. (2003). *Exploring spirituality and culture in adult and higher education.* San Francisco: Jossey-Bass.

Tissington, L., & Grow, A. (2007). Alternative certification teachers and children at risk. *Preventing School Failure, 51*(2), 23–27. doi:10.3200/PSFL.51.2.23-27

Toffler, A. (1980). *The third wave.* New York: Bantam Books.

Toffler, A. (1991). *Powershift.* New York: Bantam.

Torf, B., & Sessions, D. (2005). Principals' perceptions of the causes of teacher ineffectiveness. *Journal of Educational Psychology, 97*(4), 530–537. doi:10.1037/0022-0663.97.4.530

Tough, A. (1967). *Learning without a teacher.* Toronto: Institute for Studies in Education.

Tough, A. (1979). *The adult's learning project.* Toronto: Institute for Studies in Education.

Tucker, S. Y. (2003). Teaching and learning styles of community college business instructors and their students: Relationship to student performance and instructor evaluations. *New Horizons in Adult Education, 17*(2), 11-21. Retrieved April 30, 2009, from http://www.nova.edu/~aed/horizons/volume17no2.pdf

U.S. Bureau of Labor Statistics. (2008). *Occupational Outlook Handbook.* Retrieved May 13, 2009, from http://www.bls.gov/oco/oco2003.htm

U.S. Department of Education, Office of the Under Secretary, Policy and Program Studies Service. (2004). *National assessment of vocational education: Final report to congress.* Retrieved May 20, 2009, from http://www.ed.gov/rschstat/eval/sectech/nave/navefinal.pdf

U.S. Department of Education. (1983). *A nation at risk.* Washington, DC: Government Printing Office.

U.S. Department of Education. (2004, May). *No Child Left Behind: A toolkit for teachers.* Retrieved August 10, 2008, from http://www.ed.gov/teachers/nclbguide/nclb-teachers- toolkit.pdf

U.S. Department of Labor. (1991). *Secretary's Commission on Achieving Necessary Skills.* Washington, DC: Government Printing Office.

UNESCO. (2002). *Universal declaration on cultural diversity.* The Hague: UNESCO.

University of Alaska Anchorage. (2009) *Academics.* Retrieved May 16, 2009, from http://www.uaa.alaska.edu/pathways/career_connections.cfm

University of Alaska Fairbanks. (2009). *Student technology competencies.* Retrieved May 3, 2009, from http://www.uaf.edu/educ/technology/techcompetencies.html

Valmont, W. (2003). *Technology for literacy teaching and learning.* New York: Houghton Mifflin.

Venn, G. (1964). *Man, education, and work: Post secondary vocational and technical education.* Washington, DC: American Council on Education.

Venn, G. (1970). *Man, education, and manpower.* Washington, DC: American Association of School Administrators.

Verducci, S. (1961). The ability to respond . In Gardner, H. (Ed.), *Responsibility at work: How leading professionals act (or don't act responsibly)* (pp. 43–61). San Francisco: Jossey-Bass.

Vlastos, G. (1991). *Socrates, ironist and moral philosopher.* Ithaca, NY: Cornell University Press. doi:10.1017/CBO9780511518508

Vo, C. H. (1997). Not for my child. *Techniques, 71*(9), 20–23.

Vogel, L. J. (2000). Reckoning with the spiritual lives of adult educators. In L. M. English & M. A. Gillen (Eds.), *Addressing the spiritual dimensions of adult learning: What educators can do* (pp. 17-35). New Directions for Adult and Continuing Education, No. 85. San Francisco: Jossey-Bass.

Walter, R., & Gray, K. (2002). Teacher preparation/licensure in career and technical education: A public policy analysis. *Journal of Vocational Education Research, 27*(1), 127–149.

Wayman, J., Foster, A., Mantle-Bromley, C., & Wilson, C. (2003). A comparison of the professional concerns of traditionally prepared and alternatively licensed new teachers. *High School Journal, 86*(3), 35–40. doi:10.1353/hsj.2003.0005

Welch, L., Cleckley, B., & McClure, M. (1997). *Strategies for promoting pluralism in education and the workplace.* Westport, CT: Praeger.

West, P. (1996). Scholarships for Voc Ed training go untapped. *Education Week, 15*(28), 3–5.

White, B. A., & Bridwell, C. (2004). Distance learning techniques . In Galbraith, M. (Ed.), *Adult learning methods: A guide for effective instruction* (pp. 273–288). Malabar, FL: Krieger.

White, L. (2002). *Engaging black learners in adult and community education.* Leicester, England: National Institute of Adult Continuing Education.

Wichowski, C., Kormanik, G., & Evans, C. (2008). Pennsylvania's career support tools: An asset to students, parents, the workplace and the economy. *Techniques: Connecting Education and Careers, 83*(8), 39–42.

Wiener, R. (2005, April). How the federal government could promote academically rigorous career and technical education. In R. Kazis (Ed.), *Remaking career and technical education for the 21st century: What role for high school programs* (pp. 32-34). Boston, MA: Jobs for the Future/Aspen Institute. Retrieved May 1, 2009, from http://www. eric.ed.gov/ERICDocs/data/ericdocs2sql/content_storage_01/0000019b/80/30/b1/d6.pdf

Wilson, A. L., & Hayes, A. R. (2000). *Handbook of adult and continuing education.* San Francisco: Jossey-Bass.

Wilson, G. (1997). *The metanarrative of consequences in the pragmatism of Charles Sanders Peirce.* (ERIC ED413607). Retrieved May 12, 2009, from http://www. csa.com

Wilson, S., Floden, R., & Ferrini-Mundy, J. (2001). *Teacher preparation research: Current knowledge, gaps, and recommendations: A research report prepared for the U.S. Department of Education.* Seattle, WA: Center for the Study of Teaching and Policy.

Wirth, A. G. (1974). Philosophical issues in the vocational-liberal studies controversy (1900-1917): John Dewey vs. the social efficiency philosophers. [from http://www.csa. com]. *Studies in Philosophy and Education, 8*(3), 169–182. Retrieved June 22, 2009. doi:10.1007/BF00368858

Wonacott, M. (2000). *Vocational Education Myths and Realities. ERIC Clearinghouse on Adult, Career, & Vocational Education Myths and Realities.* Retrieved May 16, 2009, from http://www.fape.org/idea/How_it_works/voced_myths_8.html

Woods, R. G., & Barrow, R. S. (2006). *Introduction to philosophy of education* (4th ed.). London: Routledge.

Workforce Readiness Initiative. (2007). *Meeting summary report: Stakeholders strategy meeting.* The Conference Board, Research Report E-0014-07-RR, Washington, D.C.

Yermish, I. (2000). A case for case studies via video-conferencing . In Lau, L. (Ed.), *Distance learning technologies: Issues, trends and opportunities* (pp. 208–217). Hershey, PA: Idea Group Publishing.

Yiu, L., & Parker, J. (2005). Cyber action learning and virtual project teams for leadership and management development . In Jacobs, R. L., & Osman-Gani, A. M. (Eds.), *Workplace training & learning: Cases from cross-cultural perspectives* (pp. 1–14). New York: Pearson/Prentice Hall.

Zeichner, K., & Schulte, A. (2001). What we know and don't know from peer-review research about alternative teacher certification programs. *Journal of Teacher Education, 52*(4), 266–282. doi:10.1177/0022487101052004002

Zeidler, D. L. (2002). Dancing with maggots and saints: Visions for subject matter knowledge, pedagogical knowledge, and pedagogical content knowledge in science teacher education reform. *Journal of Science Teacher Education, 13*(1), 27–42. doi:10.1023/A:1015129825891

Zirkle, C. (2005). Web-enhanced alternative teacher licensure. *Teacher Educator, 40*(3), 208–219. doi:10.1080/08878730509555361

Zirkle, C., Martin, L., & McCaslin, N. (2007). *Study of state certification/licensure requirements for secondary career and technical education teachers.* St. Paul, MN: National Research Center for Career and Technical Education.

Zumwalt, K. (1996). Simple answers: Alternative Teacher Certification. *Educational Researcher, 25*(8), 40–42.

About the Contributors

Victor C. X. Wang, Ed.D., an Associate Professor, joined the faculty at California State University, Long Beach (CSULB) in 2002 and has been the credential coordinator of CTE and adult education since 2005. Dr. Wang's research and writing activities have focused on workforce education, the foundations of adult education, adult teaching and learning, training, transformative learning, cultural issues in vocational and adult education, distance education, human performance technology and curriculum development. He has published well over 100 journal articles, book chapters and books during his eight years at CSULB and has been a reviewer for five national and international journals. Currently he serves as the editor in chief of the *International Journal of Adult Vocational Education and Technology.* He has won many academic achievement awards from the universities in China and the United States, including the Distinguished Faculty Scholarly & Creative Achievement Award in 2009. Dr. Wang taught extensively as a professor in Chinese universities prior to coming to study and work in the United States in 1997. He has taught adult learners English as a second language, Chinese, computer technology, vocational and adult education courses, research methods, administrative leadership, human resource management and curriculum development for the past 20 years in university settings. Two of the books he has written and edited have been adopted as required textbooks by major universities in the United States, and in China. In addition, numerous universities worldwide including Howard University, Princeton University, Yale University, University of Chicago, Cornell University, UC-Berkeley and Rice University have cataloged his books and journal articles.

***

Jules K. Beck, Ph.D., LCSW, is an Assistant Professor at the University of Arkansas. A native of Minneapolis, Minnesota, Beck attended the University of Chicago and graduated from the University of Minnesota with an M.S.W. and Ph.D. with concentration in Human Resource Development (HRD). Beck is a Licensed Certified Social Worker (LCSW) in Arkansas and holds Social Worker Emeritus status in Minnesota. Beck has over three years experience in international community and leadership development in South and Central America, West Africa, and Eastern Europe. He was a two-year volunteer in community development on White Earth Reservation in Minnesota. Beck taught grades 4~6 in Potosí, Bolivia and high school classes in South Dakota. He was a community organizer for 10 years on the North Side of Minneapolis. Beck chaired the St. Louis Park, MN Human Rights Commission and was elected to three terms as president of the ACLU of Minnesota. Beck co-developed a disaster recovery planning system in Spanish as an information technology consultant for a U.S. accounting firm. Beck is in his eleventh year teaching university classes in adult education, human resource development, and business and industry education at both undergraduate and graduate levels. His research interests include international HRD, leadership development, and distance education. Beck advises graduate students pursuing studies in Adult Education and Human Resource Development.

Ernest W. Brewer, Ed.D., is a Professor of Educational Administration and Policy Studies and Principal Investigator/Director of Federal Programs at the University of Tennessee. Dr. Brewer has authored/co-authored over 100 books, book chapters, articles, monographs, and technical reports. He has received such awards as the Excellence in Teaching Award, the Outstanding Service Award from the IVETA, and the Outstanding Faculty Counselor Award from Kappa Delta Pi. His current research interests, that are frequently intertwined, include job satisfaction, occupational stress, and job burnout.

Jane Briggs, Ph.D., is a Financial Services Instructor at Eastland Career Center in Groveport, Ohio, and an adjunct instructor in Business Education at the Ohio State University. She holds both bachelor's and master's degrees from Bowling Green State University and a Ph.D. in Workforce Development and Education from the Ohio State University with cognates in teacher education and CTE leadership.

Lesley Farmer, Ed.D., currently is a Professor at California State University, Long Beach. Dr. Lesley Farmer has been coordinating their Librarianship program since 1999. She also taught and served as the external examiner for the University of Hong Kong's library science program, as well as worked as a library professional in K-12 school, public, special and academic libraries. Dr. Farmer earned her M.S. in Library Science at the University of North Carolina Chapel Hill, and received her doctorate in Adult Education from Temple University. She serves as the International Association for School Librarianship Vice President for Association Relations, helped edit their newsletter, and was selected for their research award. She edits the International Association of Library Association School Libraries Section Newsletter, and chaired the Education Division of Special Library Association. She has chaired the International Education SIG and the Gender Studies SIG for the Association of Library and Information Science Educators, and serves as treasurer for the Alpha Chapter of Phi Beta Delta (honor society for international scholars). Dr. Farmer presents regularly at national and international professional conferences. She has edited library journals, written twenty-four books and over a hundred articles and chapters; the most current books are titled *Teen Girls and Technology* (Teachers College Press, 2008) and *Your School Library* (Libraries Unlimited, 2009). Her research interests include information literacy, collaboration, assessment, and gendered educational technology.

Edward C. Fletcher Jr., Ph.D., earned his master's and bachelor's degrees from the University of Missouri in Business Education and CTE. He earned his Ph.D. at the Ohio State University in Workforce Development and Education. He is currently an Assistant Professor in Business Teacher Education at Illinois State University in the College of Business. His research interests include studying the effects of tracking on students' long-term status attainment, examining issues related to student teaching and teacher candidates' development, and exploring the perceptions of CTE teacher candidates and practicing teachers regarding their preparation.

Kenda S. Grover, Ed.D., is the Assistant Department Head for the Rehabilitation, Human Resources, and Communication Disorders Department in the College of Education and Health Professions at the University of Arkansas as well as program coordinator for the Workforce Development Education Program (WDED). Grover oversees operations for the online WDED undergraduate, master's and doctoral programs and coordinates the graduate student recruitment and retention initiative. Her background is in student affairs in higher education; she has developed Carl Perkins grant articulation agreements with career and technical education programs in Oklahoma, Missouri, and Kansas. Grover teaches courses in adult education and human resource development for graduate students in the WDED program and undergraduate students pursuing the department's bachelor degree completion program in HRD. Her current research focuses on student recruitment and retention, performance evaluation, branding in higher education, and diversity awareness.

Kit Kacirek, Ed.D., SPHR, is an Associate Professor at the University of Arkansas, who teaches Adult Education and Human Resource Development (HRD) in the College of Education and Health Professions. Her experience as an organization development consultant influences a research agenda that focuses on bridging the gap between theory and practice in HRD. In addition to teaching, she provides professional development services for clients of the Center for Management and Executive Education in the Sam M. Walton College of Business. Her consulting and research has led to several international assignments working with emerging business owners in Poland, strategic planning and needs assessment for a women's health clinic in Morocco, and leadership development workshops in Tunisia, Ghana, Honduras, and the Ukraine. Dr. Kacirek has published practitioner-relevant cases in the *Training and Development in Action Series*, as well as in various scholarly journals.

Judith Parker, Ed.D., has earned a doctorate degree and an M.S. degree in Adult and Continuing Education from Teachers College/Columbia University in New York, an M.S. degree in Physics from Purdue University in Indiana, and a B.S. degree in Physics and Mathematics from Notre Dame College in Ohio. Dr. Parker has over 20 years experience in leadership positions within business organizations emerging into the global market and has been instrumental in leading them toward becoming global learning organizations. She has worked extensively with technical managers and technical employees in Asia and Europe in leadership education and training and technical employee skill development. Dr. Parker's academic experience includes teaching adult learning and leadership theory and practice, staff development and training, and organizational development, in graduate programs at Teachers College/Columbia University and St. Mary's University of Minnesota using totally on-line format, totally classroom format and blended delivery. She also teaches college Physics and Astronomy at Muhlenberg College in Pennsylvania. She has presented numerous papers at conferences globally including the Academy of Management, American Association of Physics Teachers, American Society of Training and Development, College Industry Education Conference, Quality and Productivity Management Association, Business and Multimedia Conference in Ireland, Lisbon 2000 European Conference on ODL Networking for Quality Learning, and World Open Learning for Business Conferences in the UK. She has authored numerous articles in publications including the "Compendium on Uses of Distance Learning Technologies in Engineering Education" and the *Journal of the International Association for Continuing Engineering Education* and book chapters including "Cyber Action Learning and Virtual Project Teams for Leadership and Management Development" with L. Yiu in the book *Workplace Training and Learning: A Cross-Cultural Perspective* and the chapter "The Online Adult Learner: Profiles and Practices" in *Handbook of Research on E-Learning Applications for Career and Technical Education* edited by Victor Wang. She has been elected a Fellow of the American Association for the Advancement of Science, and has received the American Association of Physics Teachers Innovative Teaching Award and the Park College Educational Partnership Award.

Gregory C. Petty, Ph.D., is a Professor of Education, Health, and Human Sciences at the University of Tennessee. He received his Ph.D. from the University of Missouri, Columbia. He is a veteran of the United States Navy Nuclear Submarine Service, and is the author of more than 100 refereed articles, books, and technical reports, 54 educational videos, and has made 88 scholarly presentations at national, regional and state conferences. He has received numerous professional awards and was awarded Author of the Year by the *AATEA Journal* and Outstanding Research Manuscript (2006) for the *Journal of Industrial Teacher Education*. He most recently received the Award of Merit for Research by the National Safety Council in Anaheim California, 2008. His primary research areas are work ethic for a healthy life, behavioral issues for safety and health including occupational stress, and psychometric measures of performance, attitude, and self-efficacy. He is currently the Technical Advisor for Research for the National Safety Council, College and University Initiative and is a member of NSC's Board of Delegates.

Kristina L. Sander worked in the corporate sector for six years while earning an associates degree in Secretarial Science. She then earned a bachelor's degree in Business and Vocational Education, then the Master of Arts degree in Education, both from the Ohio State University. She is currently teaching Secondary Business and Vocational Education for South-Western City Schools, while pursuing a Ph.D. in Workforce Development and Education with cognates in CTE and Technologies of Instruction and Media. In addition, she has also been an Adjunct Instructor in CTE Curriculum and Assessment for the Ohio State University.

Leane B. Skinner, Ed.D., is an Associate Professor in CTE and Business/Marketing Education within the Department of Curriculum and Teaching at Auburn University. Her research areas of interest include professional development for CTE educators, integration of technology, industry certification for CTE educators, and distance learning.

James E. Witte, Ph.D., is an Associate Professor in Adult Education within the Department of Educational Foundations, Leadership, and Technology at Auburn University. His academic areas of interest include training program development and evaluation, individual learning styles and how learning is assessed both conventional and distance learning settings.

Maria Martinez Witte, Ed.D., is an Associate Professor in Adult Education within the Department of Educational Foundations, Leadership, and Technology at Auburn University. Her academic areas of interest include analyzing effective content, context, and processes that enhance the teaching-learning environment, learning styles, and the assessment of learning. Her skills include facilitating, coordinating, developing, and delivering educational programs.

Chris Zirkle, Ph.D., earned his bachelor's degree at Central State University. He earned two masters' degrees, one from Wright State University and the other at Ball State University. He earned his Ph.D. at the Ohio State University in Comprehensive Vocational Education. He currently is an Associate Professor of Workforce Development and Education. His research work is primarily within the broad discipline of CTE, and more specifically focused on teacher education/preparation and the utilization of distance education methodologies in CTE.

Index

W

LaVergne, TN USA
01 August 2010
191277LV00005B/2/P